D0923083

A History of

Chinese Literature

by
LAI MING

with a Preface by
LIN YUTANG

CAPRICORN BOOKS
NEW YORK

To My Wife

NOTE

THE romanization of Chinese names in this book has been
simplified for the sake of the general reader: unless two names
in one chapter must be differentiated, for instance, Chin and
Ch'in, the use of the apostrophe in denoting aspirated consonants has been omitted. The use of the umlaut is omitted.
The distinction between *tz* and *ts* sounds is not made. The rest
follows the Wade Romanization System.

PREFACE

by Dr LIN YUTANG

THE story of Chinese literature, covering as it does three thousand years, going back to the sacrificial odes of the Chou Dynasty (*c.* 1000 B.C.), may seem a formidable task for anyone to undertake writing. Yet, perhaps more clearly than in the literature of any other country, the remarkably slow evolution of Chinese literary forms makes it possible to identify a particular form of writing, or genre of literature, with a period in which this genre predominates. Thus, it is possible to speak in an exact sense of 'Tang poetry', 'Sung *tse*' (poems written to given melodies), 'Yuan drama' (of the Mongol period) and 'Ming novel'. There was, as far as we know, no evidence of epic poetry; no development of the short story till the eighth and ninth centuries; no recorded dramas before the thirteenth; and strangest of all, no development of the novel till the fourteenth and fifteenth. There was good narrative prose in *Tsochuan*, written perhaps in the fourth or fifth centuries B.C. with good human motivation; there was plenty of epic material in the wars between Wu and Yueh taking place in Confucius' own lifetime, which later became the material for the novel *Wu-Yueh Chunchiu*; there were brilliant narrative passages by Szema Chien (see Chapter 4), wonderful anecdotes in philosophical works like *Chuangtse*, *Liehtse* and jokes in *Hanfeitse* and *Huainantse*, and a lot of short supernatural tales in the third to fifth centuries. But take the supernatural tales, for instance; these were told like anecdotes in four or five lines, and were a far cry from the art tales and short stories found in the ninth century.

What was wrong? Perhaps one important factor was the classical language, which had grown more and more apart from the vernacular. It would seem almost impossible to write a good novel in Latin, and this was so with the classical language. But there was a broader and deeper reason in the general attitude of Confucianists toward imaginative literature. Literature has been classified under two categories: literature for 'carrying moral teachings' (*tsai tao*) and for 'expressing sentiments' (*chu ching*). Moralizing seemed to be an inveterate habit of the Chinese, back from Confucius and the author of *Tso-chuan* on, and even further back from some of the earliest historical documents in the *Book of History*, which contained some extraordinary moral platitudes. Shut up any Confucian scholar in a prison for three months and out comes, not an imaginative work, but a book of moral proverbs and reflections on life. Any scholar would be too ashamed to be known writing a novel for sheer entertainment. The Confucianism which did not stop love and courtship, nevertheless stopped social dancing and the cultivation of the musical arts in general, such as an opera. When the theatre thrived in the fifteenth and sixteenth centuries, Confucian scholars were not above going to see some plays with their wives or being seen enjoying themselves, but they would be certainly far more at ease if they were moralizing on righteousness and justice at court or writing eulogies to the emperor.

Thus it happened that there existed two strata of thinking and feeling, an effete intellectualism subsisting on moral morsels of wisdom, and the great common people of China who went on enjoying themselves anyway, talking and singing in the vernacular.

These social elements, so clearly pointed out in this volume, explain the periodic cycles of growth and decay in Chinese literary forms. Such forms always grow from the soil of popular entertainments and music. When the last nuances of a certain form of literary expression, such as Tang poetry, were exhausted, new life came from some form of vigorous popular art. The Sung lyrics simply came from the sing-song girls, and the novel, or art of story-telling, from the tea-house. The great novels, such as the *Three Kingdoms* or *Water Margins* (*All Men Are Brothers*), were simply compilations from romance cycles already known and made popular in the tea-houses. The Chinese scholars had a habit of 'copying ancients'. When they had copied themselves to death, in technique and in vocabulary, again some innovation borrowed fresh life from the popular forms of entertainment.

Thus came about the periodic effemination and renewal of Chinese literary forms. It is the distinction of this History of Chinese Literature that it has brought this out clearly. As will be seen in the Introduction, the periodic cycles, the influence of Buddhism and of the musical arts, have been made the framework against which the story is told. The author has deftly interwoven the social factors and the life of a representative poet or writer with the evolution of a particular period and has thus made the whole book a delight to read.

CONTENTS

CONTENTS

CONTENTS

ACKNOWLEDGMENTS

THE author wishes to thank the following copyright-holders for permission to reproduce extracts from the publications cited:

Messrs Abelard-Schuman Ltd (*Poems of Solitude* trs. Michael Bullock and Jerome Ch'en); Allen & Unwin Ltd (*Book of Songs*, *Chinese Poems* and *Monkey* trs. Arthur Waley); The Bodley Head Ltd (*Stories from a Ming Collection* trs. Cyril Birch); Miss Pearl Buck and Methuen & Co Ltd (*All Men Are Brothers* trs. Pearl Buck); Clarendon Press (*Ch'u Tz'u: The Songs of the South* trs. David Hawkes); Constable & Co Ltd (*Lyrics from the Chinese* trs. Helen Waddell); Gerald Duckworth & Co Ltd (*Modern Chinese Poetry* trs. Harold Acton); Alfred A. Knopf Inc (*The Jade Mountain* trs. Witter Bynner. Copyright 1929 by Alfred A. Knopf Inc. Renewed 1957 by Witter Bynner); Dr Lin Yutang (*The Importance of Understanding*, World Publishing Co, Cleveland. *My Country and My People*, Wm. Heinemann Ltd. *The Wisdom of China and India*, Random House, New York. *The Wisdom of Confucius* and *The Wisdom of Laotse*, Random House and Michael Joseph Ltd); Mr Robert Payne (*The White Pony*); Arthur Probsthain (*The Works of Motse* trs. Y. P. Mei); Routledge & Kegan Paul Ltd (*The Golden Lotus* trs. Clement Egerton); UNESCO (*Flowers in the Mirror* trs. Lin Tai-yi).

INTRODUCTION

WHENEVER the Chinese discuss the civilizations of the world, they are apt to say, with pride, that they are the descendants of Huang Ti, meaning that theirs is among the oldest in the world. According to *Tse Hai*, one of the two outstanding contemporary Chinese dictionary-encyclopaedias, Chinese dynasties started with that of Huang Ti who ascended the throne of China in 2698 B.C., fifty-two years after the establishment of Babylon. The Chinese Nationalist Government, too, holds yearly memorial services for Huang Ti on 6 April, the National Memorial Day. The evidence now available of the earliest Chinese dynasty, however, only dates back to King Pan Keng, the first king of the Yin Dynasty, who reigned from 1401 to 1373 B.C. We cannot, of course, say that Chinese history began, therefore, with King Pan Keng. But even if one left the tracing of Chinese history to the archaeologists and historians and picked up the thread of Chinese civilization from King Pan Keng, it would be a tremendous task if one were to attempt to analyse even one facet of it—for instance, literature—in detail. This would require a team of scholars to devote their lives to it. The result of their expertise and labour would contribute greatly to the appreciation and understanding of Chinese literature, and consequently, Chinese civilization. The pity of it is that such an enterprise has yet to be undertaken.

In the absence of such a work, however, the curiosity of the Western reading public about Chinese literature must be satisfied by less detailed studies. It has been my aim in this volume to introduce to Western readers the history of Chinese literature in a simple, informative and interesting way without having to list the names of Chinese authors and their works in their myriad variety and losing the reader in a forest of foreign names and terms. There are, in fact, four striking features in the development of Chinese literature by means of which we can approach the subject, and thus satisfy the needs of the general reader.

1. *The golden ages and outstanding exponents of each form of the various genres of Chinese literature are generally recognized.*

The most outstanding feature in the story of Chinese literature is that we can say quite definitely who are the most outstanding poets, essayists, novelists and playwrights of the various periods during which one form or another of Chinese literature flourished, for their major works tower over those of their contemporaries, and are easy landmarks to cite.

Specifically, the poems collected in the *Book of Poetry* are the best of Chinese poetry from the early Yin Dynasty (1401 B.C.) to the middle Chun Chiu Period (570 B.C.), and Chu Yuan's *Tsu Tse* the best collection of poems up to the Warring States Period (403–246 B.C.).

Chuangtse's *Chuangtse* is the most beautiful piece of prose-writing up to the Warring States Period and Szema Chien's *Historical Record* the most moving piece of descriptive prose of the Han Dynasty (206 B.C.–A.D. 219). *Fu* was the form of poetry most practised in the Han Dynasty, while from the folk songs of the same period, which are contained in *Yueh Fu*, evolved the best of the 'five-word' poems by Tao Chien.

Folk songs of the Northern-Southern Dynasties were also the forerunners of the great 'new style' poetry of the Tang Dynasty (A.D. 618–906), epitomized by the works of Li Po and Tu Fu. The 'Classical Prose Movement' of the Tang Dynasty led by Han Yu revitalized Chinese prose, which had become overburdened with the impositions of sentence construction and tonal values of words, by re-emphasizing the importance of content and the simplicity of style. This led to the flowering of the short story, or *Chuan chi hsiao shuo*, which Yuan Chen, Tu Kuang-ting and others made famous.

In the Sung Dynasty (960–1276), Su Tung-po, Liu Yung and Hsingchi-chi's *Tse*, and in the Yuan Dynasty (1277–1367), Kuan Han-ching, Ma Chih-yuan and Wang Shih-fu's *Chu* comprised the greatest achievements of Chinese poetry in their two succeeding poetic forms.

Kuan Han-ching's *Tou O Yuan* and Wang Shih-fu's *Hsi Hsiang Chi* (*Western Chamber*) are the best Northern drama, or *Tsa Chu*, of the

Yuan Dynasty, while Tang Hsien-tsu's *Mou Tan Ting* (*Peony Pavilion*) is the best Southern drama, or *Chuan chi*, of the Ming Dynasty (1368–1643).

Novels flourished in the Ming and Ching Dynasties (1644–1911), the most outstanding of which are Lo Kuan-chung's *Three Kingdoms*, Wu Cheng-en's *Hsi Yu Chi* (*Monkey*), Shih Nai-an's *Shui Hu Chuan* (*All Men are Brothers*), Hsiao Hsiao Shen's *Chin Ping Mei* (*Golden Lotus*), Tsao Hsueh-chin's *Hung Lou Meng* (*Red Chamber Dream*), Wu Ching-tse's *Ju Lin Wai Shih* (*The Scholars*) and Li Ju-chen's *Ching Hua Yuan* (*Flowers in the Mirror*).

Prose, too, showed its vitality in the late Ming and the early Ching dynasties in the flowering of *Hsiao Pin Wen*, a form of prose written in the personal style, represented by Yuan Chung-lang, Chen Chi-ju, Chang Tai, Chin Sheng-tan and others.

In modern China, Mao Tun's novels, Lu Hsun's and Shen Tsung-wen's short stories, the prose of Chou Tso-jen, Lu Hsun and Lin Yutang, Tsao Yu's plays and Hsu Chih-mo's and Feng Chih's poems are considered to be the best of their genre.

2. *Buddhist literature has had immense influence on Chinese literature since the East Chin Period.*

The second significant feature in the development of Chinese literature is the immense influence of Buddhist literature on the development of every sphere of Chinese literature since the East Chin Period (A.D. 317). We cannot say that without this influence Chinese literature would have remained static and only poetry and prose been its principal literary forms, but we can safely say that it certainly would have been different from what it is today.

Buddhism was brought to China some time before the reign of Emperor Ming of the Han Dynasty (A.D. 58–75). But, because of a lack of trained translators, few Buddhist sutras were available in accurate Chinese editions. It was not until the East Chin and Northern-Southern Dynasties when more and more Chinese, weary of wars and the prevalent chaos in the country, turned to the Buddhist faith for consolation and promise of a future life, that better translated Buddhist sutras began to appear.

The great difficulty in translating Buddhist sutras from Sanskrit into Chinese was that, coupled with the fact that Sanskrit is alphabetical while Chinese is monosyllabic and ideographic, the literary form of the sutras combined prose and rhymed verses, a literary form then unknown in China. It was possible to convey the meaning, but impossible to retain the sonorous quality of the original, let alone the tonal harmony and beauty of the verses. Huei Chiao,[1] in his *Biographies of Great Buddhist Monks*, said, 'Since Buddhism was introduced to the East, many people have engaged in translating the meaning of Buddhist sutras, but few tried also to convey their tonal beauty. This is because Sanskrit is polyphonic and Chinese is monophthongal. The Chinese language when read in polyphonic manner is apt to sound hurried and abrupt. And to chant the Sanskrit verses in monophthongal Chinese would lengthen the verses so greatly that the rhymes are apt to be lost.'

In order that translated sutras should be pleasing to the ear when the prose was intoned, and moving when the verses were chanted, Chinese had to be adapted to the polyphonic sounds of Sanskrit and greater attention paid to *fan chieh*.[2] As a result of this, the tones of each monophthongal Chinese sound were better and more accurately defined and the four tonal differences of the Chinese language were established. These are *ping* or 'soft' tone, and three 'hard' tones, namely *shang* or acute tone, *chu* or grave tone, and *ju* or abrupt tone. About this, Professor Chen Yin-keh said, 'On the twentieth day of the second month in the seventh year of Yung Ming (A.D. 489), Tse Liang, Prince of Ching Ling, called a conference of Buddhist monks at his palace in the capital to differentiate between and define the tones of the Chinese language for reading Buddhist sutras and chanting the verses contained therein. This was a most important occasion. Chou Yu and Shen Yueh became the propounders of this new theory, called the "Theory of Four Tones".'[3]

Because of the general acceptance of the Theory of Four Tones, a new prosody of Chinese poetry came into being. Instead of using a single rhyme for a poem, poets started to write poems which changed rhymes every two, four or eight lines and more attention was paid to the balance of tonal values. The 'new style' poetry of the Tang Dynasty, *tse* of the Sung Dynasty and *chu* of the Yuan Dynasty, all followed basically the same theory which had grown out of the necessity to adapt the Chinese language to translating Buddhist sutras and propagating Buddhism.

The immediate effect of this emphasis on tonal value was the emergence of *pien-ti wen*, a form of prose which, apart from its require-

4

ments as to the tones of certain words in a sentence, consists of parallel sentences of alternately four and six words. These rules restricted the flow of thought to such an extent that from the Chi and Liang Dynasties on to the beginning of the Tang Dynasty, when this style was in great vogue, no good prose was written, except for a few short lyrical pieces. However, because of its pleasing tones and flowery phrases, *pien-ti wen* brought about greater consciousness of the difference between works of philosophy and history and works of creative literature, as attested by the sudden increase of works of literary criticism. Prince Chao Ming, when he edited his famous *Selected Literary Masterpieces*, left out for the first time philosophical, historical works, etc., which heretofore had been considered part and parcel of literature. This consciousness of different forms of writing and the realization of the importance of the imagination in creative writing are, to my mind, the greatest influence Buddhist literature had on Chinese literature. More specifically, perhaps, we can say that the influence of translated Buddhist literary masterpieces such as *Buddha Charita* by Asvagosha, contributed to the great superiority of *Monkey*, for instance, as a work of imagination over the short and outline-like ghost stories of the Northern-Southern Dynasties collected in Wang Yen's *Ming Hsiang Chi* and Yen Chih-tui's *Yuan Hun Chi*, etc.

At the same time, Buddhist monks of that period went to great trouble to explain the often obscure meaning of Buddhist sutras by telling anecdotes with a moral and describing in moving detail the horrors of Hell, etc., in order to arouse and hold the interest of the people and persuade them to believe in Buddhism. Huei Chiao referred to this in his *Biographies of Great Buddhist Monks*: 'When the Priests talked about the transience of life, the audience was seized by fear and trembled; when they described the scenes in Hell, the audience burst into tears of shock; when they examined the causes of tragedy, the audience felt that they were witness to the wrong-doings; when they preached the moral of their stories, the audience anticipated the punishment which was to follow; when they described happiness, the audience felt comforted and contented; when they portrayed sorrow, the audience wheezed and sobbed. Thus, audiences were moved and won over. The people left their seats to kneel down and repent. And then everyone joined in intoning Buddhist sutras and felt happy.'

As this became the prevalent practice, Buddhist sutras gradually became popularized and were expounded in story-telling form, so that, at last, a new literary form, *pien wen*, evolved, combining straight narration with rhymed verses, descriptive prose and allegories. For propagating Buddhism, *pien wen* proved to be very effective and popular. Inevitably, it was adapted for other purposes. Among the manuscripts, scrolls and antiques which were brought out from Tunhuang by A. Stein and Paul Pelliot and which are now housed in the British Museum and the Bibliothèque Nationale, others which were bought by the Japanese from private parties and stored at the Museum of Calligraphy in Tokyo and still others which were saved by the Chinese Government and are stored now in the Peking Library, fortyodd kinds of stories have been discovered written in the form of *pien wen*. Of these, *Shuntse Chih Hsiao Pien Wen* (*The Most Filial Shuntse*), *Lieh Kuo Chih Pien Wen* (*The Story of Lieh Kuo*), *Ming Fei Pien Wen* or *Ming Fei*, *Chiu Hu Pien Wen* or *Chiu Hu*, etc., have nothing to do with Buddhism in subject, but are historical or legendary stories retold in the literary form of *pien wen*. The narrative parts of these non-Buddhist *pien wen* veered away, in varying extent, from the *pien ti wen* style of prose and toward that of vernacular language. In *Chiu Hu Pien Wen* this is particularly noticeable. The style of the questions and answers contained therein is practically that of the professional storyteller of the Sung Dynasty. This and other popular *pien wen*, including *Tai Tsung Ju Ming Chi* (*Emperor Tai Tsung's Experience in the Nether World*), are very close in style to *hua pen* or the texts of story-tellers of the Sung Dynasty, and are in fact the forerunners of the latter. And it is in bringing about the emergence of *hua pen* that Buddhist literature contributed to the development of Chinese novels. For Chinese novels as a literary form evolved from and adopted almost indiscriminately features of *hua pen*.

The influence of *pien wen* and indirectly of Buddhist literature on the development of Chinese drama is less apparent. Chinese scholars, however, are agreed to a varying extent that since *pien wen* is the first of the literary forms in China to have contained both prose and rhymed verse, it must have contributed to the emergence of an art form of the Sung and Chin Dynasties called *chu kung tiao* which consists of sets of lyrics composed according to musical scores in various keys and linking descriptive passages and dialogue, and from which Northern drama or *tsa chu* evolved. They are probably right, but one wishes that this opinion could be better substantiated by extant scripts and books, as in the case of the development of Chinese novels. But we may safely say that *pien wen* is one of the important influences in the emergence of *chu kung tiao* and contributed indirectly to the birth of Chinese drama.

3. *The flowering of Chinese poetry, novels and the drama in their various forms generally sprang from the spontaneous expression of the common people.*

Wang Kuo-wei[4] said in his famous *Jen Chien Tse Hua* (*Comments on Tse*) that 'after a literary form has been prevalent for a long time, sets of refinements and restrictions will, because of the great number of practitioners, be imposed upon it. Even talented writers will find it difficult to abide by these, and still express their feelings. Therefore, they will turn to another form of literature to free themselves of the restrictions. This is why all literary forms decline sooner or later after a period of flowering.'

As far as the development of Chinese literature goes, he is right. But he forgot to mention that other literary forms are invariably created, however crudely, by the common people and not by the scholars. In fact, the history of almost every branch of Chinese literature always began as a popular form of literature, adopted and adapted and later developed by Chinese *literati*. This is the third important feature in the development of Chinese literature, and it is most striking in the development of its poetry.

It is common knowledge that one hundred and sixty *feng* poems, or more than half of the poems collected in the *Book of Poetry*, are folk songs. The four-word poem, as represented by these songs, gradually lost its force in the Chin Dynasty or early Han Dynasty. But before this, Chu Yuan created a new form of poetry called *sao ti* during the Warring States Period, which was greatly influenced by the folk songs of his country, Tsu. *Chiu Ko*, one set of his poems, for instance, was based on the then prevalent Wu songs, or songs of the priests in Tsu.

Throughout the Han Dynasty, poets either imitated the style of Chu Yuan's poems or devoted their time and energy to writing *fu*, a kind of prose-poetry which became in effect an exhaustive cataloguing of terms having anything at all to do with the theme of a poem. When the need for a new poetic form was felt, again it was the folk songs from which it sprang, this time, the 'five-word' poem, the classic examples of which are the famous *Nineteen Old-Style Poems* and those of Tao Chien.

In the two hundred-odd years from the Northern-Southern Dynasties to the Sui and early Tang Dynasties, poets tried incessantly to create new forms of poetry in accordance with the Theory of Four Tones. The five-word and seven-word 'stop-short'[5] and 'regular'[6] poems of the Tang Dynasty which are justifiably famous gradually developed during this period. Of these, five-word and seven-word 'stop-short' poems, although they first appeared at the end of the Han Dynasty, were not widely adopted by the poets as a form of expression. It was in the folk songs of Northern-Southern Dynasties, especially those in Southern China such as *Wu Shen Songs* and *Hsi Chu Songs*, that the 'stop-short' form of verses appeared most frequently. It is generally agreed that 'stop-short' verses as a literary form were not completely established until the reign of Emperor Wu of the Liang Dynasty (A.D. 464–549). But from the fact that most poets of that period used titles of folk songs in *Yueh Fu*, it appears that they acknowledge the influence of folk songs in their efforts to write poetry.

The five-word and seven-word 'stop-short' and 'regular' forms of poetry reached the peak of their development in the periods of Kai Yuan[7] and Tien Po[8] of the Tang Dynasty. Not long after this, these forms of poetry developed such refinements or restrictions that poets started again to look for other forms of expression. Liu Yu-hsi and Po Chu-yi were among the first to use *tse*, which had originally made its appearance during the reign of Emperor Wu of the Liang Dynasty, but had until now remained an art form of the common people.

Tse is essentially not unlike the lyrics of songs, because it also is written to the arrangements of sharp and soft tones and irregular metres of various airs. Before Liu Yu-hsi and others attempted this form of poetic expression, the wording of *tse* was, as a rule, crude and undeveloped. This might well have been the reason why poets were attracted to it—it was a new frontier for pioneers to explore and conquer.

So *tse* gradually developed during the Tang Dynasty. There were many excellent *tse* written during the Five Dynasties Period (A.D. 907–959), and in the Sung Dynasty *tse* became the most popular form of the time. Again, however, in the Southern Sung Dynasty, *tse* became so much burdened with refinement in form, tonal values, rhymes and rhetoric that only a few connoisseurs were able to write and appreciate its finer points. Following the importation of foreign music and its acceptance by the people, a form of popular ditty emerged and the poets again took over this crude poetic form and developed it into *chu*, which is in many ways the best form of poetic expression of China, and constitutes the libretti of Chinese drama of the Yuan and Ming Dynasties. The development of Chinese poetry is, then, a process of the poets periodically going back to and adopting folk songs or other poetic forms of expression of the common people for new styles. Poems in the styles of the Tang, Sung and Yuan Dynasties are still being written in China now, but since the Literary Revolution of 1919,[9] poetry has modelled itself upon that of the West, and, unlike the earlier forms of poetry, it is not closely connected with music.

In the development of the Chinese novel, the part played by folklore or spontaneous expression from the heart of the people is also great. We know that in the Tang Dynasty, *shuo shu*, or public story-telling, was already very popular. Yuan Chen[10] the poet said, 'I once heard a story-teller tell the story of *I Chih Hua* at the house of Hsin An. He started at three in the afternoon and was still at it two hours later.'[11] In fact, Pai Hsing-chien's[12] *The Story of Li Wa*, one of the most famous short stories of the Tang Dynasty, was based on the story of *I Chih Hua*. With the emergence of *pien wen*, this form of entertainment became more highly developed. In the Sung Dynasty, many people earned their living by specializing in telling certain kinds of stories. According to *Reminiscences of Things that Happened in Wu Ling*,[13] there were ninety-three famous story-tellers in Hangchow during the last years of the Southern Sung Dynasty, of whom fifty-two specialized in telling novels and short stories, twenty-three in historical novels. The popularity of the short stories and novels and the fierce competition among story-tellers led to the greater use of the spoken or vernacular language to describe better the dramatic scenes and emotional involvements of the leading characters. In the extant famous collections[14] of the texts of story-tellers, there are a few features which were brought about by the expedients of story-telling as a trade. Because of the necessity to attract and hold the interest of the listeners, story-tellers recited a poem and explained the theme of each chapter by way of introduction, or even told a short short-story as a curtain-raiser. They always ended each session at a crucial moment in the story, saying, 'If you want to know what happened next, please come back and listen to the next chapter.' Curiously enough, these expedients were carried into novel-writing, where they no longer served a purpose.

Story-telling remains a popular form of entertainment in China today. But in its long history, especially from the Sung Dynasty to the Ming Dynasty, the influence of story-telling on Chinese novels was not limited to their presentation. Many famous novels were actually based on the texts of the story-tellers. *All Men Are Brothers*, for instance, was based on *Ta Sung Hsuen Ho Yi Shih* (*The Story of the Hsuen Ho*[15] *Period of the Sung Dynasty*).

Chinese drama, with singers acting various roles in operas, was a late development. As late as the Sung Dynasty, public entertainment consisted only of puppet shows, shadow plays, humorous sketches, song and dance acts and story-telling with musical accompaniments, but no real plays or operas. Before the appearance of the opera of the Yuan Dynasty, the nearest thing to it was *chu kung tiao*. In fact, Wang Shih-fu's famous *Western Chamber* was based on Tung Chieh-yuan's *Hsien So Hsi Hsiang*, one of the three existing *chu kung tiao*.

According to all available accounts, Kung San-chuan was the creator of *chu kung tiao*. In *Pi Chi Man Chi*[16] (*Random Jottings in Pi Chi*), for instance, it is said, 'In the period from the reign of Emperor Shen Chung to that of Emperor Cheh Chung (A.D. 1068–1086), Chang Shen-jen of Yenchow was the best comedian in the capital and excelled in telling jokes. And Kung San-chuan of Tsechow was the creator of *chu kung tiao* which was popular even with officials and scholars.' There is no record of Kung's life, but he was everywhere mentioned in connection with popular entertainers. It is safe to say, therefore, that Chinese drama is also an art form created by the common people and adapted and developed by the *literati*.

4. There is a close relationship between music and Chinese literature.

The fourth and last significant feature of the development of Chinese literature is its close relationship to music. Chinese drama, as I have just mentioned, is in fact opera. Its relationship to music is obvious. Straight plays were unknown in China until 1919 when the 4 May Literary Movement introduced to the country plays by Western playwrights.

In poetry, the earliest collection of Chinese poems, the *Book of Poetry*, contains three hundred and five poems, all of which are really songs. According to Szema Chien (145–86 B.C.?) the greatest Chinese historian of the Han Dynasty, 'Confucius (551–479 B.C.) personally sang all three hundred and five songs and played the music on a stringed instrument.'[17] After the *Book of Poetry* the most brilliant achievement in Chinese poetry is Chu Yuan's *Tsu Tse*, which was greatly influenced by the music of the Tsus.

There is an entry in *Tso Chuan*[18] which states, 'The Duke of Chin once visited the armoury where prisoners were kept. He saw Chung Yi and asked, "Who is the prisoner with the cap of Tsu?" The warder answered, "A prisoner from Tsu who was captured and sent to us by the people of Cheng." The Marquis ordered that a *chin*[19] be given to the prisoner and asked him to play. The prisoner played airs of Tsu. . . .' Chu Yuan in writing his poems was influenced by the music of Tsu. *Chiu Ko*, one set of his poems, for instance, was based on Wu songs, or the songs of the priests.

Poems collected in *Yueh Fu* of the Han Dynasty, except for a few written by scholars, are all folk songs, some of which were even sung to music imported from Pei Ti, or Northern Barbarians.[20] From these folk songs evolved the five-word poems, while the 'new-style' poetry of the Tang Dynasty was developed from the folk songs of the Northern-Southern Dynasties which were sung in accordance with more than a hundred different musical scores. Of the two forms of 'new-style' poetry, namely 'regular' and 'stop-short', the latter were still songs and were sung by the people. There is an interesting anecdote about this in *Chi Yi Chi*[21]:

During the period of Kai Yuan, Wang Chih-huan, Wang Chang-ling and Kao Shih, all well-known poets, went together to an inn one day to have a few drinks. Upon entering, they found ten to twenty girl singers of Li Yuan[22] having a party there. They went over to a corner table by a fireplace and sat down to have their drinks while watching the singers. After a while, four young girls began to sing. What they sang were all poems of famous poets. The poets decided, 'We three are well-known poets but have never known which one among us is the most popular. Let's now decide this by the songs the girls sing. The one whose poems are sung in greatest number must be the most popular poet of us.' As it turned out, one of Chang-ling's poems was first sung, then one of Kao Shih's, and then again, one of Chang-ling's. Embarrassed, Chih-huan, who was a poet of long standing, pointed to the most beautiful of the girls and said, 'Wait till she sings. If she doesn't sing one of my poems, I will not consider myself a poet of equal standing with you two.' But as it turned out, the girl saved the day by singing one of Chih-huan's poems. The poets burst out laughing and joked hilariously with one another. The girl singers came over and made inquiries. When told the reason for the laughter, they curtsied and asked the poets to join their party. The three consented and drank with the girls for the rest of the day.

Tse, which flourished in the Sung Dynasty, is a kind of lyric composed to the requirements in tonal values, rhymes and the different metres of musical airs. In this respect, it is different from the 'stop-short' poems of the Tang Dynasty for which musical scores were composed. *Chu*, or dramatic poetry, of the Yuan and Ming Dynasties, had also to conform to the exigencies of operatic airs. These various traditional forms of poetry are considered *passé* by the young since the Literary Revolution of 1919. In the meantime, *pai hua* or vernacular poetry, which came into being under the influence of Western poetry, has not yet found a really outstanding exponent, and the close relationship between Chinese poetry and music seems to have been severed.

I mentioned earlier that Chinese novels developed from *hua pen*, or the tales of story-tellers of the Sung Dynasty. In some of these, notably *Kuai Tsui Lee Tsui-lien* (*The Sharp-tongued Lee Tsui-lien*) and *Chiang Shu-chen Wen Ching Yuan Yang Huei* (*The Meeting of Chiang Shu-jen with Her Beloved*), a great part of the texts is in verse. In the latter, sentences such as 'May I bother the accompanist to play again the tune he just played', were followed by paragraphs of verse.

It is clear that *hua pen* also depended much on music for the singing of the verse. But as *hua pen* gradually came to contain more and more vernacular prose, verses were proportionately reduced and the relationship between music and *hua pen* became less obvious. Therefore, when Chinese novels came into being, it was difficult to see that music had anything to do with their development. However, from the fact that *hua pen* first gained popularity because of its musical content, we may say that music contributed to the development of Chinese novels through its close relationship with its predecessor, *hua pen*.

These, then, are the four important features in the development of

Chinese literature, and it is with them always in mind that I have approached the task of writing this book. As the trends leading to the flowering of each form of literature essentially stem from the interplay of the last three named characteristics, the task of presenting a general picture of the development of Chinese literature becomes the tracing and outlining of the evolution of literary forms, which, under political and economic and/or social situations produced masterpieces or works of excellence.

This approach also allows me to concentrate on the outstanding literary figures and their works. More than two-thirds of the book is devoted to the presentation of the lives of outstanding literary figures and their works, which generally speaking are arranged as the second and third sections of each chapter, while the first section of each chapter depicts the background or trends leading to the flowering of each genre. I have compiled with some care a bibliography of Chinese literature and translated Chinese works in the hope that these will be helpful to readers of this book. A table of Chinese dynasties is also given in the Addenda.

CHAPTER I

The Poetry and Folk Songs of the Yin and Chou Dynasties and the Spring-Autumn Period

I. *THE EARLY RECORDED SONGS*

IN 1898, Chinese peasants in Hsiao-tun village in An-yang county, Honan, turned up from the earth many animal bones and tortoise shells while they were ploughing their fields. They must have been very annoyed by the large number of bones and shells which they found, which greatly added to their work. Apart from those which must have been destroyed, some ten thousand catties (a catty is equivalent to 1⅓ lb.) of these bones and shells had survived. Imagine the labour involved in removing this heap of bones and shells from the fields! But it was not an altogether thankless task. Soon, some local chemists came forward and took the bones off the peasants' hands, and paid them for their labour. The chemists thought that these fossilized bones were 'dragon bones', a useful ingredient for curing certain diseases. But they could not dispose of all the bones there were, and after a certain length of time some antique dealers heard of them and of the peculiar inscriptions and pictographs on the bones and shells. They were, however, uncertain of their value. Perhaps out of curiosity, or because they wanted to make some profit, they showed some of the bones and shells to clients, who were scholars, or maybe the scholars came to notice them by chance. In any case, Chinese scholars soon began to study and decipher the pictographs. The first to make some sense out of them was Sun Yi-jang, who believed that these pictographs were in fact the earliest form of Chinese characters. He wrote *Chi Wen Chu Lieh* to explain his theory, and many scholars, notably Wang Kuo-wei, Lo

Chen-yu, Liu O, S. Couling, F. H. Chalfant and L. C. Hopkins, followed with other works of research.

It is now established that Hsiao-tun was the capital of the Yin Dynasty under King Wu Yi, who reigned from 1198–1194 B.C., and that these bones and shells were principally records of oracles, inscribed by priests. From these records it can be seen that the people of Yin had not yet learned to use any iron implements but were dependent on bronze and even stone tools, and that during King Pan Keng's reign they were only starting to settle down, changing from nomadic lives to cultivating the land and raising crops. They depended very much on oracles in the way they conducted their lives. They consulted the deity, or deities, for predictions on the weather, on their harvests, on their journeys, battles, hunting and, especially, sacrificial rites. Of the existing 1,169 pieces of oracular bones, inscriptions on 538 pieces are about these rites and Wu, or priests, are also mentioned in some of these inscriptions. It would seem, therefore, that priests occupied quite an important position in society. The pictographs also show that there existed as yet no definite forms of writing to convey definite meanings. There were, for instance, forty-five different ways of conveying the word 'sheep'. Neither was the manner in which records were put down defined. Inscriptions on the bones and shells may go from left to right, may be in vertical lines running from top to bottom, or they may be in horizontal lines, starting from right to left. All in all, these oracular bones show that in the Yin Dynasty, Chinese characters were still evolving from the pictograph stage. The peasants in Hsiao-tun certainly could not have known that in finding the bones and shells, they had furnished proof of the existence of a dynasty and its culture which up to then was considered by some to be only legendary.

From the research of many scholars, we now know the meaning of some of the simple songs contained in the oracular records, such as:

> God wills rain (for a) good harvest.
> God wills (insufficient) rain (for a) poor harvest.

and:

> (Will) it rain today?
> Will the rain come from the West,
> Will the rain come from the East,
> Will the rain come from the North,
> Will the rain come from the South?

These oracular records also mentioned various musical instruments, including drums; *ching*, a kind of musical stone; *yao*, a short bamboo flute with three holes; and hand cymbals; and various dances. It is probable that music and dances were used mostly in connection with religious and sacrificial rites, and that many songs were sung at these rites. It is unfortunate that these songs were not recorded.

Apart from these oracular bones, *I-ching* is the most ancient source of Chinese literature. This is also a book of oracles, edited perhaps in the last years of the Yin Dynasty, or the early years of the Chou Dynasty by priests, and which, because of its nature, was not ordered to be burned by the first Emperor of the Ch'in Dynasty (246–205 B.C.), as were so many other Chinese classics. From the oracles in *I-ching*, we may surmise that the Yin people and the early Chou people were still in the process of changing from the nomadic life to become cultivators of land, for there were fewer oracles about agriculture than about cattle, the loss of a cow, a horse or a lamb. There are many oracles about wine vessels and drinking, and others about merchants and trading. Apparently, then, agriculture was being more widely practised then than in King Pan Keng's reign, and this led to the beginning of trade. Ways of writing Chinese characters seemed to have become more standardized and the art of writing songs, too, was much more advanced. There is a song which depicts the custom of carrying off and marrying girls by force:

> White, white
> White is the horse (the man rides),
> (He comes) not to rob us,
> But to marry one of our girls.
>
> On the horse that turns and hesitates
> (The girl) weeps and snivels.

However, monogamous marriage as an accepted custom was gradually taking root. There is the following song:

> Cranes keep away from land,
> So—when the husband is away
> A wife should not (mingle with other men)
> And get herself with child.

This was perhaps one of the first poems to use the technique of alluding to things in nature as a means of illustrating the sentiment people wanted to convey; metaphor is often used by the poets in the *Book of Poetry*.

But the sweetest of the *I-ching* songs, I think, is the following, from which the reader may derive a clear visual image of the feeling of the song:

> In the shade, a stork calls
> And softly his mate answers;
> Oh! I have brought excellent wine,
> Come, come and share it with me!

The technique of poetry-writing continued to advance, so that when Confucius edited the *Book of Poetry*[1] after his return to the state of Lu from his wanderings in various states in about 475 B.C., the poems he collected were more varied in their subjects, expressed better the feelings of the people and generally reflected the lives of the people from the early Chou Dynasty (1100 B.C.) to the middle of the Spring-Autumn Period (570 B.C.). There is, for instance, a poem entitled *Ming* which tells of a love affair from its very beginning to its bitter end; another, entitled *July*, depicts the farmers' lives of that period; and five, namely *Sheng Min, Kung Liu, Mien Mien Kua Ti, Huang Yu* and *Ta Ming*, together form an epic, a genre which is very rare in Chinese poetry. Szema Chien, the famous historian of the Han Dynasty, said in *The Life of Confucius* that Confucius in editing the *Book of Poetry* selected 305 poems from more than 3,000. It is, however, difficult to see how anyone can be certain as to the number of folk songs of any given period, of which, incidentally, more than half of the poems collected in the *Book of Poetry* consist. We also do not know what Confucius' criteria were in selecting the poems. Nevertheless, although there were Neo-Confucians of the Sung Dynasty who thought that some of the poems were lascivious and should be deleted, because of the prestige his name carried, they dared not touch the work of the Master and these poems remain for us to enjoy today.

2. THE LIFE OF CONFUCIUS

Although it is highly improbable that Confucius spoke only in aphorisms, that, nevertheless, is the popular notion of him. During the Second World War, there was a fad in western countries, particularly in America, to prefix 'Confucius said' to any catchphrase of the moment whereby the man was treated with a disrespect which bordered upon ridicule. At the other extreme, we have the Neo-Confucians of the Sung Dynasty who in their extreme reverence for Confucius wanted to turn him into a saint by denying him any human emotions and hiding the fact that he was illegitimate. They also denied that Confucius was capable of doing anything wrong. 'No! Confucius would not have done that!' they said, and whatever evidence to the contrary might exist must have been forged. The pity of it all was that Confucius himself did not write a book about his teachings or his life. *Lun Yu*[2] (*The Analects*) is only a collection of piecemeal records of what he said and how he acted, hardly adequate to give us a full picture of Confucius, the man.

This may have been due to the fact that during Confucius' lifetime, the art of prose writing was still at a rather rudimentary stage. *Chun Chiu* (*Spring-Autumn*), the historical record which Confucius wrote, is not much more stylistic than an account book. The writing of Motse, who lived some time after Confucius, remains rather bald in style. Nevertheless, from available records of his doctrine, we know that Confucius stood for a rationalized social order through the ethical approach, based on cultivation of personal character. This identification of politics with ethics led him to propound the idea that only capable and virtuous men should help to rule the country, to re-establish the feudal order, set up *li fa*, or a code of social behaviour, and to improve the lot of the people.

In common with those of other great philosophers, Confucius' doctrine met the need of his time. For Confucius was born in 551 B.C. during the Chun Chiu period of Chinese history when the Royal House of Chou was reduced to figureheads and the country was carved up into more than one hundred states, ruled by dukes, earls, barons, etc. It was also a tumultuous era when wars were incessant, old social orders being destroyed, and the lives of people being ruthlessly sacrificed. Many aristocratic families suddenly found themselves among the rootless paupers, and the common people longed for peace and a stabilized country. Confucius' idea reflected the wish of the people, and, in insisting on the appointment of men of character and ability to help rule the country, represented a bold reform. For official positions and social status were still inherited. ('Workers' sons are always workers' sons. Farmers' sons are always farmers' sons.') For persons other than the sons of aristocrats and officials to aspire to official positions, let alone demand the right to them, was nothing short of revolutionary.

Confucius himself was one of the aristocrats of reduced means. He himself said that when he was young he was poor and that was why he knew how to do many lowly tasks. Mencius also said that Confucius worked once as a keeper of stores and at another time was in charge of pastures. Although impoverished, Confucius still managed to study Chinese history. He himself often talked about his love of study. He said that he was not one of those who were 'born to know the truth', but that he was tireless in his search for knowledge and learning. He also admitted that in every hamlet of ten families there were men as righteous and honest as himself, but none who loved learning as much as he did. He probably became one of the most learned men of his time when he was still quite young and gradually attracted a group of young followers who discussed with him ways to cultivate their character and improve their knowledge, generally preparing for the day when they should be summoned to serve the rulers and the people. We see that when the man, in his later wandering days, was surrounded by the people of Kuang who threatened to kill him, he said to his disciples who were frightened, 'Since King Wen died, is not the moral tradition of King Wen (who, Confucius thought, carried out an ideal system of government during his reign) in my keeping? If it be Heaven's will that this tradition should be lost, posterity shall never share in the knowledge of it. But if it be Heaven's will that this tradition should not be lost, what can the people of Kuang do to me?' He saw himself then as the keeper of the best of Chinese moral tradition. This incident happened when he was about fifty-five years old. If, at an age when a man is supposed to have mellowed, Confucius was still so arrogant, it is probable that in his youth, he was quite a cocky and self-satisfied fellow. Perhaps that explained why when he went to Chou and studied the ancient rites and ceremonies and met Laotse, the wise old sage gave him this advice: 'A man who is brilliant and thoughtful is often in danger of his life, because he likes to criticize people. A man who is learned and well-read and clever at argument often endangers himself because he likes to reveal people's foibles. Do not think of yourself only as a son or a minister at court.'

But whatever his character might have been he more than made up for it by his great gift as a teacher. He himself said that he never refused to teach anyone, even those who presented him with dried meat instead of a fee. At a time when learning was a privilege enjoyed only by the aristocrats, this was as significant as the setting up of the universities in Alexandria, and at other places during the Renaissance period, or of compulsory education in modern times. But apart from the fact that he was the first man to set up a school which was open to the public, Confucius was also a teacher who was very close to his disciples. In *The Analects* there are many instances which show clearly this informal and close relationship between the Master and his students.

Confucius remarked one day to two or three of his disciples, 'Do you think that I have hidden anything from you? I certainly have not. There is nothing that I do that I do not share with you.' Another time: Tsekung loved to criticize people, and Confucius said, 'Ah Sze, you are very clever, aren't you? I have no time for such things.'

Confucius knew the different personalities of his students thoroughly, and when he answered their identical questions, he knew how to reach the heart of each man. Also, as is common with all true scholars, Confucius was not afraid to say that he did not know the answer to a question, or to admit that he was wrong. But rarest of all, perhaps, was that he was himself always in front of his students, freely expressing what he thought and joking with them, and was never embarrassed or angry when his disciples, too, spoke their mind.

Once, Confucius talked derisively about what one of his disciples had been doing and when the disciple showed his astonishment Confucius explained that he was only joking. At another time, Tselu, one of his disciples, asked if the ruler of Wei State were to put him in power what he would do first. Confucius said that he would first establish the exact meaning of terms (*cheng ming*). Tselu said, 'Is that so? How pedantic you can be! What do you want to do that for?' Confucius was not angry. 'You are simple-minded indeed,' he said, and went on to explain why he thought it necessary to establish the exact meanings of terms. Again, commenting on a poem in the *Book of Poetry*, in which a girl said that it was not that she did not think of her lover, but that 'his house was so far away', Confucius said, 'She *really* did not think of him at all, otherwise how could his house seem so far away?'

It was, however, a sense of mission which drove the man on in his studies and bound him to his disciples. They wanted to help the rulers of various states take the famous kings of old as examples for, according to Confucius, these united the country in peace and order, established the feudal order and code of social behaviour and delivered the people from suffering. The only way open to the disciples was to try to persuade the rulers to put into practice the doctrines Confucius believed in. But few, if any, of the rulers were convinced of the practicability of his theories. Confucius himself was partly responsible for this. For whenever a ruler asked him how to rule a country, Confucius would invariably give a doctrinal or seemingly impertinent answer, such as telling Baron Chi Kang first to learn to govern himself before trying to govern his country, which must have seriously affected his standing with the Baron. It is no wonder, then, that Confucius was unsuccessful in winning himself an official position, still less in putting into practice his theory of government. Szema Chien said that Confucius was not appointed to an official position until he was forty-nine years old, and was compelled by circumstances to resign after having served consecutively as magistrate, Secretary of Labour and Secretary of Justice for a total of only six years in the State of Lu. Many scholars have since cast doubt on this account, saying that there is no reliable direct evidence of Confucius ever having held any position of importance. But even if Szema Chien's account were true, he did not say that Confucius put into practice any of his doctrines, or accomplished anything of importance, or that any of his disciples whom he had trained as officials helped him in his work during his tenure of office. It seems safe to say that when he set out from Lu at the age of fifty-five to tour various states, hoping to persuade one of the rulers to put his theories of government into practice, Confucius had not had much of a political career. But the fact that he made this tour at an age when people normally think of retiring, and was still as full of energy as ever, is the measure of the man. There is a passage in *The Analects*: Tselu was stopping for the night at the Stone Gate. The gatekeeper asked him, 'Where are you from?' 'I am from Confucius,' replied Tselu. 'Oh, is he the fellow who knows a thing cannot be done and still wants to do it?' This was perhaps the best description of Confucius' state of mind when he set out on this journey. He was frustrated, but not bitter; he tried his best.

For fourteen years Confucius wandered from one state to another. While in most of these states he was received with courtesy, his advice when sought was never taken. On top of this, he and his party met with many unexpected difficulties. Once, he was mistaken for someone else and surrounded by hostile people who threatened to kill him and his disciples. At another time, they ran out of food and many in his party fell sick. On all occasions Confucius took such adversities calmly even humorously. For instance, when Confucius and his disciples lost track of each other, the latter finally heard from the crowd that there was a tall man with a high forehead standing at the East Gate who looked like an ancient emperor, but who was crestfallen like a homeless, wandering dog. On being told of this remark when the disciples finally found him Confucius replied, 'I don't know about looking like an ancient emperor, but as for looking like a homeless wandering dog, he was quite right! Quite right!'

Nevertheless, humour and even confidence can be worn quite thin. Once, out of desperation, Confucius even considered joining forces with the notorious magistrate of a city and only gave up the notion after Tselu protested strongly. At the end of his wandering, however, when Confucius had admitted failure to himself and was going back to his native country to devote himself to editing and writing, he compared himself and his disciples to a band of nondescript animals, 'neither buffalo nor tiger', who wandered in the wilds, and asked his disciples what was wrong with him. Tselu replied, 'Perhaps we are not great enough and have not been able to win people's confidence. Perhaps we are not wise enough and people are unwilling to follow our teachings.' Tsekung answered, 'The Master's teachings are too great for the people, and this is why the world cannot accept them. Why don't you come down a little from your heights?' Confucius was not satisfied with the answers and asked Yen Huei what he thought. Yen Huei said, 'The Master's teachings are so great. That is why the world cannot accept them. However, you should just do your best to spread your ideas. What do you care if they are not accepted? The very fact that your teachings are not accepted shows that you are a true gentleman. If the truth is not cultivated, the shame is ours; but if we have cultivated the teachings of a moral order and they are not accepted by the people, it is the same with those in power. The very fact that you are not accepted shows that you are a gentleman.' Confucius was pleased and said with a smile, 'Is that so? Oh, son of Yen, if you were a rich man, I would be your valet!'

It seems to me that Confucius knew all three answers were right, but he had decided that whatever people might think of his teachings, he had to do his best. He was of course disappointed that his doctrines were not accepted, but there was nothing he could do about it. He had to go on teaching. Thus, we see quite clearly his sense of relief when he realized that his favourite pupils understood him. What he said showed once again how his sense of humour sustained him in his disappointment.

His love of music and poetry, too, made him not a man to dwell too long in despair. We see that once when he was surrounded by soldiers in Chen, Confucius kept on reading and singing and accompanying himself on a stringed instrument. It is also recorded that when he heard someone sing and liked it, he would ask for an encore and join in the refrain. Although it may have been an exaggeration that when he heard the music of Hsiao (symbolic dance music ascribed to Emperor Shun (2255–2204 B.C.)), he forgot the taste of meat for three months, his love of music and songs led him to edit the *Book of Poetry*, all 305 poems of which he could sing himself. He once said of this work, 'Since my return to Lu from Wei, I have been able to restore the musical tradition and classify the music of Sung and Ya[3] and restore the poems to their respective original music.'

In *The Analects* Confucius referred most frequently to the *Book of Poetry*. He once said to a group of his disciples, 'Why don't you people study *Poetry*? *Poetry* will stir your imagination, help you to be more observant of things, more understanding of others and more moderate in your opinions. It is helpful to one in serving one's father and one's king. Furthermore, it will help one to know more about plants, trees, birds and beasts.'

One of the most interesting entries in *The Analects* tells of Chen Kang asking Confucius' son if his father had taught him anything special:

Chen Kang asked Po-yu, 'Is there anything special that you were taught by your father?' Po-yu replied, 'No. One day he was standing alone when I ran past in the court, and he asked me, "Have you learned the *Book of Poetry* yet?" and I said, "Not yet." "If you don't study the *Book of Poetry*," he said, "you won't be able to express yourself well . . .!" '

Confucius seemed to think that studying the *Book of Poetry* was the most useful task a scholar could take upon himself. He said, 'A man may have studied the "three hundred poems", but if he is ineffective when given a government post, at a loss for words when sent on a diplomatic mission, even if his learning were extensive, of what use is it?'

He was most pleased when his disciples were able to make use of the poems:

Tsekung asked, 'What do you think of a person who is not subservient to the rich when he is poor, and not conceited when he is rich?' Confucius replied, 'That's fairly good. It would be better if he were happy when he is poor, and had self-discipline when he is rich.' Tsekung said, 'In the *Book of Poetry* there is this phrase: "As things cut, as things filed, as things chiselled, as things polished." Can it be that expresses exactly what you mean?' Confucius said, 'Sze is worthy to discuss the *Book of Poetry* with me. I tell him something, and he comes back with a fresh suggestion.'

Once Tsehsia asked (concerning a passage in the *Book of Poetry*), 'What is the meaning of the passage, "She has a winning smile, and her eyes are so clear and bright. Her dress is of a coloured design on a plain background"?' Confucius said, 'In painting, we must have a plain background.' 'Does that mean that the ceremonial forms of Li must be laid on a background of simplicity of character?' Confucius said, 'Now you have contributed a fresh thought, Ah Shang! You are worthy to study the *Book of Poetry*.'[4]

Undoubtedly, such seemingly fanciful interpretations of the meanings of the poems contributed to the belief of many later Confucians that the love poems in the *Book of Poetry* contained hidden allegorical meanings. But, during the Spring-Autumn Period, to quote poems from the *Book of Poetry* and indulge in interpreting the meaning of the poems was an occupation which was not confined to Confucius. In fact, the *Book of Poetry* seemed to have been one of the textbooks of the diplomatists of that period, and clever interpretations of the poems one of the necessary techniques of their calling. In *Tso Chuan*, for instance, free interpretations of 219 poems were given by ministers and statesmen at banquets and meetings, among which more than ten were not recorded in the *Book of Poetry*.

Whatever were the reasons for the importance attached to the *Book of Poetry*, Confucius himself, partly because of his love of music and poetry, was able to face a life of frustration without bitterness. Perhaps that was also why he said a man's education should begin with poetry, be strengthened by proper conduct and 'consummated by music'.

He was indeed a man of curious sensitivity and deep emotion. When he was in the company of people in mourning, he lost his appetite, and if he should cry (at a funeral ceremony), he would not sing that day. Once he happened to pass by while a funeral service of one of his old acquaintances was being conducted. He went in, and moved by the weeping of others, also wept. When he came out, he asked one of his disciples to take a present to the family of the deceased and said, 'Take it as my formal present. I hate this weeping without reason.' At the death of his favourite disciple, Confucius wept bitterly. When asked why he wept so hard and was so shaken, he replied, 'If I don't weep bitterly at the death of such a person, for whom should I weep bitterly?'

And he was known to lose his temper. In *The Analects* this incident is recorded:

Yuan Jen (who was reputed to have sung at his mother's death) squatted in Confucius' presence and Confucius said, 'As a child, you were impudent; since you have grown up, you have done absolutely nothing; and now in your old age, you refuse to die! You are a thief!' Confucius thereupon struck him on the shin with a cane.

Another incident recorded in the same book reveals Confucius as capable of being really rude:

Ju Pei wanted to see Confucius and Confucius declined by saying that he was sick. When the man was just outside the door, Confucius took a stringed instrument, the *seh*, and sang, in order to let him hear (and know that he was not sick after all).

By being completely himself in front of his disciples, and by being a man, as he described himself, 'who forgets to eat when he is excited about something, forgets all his worries when he is happy and is not aware that old age is coming on', Confucius completely won the respect and affection of his disciples. For it was perhaps his personality, his joy of living, enthusiasm and stubborn determination to do something for the people, more than his teachings, which left the most profound impression on his disciples. Yen Huei, for instance, literally worshipped him, comparing him to a great mysterious power: 'You look up to it and it seems so high. You try to drill through it and it becomes hard. You seem to see it in front of you, and all of a sudden it appears behind you.' Tsekung was more straightforward. When someone tried to belittle the greatness of Confucius, Tsekung said, 'Confucius is like the moon and the sun, which you can never reach. A man can shut his eyes to the sun and the moon, but what harm can that do to the sun and the moon? You are just trying to do the impossible.'

When Confucius died in 479 B.C., a few years after his return to Lu from wandering in various states, at the age of seventy-two, his disciples all observed the regular mourning of three years. It may seem strange that these disciples, all men in the prime of their lives, should have devoted such a long time to mourning their Master, but such was the impact of Confucius on his students. Through his disciples, Confucius' influence persisted throughout the ages, and in this respect we think of other great teachers of the past, men like Socrates and St Francis of Assisi, whose personality more than their scholarship seemed to account for their great influence.

3. *THE* BOOK OF POETRY

Of the 305 poems in the present *Book of Poetry*, we know definitely the authors of five of them, and from the content of the poems and other data, we may ascertain the authorship or date of another sixteen poems. Generally speaking, the *Book of Poetry* contains poems written during the period between the early Chou Dynasty (*circa* 1100 B.C.) and the middle of the Spring-Autumn Period (*circa* 570 B.C.). In these five hundred-odd years, the Chou Dynasty, because of the progress in agriculture and the establishment of a feudal order, at first passed through a prosperous period. In the reigns of Kings Chen and Kang, for forty years no one had to be brought before the courts and punished. But its power gradually declined after the reigns of Kings Chao and Mu. Of the last three kings of the West Chou Period, King Li, who reigned from 878–827 B.C., was exiled and King Yu, who reigned from 781–771 B.C., was killed.

After King Ping moved his capital to Loyang, the prestige of the Royal House of Chou was further reduced, and from 722 B.C. on, the kings reigned only in name, and the country was thrown into extreme chaos. These changes and their effect on the lives of the people were reflected in the *Book of Poetry* and gave birth to the diverse poems contained in it which are so much admired.

There have been various opinions concerning the classification of the poems. Some scholars ignore the traditional way of classification, and group the poems according to their subject. Indeed, the traditional way of dividing the poems into three categories, namely *feng* or folk songs of fifteen states, *ya* or verses of songs sung at Court, and *sung* or verses of songs sung at sacrificial rites held for the royal house or ducal houses, is not entirely satisfactory. Poems that should be put into one category are sometimes put into another. Nevertheless, this classification does have some advantages. We know, for instance, that *feng* poems are principally lyrical love songs, *ya* poems are narrative verses and *sung* poems are poems sung when people were dancing as an accompaniment to music. From the point of view of Western readers, it is more important to understand at a glance the nature of these poems than to know what their subjects are, which, incidentally, the method of classifying by subject cannot really convey unless a great number of headings are made, which would defeat its own purpose. For this reason, I have kept to the traditional way of classification in giving examples of the poems.

A word about the form of the poems. The majority of the poems have four words in a line, but the number of lines in a stanza vary. The rhyming comes most often at the end of a line. Principally, there are three variations, i.e. in quatrains every line rhymes, every other line rhymes or the first and second lines rhyme with the fourth line. Head rhyme, internal rhyme and alliteration, as found in Western poetry, are seldom used. It can be said, then, that the form and method of rhyming in poems were not definitely established at the time, and that the poems were, perhaps, the natural expression of the feelings of the people.

A. *Feng* Poems

There are 160 *feng* poems in the *Book of Poetry*, or more than half of the total number of poems in the book. These are the poems which are considered to be lascivious by many of the Neo-Confucians of the Sung Dynasty. Confucius himself, however, rather liked them. This can be seen from the fact that he urged his son to study them, saying that one who has not studied them is like a man who is standing with his face to a wall. Indeed, these poems are fresh and direct, and the most moving and vivid of all the poems, principally because the great majority of them are love songs, expressing the changing facets of this universal human emotion. There is, for instance, one in which a girl blames a boy for not coming to see her:

> Oh, you with the blue collar,
> On and on I think of you.
> Even though I do not go to you,
> You might surely send me news?

> Oh, you with the blue collar,
> Always and ever I long for you.
> Even though I do not go to you,
> You might surely sometimes come?
>
> Here by the wall-gate
> I pace to and fro.
> One day when I do not see you
> Is like three months.[5]

Another one is a variation of the same theme:

> I cannot come to you. I am afraid.
> I will not come to you. There, I have said.
> Though all the night I lie awake and know
> That you are lying, waking, even so.
> Though day by day you take the lonely road,
> And come at nightfall to a dark abode.
>
> Yet if so be you are indeed my friend,
> Then in the end,
> There is one road, a road I've never gone,
> And down that road you shall not pass alone.
> And there's one night you'll find me by your side
> The night that they shall tell me you have died.[6]

Still, one may be in love, but one cannot stand being taken for granted. As this girl says:

> If you tenderly love me,
> Gird your loins and wade across the Chen;
> But if you do not love me—
> There are plenty of other men,
> Of madcaps maddest, oh!
>
> If you tenderly love me,
> Gird your loins and wade across the Wei;
> But if you do not love me—
> There are plenty of other knights,
> Of madcaps maddest, oh![7]

Another girl was torn between her love for the man and her fear of her parents, brothers and all the rest of the world:

> Don't come in, sir, please!
> Don't break my willow-trees!
> Not that *that* would very much grieve me;
> But alack-a-day! What would my parents say?
> And love you as I may,
> I cannot bear to think what that would be.
>
> Don't cross my wall, sir, please!
> Don't spoil my mulberry-trees!
> Not that *that* would very much grieve me!
> But alack-a-day! What would my brothers say?
> And love you as I may,
> I cannot bear to think what that would be.
>
> Keep outside, sir, please!
> Don't spoil my sandal-trees!
> Not that *that* would very much grieve me;
> But alack-a-day! What would the world say?
> And love you as I may,
> I cannot bear to think what that would be.[8]

The poem which describes most poignantly a love story from its
very beginning to the sad ending is perhaps the following:

> You seemed a guileless youth enough,
> Offering for silk your woven stuff;
> But silk was not required by you:
> I was the silk you had in view.
> With you I crossed the ford, and while
> We wandered on for many a mile
> I said, 'I do not wish delay,
> But friends must fix our wedding day—
> Oh, do not let my words give pain,
> But with the autumn come again.'
>
> And then I used to watch and wait
> To see you passing through the gate;
> And sometimes when I watched in vain,
> My tears would flow like falling rain;
> But when I saw my darling boy,
> I laughed and cried aloud for joy.
> The fortune-tellers, you declared,
> Had all pronounced us duly paired;
> 'Then bring a carriage,' I replied,
> 'And I'll away to be your bride.'

The mulberry-leaf, not yet undone
By autumn chill, shines in the sun,
O tender dove, I would advise,
Beware the fruit that tempts thy eyes!
O, maiden fair, not yet a spouse,
List lightly not to lovers' vows!
A man may do this wrong, and time
Will fling its shadow o'er his crime,
A woman who has lost her name
Is doomed to everlasting shame.

The mulberry-tree upon the ground
Now sheds its yellow leaves around,
Three years have slipped away from me,
Since first I shared your poverty;
And now again, alas the day!
Back through the ford I take my way,
My heart is still unchanged, but you
Have uttered words now proved untrue;
And you have left me to deplore
A love that can be mine no more.

For three long years I was your wife,
And led in truth a toilsome life;
Early to rise and late to bed,
Each day alike passed o'er my head.
I honestly fulfilled my part;
And you—well, you have broke my heart,
The truth my brothers will not know,
So all the more their gibes will flow.
I grieve in silence and repine
That such a wretched fate is mine.

Ah, hand in hand to face old age!—
Instead, I turn a bitter page.
Oh for the river-banks of yore;
Oh for the much-loved marshy shore;
The hours of girlhood, with my hair
Ungathered, as we lingered there.
The words we spoke, that seemed so true,
I little thought that I should rue;
I little thought the vows we swore
Would some day bind us two no more.[9]

Other *feng* poems depict misfortunes in marriage, sad feelings of impoverished aristocrats, the lives of peasants, etc. There are also many anti-war poems. The following is one:

> How few of us are left, how few!
> Why do we not go back?
> Were it not for our prince and his concerns,
> What should we be doing here in the dew?
>
> How few of us are left, how few!
> Why do we not go back?
> Were it not for our prince's own concerns,
> What should we be doing here in the mud?[10]

B. *Ya* Poems

There are 105 *ya* poems in the *Book of Poetry*. These poems are chiefly verses of songs sung at banquets or meetings of the Court. They are, as a rule, longer than the *feng* poems, and their choice of words better. There are some poems which by their nature seem to have been included in this category by mistake. This could have been due to interpolations. It may also be that these poems were arranged according to their musical score, and all the poems that were sung with a certain type of music were grouped together. Some Chinese scholars have advanced the theory that all the poems in the *Book of Poetry* were indeed classified on this basis. It was said that in the early Han Dynasty, some five hundred years after Confucius' time, musicians could still sing the 'Three Hundred Poems'. Unfortunately, we now have no means of finding the reasons for including in this category poems of obviously a different nature.

Ya poems are mainly narrative poems. Of these, the five epic poems *Sheng Ming, Kung Liu, Mien Mien Kua Ti, Huang Yu* and *Ta Ming* tell of the events leading to the establishment of the Chou Dynasty. There have been few epics in Chinese literature and considerable importance is attached to these five poems by Chinese scholars. Of these, *Mien Mien Kua Ti* is perhaps the best:

> The young gourds spread and spread.
> The people after they were first brought into being
> From the River Tu went to the Chi.

Of old, Tan-fu the duke
Scraped shelters, scraped holes;
As yet they had no houses.

Of old, Tan-fu the duke
At coming of day galloped his horses,
Going west along the river bank
Till he came to the foot of Mount Chi.
Where with the lady Chiang
He came to look for a home.

The plain of Chou was very fertile.
Its celery and sowthistle sweet as rice-cakes.
'Here we will make a start; here take counsel,
Here notch our tortoise.'
It says, 'Stop,' it says, 'Halt.
Build houses here.'

So he halted, so he stopped.
And left and right
He drew the boundaries of big plots and little,
He opened up the ground, he counted the acres
From west to east;
Everywhere he took his task in hand.

Then he summoned his Master of Works,
Then he summoned his Master of Lands
And made them build houses.
Dead straight was the plumb-line,
The planks were lashed to hold the earth;
They made the Hall of Ancestors, very venerable.

They tilted the earth with a rattling,
They pounded it with a dull thud,
They beat the walls with a loud clang,
They pared and chiselled them with a faint ping, ping;
The hundred cubits all rose;
The drummers could not hold out.

They raised the outer gate;
The outer gate soared high.
They raised the inner gate;
The inner gate was very strong.
They raised the great earth-mound,
Whence excursions of war might start.

33

And in the time that followed they did not abate their sacrifices,
Did not let fall their high renown;
The oak forests were laid low,
Roads were opened up.
The Kun tribes scampered away;
Oh, how they panted!

The peoples of Yü and Jui broke faith,
And King Wen harried their lives.
This I will say, the rebels were brought to allegiance,
Those that were first were made last.
This I will say, there were men zealous in their tasks,
There were those that kept the insolent at bay.[11]

C. *Sung* Poems

There are forty *sung* poems in the *Book of Poetry*, and the Chou *sung* poems in the group are the most ancient of the 'Three Hundred Poems'. *Sung* poems were principally sung by dancers during the performance of sacrificial rites held for the royal house or ducal houses. Chinese scholars tend to think that there were dances at such rites and that five poems of the Chou *sung* group, namely *Wei Ching, Chüeh, Heng, Lai* and *Pan*, were sung by dancers of certain mime and war dances. It is not possible to say exactly what sort of dances these were.

Among the poems sung at sacrificial rites to ancestors is the longest poem in the whole book. Here is a short one which praises the exploits of the ancestors, in this case Kings Wen and Wu:

Oh, great were you, King Wu!
None so doughty in glorious deeds.
A strong toiler was King Wen;
Well he opened the way for those that followed him.
As heir Wu received it.
Conquered the Yin, utterly destroyed them.
Firmly founded were his works.[12]

Some poems were sung after the harvest was in, expressing the people's thanks to the ancestors at sacrificial rites. Here is one example:

Abundant is the year, with much millet, much rice;
But we have tall granaries,
To hold myriads, many myriads and millions of grain.
We make wine, make sweet liquor,
We offer it to ancestor, to ancestress,
We use it to fulfil all the rites,
To bring down blessings upon each and all.[13]

CHAPTER II

The Prose of the Spring-Autumn and Warring States Periods

1. *THE EVOLUTION OF PROSE*

THE most ancient collection of Chinese prose pieces is to be found in *Shu Ching* (*The Book of History*). This is in the form of speeches and declarations made by various kings of the Yu Hsia, Shang, Yin and Chou Dynasties. It is believed that these speeches and declarations were taken down by officials exactly as the kings made them; in other words, they were vernacular prose, so that as spoken words evolved, the meaning of the words in the texts became more and more difficult to understand, and the style of the prose bore less and less resemblance to that of later prose, even to that of *Tao Te Ching*, the earliest but one of the ancient books of prose. To translate the meaning of these speeches and declarations would serve no purpose in the study of the evolution of prose.

But let us consider the *Tao Te Ching*, which is a record of Laotse's sayings taken down by his disciples. A great part of the prose in it is rhymed. Some people think that it is an example of Chinese prose in its earliest stage of development. Whether this is true or not, the meaning of the text in *Tao Te Ching* is certainly often ambiguous, and this can be due to an incomplete mastery of the technique of writing. The meaning of the first four lines of the first chapter of the book, for instance, has long been a matter of controversy. Many scholars think that they mean:

> The Tao that can be told of
>   Is not the Absolute Tao;
> The Names that can be given
>   Are not absolute Names.
> The Nameless is the Origin of Heaven and Earth;
> The Named is the Mother of All Things.[1]

Other equally eminent scholars give the lines a different interpretation:

> Tao explains the Absolute Tao
> And Names express the Absolute Names.
> 'Non-being' is the Origin of Heaven and Earth;
> 'Being' is the Mother of All Things.[2]

In form, the prose in *The Analects* is similar to that of *Tao Te Ching*, in that it also consists of short chapters, each made up of several sentences, in some cases only a single sentence. The meaning of the sentences in *The Analects* is clearly conveyed, but the book gives its readers a sense of abruptness, or even frustration, because no event is ever completely recorded, and its contents appear scrappy and unedited. This perhaps represents the stage of development of prose in that period, as almost the same style of writing was used by Confucius in writing *Spring-Autumn*, the book by which he wished to be judged.

From the quotations in the preceding chapter, we have seen the style of writing in *The Analects*. Here is an example of the style of *Spring-Autumn*:

> In the second year of the reign of Duke Huan, in spring, on the Mou-shen day of the first month, Tu murdered Yu-yi, the Duke of Sung, and Kung Fu, a Tai-fu. The Baron of Teng had an audience with the King.
>
> In summer, in the fourth month, the Duke took the great sacrificial vessel of Kao from Sung. On the Mou-shen day, he installed it at the ancestral temple of the Royal House.

This résumé-like or telegraphic style of writing finally developed into one of comparatively well-organized, more detailed dissertations of greater length, when China entered the Warring States Period. With the invention of iron tools, agricultural productivity greatly increased, and the land value increased with it. The nobility therefore heeded even less the kings of the Chou Dynasty and fought to annihilate each other and snatch the land. The hundred-odd states of the Spring-Autumn Period were merged into seven larger states. In carrying out their aggression, the rulers of these states were helped by the scholars, for new production tools and methods had brought about drastic changes in the social structure and personal fortunes, and the scholars, either for selfish reasons or acting for the good of the people, pleaded the cause of peace and the unification of the country, and were heard. The result was that in this chaotic period of Chinese history, for the first time— and for the last—there arose many schools of thought which contended with each other freely and fiercely as to what was good government. To gain the ear of the rulers of the seven states and convince them that they had the opportunity to become as great as the kings of the past, the scholars had to rely on the eloquence of their speeches and writings. As a result of this, the art of prose writing advanced rapidly.

Among the first to write well-reasoned and well-organized discourses was Motse. But perhaps he concentrated too much on logic and not enough on style and rhetoric, for there is still a baldness of style in his writing.

The following is one of his pieces on 'Universal Love':

Motse said: The purpose of the magnanimous is to be found in procuring benefits for the world and eliminating its calamities.

But what are the benefits of the world and what its calamities?

Motse: Mutual attacks among states, mutual usurpation among houses, mutual injuries among individuals; the lack of grace and loyalty between rulers and ruled, the lack of affection and filial piety between father and son, the lack of harmony between elder and younger brothers—these are the major calamities in the world.

But whence did these calamities arise, out of mutual love?

Motse said: They arise out of want of mutual love. At present feudal lords have learned only to love their own states and not those of others. Therefore they do not scruple about attacking other states. The heads of houses have learned only to love their houses and not those of others. Therefore they do not scruple about usurping other houses. And individuals have learned only to love themselves and not others. Therefore they do not scruple about injuring others. When feudal lords do not love one another there will be war in the fields. When heads of houses do not love one another they will usurp one another's power. When individuals do not love one another they will injure one another. When ruler and ruled do not love one another they will not be gracious and loyal. When father and son do not love each other they will not be affectionate and filial. When elder and younger brothers do not love each other they will not be harmonious. When nobody in the world loves any other, naturally the strong will overpower the weak, the many will oppress the few, the wealthy will mock the poor, the honoured will disdain the humble, the cunning will deceive the simple. Therefore all the calamities, strife, complaints and hatred in the world have arisen out of want of mutual love. Therefore, the benevolent disapproved of this want.[3]

Motse's emphasis on logic had considerable influence on the other schools of thought. The one school which carried logic to the extreme was that of the Sophists, such as Hueitse and Kungsun Lung, of whose sophistries Chuangtse mentioned these examples:

The egg contains hair (latent in the embryo). A chicken has three legs (two plus the will which moves them). Ying (a small country) possesses the world (being identical in nature with the rest). A dog can be a sheep and a horse lays eggs (all being questions of nomenclature). The frog has a tail (though it is atrophied). Fire is not hot (heat being subjective). Mountains have mouths (they echo). The wheel never touches the ground (except one point at a time). The eye does not see (for it is the brain which does). The finger does not point to a thing, but rather points endlessly beyond it. The tortoise is longer than the snake (relativity of notions of size).[4]

Somewhat later than Motse came Mencius, who as one of the leaders of the then decaying school of Confucianism was an eloquent writer and ever anxious to spread the teaching of Confucius. He sometimes appears dogmatically critical in his attacks on other schools of thought, especially those of Motse and Yang Chu, which were said to have captured between them the hearts of all the people. Mencius said, 'Yang Chu's egoism denies the claim of a sovereign and Motse's universal altruism denies that of a father. He who denies the claim of either a sovereign or father is a brute beast.' No wonder one of his disciples told him that people thought him argumentative. But as he himself said, he had to be. And this compelling need to win the support of the rulers and the people for Confucianism must have been an important contributing factor to the gusto and eloquence we find in his writing, which has a captivating quality which many later prose writers, including Szema Chien and Su Tung-po, greatly admired and tried to imitate, and which was used as one of the criteria for the judgment of prose writing.

Here is an example of Mencius' writing. In a passage expounding the goodness of human nature, he wrote:

> Kaotse said, 'The desires for food and sex are born in us. Benevolence comes from within and is not something external, while righteousness is something external, and does not come from within.' Mencius replied, 'What do you mean by saying that benevolence comes from within while righteousness (or righteous conduct) is something external?' 'When I see a tall man and call him tall,' Kaotse replied, 'it is not I who am tall (or that tallness is not within me), just as when something is white and I call it white, I observe its external white appearance merely. Therefore, I say righteous conduct is external.' 'Now,' said Mencius, 'the whiteness of a white horse in no way differs from the whiteness of a white person. But do you think that the tallness of a tall horse is in no way different from the tallness of a tall person? Now is the tall person or horse *right* [same word as "righteous"] or the man who calls it tall or regards it as tall *right* (*the right conception of "tallness" is a subjective element belonging to the observer*).' 'But,' said Kaotse, 'I love my own brother, but I do not love the brother, say, of a man from the country of Ch'in. That shows that love comes from myself and is therefore regarded as something from within. On the other hand, I equally respect the elders of Ch'u as well as my own elders. That shows that what pleases me is the fact of their being elders, and this respect (a virtue of righteous conduct) is therefore something external.' Mencius replied, 'But we love the roast pork of the Ch'in people as much as we love our own roast pork. That is so even with respect to material things. Then are you going to say that this love of roast pork is also something external?'[5]

In common with other writers of that period, there was also irony and humour in Mencius:

> A man of Ch'i had a wife and a concubine, and lived together

with them in his house. When their good-man went out, he was sure to get himself well filled with spirits and flesh, and then return, and on his wife's asking him with whom he had been eating and drinking, they were sure to be all men of wealth and rank. The wife informed the concubine, saying, 'When the good-man goes out, he is sure to come back having partaken plentifully of spirits and flesh, and when I ask him with whom he has been eating and drinking, they are all men of wealth and rank. And yet no man of distinction ever comes (here). I will spy out where our good-man goes.' (Accordingly) she got up early in the morning, and privately followed the good-man to where he was going. All through the city there was nobody who stood and talked to him. At last he came to those who were sacrificing among the tombs outside the outer wall on the east, and begged what they had left. Not being satisfied, he looked round him and went to another party; and this was the way in which he got himself satiated. His wife went home, and informed the concubine, saying, 'It was to the good-man that we looked up in hopeful contemplation, and with whom our lot is cast for life[6]; and these are his ways.' (On this) she and the concubine reviled their good-man, and wept together in the middle courtyard. (In the meantime) the good-man, knowing nothing of all this, came in with a jaunty air, carrying himself proudly to them.

According to the view which a superior man takes of things, as to the ways by which men seek for riches, honours, gain and advancement, there are few of their wives and concubines who might not be ashamed and weep together because of them.[7]

In Mencius' time, then, prose had developed to the stage where it could sustain lengthy discussions. The greatest prose master, however, was, by common consent, Chuangtse. Of other prose writers of that period, the prose of Hsuntse was unadorned and concise, that of Hanfeitse was polished and precise, but from the standpoint of the evolution of prose writing, they are considered to be of only secondary importance.

2. CHUANGTSE, THE MAN

The Chinese are extremely careless biographers of their famous sons, as a rule. As a result, needless controversies arise: had there really been a man called Laotse? Was Laotse the man's name? When was Confucius born? Who was his father? Did Chu Yuan, the poet, really exist? There have been arguments even as to where and when Li Po, the great Chinese poet of the Tang Dynasty, a comparatively recent period in Chinese history, was born and how he died. The last question has also beset the admirers of Tu Fu, another great poet of the same period.

The same difficulty applies to the life of Chuangtse. Szema Chien dealt with him in a few sentences: 'Chuangtse's name was Chou. He was a native of Meng and was at one time an official of the "Varnish Grove". He was a contemporary of King Huei of Liang and King Hsuan of Chi. . . .' We can deduce, however, from the people mentioned in his book, that Chuangtse was born some time in the early years of the reign of King Huei of Liang (*circa* 368–363 B.C.) and died some time in the early years of the reign of King Huei of Chao (297–292 B.C.) when he was seventy or eighty years old.

During Chuangtse's lifetime China was in one of her most chaotic periods. Wars were being incessantly waged against one another by the states, the old social order was being destroyed, laws disregarded and the people suffered. It was a time when might was right, when 'one who steals hooks is killed, and who usurps the power of a state becomes a marquis'. Chuangtse, like Laotse before him, considered this to be the result of the quest of knowledge by the 'sages'. Thus, he said, 'When the sages arose, gangsters appeared. Overthrow the sages and set the gangsters free and then will the Empire come to order.' He attacked almost every leader of the different schools of thought except Mencius whom he never once mentioned in his book. Considering the fact that Mencius was his contemporary, one wonders if this was a deliberate slight. However, it was Confucius whom Chuangtse attacked and ridiculed most. Confucius was mentioned more than forty times in Chuangtse's book, and almost every time, he was either being lectured or ridiculed. For instance:

Confucius was going west to give his books to the Chou Imperial Archives. And Tselu thought and said to him, 'I have heard that there is a keeper of the archives at (the Capital) Chou. His name is Lao Tan. He has retired and is living at his home. If you want to entrust your books for safe-keeping, why don't you go and give them to him?'

'Good,' said Confucius.

So Confucius went to see Lao Tan and Lao Tan would not accept the books. Confucius spread the Twelve Classics before him, and tried to explain what he had done. Before Confucius had finished, Lao Tan interrupted him, saying, 'You are trying to cover too much material. Tell me the essence of your ideas.'

'The essence is in the teachings of humanity and justice,' said Confucius.

'May I ask, are humanity and justice a part of the nature of man?'

'Yes,' replied Confucius. 'A gentleman's character is not complete without the principle of humanity, and his life is not correct if he does not follow the principle of justice. Humanity and justice are truly a part of the nature of man. What else can they be?'

'May I ask what you mean by humanity and justice?' said Lao Tan.

'To share the happiness with others and to love all mankind without partiality—this is the essence of humanity and justice.'

'Alas,' replied Lao Tan. 'You talk like the latter-day prophets. Isn't it abstruse to talk of love for all mankind? Impartiality implies the recognition of partiality (for individuals). If you want the world to find again its lost shepherd, remember that there is already a constant law governing heaven and earth, the sun and the moon are shining in the sky, the constellations are in their proper places, and the fowl of the air and the beasts of the earth already thrive in flocks and herds, and trees already grow and prosper. Why don't you just follow the natural bent of your character and the laws of Tao? Why do you create such a commotion, holding the banner of humanity and justice like one who has lost his son and is beating a drum to look for him? Alas! I am afraid you are disturbing the nature of man.'[8]

Lao Tan was, of course, Laotse.

Chuangtse was equally impatient with those who claimed to sympathize with him: 'The hypocrites are those people who regard as good whatever the world acclaims as good, and regard as right whatever the world acclaims as right. . . . All their lives they call themselves "Men of Tao" and all their lives they remain hypocrites. They know how to make a good-sounding speech and tell appropriate anecdotes to attract the crowd, but from the very beginning to the very end they don't know what it [Tao] is all about.' And from the following quotation,

43

one might suspect that Tunkuotse might be one of these sympathizers, or Chuangtse would not have been so short-tempered with him:

> 'Where is this so-called Tao?' asked Tunkuotse of Chuangtse.
> 'Tao is everywhere,' replied Chuangtse.
> 'But you must specify.'
> 'It is in the ants,' was the reply.
> 'Why, is it so low?'
> 'It is in the tare-seeds,' said Chuangtse again.
> 'It is getting lower still,' exclaimed Tunkuotse.
> 'It is in the jars and bricks.'
> 'It is getting worse and worse!'
> 'It is in the excrement,' said Chuangtse.[9]

Tunkuotse did not speak any more, and Chuangtse relented. He said:

> What you asked me just now is a question which is a difficult one for me to answer and substantiate with examples. When Corporal Huo went to the head of the market to buy pigs, he looked for the pig's hoofs (as the best place to judge a pig). You should not have asked me to specify, for thus you cannot get away from the material. Great truths are (elusive) like this, and so are great teachings.[10]

Chuangtse's was a complicated personality. Unlike Confucius, Motse, Mencius and others, he was not bent on persuading the rulers to putting his theories of government into practice. Thus we see him declining the summons of the Prince of Tsu:

> Chuangtse was fishing on the P'u River when the Prince of Tsu sent two high officials to see him who said, 'Our Prince desires to burden you with the administration of the Tsu State.'
> Chuangtse went on fishing without turning his head and said, 'I have heard that in Tsu there is a sacred tortoise which died when it was three thousand (years) old. The Prince keeps this tortoise carefully enclosed in a chest in his ancestral temple. Now would this tortoise rather be dead and have its remains venerated, or would it rather be alive and wagging its tail in the mud?'
> 'It would rather be alive,' replied the two officials, 'and wagging

44

its tail in the mud.' 'Begone!' cried Chuangtse. 'I too will wag my tail in the mud.'[11]

Yet, he was not without ambition, and not even Hueitse, his closest friend, could be very sure of his intentions.

> Hueitse was Prime Minister in the Liang State, and Chuangtse was on his way to see him.
> Someone remarked, 'Chuangtse has come. He wants to be Minister in your place.'
> Thereupon Hueitse was afraid, and searched all over the country for three days and three nights to find him.
> Then Chuangtse went to see him and said, 'In the south there is a bird. It is a kind of phoenix. Do you know it? When it starts from the South Sea to fly to the North Sea, it would not alight except on the *Wu-t'ung* tree. It eats nothing but the fruit of the bamboo, drinks nothing but the purest spring water. An owl which had got the rotten carcase of a rat looked up as the phoenix flew by, and screeched. Are you not screeching at me over your kingdom of Liang?'[12]

It would seem as though Chuangtse had not learned from Laotse the qualities of humility and tolerance, which the latter spent so much time propounding. Why was he so caustic, even to his closest friend? Could it be that Chuangtse was angry only because Hueitse's suspicions were not baseless? And when he was on his way to Tsu and saw a skull with a sharp contour, why had Chuangtse to strike it with a horsewhip, ask about the knife the skull (man) had had and then use the skull as a pillow and go to sleep on it?

Indeed, although Chuangtse preached the necessity of preserving one's spiritual power through tranquillity and the 'levelling of all things', he himself could not avoid getting angry. Here is one illustration of his bad temper:

> Once Chuangtse was reduced to such extremities that he was obliged to go to Marquis Wen of Wei and ask for some millet. Marquis Wen of Wei said, 'Of course. I shall receive at the end of this year the rent and taxes of the people. I shall then be pleased to lend you three hundred pieces of coin. Will that be all right?'

45

Chuangtse said, flushed with anger, 'On my way here yesterday, I suddenly heard a voice calling for help. Looking around me, I found a gudgeon in the cart-track. "Gudgeon," I said, "what are you doing here?" "I am an exile from the East Sea," it replied. "Could you give me a small amount of water and save my life?" And I said to it, "Of course. I shall soon be going to the South to visit the Kings of Wu and Yueh. I will ask them to dam the West River, so that it will flow your way. Will that be all right?" "I am out of my usual surroundings and don't know what to do here. Only a small amount of water will be enough to sustain me," said the gudgeon, flushed with anger. "If you propose to do as you said, you might save yourself the trouble and go and find me in the dried-fish shop." '[13]

Nor was Chuangtse above being mean and caustic:

A scholar of Sung once went to see the King and returned in glory, with a number of carriages and a retinue presented to him by the King. The scholar was very proud of the success of his visit, and Chuangtse said to him, 'There was once a King of Chin who was ill. He gave one carriage to a physician who lanced his tumour, but five carriages to one who cured his piles. The lower down you go, the richer the reward. Did you cure the King's piles?[14]

Could all this be an expression of a deep frustration he felt about the life he was leading, which was virtually nothing but an enforced retirement? Anyway, in trying to overcome his frustration—if it was frustration—and seeing the misery of other people's lives: 'All these people follow their routine year in, year out, submerged in their own affairs, and cannot get free of them. They let their bodily desire run away with them and get tangled up in a thousand and one affairs till they die. Alas!' Chuangtse turned his mind to such questions as 'What are life and death? Am I one with the Universe? Where do the spirits move? Whither do they go and where do they disappear, so mysteriously and suddenly?' And he was especially fascinated by the question of life and death. He said that 'Human life in this world is but as the form of a white pony flashing past a rock crevice. In a moment it is gone. Suddenly waking up, all life is born; suddenly slipping off, all silently creep away. With one change, one is born, with another one dies.' Also, 'Who can appreciate the connection between the two?

When a man is born, it is but the embodiment of a spirit. When the spirit is embodied, there is life, and when the spirit disperses, there is death. But if life and death are companions to each other, why should I be concerned? Therefore, all things are one. What we love is the mystery of life. What we hate is corruption in death. But the corruptible in its turn becomes mysterious life, and this mysterious life once more becomes corruptible.'[15] And yet, he seemed not to have been satisfied with this theorizing, and tried to reassure himself, apparently with little success:

How do I know that love of life is not a delusion after all? How do I know but that he who dreads death is not as a child who has lost his way and does not know his way home?

The Lady Li Chi was the daughter of the frontier officer of Ai. When the Duke of Chin first got her, she wept until the bosom of her dress was drenched with tears. But when she came to the royal residence, shared with the Duke his luxurious couch, and ate rich food, she repented of having wept. How then do I know but that the dead may repent of having previously clung to life?

Those who dream of the banquet, wake to lamentation and sorrow. Those who dream of lamentation and sorrow wake to join the hunt. While they dream, they do not know that they are dreaming. Some will even interpret the very dream they are dreaming, and only when they awake do they know it was a dream. By and by comes the great awakening, and then we find out that this life is really a great dream. Fools think they are awake now, and flatter themselves they know—this one is a prince, and that one is a shepherd. What narrowness of mind! Confucius and you are both dreams and I who say you are dreams—I am a dream myself. This is a paradox. Tomorrow a Sage may arise to explain it; but that tomorrow will not be until ten thousand generations have gone by. Yet you may meet him around the corner.[16]

Seen in this light, when he wrote about his own dream in which he appeared to be a butterfly—'I don't know whether I was then dreaming that I was a butterfly or whether I am now a butterfly, dreaming I am a man'—it could only have been an effort to reassure himself by a man who loved life too dearly to contemplate ever giving it up. In the same light, his apparently nonchalant, cynical and detached attitude at the

47

death of his wife could have been a heart-rending attempt at bravado:

Chuangtse's wife died and Hueitse went to offer his condolence. The visitor found him squatting on the ground and singing, beating on a basin to keep time.

'Someone has lived with you and raised children for you and now her old body dies. Is it not enough that you should not weep, but that you should be singing to the music of a basin? Isn't it too much?'

'No,' replied Chuangtse. 'When she died, how could I but feel very sorry? But I began to think and I realized that originally she had no life, and not only no life, she had no form, and not only no form, she had no spirit (*yin* and *yang*). She was a part of a mass of formlessness. Then she changed and received spirit, the spirit changed, and she was given form, form changed and she was given life, and now she changes once more and goes to her death. She merely goes through a process resembling the rotation of spring, summer, autumn and winter. There she lies now peacefully in a big house. If I should break down and cry out loud, I would behave like one who does not understand destiny. Therefore, I stopped.'[17]

And what he said when death was claiming him may have sounded poetic, but it was not difficult to detect the pathos and despair he must have been burdened with at having no escape from corruption in death:

Chuangtse was about to die, and his disciples wanted to give him a sumptuous funeral.

'I regard the heaven and earth as my coffin and outer coffin, the sun and the moon as a pair of jade gifts and the constellation as my burial jewels. And the whole creation shall come to my funeral. Will it not be a grand funeral? What more could I want?'

'We are afraid that vultures and crows will come and eat our Master,' said the disciples.

'Above the ground, I shall be eaten by vultures, and underground, I shall be eaten by the ants. Why rob the one to give it to the other? Why are you so partial (to the ants)?' Chuangtse replied.[18]

However he seemed to deplore sentimentality, friendship was the one thing Chuangtse treasured in life. He might have been angry at Hueitse. Nevertheless, he thought rather highly of him, and was sorry that Hueitse wasted his talents on sophistries. Incidentally, although Chuangtse did not think too highly of sophistry and considered arguments futile, he was not above arguing with Hueitse:

> Chuangtse and Hueitse had strolled on to the bridge over the Hao, when the former observed, 'See how the small fish are darting about! This is the happiness of the fish.'
>
> 'You not being a fish yourself,' said Hueitse, 'how can you know the happiness of the fish?'
>
> 'And you not being I,' retorted Chuangtse, 'how can you know that I do not know?'
>
> 'If I, not being you, cannot know what you know,' urged Hueitse, 'it follows that you, not being a fish, cannot know the happiness of fish.'
>
> 'Let us go back to your original question,' said Chuangtse. 'You asked me *how* I knew the happiness of the fish. Your very question shows that you knew that I knew. I knew it (from my own feeling) on the bridge.'[19]

The friends were often together, and once, after Hueitse had died, Chuangtse walked past his tomb and said to those who were with him:

> Once there was a wall-plasterer who loathed to have any plaster, even a tiny speck no thicker than the wing of a fly, fall on his nose. Whenever this happened, he would ask his assistant, Shih, to remove it. While Shih was slicing the speck of plaster clean off his nose by brandishing an adze with such a force that the air whistled, the plasterer would stand stock still, without batting an eye.
>
> Yuan, Prince of Sung, heard of this and sent for Shih, saying to him, 'I should very much like you to show me how you do it.' Shih replied, 'It is true that I used to do it. But I need a proper partner to do it with. And my partner died long ago.'
>
> Since Hueitse died I, too, have lost my partner. I have no one with whom I can really talk.[20]

3. CHUANGTSE, *THE BOOK*

Almost every literate person in China likes, or says he likes, *Chuangtse*, the book. This is because although Chuangtse might not have written his book strictly according to the generally recognized rules, his lively imagination and rich vocabulary make the reading of his book a very pleasant spiritual journey, filled with surprises. For *Chuangtse* the book is like the eloquent outpourings of a learned and charming rogue who has had no one to talk to for a long time. He tends to talk on for too long at times, a weakness he knows, and yet, having so much to say and having been in solitude for so long, he just has to go on talking. And knowing human nature, he throws in, here and there, an allegory, an anecdote, to keep the listener from getting bored. So it is that in reading *Chuangtse*, we are now following a well-reasoned argument, and the next moment, reading a fantastic allegory about 'General Cloud' and 'Great Nebulous', or, much to our surprise, finding Confucius being lectured. What is the author trying to say? He is almost sacrilegious! Yet, the analogy does not seem completely irrelevant. Hm. From this point of view—well, yes. Confucius? Ha! And if one has not been too lucky in life, one is more apt to say, Confucius? Ha, ha, ha! For until quite recently, Confucius and his teaching have had very much to do with one's social standing and career advancement. From the often expressed truism that Chinese officials like Confucianism openly, Chuangtse and Laotse secretly, and that retired and resigned officials and writers and poets like Chuangtse and Laotse openly, one may deduce the attraction that Chuangtse's writing had for the *literati*. Indeed, with Chuangtse, words were like colours in the hands of a great painter, which he splashed boldly on to the canvas, making dazzling pictures which inevitably caught the eye. I say the attraction of Chuangtse's writing, for Laotse's contribution to literature is the profundity of his thought; *Tao Te Ching* is not known for the brilliance of its style.

I think Chuangtse's appraisal of his own writing is good:

> With unbridled fancy, facetious language and romantic nonsense, he gives free play to his spirit without restraint. . . . His 'goblet words' are a continuous pouring forth, his 'serious words' are true, and his 'allegories' are broad with implication. Although his books dazzle and spin out lengthy discourse, this is a minor blemish. Though his language is uneven (shifting from the serious to the facetious), it is lively and good reading, for it overflows from the fullness of his thoughts and he cannot stop himself. . . .[21]

Apparently his readers agreed, and in appreciation of his contribution to the propagation of Taoist thought through his brilliant writing, Taoism became known as the 'philosophy of Lao(tse) and Chuang(tse)', and people no longer referred to it as the 'science of Yellow Emperor and Laotse'.

The extant text of *Chuangtse* consists of thirty-three chapters in eight volumes. Like other Chinese classics, parts of the book are considered to be forged by later writers. Some scholars even go so far as to say that only seven chapters in the book are genuine. The general view seems to be that although anecdotes might have been added by later generations to the extremely loose structure of the chapters, perhaps only four of the chapters, namely the twenty-eighth, twenty-ninth, thirtieth and thirty-first, were not written by him. Here I quote part of 'Autumn Floods', which is, I think, the most beautiful of all the chapters in the book.

In the time of autumn floods, a hundred streams poured into the river. It swelled in its turbid course, so that it was impossible to tell a cow from a horse on the opposite banks or on the islets.

Then the Spirit of the River laughed for joy that all the beauty of the earth was gathered to himself. Down the stream he journeyed east, until he reached the sea. There, looking eastwards and seeing no limit to its wide expanse, his countenance began to change. And as he gazed over the ocean, he sighed and said to the Spirit of Ocean, 'A common proverb says that he who has heard a great many truths thinks no one equal to himself. And such a one am I. Formerly when I heard people detracting from the learning of Confucius or underrating the heroism of Po Yi, I did not believe it. But now that I have looked upon inexhaustibility—alas for me! Had I not reached your abode, I should have been forever a laughing-stock to those of great enlightenment!'

To this the Spirit of the Ocean replied, 'You cannot speak of ocean to a well-frog, which is limited by its abode. You cannot speak of ice to a summer insect, which is limited by its short life. You cannot speak of Tao to a pedagogue, who is limited in his knowledge. But now that you have emerged from your narrow sphere and have seen the great ocean, you know your own insignificance, and I can speak to you of great principles.

'There is no body of water beneath the canopy of heaven which is greater than the ocean. All streams pour into it without cease, yet it does not overflow. It is being continuously drained off at the Tail-Gate,[22] yet it is never empty. Spring and autumn bring no change; floods and droughts are equally unknown. And thus it is immeasurably superior to mere rivers and streams. Yet I have never ventured to boast on this account. For I count myself among the things that take shape from the universe and receive life from the *yin* and *yang*, but as a pebble or a small tree on a vast mountain. Only too conscious of my own insignificance, how can I presume to boast of my greatness?

'Are not the Four Seas to the universe but like ant-holes in a marsh? Is not the Middle Kingdom to the surrounding ocean like a tare-seed in a granary? Of all the myriad created things, man is but one. And of all those who inhabit the Nine Continents, live on the fruit of the earth, and move about in cart and boat, an individual man is but one. Is not he, as compared with all creation, but as the tip of a hair upon a horse's body?

'The succession of the Five Rulers,[23] the contentions of the Three Kings, the concerns of the kind-hearted, the labours of the administrators, are but this and nothing more. Po Yi refused the dignity of the throne. Chungni (Confucius) discoursed to get a reputation for learning. This over-estimation of self on their part— was it not very much like your own previous self-estimation in reference to water?'

'Very well,' said the Spirit of the River, 'am I then to regard the universe as great and the tip of a hair as small?'

'Not at all,' said the Spirit of the Ocean. 'Dimensions are limitless, time is endless. Conditions are not constant, terms are not final. Thus, the wise man looks into space and does not regard the small as too little, nor the great as too much; for he knows that there is no limit to dimensions. He looks back into the past, and does not grieve over what is far off, nor rejoice over what is near; for he knows that time is without end. He investigates fullness and decay, and therefore does not rejoice if he succeeds, nor lament if he fails; for he knows that conditions are not constant. He who clearly apprehends the scheme of existence does not rejoice over life, nor repine at death; for he knows that terms are not final.

'What man knows is not to be compared with what he does not know. The span of his existence is not to be compared with the span of his non-existence. To strive to exhaust the infinite by means of the infinitesimal necessarily lands him in confusion and unhappiness. How then should one be able to say that the tip of a hair is the *ne plus ultra* of smallness, or that the universe is the *ne plus ultra* of greatness?'

'Dialecticians of the day,' replied the Spirit of the River, 'all say that the infinitesimal has no form, and that the infinite is beyond all measurement. Is that true?'

'If we look at the great from the standpoint of the small,' said the Spirit of the Ocean, 'we cannot reach its limit; and if we look at the small from the standpoint of the great, it eludes our sight. The infinitesimal is a subdivision of the small; the colossal is an extension of the great. In this sense the two fall into different categories. This lies in the nature of circumstances. Now smallness and greatness presuppose form. That which is without form cannot be divided by numbers, and that which is above measurement cannot be measured. The greatness of anything may be a topic of discussion, and the smallness of anything may be mentally imagined. But that which can be neither a topic of discussion nor imagined mentally cannot be said to have greatness or smallness.

'Therefore, the truly great man does not injure others and does not credit himself with charity and mercy. He seeks not gain, but does not despise the greedy. He acts differently from the vulgar crowd, but does not place high value on being different or eccentric; nor because he acts with the majority does he despise those that flatter a few. The ranks and emoluments of the world are to him no cause for joy; its punishments and shame no cause for disgrace. He knows that right and wrong cannot be distinguished, that great and small cannot be defined.

'I have heard say, "The man of Tao has no (concern for) reputation; the truly virtuous has no (concern for) possessions; the truly great man ignores self." This is the height of self-discipline.'

'But how then,' said the Spirit of the River, 'arise the distinctions of high and low, of great and small in the material and immaterial aspects of things?'

'From the point of view of Tao,' replied the Spirit of the Ocean, 'there are no such distinctions as high and low. From the point of view of individuals, each holds himself high and holds others low. From the vulgar point of view, high and low (honour and dishonour) are something conferred by others.

'In regard to distinctions, if we say that a thing is great or small by its own standard of great or small, then there is nothing in all creation which is not great, nothing which is not small. To know that the universe is but as a tare-seed, and the tip of a hair is (as big as) a mountain—this is the expression of relativity.

'In regard of function, if we say that something exists or does not exist by its own standard of existence or non-existence, then there is nothing which does not exist, nothing which does not perish from existence. If we know that east and west are convertible, and yet necessary terms, in relation to each other, then such (relative) functions may be determined.

'In regard to man's desires or interests, if we say that anything is good or bad because it is either good or bad according to our individual (subjective) standards, then there is nothing which is not good, nothing which is not bad. If we know that Yao and Chieh each regarded himself as good and the other as bad, then the (direction of) their interests becomes apparent.

'Of old Yao and Shun abdicated (in favour of worthy successors) and the rule was maintained, while Kuei (Prince of Yen) abdicated (in favour of Tsechih) and the latter failed. T'ang and Wu got the empire by fighting, while by fighting, Po Kung lost it. From this it may be seen that the value of abdicating or fighting, or acting like Yao or like Chieh, varies according to time, and may not be regarded as a constant principle.

'A battering-ram can knock down a wall, but it cannot repair a breach. Different things are differently applied. Ch'ichi and Hualiu (famous horses) could travel 1,000 *li* a day, but for catching rats they were not equal to a wild cat. Different animals possess different aptitudes. An owl can catch fleas at night, and see the tip of a hair, but if it comes out in the daytime it can open wide its eyes and yet fail to see a mountain. Different creatures are differently constituted.

'Thus, those who say that they would have right without its correlate, wrong; or good government without its correlate, misrule, do not apprehend the great principles of the universe, nor the nature of all creation. One might as well talk of the existence of Heaven without that of Earth, or of the negative principle without the positive, which is clearly impossible. Yet people keep on discussing it without ceasing; such people must be either fools or knaves.

'Rulers abdicated under different conditions, and the Three Dynasties succeeded each other under different conditions. Those who came at the wrong time and went against the tide are called usurpers. Those who came at the right time and fitted in with their age are called defenders of right. Hold your peace, Uncle River. How can you know the distinctions of high and low and of the houses of the great and small?'

'In that case,' replied the Spirit of the River, 'what am I to do about declining and accepting, following and abandoning (courses of action)?'

'From the point of view of Tao,' said the Spirit of the Ocean, 'how can we call this high and that low? For there is (the process) reverse evolution (uniting opposites). To follow one absolute course would involve great departure from Tao. What is much? What is little? Be thankful for the gift. To follow a one-sided opinion is to diverge from Tao. Be exalted, as the ruler of a State whose administration is impartial. Be expansive, like the points of the compass, boundless without a limit. Embrace all creation, and none shall be more sheltered or helped than another. This is to be without bias. And all things being equal, how can we say which is long and which is short? Tao is without beginning, without end. Material things are born and die, and no credit is taken for their development. Emptiness and fullness alternate, and their relations are not fixed. Past years cannot be recalled; time cannot be arrested. The succession of growth and decay, of increase and diminution, goes in a cycle, each end becoming a new beginning. In this sense only may we discuss the ways of truth and the principles of the universe. The life of things passes by like a rushing, galloping horse, changing at every turn, at every hour. What should one do, or what should one not do? Let the (cycle of) changes go on by itself.'

'If that is the case,' said the Spirit of the River, 'what is the value of Tao?'

'Those who understand Tao,' answered the Spirit of the Ocean, 'must necessarily apprehend eternal principles and those who apprehend eternal principles must understand their application. Those who understand their application do not suffer material things to injure them.

'The man of perfect virtue cannot be burnt by fire, nor drowned by water, nor hurt by the cold of winter nor the heat of summer, nor torn by bird or beast. Not that he makes light of these; but that he discriminates between safety and danger, is happy under prosperous and adverse circumstances alike and cautious in his choice of action, so that none can harm him.

'Therefore it has been said that Heaven (the natural) abides within, man (the artificial) without. Virtue abides in the natural. Knowledge of the action of the natural and·of the artificial has its basis in the natural, its destination in virtue. Thus, whether moving forward or backward, whether yielding or asserting, there is always a reversion to the essential and to the ultimate.'

'What do you mean,' inquired the Spirit of the River, 'by the natural and the artificial?'

'Horses and oxen,' answered the Spirit of the Ocean, 'have four feet. That is the natural. Put a halter on a horse's head, a string through a bullock's nose. That is the artificial.

'Therefore it has been said, do not let the artificial obliterate the natural, do not let will obliterate destiny; do not let virtue be sacrificed to fame. Diligently observe these precepts without fail, and thus you will revert to the True.'[24]

CHAPTER III

The Poetry of the Warring States Period

1. *FROM THE* BOOK OF POETRY *TO* TSU TSE

IN the Warring States Period, Chinese poetry also evolved from the rather simple, narrative poems and short love poems as contained in the *Book of Poetry* and presented a dazzling display of romantic and imaginative poems as epitomized by *Li Sao* and other poems written by Chu Yuan. Chinese scholars tended to think that these poems were direct descendants of the 'Three Hundred Poems'. Szema Chien, for instance, said, 'The songs of the States (*feng* poems) are sensual without being licentious, the lesser *ya* poems are plaintive without being seditious. *Li Sao* may be said to combine these two virtues.'[1] And Cheng Chiao, an illustrious historian of the Sung Dynasty, said, 'The area between Kiang (Yangtse) and Han (River) was formerly the territory of Chou Nan and Shao Nan where poetry originated. Since Chu Yuan and Sung Yu's[2] time, most poets have been born in this area. That was why Chungni (Confucius) also thought poetry originated in Chou Nan and Shao Nan.'[3] But to explain the relation between the *Book of Poetry* and *Tsu Tse*[4] solely from a moralistic or geographical point of view would be to invite argument. The fact is, as I mentioned earlier, the *Book of Poetry* was one of the most important textbooks for scholars and diplomatists during the Spring-Autumn and Warring States Periods. In *Tso Chuan* there are many entries about diplomatists from the State of Tsu who quoted the poems in the book to help them in their diplomatic manœuvres. Chu Yuan was a statesman who 'was responsible for receiving state visitors and carrying out diplomatic discussions with the heads of other states'.[5] It seems fairly certain that he was influenced by the poems in the *Book of Poetry* when he was writing his own poems. This can be evidenced by the fact that the 'empty words'[6] which are found in *Tsu Tse* were found to have an affinity with those which are contained in the poems in the *Book of Poetry*. For instance, the 'empty word' *hsieh* which for a time was considered to be limited to *Tsu Tse* is now known by scholars to be a derivative of another 'empty word' *sze* which appeared in the *Book of Poetry*. Other 'empty words' like *hsi*, *yeh* and *chih*, which are to be found in the *Book of Poetry*, were put to more standardized uses with richer connotation in *Tsu Tse*.

Influence aside, *Tsu Tse* stands as a body of original work created mostly by a single poet, as opposed to the 'Three Hundred Poems' which were collected and improved upon by unknown poets from folk songs. The lines in *Tsu Tse* are longer and the metres more varied than those of the 'Three Hundred Poems'. Moreover, the work is concerned not only with a poet's reflections on life, but also has religious meaning. The creative imagination of the poet made use of legends, and employed flowers and plants as symbols or metaphors. How did this new form of poetry come about?

To answer this question we must first note that after the Yin Dynasty was overthrown in 1123 B.C., the Chou people, being realists, took only part of the Yin culture as their own, and almost completely ignored the animistic religious attitude of the Yins. During their sacrificial rites, the Chou people thanked the gods and their ancestors for their blessings as a matter of form only, and did not speculate about the supernatural world, so far as we know. *Liki* sums up the difference between the Yin and the Chou peoples rather neatly:

'The Yin people revered the gods. Their leaders led the people to pay homage to the gods. They looked after the spirits first, and then after themselves. . . . The Chou people lived by their moral standards and were practical. They paid tribute to the spirits and gods, but never let their religious feelings interfere with their affairs.'[7]

But in the South the religious spirit of the Yin people remained unabated and influential. This might have been partly due to the natural environment of the South, where unexplored high mountains, virgin forests, broad and deep rivers and lakes, and the ever-changing hues of the clouds, mist and fog aroused in the people a sharp consciousness and profound awe of unknown phenomena, an awareness of the transience of man and a curiosity concerning man's relationship with the multitudinous representations of the Unknown. Therefore, 'the

Tsu people (in the South) believed in wu^8 and spirits, and laid great stress on sacrificial rites'.[9] Wang Yi said in his preface to *Chiu Ko*, 'In the county of Ying, between the Yuan and Hsiang Rivers in the State of Tsu, the people believed in spirits and liked sacrificial rites. Whenever these rites were held they sang and danced to musical accompaniment so as to amuse the gods.' All this must have been conducive to the preservation of legends and myths and the development of song and dance in the people. From this, Chu Yuan drew inspiration and material for his poetry.

It was, in fact, the music of the South which had the greatest influence on the evolution of the poetic form in *Tsu Tse*. I mentioned in Chapter I that the poems in the *Book of Poetry* were sung to the accompaniment of flute, bamboo-pipes and *hsiao*, which is a series of pitchpipes. During the Warring States Period, the merging of the hundred-odd states into seven, as already mentioned, caused increased contact between the peoples and the barbarian tribes such as Yuan, Chin, Hsien-yun, etc., and must have brought into use new musical instruments. A new kind of music came into being. We find, in the chapter under the heading of *Yochi* in *Liki*, for instance, an interesting episode:

Baron Wen of Wei asked Tsehsia, the disciple of Confucius, 'Why is it that I feel sleepy every time I listen to classical music in my official dress, and never feel tired when I listen to the music of the states of Cheng and Wei? Why is it that the classical music is like that and this music is like this?'

'In ancient music,' replied Tsehsia, 'the dancers move in formation forward and backward in an atmosphere of peace and order and a certain luxury of movement. . . . The music begins with the civil dance movements and ends with the military dance movements, and there is a continuity of movement from beginning to end, while the measure of the classical music prevents or checks the dancers who are inclined to go too fast. . . . Now in this new music, people bend their bodies while they move back and forth, there is a deluge of immoral sounds without form or restraint, and actors and dwarfs, dressed like monkeys, mix with the men and women, behaving as if they didn't know who were their parents or children. . . . Now you ask me about music, but what you are really interested in is just sounds. Music and sounds are of course related, but they are two different things.'

'What do you mean?' asked the Baron.

'In ancient times,' said, Tsehsia, '. . . after the world was brought into order, the Sages set the right standards for the six pitch-pipes and the five keys. People then began to sing songs and anthems to the accompaniment of Hsuan stringed instruments, and this was ritual music and ritual music was true music. . . . But what your Highness is interested in is merely a jumble of lewd sounds.'

'May I ask, where do the lewd sounds come from?' asked the Baron.

'The music of Cheng,' replied Tsehsia, 'is lewd and corrupting, the music of Sung is soft and leads to effeminacy, the music of Wei is repetitious and monotonous and the music of Ch'i is harsh and makes one haughty. These four kinds of music are all sensual music and undermine the people's character, and that is why they cannot be used at the sacrifices. . . .'[10]

Chinese music, then, had changed a great deal in Tsehsia's time. In *Tso Chuan*, in the record of the ninth year of the reign of Duke Chen of Chin, it was recorded that, 'When the Duke visited the armoury where prisoners were kept, he saw Chung Yi and asked, "Who is the prisoner with the Southerner's cap?" The warden replied, "He is a native of Tsu whom the people of Cheng captured and presented to us." The Duke ordered that a *chin*, a seven-stringed musical instrument, be given to the captive, and asked him to play. With the *chin*, the man played the music of the South. . . .'

The music of Tsu was, then, different from that of the North. It is impossible to say exactly what it was like. It is, however, generally conceded that it was languorous in mood, pleasing to the ear and had more variety than that of the North. Poems sung to the accompaniment of this kind of music must necessarily have been different from those to be found in the *Book of Poetry* and those of other states where the rhythm and beat of music was different. The songs of the Wu's (or priests) of Tsu, which were the product of the religious and superstitious inclination of the people, and their music, perhaps presaged the creation of *Tsu Tse*. For a great majority of the poems in *Chiu Ko*, which form part of the works of Chu Yuan, are now generally agreed to be based on the songs of priests.

There are other songs of the South to be found in ancient Chinese books, from which we may roughly trace the evolution of *Tsu Tse*.

There is, for instance, the 'Song of a Native of Yueh', which is said to be the song a boatman sang when he rowed the ruler of Yao on a river pleasure trip. The boatman sang in his own dialect and the ruler of Yao, unable to understand the meaning, asked someone to translate it for him into the language of Tsu. The following is the translated version which is, incidentally, the earliest recorded translated poem in Chinese.

> What an evening this is
> To sail past the islet in mid-stream;
> What a day this is,
> To be in the same boat with a prince.
>
> Treating alike the weakness and foibles of people,
> You do not blame them when they err.
> I was worried and confused,
> But my spirit is not crushed.
> And now I have met you, O Prince!
>
> Great is the number of branches in a tree
>   And of the trees on the mountains;
> Equally great is my admiration for you,
>   Only of it you are unaware.[11]

Another is the 'Song of the People of Hsu'. It is said that when Chitse of Yuan-ling passed through the State of Hsu on a visit to the North, the ruler of Hsu saw the sword he carried and wished that he could have it. Chitse sensed this and promised himself that when he returned and had less need of the sword, he would present it to the ruler of Hsu. But when he came again, the ruler of Hsu had died. In order to carry out his promise, although it had not actually been made, Chitse left his sword on the ruler's tomb and went home. The people of Hsu were greatly moved and a song was composed in praise of Chitse.

> Chitse of Yuan-ling, he is
> One who does not forget his friends;
> Leaving on his friend's tomb his precious sword
> Graciously—that's how he keeps his word.[12]

In the *Book of Mencius*, there is also a 'Song of Children' which Confucius was said to have heard when he visited Tsu:

When the water in the Chan-lang River is clear,
  I'll wash the tassels of my hat in it;
When the water in the Chan-lang River is muddy,
  I'll wash my feet in it.

These are songs of Tsu and her neighbouring states. They had all broken away from the style of the 'Three Hundred Poems' which mostly contained four words to a line. These songs have, respectively, eight, nine and eleven words in a line, and use the 'empty word' *hsi* to connect up two segments in each of their lines. The varying lengths of a line of verse and the usage of 'empty words' were later adopted and developed by Chu Yuan and became the most common features in his poems.

2. *THE LIFE OF CHU YUAN*

Chu Yuan is the greatest poet of ancient China. In fact, he is the only one of all the poets before the Ch'in Dynasty (221–207 B.C.) to leave us a collection of his works, probably because his poems were considered to be the best, and so were preserved by his admirers. He was born in 340 B.C. and according to Szema Chien, belonged to the Royal House of Tsu. We know very little about his family except that his father's name was Po-yung. Chu Yuan was an intelligent and well-educated man. When still in his twenties he was appointed Tso-tu, a post perhaps second only to that of Prime Minister in its importance. We do not know for how long he held this post, but however long or short, these were the only years of his life when he had the opportunity to serve his country, and was at peace with the world. 'At court, he planned and discussed matters of state with the King and decided what decrees were to be promulgated; outside, he was responsible for receiving state visitors and carrying out diplomatic discussions with heads of other states. The King trusted him completely.'[13] From this experience, Chu Yuan became thoroughly familiar with the international situation of his time and formed strong views on the policy of Tsu. Here it is necessary to point out that during Chu Yuan's lifetime, Chin, Chi and Tsu were the three strong powers of the seven states which existed during the Warring States Period, and of them, Chin was the strongest. Tsu had only two alternatives in her foreign policy: to yield to Chin, or to ally herself with Chi and oppose Chin. Judging from Szema Chien's 'The Life of Chu Yuan', we gather that Chu Yuan was one of the very few, if not the only official at court, who insisted on resisting Chin. His reasons seemed to be that Tsu was, after all, the second strongest state and occupied the vast, fertile land in the South. She could ally herself with Chi and other states to resist and defeat Chin. But the most important factor which decided Chu Yuan in favour of an uncompromising attitude toward Chin was that he believed in the teaching of Confucius. He wanted to see a united country and help his king to emulate the famous kings of olden time and set up the *li fa* system, or Code of Social Behaviour. This may seem odd, since the South was where Taoism originated. Laotse and Chuangtse were both from the Southern states. However, in Chu Yuan's time, Confucianism had already spread to the South, and there were Confucian scholars in Tsu whose scholarship was comparable to that of Northern scholars. Apparently, Chu Yuan had more sympathy with their doctrine than with that of Laotse and Chuangtse.

We know, from the *Book of Mencius*, of several Confucian scholars of the South.

'Chen Liang is a native of Tsu. He admires the teachings of the Duke of Chow and Chungni (Confucius) and comes to study in the North. The scholars of the Northern States cannot excel him in the study of Confucianism. He is really an outstanding scholar.'

The *Book of Mencius* also mentions two of Chen Liang's students going up to the North to study Confucianism. It is not strange, then, that Chu Yuan should have been influenced by Confucianism and accepted this school of thought. In his masterpiece *Li Sao* Chu Yuan reflected Confucius' admiration for the kings Yao, Shun, Yu, Tang and Wen.

Chu Yuan wanted King Huai of Tsu to follow the example of the 'model kings' and use only people of virtue and ability to help him rule the country, and unite it.

He wrote:

> I hurried about your chariot in attendance
> Leading you in the tracks of the kings of old.[14]

And he told King Huai:

> High God in Heaven knows no partiality;
> He looks for the virtuous and makes them his ministers.
> For only the wise and good can ever flourish
> If it is given them to possess the earth.[15]

This, then, was Chu Yuan's ideal. And it was because of it that he wanted Tsu to fight, and not yield to Chin. I believe that it was his stern moral judgment and insistence upon appointing only virtuous and able men to serve king and country that alienated the other aristocrats, including Tse Lan, younger son of the King. This attitude caused them to attack Chu Yuan and finally changed the King's own feelings toward him. For it seems probable that at that time, most official posts were still hereditary, at least the aristocrats received special consideration for official appointments. Chu Yuan's ideas were, therefore, a threat to their interests. In 'The Life of Chu Yuan', Szema Chien said, 'The lord of Shang-kuan . . . slandered him (Chu Yuan) to the King, saying that whenever the King employed Chu Yuan to frame a law, he always boasted after its promulgation that only he was capable of performing such a service. The King was angry and became estranged from Chu Yuan.'[16]

However, considering the fact that King Huai had hitherto trusted Chu Yuan completely this seems to me but part of the story of his downfall. The rest of the story of his fall from favour might have been due to his temper. It is conceivable that Chu Yuan, believing in his mission and the teaching of Confucius, should have treated his colleagues with contempt and condescension, as many idealistic young men are prone to do when their ideals and ideas are not understood. Given time, perhaps he would have mellowed. But he was still in his late twenties, or at most, early thirties. He wrote of his colleagues who attacked him because he would not compromise and co-operate:

> It is this that my heart takes most delight in,
> And though I died nine times, I should not regret it.[17]

and

> But I would rather quickly die and meet dissolution
> Before I ever would consent to ape their behaviour.[18]

As a result, Chu Yuan was sent on an embassy to Chi. Upon his return, King Huai, against his advice, decided to accept King Chao of Chin's invitation to a conference in Chin. It was probably at this time that Chu Yuan was banished to an area north of Han River. When King Huai went to Chin, however, he was ambushed and forcibly detained and later died there. Meanwhile, King Ching Hsiang had acceded to the throne of Tsu, and upon hearing of his father's death in the third year of his reign, broke off relations with Chin. Although this had nothing to do with Chu Yuan, it nevertheless proved him to be right. It is probable that Chu Yuan returned to Tsu at that time, and King Ching Hsiang promised him that he would form an alliance with Chi to oppose Chin. However, because his younger brother Tse Lan was against such an alliance and spoke ill of Chu Yuan, the King kept putting it off. In the sixth year of the reign of King Ching Hsiang (293 B.C.), Chin sent General Po Hsu to attack the State of Han. After Po Hsu had gained a great victory over the armies of Han, he sent a message to King Ching Hsiang threatening to invade Tsu. King Ching Hsiang was intimidated and decided to restore relations with Chin. The following year he married a princess of Chin, and Tsu and Chin became friendly again.

This was a severe blow to Chu Yuan. The opportunity of making his country strong and realizing his ambition of helping his King to become a great monarch in the style of the kings of ancient times, was snatched away when it appeared to be within reach. Perhaps that is why he complained in *Li Sao*:

> You have originally made an agreement with me,
> Why should you now regret and change your mind?

The King no longer thought of his promise to Chu Yuan, but Chu Yuan remembered. It was as though he did not know that the King was now married to a princess of Chin. So, a year or two later, he was banished again, this time to the south of the Yangtse, and the banishment lasted for fourteen years until he drowned himself.

During this period he had plenty of time to think of his undeserved fate and worry about the sapping away of the strength of his country. In despair, he thought of leaving Tsu and going to live and work in another state. Confucius, Motse, Mencius and others had all tried to serve in countries other than their own: he could do the same. In *Li Sao*, then, when Wu Hsien told him, 'To and fro on earth you must everywhere wander, seeking for those whose thoughts are at one with yours', it is not inconceivable that the man was addressing himself.

But the people of Tsu were a proud people. In the 'Annals of the Royal House of Tsu' in the *Historical Record*, for instance, it is said that when 'Tsu invaded Sui, Sui complained. Tsu said, "We are barbarians. . . . We would like the Royal House of Chou to recognize the title of our Ruler." ' It is, to say the least, a great thing when a strong country will admit that she is uncivilized when she is attacking another country. Great powers of today come out rather poorly in comparison. All they can manage to say is that when they fight the wars are just wars. So far as I know, Tsu was the only state which was big enough to say that they were barbarians and expect others to respect them for it.

Chu Yuan was no less proud than his compatriots. It was not easy for him to leave Tsu. In *Chu Sung* (*In Praise of the Orange Tree*), a poem he wrote when he was young, he said:

Fairest of all God's trees, the orange came and settled here,
Commanded by Him not to move, but only grow in the south country.
Deep-rooted, firm and hard to shift: showing in this his singleness of purpose;

Pure and apart and free from sin, and strong in the order of your ways:
Though young in years fit to be a teacher of men;
In your acts like Po Yi; I set you up as my model.[19]

The decision not to leave his country must have been taken after long and painful soul-searching. In *Chao Hun*, the poem he wrote when he heard of King Huai's death in Chin, he was probably writing about the vicissitudes that might overtake him should he decide to leave Tsu:

O soul, come back! In the east you cannot abide,
O soul, come back! In the south you cannot stay.

O soul, come back! In the south you may not linger,
O soul, come back! For the west holds many perils:

O soul, come back! Lest you bring on yourself perdition.[20]

However, it was during this period of his banishment, in this comparatively remote region where the people believed in spirits and liked sacrificial rites, and whenever such rites were held, they (the people) sang and danced to the accompaniment of music so as to amuse the gods, that Chu Yuan came into much closer contact with the animistic religious songs, rites and legends and came into his own. He began to let his imagination soar. Another side of his personality began to develop, and he expressed his despair and nagging hope of a summons from the King in a new poetic form which was used by the priests at such religious rites, which allowed for freer expression of feeling, and which he improved upon. His poems became the most imaginative and passionate of his time, and were admired and imitated by many poets of later periods.

From the standpoint of his stature as a poet, Chu Yuan benefited from his exile. But the *raison d'être* of his life was to serve his king and country, and when the summons from the King never came, Chu Yuan realized that he was to stand helplessly aside and watch, while his King and ministers, hypnotized by the false sense of security brought about by friendly relations with the much stronger and ruthless State of Chin, thought only of personal comfort and indulged in petty feuds, ignoring the welfare of the people. Chu Yuan felt that if things went on this way, Tsu was doomed to be conquered by Chin, which was only waiting for a chance to pounce on his country, and he was aghast at the thought of the outcome. In his long and dark years of banishment, this nightmare haunted him relentlessly. In his frustration, Chu Yuan became more and more introspective, and he had plenty of time to find reasons for his personal failure. But he could not see how he could have acted differently. Everything was clear to him. It was the fault of his selfish and short-sighted rivals. If only the King had listened to his advice! Why should he suffer this fate because of his loyalty? His imagination ran away with him. There was no justice at all. Even in Heaven, he said in *Li Sao*, the gate-keeper would not let him in, but would look at him with contempt. He could not find the answer to his and his country's dilemma, and his anxiety and anguish reduced him to a nervous wreck.

In the twenty-first year of King Ching Hsiang's reign (278 B.C.), General Po Hsu of Chin captured Ying, capital of Tsu, and King Ching Hsiang was forced to move his government to Chen. The country was thrown into turmoil and the people suffered great loss in lives and property. It seemed to Chu Yuan that the end which he had dreaded for so long had come at last. On the fifth day of the fifth month of that year, he threw himself into the Milo River and perished. He was sixty-two.

Chu Yuan's life was a tragedy, the tragedy of an idealist who was forced to play the game of politics without knowing how. It is also the story of the first of the Confucian martyrs who in the long course of Chinese history sacrificed their lives in futile efforts to persuade their kings to follow Confucian teachings. A scholar nowadays does not have to go into politics, nor do politicians have to be scholars. But until quite recently, Chinese scholars have traditionally sought official careers. It was expected of them. The tragedy of Chu Yuan lies perhaps in his pride in being a Confucian and a patriot, and in his inability to see that even poets have to compromise in politics. But for his imaginative and creative powers, he might have died like so many unknown patriots.

Chu Yuan's political career was, then, a failure. However, when Chin united China and ruled the country in tyranny, the people became discontented and they thought of Tsu, believing that their lot might have been better had Tsu still existed. They remembered Chu Yuan, an important minister of Tsu who was banished because of his anti-Chin feelings. Gradually, there came into being the Festival of Tuan-wu around which the legend of Chu Yuan's death was built, which is celebrated to this day. On the fifth day of the fifth month, it is the custom to race dragon boats which symbolize the people's wish to save Chu Yuan from drowning, and to throw glutinous rice balls wrapped in bamboo leaves into the river so that Chu Yuan's spirit will not be short of food. Seldom has a poet been so highly respected and loved by the Chinese.

3. TSU TSE

Szema Chien, in his 'Life of Chu Yuan', said that Chu Yuan wrote five poems: *Li Sao* (*On Encountering Sorrow*), *Tien Wen* (*Questions asked of Heaven*), *Ai Ying* (*A Lament for Ying*), *Chao Hun* (*The Summons of the Soul*) and *Huai Sha* (*Embracing the Sand*). But Pan Ku (A.D. 39–92), in the 'Record of Arts and Letters' in his *History of Han Dynasty*, said that Chu Yuan wrote twenty-five poems. Wang I, in his *Tsu Tse Chang Chu* (*Annotations of Tsu Tse*), based himself perhaps on the *History of Han Dynasty* and said that the poems which Chu Yuan wrote were *Li Sao*, *Chiu Ko* (*Nine Songs*), *Tien Wen*, *Chiu Chang* (*Nine Declarations*), *Yuan Yu* (*The Far-off Journey*), *Pu Chu* (*Divination*) and *Yu Fu* (*The Fisherman*), making a total of twenty-five poems. He also said that *Chao Hun* was written by Sung Yu and not Chu Yuan. There have been controversies involving Chinese scholars and Western sinologists as to which poems were really written by Chu Yuan. Generally speaking, it is now agreed that Chu Yuan wrote the following: *Li Sao*, *Tien Wen*, *Chao Hun*, *Chiu Chang* and *Chiu Ko*. These

68

poems are here referred to as *Tsu Tse*, although the term *Tsu Tse* can also be used to designate poems written in Chu Yuan's style.

Because the technique of writing had greatly advanced in the Warring States Period, Chu Yuan's poems expressed more complicated events and finer emotions than those to be found in the *Book of Poetry*. The most important factor was that Chu Yuan had broken away from the limitations of the four-word poems and was able to express himself freely. This was, in turn, perhaps, due to the influence of folk songs, particularly those of the priests. Indeed, in his poems we see how he alluded to the legends and myths which abounded in the songs of the priests to express his various feelings. But it would be sheer speculation to say to what extent his poems were influenced by these songs.

Chiu Ko was based on the songs of the Wus collected from various places in Tsu. From the verse in *Li Sao*:

> In the Nine Variations and Nine Songs of Chi,
> The House of Hsia made revelry and knew no restraint,[21]

it seems certain that *Chiu Ko* was the name of a set of sacrificial songs, and 'Nine' did not signify the number of songs it comprised. From the musical instruments, songs, dances, props and the numbers of persons mentioned in it, *Chiu Ko* was probably sung and performed only at court during sacrificial rites on national festivals or state occasions. There are eleven poems in *Chiu Ko*: *Tung Huang Tai I* (*God of Heaven*), *Yun Chung Chun* (*God of the Clouds*), *Hsiang Chun*, *Hsiang Fu Jen* (*Goddess of Love*), *Ta Sze Ming*, *Hsiao Sze Ming* (*Gods of Fate*), *Tung Chun* (*God of the Sun*), *Ho Po* (*God of the River*), *Shan Kuei* (*Spirit of the Mountains*), *Kuo Shang* (*The Spirit of the Fallen*) and *Li Hun* (*Epilogue*). Because these were poems sung at sacrificial rites to different gods, their moods vary. The mood of *Kuo Shang*, which was sung in rites held for the Spirit of the Fallen, for instance, was sorrowful and valiant:

> Grasping our great shields and wearing our hide armour,
> Wheel-hub to wheel-hub locked, we battle hand to hand.
> Our banners darken the sky; the enemy teem like clouds:
> Through the hail of arrows the warriors press forward.
> They dash on our lines; they trample our ranks down.
> The left horse has fallen, the right one is wounded.
> Bury the wheels in; tie up the horses!
> Seize the jade drumstick and beat the sounding drum!

The time is against us: the gods are angry.
Now all lie dead, left on the field of battle.
They went out never more to return:
Far, far away they lie, on the level plain,
Their long swords at their belts, clasping their elm-wood bows.
Head from body sundered: but their hearts could not be vanquished.
Both truly brave, and also truly noble;
Strong to the last, they could not be dishonoured.
Their bodies may have died, but their souls are living:
Heroes among the shades their valiant souls will be.[22]

Hsiang Chun and *Hsiang Fu Jen*, which were sung at rites held for the Goddesses of Love, are rather romantic poems:

Far out I gaze to the mooring at Ts'en-yang
And over the great river waft my spirit:
Waft, but my spirit does not reach her;
And the maiden many a sigh heaves for me:
While down my cheeks the teardrops in streams are falling
As with grieving heart I yearn for my lady.
The cassia oars, the sweep of orchid
Churn the waters to foaming snow.
Would you gather the wild-fig in the water?
Or pluck the lotus-flower in the tree-tops?
Unless two hearts are both as one heart,
The matchmaker only wastes her labours,
And love not deep is too quickly broken.[23]

And:

The Child of God, descending the northern bank,
Turns on me her eyes that are dark with longing.
Gently the wind of autumn whispers;
On the waves of the Tung-ting lake the leaves are falling.
Over the white sedge I gaze out wildly;
For a tryst is made to meet my love this evening.
But why should the birds gather in the duckweed?
And what are the nets doing in the tree-tops?
The Yüan has its angelicas, the Li has its orchids:
And I think of my lady, but dare not tell it,
As with trembling heart I gaze on the distance
Over the swiftly moving waters.[24]

These and other passages in *Chiu Ko* which seem to depict a court-ship between the gods and the priests have led some scholars to speculate on the existence of an erotic religion in Tsu. But what is more probable is that the Tsu people, like the Greeks, believed that gods were like human beings, having the same desires and emotions, and so it was natural for them to perfume themselves and dress in beautiful costumes when they sang to please the gods. As recently as the 1940s, there still prevailed in Hunan province, which was part of Tsu, the custom of priests singing songs at sacrificial rites, and what they sang were not only songs of love, but sometimes songs of a rather coarse and obscene nature. And there certainly was no erotic religion in Hunan.

Tien Wen consists of 170 questions. As we do not know all the legends referred to in these questions it is impossible to say why Chu Yuan raised these questions, the style of which is so very different from that of his other poems. The difficulty with *Chao Hun* is that there have long been controversies over its authenticity. Recently, however, Chinese scholars have been inclined to agree that judging from its content, *Chao Hun* was written by Chu Yuan, to summon back to Tsu the soul of King Huai when the latter died in Chin. The style of this poem is also different from that of Chu Yuan's other poems. It describes the horror and the tragic end which the wandering soul will meet with in the east, west, south, north, and in Heaven and Hell. It tells of the pleasures which await the soul if it comes back to its own country. The effect of this poem is impressed upon the reader by exaggerated details of its subject matter. The style of writing in this poem had the most telling influence on *fu*, which was the prevalent form of poetry in the Han Dynasty.

Chiu Chang is made up of nine poems, i.e. *Chu Sung* (*In Praise of the Orange Tree*), *Pei Hui Feng* (*Grieving at the Eddying Wind*), *Hsi Sung* (*Grieving I Make My Plaint*), *Chou Sze* (*The Outpouring of Sad Thoughts*), *Sze Mei Jen* (*Thinking of a Fair One*), *Ai Ying* (*A Lament for Ying*), *Sheh Kiang* (*Crossing the River*), *Huai Sha* (*Embracing the Sand*) and *Hsi Wang Jih* (*Alas for the Days Gone By*). These are not quite a set of songs, but were written at different times and places by Chu Yuan. It is generally agreed that *Chu Sung* was written when Chu Yuan was quite young, *Chou Sze* and *Sze Mei Jen* when he was banished for the first time to the north of Han River, and *Ai Ying* when Ying was over-run by the armies of Chin. Because in *Huai Sha* there are the lines:

'I know that death cannot be avoided, therefore, I will not grudge his coming. To noble men I have plainly declared that I will be numbered with such as you,' and in *Hsi Wang Jih*: 'I will stand above the Yuan's dark waters, And steel myself to plunge in the flowing stream. . . . With much left unsaid, I could plunge into the waters; But I grieve for my blinded Lord who cannot understand,' these two poems are thought to have been written shortly before the poet drowned himself. It is impossible to say when and where the other poems in *Chiu Chang* were written. Of the nine poems, *Ai Ying* is perhaps the most moving. It describes the poet's passionate love of his country and his deep sorrow at going into exile:

> As I set out from the city and left the gate of my village,
> An endless turmoil started in my mind.
> And as the oars slowly swept in time,
> I grieved that I should never look on my prince again.
> I gazed on the high catalpa trees and heaved a heavy sigh,
> And the tears in torrents, like winter's sleet, came down.
>
> My mind was drawn with yearning and my heart was grieved.
> So far! I knew not whither my way was leading.
> But I followed the wind and waves, drifting on aimlessly—
> A traveller on an aimless journey, with no hope of return.[25]

Li Sao is by common consent the greatest of Chu Yuan's poems. It is in this poem that his imagination soars and he alludes to myths and legends and flowers and plants to help him express his feelings. Here also, he adopted the forms of the folk songs of Tsu, which, influenced by local music, offered greater freedom of expression. The result is a fascinating and captivating poem, sad and yet full of surprises. Seldom has China produced such a long and moving poem, full of symbolism and romanticism. I believe it is because of this, rather than its being a new style of poetry, that *Li Sao* is so highly thought of.

Here is a passage from *Li Sao* (*On Encountering Sorrow*)[26] which is much admired:

> I searched for the holy plant and twigs of bamboo,
> And ordered Ling Fen to make divination for me.
> He said, 'Beauty is always bound to find its mate.
> Who that was truly fair was ever without lovers?
> Think of the vastness of the wide world.

Here is not the only place where you can find your lady.
Go farther afield,' he said, 'and do not be faint-hearted.
What woman seeking handsome mate could ever refuse you?

'What place on earth does not boast some fragrant flower?
Why should you always cleave to your old home?'
The world is blinded with its own folly:
How can you show men the virtue inside you?
Most people's likings and loathings are quite separate:
Only *these* men differ in this respect.
For they wear mugwort and cram their waistbands with it;
While the lovely valley orchids they say are not fit to wear.

Since beauty of flower and of shrub escapes them,
What chance has a rarest jewel of gaining recognition?
They gather up muck to stuff their perfume-bags with;
But the pepper-shrub they say has got no fragrance.
I wanted to follow Ling Fen's auspicious oracle.
But I faltered and could not make my mind up.
I heard that Wu Hsien was descending in the evening,
So I lay in wait with offerings of peppered rice-balls.

The spirits came like a dense cloud descending,
And the host of Chiu I mountain came crowding to meet him.
His godhead was manifested by a blaze of radiance,
And he addressed me in these auspicious words:
'To and fro in the earth you must everywhere wander,
Seeking for one whose thoughts are of your own measure.
T'ang and Yü sought sincerely for the right helpers;
So I Yin and Kao Yao worked well with their princes.

'As long as your soul within is beautiful,
What need have you of a matchmaker?
Yüeh laboured as a builder, pounding earth at Fu Yen,
Yet Wu Ting employed him without a second thought.
Lü Wang wielded the butcher's knife at Chao Ko,
But King Wen met him and raised him up on high.
Ning Ch'i sang as he fed his ox at evening;
Duke Huan of Ch'i heard him and took him as his minister.

'Gather the flower of youth before it is too late,
While the fair season is still not yet over.
Beware lest the shrike sound his note before the equinox,
Causing all the flowers to lose their fine fragrance.'

73

How splendid the glitter of my jasper girdle!
But the crowd make a dark screen, masking its beauty.
And I fear that my enemies, who never can be trusted,
Will break it out of spiteful jealousy.

The age is disordered in a tumult of changing:
How can I tarry much longer among them?
Orchid and iris have lost all their fragrance;
Flag and melilotus have changed into straw.
Why have all the fragrant flowers of days gone by
Now all transformed themselves into worthless mugwort?
What other reason can there be for this
But that they all have no more care for beauty?

I thought that Orchid was one to be trusted,
But he proved a sham, bent only on pleasing his masters.
He overcame his goodness and conformed to evil counsels:
He no more deserves to rank with fragrant flowers.
Pepper is all wagging tongue and lives only for slander;
And even stinking Dogwood seeks to fill a perfume-bag.
Since they only seek advancement and labour for position
What fragrance have they deserving our respect?

Since, then, the world's way is to drift the way the tide runs,
Who can stay the same and not change with all the rest?
Seeing the behaviour of Orchid and Pepper flower,
What can be expected from cart-halt and selinea?
They have cast off their beauty and come to this:
Only my garland is left to treasure.
Its penetrating perfume does not easily desert it,
And even to this day its fragrance has not faded.

I will follow my natural bent and please myself;
I will go off wandering to look for a lady.
While my adornment is in its pristine beauty
I shall travel all around looking both high and low.
Since Ling Fen had given me a favourable oracle,
I reckoned a lucky day to start my journey on.
I broke a branch of jasper to take for my meat,
And ground fine jasper-meal for my journey's provisions.

'Harness winged dragons to be my coursers;
Let my chariot be of fine work of jade and ivory!
How can I live with men whose hearts are strangers to me?

I am going a far journey to be away from them.'
I took the way that led towards the K'un-lun mountain:
A long, long road with many a turning in it.
The Cloud-embroidered banner flapped its great shade above us;
And the jingling jade yoke-bells tinkled merrily.

I set off at morning from the Ford of Heaven;
At evening I came to the world's western end.
Phoenixes followed me, bearing up my pennants,
Soaring high aloft with majestic wing-beats.
'See, I have come to the desert of Moving Sands!'
Warily I drove along the banks of the Red Water;
Then, beckoning the water-dragons to make a bridge for me,
I summoned the God of the West to take me over.

Long was the road that lay ahead and full of difficulties;
I sent word to my other chariots to take a short route and wait.
The road wound leftwards round the Pu Chou Mountain:
I marked out the Western Sea as our meeting-place.
There I marshalled my thousand chariots,
And jade hub to jade hub we galloped on abreast.
My eight dragon-steeds flew on with writhing undulations;
My cloud-embroidered banners flapped on the wind.

I tried to curb my mounting will and slacken the swift pace;
But the spirits soared high up, far into the distance.
We played the Nine Songs[27] and danced the Nine Shao Dances:
I wanted to snatch some time for pleasure and amusement.
But when I had ascended the splendour of the heavens,
I suddenly caught a glimpse below of my old home.
The groom's heart was heavy and the horses for longing
Arched their heads back and refused to go on.

ENVOI

Enough! There are no true men in the state: no one to understand me.
Why should I cleave to the city of my birth?
Since none is worthy to work with in making good government,
I will go and join P'eng Hsien in the place where he abides.

CHAPTER IV

The Prose of the Han Dynasty

1. *THE LINEAGE OF THE* HISTORICAL RECORD[1]

PARALLEL to the development of discursive prose during the Warring States Period, narrative prose also developed quite rapidly, as exemplified by that to be found in *Tso Chuan*.

Tso Chuan was previously supposed to have been written by Tso Chiu-ming, one of Confucius' disciples, solely to explain the meaning of, or to annotate the events recorded in, Confucius' *Spring-Autumn*. It is now generally conceded that judged from the style of the prose writing, *Tso Chuan* could not have been written during the Spring-Autumn Period, but must have been written by an unknown author at a much later date, perhaps during the Warring States Period. *Tso Chuan* is nevertheless based on the outline of the *Spring-Autumn*, and the author had probably also used data from other books. Its prose is concise. The following is an example:

In September, on the day of Chia Wu, the Marquis of Chin and Earl of Ch'in laid siege to Cheng, because Cheng had been impudent towards Chin and switched her allegiance to Tsu. The armies of Chin besieged Han Ling, while those of Ch'in invested Fan Nan. Yi Chih-fu said to the Earl of Cheng, 'Our country is in grave danger, but if you send Shu Tse-wu to see the Earl of Ch'in, the armies of Ch'in will certainly lift the siege and withdraw.' The Earl agreed and asked Shu to go. Shu refused, saying, 'When I was young, my service was not held in esteem. Now I am old, I cannot undertake this mission.' The Earl said, 'I was wrong not to have availed myself of your services, and now, in dire need, have to beg for your help—

all this is my fault. But if Cheng is conquered, your life will also be adversely affected.' Shu relented.

That night, he let himself down by a rope from the rampart of the city wall and went to see the Earl of Ch'in, and said to him, 'The people of Cheng know that they cannot hope to resist the armies of Ch'in and Chin. If to destroy Cheng will benefit your Excellency, your efforts would be worthwhile. But as you well know, it is very difficult to control a country which is on the other side of your neighbouring country, Chin. Why should you bother to conquer Cheng only to add to the power of Chin? A stronger neighbouring country would make you in turn the weaker. But if you spare Cheng and let her remain an independent state, then the people of Ch'in, when travelling to the east, can have their needs and comforts taken care of in Cheng. This will certainly not harm Ch'in. Furthermore, the Marquis once promised to cede to you the counties Chiao and Hsia, but once he had crossed the River, he had military installations built to guard against you and did not keep his promise. This, of course, you know. Chin is insatiable in her quest for territorial expansion. Having annexed Cheng to the east, she must necessarily expand to the west. To do that, she will have to carve land from you. Whether you will sacrifice your territory to enhance the power of Chin is a matter which only you can decide.' The Earl of Ch'in was swayed by Shu's reasoning and entered into an alliance with Cheng.

The fact that the fate of a country could depend on the eloquence of a person may seem strange and exaggerated to the Western reader. Nevertheless, during the Warring States Period, scholars influenced the rulers of the various states to adopt their policies or saved them from defeat, embarrassment and other emergencies by just this kind of persuasive eloquence. The most famous of these was Su Chin, who urged six of the then remaining seven states to ally themselves in opposition to Ch'in, the strongest state, and became simultaneously premier of the six states. Another was Chang I, who helped Ch'in to break up the alliance and go on to conquer the six states.

Chankuotseh (The Book of Warring States), which represents a further advance in the art of prose writing, records stories of the eloquence of these and other diplomats. The author or authors of *Chankuotseh* are unknown. The extant copy consists of thirty-three volumes and was edited by Liu Hsiang (79–8 B.C.) of the Han Dynasty. Here is an example of its prose:

Ch'in laid siege to Han Tan, capital of Chao, and King An Li of Wei sent General Chin Pi to Chao's rescue. General Chin Pi was, however, afraid to challenge the armies of Ch'in and held his troops in Tangyin to await developments. The King of Wei then sent General Hsin Yuan-yen to slip into Han Tan for the purpose of speaking to the King of Chao with the help of Prince Ping Yuan: 'Ch'in is laying siege to Chao because the King of Ch'in used to compete with King Min of Chi for the title of Emperor but failed. Now, Chi is getting weaker and weaker and Ch'in is the strongest state. The purpose of Ch'in in besieging Han Tan is not to capture it, but to claim the title of Emperor. If Chao sent an emissary to honour the King of Ch'in as Emperor, Ch'in would be pleased and withdraw her armies.' Prince Ping Yuan was undecided. At that time, Lu Chung-lien happened to be in Han Tan. He heard of Wei's suggestion and went to see Prince Ping Yuan. 'What are you going to do?' he said.

'What am I going to do? The armies of Chao have been defeated in battle and Ch'in has now laid siege to Han Tan. Now the King of Wei has sent General Hsin Yuan-yen to ask Chao to honour the King of Ch'in as her Emperor. He is still here. What am I going to do?'

'I thought that you were the best prince in China. Now I know you are not. Where is this Hsin Yuan-yen? Let me reprove him and send him home!'

'I will ask him to see you,' said Prince Ping Yuan. He went to see General Hsin Yuan-yen and said, 'Mr Lu Lien of Chi is here, I would like him to meet you.'

'I have heard Mr Lu Lien is a great scholar of Chi,' said Hsin Yuan-yen, 'but as I am sent here by my King on a mission, I would rather not see him.'

'I have already told him of your mission.'

Hsin then agreed to see Lu Lien.

When Lu Lien saw Hsin Yuan-yen, he was silent. And Hsin Yuan-yen said to him, 'The people in this besieged city all have something to ask of Prince Ping Yuan. To judge from your appearance, you don't want anything from the Prince. Why do you stay here for so long and not leave?'

'People who think Pao Chiao, the hermit, did not face death with equanimity are wrong, so are the others who think Pao Chiao only thought of himself,' said Lu Lien. 'Ch'in is a country which ignores propriety and justice and rewards her people according to the number of the enemy heads they chop off. Its government rules the country by force and enslaves the people. Should the King of Ch'in recklessly proclaim himself Emperor and his wrong-doings be made to look righteous, I will have no choice but to drown myself in the East Sea. I will never debase myself and become one of his subjects! I have come to see you in order to help Chao.'

'How are you to help Chao?'

'I shall persuade Wei and Yen to help Chao. There is no doubt that Chi and Tsu will help her.'

'You may be able to persuade Yen,' said Hsin Yuan-yen. 'As for Wei, I am from Wei, how can you persuade Wei to help Chao?'

'The thing to do is to make Wei see the grave consequence once the King of Ch'in is proclaimed Emperor,' said Lu Lien. 'When Wei realizes this, she will surely help Chao.'

'What will be the consequences?'

'King Wei of Chi[2] was mindful of propriety and justice, and although the Royal House of Chou was poor and powerless, he was the only one among the rulers of the nominal vassal states of Chou to pay it homage. More than a year later, King Lieh of Chou died. All the rulers of the various states went to Chou to mourn with the Royal House on the passing of the King, but the Ruler of Chi was slow in going. The King of Chou was angered and sent to Chi an announcement about the death of King Lieh and told King Wei of Chi, "The Sovereign has passed away. It is as if the sky had fallen and the earth cracked open. But you, Tien Yin, vassal of the eastern state of Chi, impudently tarry in mourning over the death of the King. You should be beheaded!" King Wei of Chi was furious and burst out, "What rubbish! Your mother was a servant!" This made King Wei of Chi a laughing-stock among all the rulers of the various states. However, it was because King Wei of Chi could not stand the demands of Chou that he acted contradictorily. On the other hand, it was only natural for Chou to have so acted, for she was after all the reigning House of the Country.'

'Haven't you ever noticed how it is with servants?' Hsin Yuan-yen asked. 'Is it because they are weaker in strength or less intelligent than their masters, that ten servants will obey one Master? No. They are afraid of him.'

'Are you comparing the relations between Wei and Ch'in to that of servant and master?'

'Yes.'

'Well, then I shall tell the King of Ch'in to boil and to chop to pieces the King of Wei.'

Hsin Yuan-yen was offended. 'You have gone too far!' he said. 'How can you tell the King of Ch'in to boil and to chop to pieces the King of Wei?'

'Of course I can!' Lu Lien said. 'Let me tell you this: Marquis Kwei, Marquis Ao and Chi Chang were the most important ministers in the reign of King Chou of the Yin Dynasty. Marquis Kwei had a talented son who could be of service to the King. One day he recommended his son to King Chou. King Chou, however, thought the young man had no talent whatsoever and gave orders that Marquis Kwei should be put to death by being chopped to pieces. Marquis Ao hastily spoke up against the order and argued vehemently with the King and the King ordered that he, too, should be killed and his body be dried and preserved. Chi Chang heard of this and heaved a sigh and the King had him imprisoned for one hundred days in the armoury of Yu Li, thinking that he could not survive the experience. Now, why should one want to tell the King to proclaim another Emperor, and risk the fate of being chopped to pieces and having his body made into preserved meat? On the other hand, when King Min of Chi was going to the State of Lu, Yi Wei-tse was assigned to accompany the King. Before they went into Lu, Yi Wei-tse asked the ministers of Lu, "How are you going to serve my Sovereign?" "We shall serve your sovereign with ten cows, ten lambs and ten pigs." "On what do you base your manner in treating my Sovereign?" said Yi Wei-tse. "My Sovereign is the Son of Heaven. Now, when the Son of Heaven visits the vassal states, the Rulers of these States should move out of their houses, roll up their sleeves to move and set the dinner tables and then supervise the preparations of the banquets somewhere below where the Son of Heaven was dining. After the Son of Heaven has dined, he will then receive the rulers." The officials of Lu threw away the keys and refused to receive King Min of Chi and his party. The King then decided to go through Tsou to Hsueh. It happened that the Ruler of

Tsou died and King Ming wanted to go to the capital of Tsou to mourn his death. Yi Wei-tse told the heir, "When the Son of Heaven comes to console with you on the passing of your father, you must put the body in a bigger coffin which should be placed on the southern side of a hall facing north. When this is done, the Son of Heaven may pay his respects to the dead, standing facing south." The officials of Tsou said, "We would rather die fighting than comply with your demand." And King Ming and his party did not dare go into Tsou. The officials of Tsou and Lu lead a hard life, and when they die, their families cannot even afford the burials they are entitled to. Nevertheless, when they were asked to treat King Min of Chi as their Emperor, they refused to receive him. Now Ch'in has ten thousand chariots, and Wei also has the same number. The Rulers of these two states have both proclaimed themselves kings. The ministers of Wei[3] in urging the installation of the King of Ch'in as the Emperor of China simply because Ch'in has won a battle, have made themselves less worthy of their King than the officials of the lowest rank of Tsou and Lu. Furthermore, Ch'in is insatiable. Once the King of Ch'in becomes Emperor, he will make changes in the administrations of the various states. He will appoint those he trusts as ministers to replace those of whom he is suspicious, and take away possessions from those whom he dislikes in order to reward those to whom he is partial. He will also have the Rulers of these states marry the girls from Ch'in. When this happens and the girls of Ch'in live in the palace of Wei, will the King of Wei live in peace? Will you, General, continue to enjoy the favours of the King?'

At that, Hsin Yuan-yen stood up, bowed and apologized to Lu Lien, saying, 'I thought you were just a mediocre fellow. Now I know you are a great scholar! I will take leave of you now and never again talk of installing the King of Ch'in as Emperor.'

When the General who led the armies of Ch'in heard of this, he withdrew his troops fifty *li* (about seventeen miles) from Han Tan. At that juncture, by coincidence, Prince Wu Chi of Wei took over from General Chin Pi the command of the armies of Wei and was coming to Chao's rescue. The Ch'in general then decided to withdraw his troops to Ch'in. Prince Ping Yuan, therefore, wanted to reward Lu Lien by ennobling him. Lu Lien refused the honour. Prince Ping Yuan then gave a banquet in his honour. When everyone was feeling happy, Prince Ping Yuan got up, walked over to Lu Lien and presented him with one thousand gold pieces. Lu Lien laughed and said, 'Great scholars are respected because they settle problems, troubles and disputes for others without gain. For them to gain anything from their efforts is to become merchants and traders. I would not think of myself as a merchant.' He then took leave of Prince Ping Yuan and did not see him again all his life.

From this it can be seen that prose writing had significantly advanced in the Warring States Period from the laconic style of Confucius' day. Not only was the narration of events more cohesive; dialogue, too, was used successfully to depict the personalities of the characters in a story.

When Ch'in successively defeated the other six states and united China in 246 B.C., she set about establishing a centralized government, the promulgation of strict laws, the institution of a legal system, the adoption of a national currency system, the inauguration of a standardized system of weights and measures and the definition and proclamation of a standard of written characters. In many ways, the establishment of the Ch'in Dynasty represented the realization of the people's wish for a united, stabilized country. However, the first Emperor of Ch'in not only banned the existing various schools of thought, burned the books of these schools, of literature and poetry,[4] and buried alive Confucian scholars, he also ignored the people's wish for a peaceful period to recuperate from the struggle and suffering they had undergone. Three hundred thousand people were sent to build the Great Wall; 700,000 were put to work to build palaces for him, and 500,000 people were exiled to the then unexplored regions of South China. The Emperor increased the agricultural tax to two-thirds of the proceeds of the farmers. The people's welfare was ignored, so that in 209 B.C. there began a series of uprisings by farmers and the aristocrats of the six conquered states, and in about three years the Ch'in Dynasty was overthrown.

For almost seventy years after the establishment of the Han Dynasty (206 B.C.–A.D. 219), successive emperors and empresses realized that after the long warring years what the people wanted was to be left alone to pursue their own business. They accordingly adopted a *laisser-faire* policy, with the result that when Emperor Wu ascended the throne in 140 B.C. it was said that 'every family has everything it can want. In the cities and towns, government granaries are filled and revenue is more than enough to pay for the expenses of all local governments. In the capital, the Treasury has accumulated such a huge amount of surplus money that the strings used to hold the (pierced) coins have rotted. In the Imperial granaries, grain collected in successive years is heaped one kind upon another and overflows from the granaries and is spoiled . . . even gatekeepers are having the best kind of grain and meat to eat.'[5]

Emperor Wu established an examination system for selecting officials and encouraged literary activities. He also built grand palaces, toured the country and held sacrificial rites on top of great mountains, praying for the blessing of the gods, and even sent people overseas to search for the drugs of immortality. Abroad, Emperor Wu waged a series of military campaigns. His troops conquered Korea, Indo-China, pacified barbarian tribes in the Western Regions, defeated the Huns and opened up the famous 'silk road' through Chinese Turkestan to Persia. Through international and domestic trade, China grew more prosperous and enjoyed prestige, influence and other benefits that came with being the most civilized and strongest country in Asia. The power of China was at its zenith, and to this day, Chinese refer to themselves as *Han jen*, or the people of Han.

In this, one of the greatest and most prosperous periods of Chinese history, the art of prose writing also greatly advanced. Tsao Tsuo's *Memoir on Ways to Raise the Value of Rice*, Chia Yi's *Comments on the Rise and Fall of Ch'in* and others are all noted for their clarity and unornamented style. But the best prose writer was Szema Chien. The prose in his *Historical Record*, the first comprehensive Chinese history book, is so skilfully written that its literary merits are perhaps more generally admired by the Chinese than the book's function as a record of historical events.

2. THE LIFE OF SZEMA CHIEN

Chinese teachers like to tell their students when they are learning to write a composition, 'Read tens of thousands of books and travel tens of thousands of miles', meaning that books broaden one's learning, and first-hand experience helps a writer to write convincingly. Often when they say this, they have Szema Chien in mind.

Szema Chien's travels covered a wide area. He went westward as far as what is now Shensi, Kansu and Sikang provinces, east to Shantung province and the coastal areas of Kiangsu and Chekiang provinces, north to Hopei and Suiyuan and south to Hunan, Kweichow and Yunnan provinces. Everywhere he went, he observed people's customs, the landscape, and asked the elders about things of the past. This helped him when later he started writing his *Historical Record*. His style, which the Chinese so admire, however, stemmed more from his scholarship and the teachings of his father, Szema Tan.[6] For it was undoubtedly his determination—arising from several causes which I shall later describe—to write what is in fact the first book of Chinese history, and his scholastic and literary gifts which gave to his prose its force and vitality.

In his early years, however, Szema Chien did not really accomplish much. Once he went to what is now Yunnan to appease the tribes there. Otherwise, he served only as Lang-chung, or a clerk in the Imperial Secretariat.[7] When he was thirty-six, his father died, which proved to be the turning-point of Szema Chien's life.

His father was a *ta-shih-ling*, whose job it was to look after the official collection of books and archives, keep official records of the important events of the day and serve as the royal astronomer. Thus, Szema Tan had the chance to read all kinds of books which had been collected in the imperial library during nearly a hundred years of peace since the Han Dynasty was established. He was determined to write a comprehensive book on Chinese history, emulating the example set by Confucius. He had collected much material and started writing,[8] but his duties as royal astronomer also involved planning and overseeing the sacrificial rites which Emperor Wu frequently wanted held in honour of the great mountains and rivers of his realm. He was kept very busy and died before realizing his lifelong ambition. In his preface to *Historical Record*, Szema Chien wrote movingly of what his father told him before he died:

He held my hand and said, weeping, 'Our ancestors were official historians of the Chou Dynasty. . . . After I die, you must get yourself appointed as the official historian. Once appointed, you must not forget to write the book I have been wanting to do myself. . . . Since the reigns of Kings Yu and Li, kings have misruled and moral standards have decayed. Confucius rescued from oblivion moral standards and customs of old, commented on Shih and Shu[9] and wrote *Spring-Autumn*. To this day, scholars model themselves on him. It is now more than four hundred years since Confucius' time. There have been incessant wars between the feudal lords and no historical records have been kept. Now Han has again united the kingdom, but I, the official historian, have not yet recorded the accomplishments of the emperors and lords and the deeds of loyal ministers and martyrs and so have failed to keep a historical record for the country. This is the greatest regret of my life. You should always keep this in mind and try to fulfil my unrealized ambition.' I bowed my head and greatly touched, replied, 'I am not worthy of the task, but I will try my best to compile an historical record based on all the material you have collected.'

Szema Chien was, moreover, an ambitious man. He said of himself that 'I was unruly in my conduct when I was young, so that when I grew up, I was not known for any special talents in my village. Because of the services rendered by my father, His Majesty was kind enough to make use of my meagre talent at Court. I was determined not to allow myself to be distracted from making a name for myself. I declined to entertain guests socially and did not attend to the well-being of my family. Day and night, I thought only of how best to devote myself to fulfilling my duties, hoping thus to please and to win the favour of His Majesty.'[10] So it was that when his father died in 110 B.C., he did not mourn his passing by going into seclusion as was required by custom, but in the same year went with Emperor Wu up to Tai-shan to hold sacrificial rites for the Mountain God, and then toured the northern frontiers. Two years later, when he was thirty-eight years old, he was appointed *ta-shih-ling*. He must have been very happy. This was what his father had wanted him to be. He started in that year to collect material and generally prepare to write the book he had promised his father. He even wrote to a hermit asking him to give up his secluded life and join the government service.

In 104 B.C. he started and was put in charge of the tremendous work of establishing a new calendar, based on the calendar used during the Hsia Dynasty. It is interesting to note that in *The Analects*, when Yen Hui asked Confucius about the organization of government, the first thing Confucius mentioned was: 'Use the calendar of Hsia Dynasty.' It seems clear that aside from other practical reasons, Szema Chien was influenced by this opinion of Confucius. For, in the same year, when the new calendar was introduced, he chose to start writing his *Historical*

Record, saying, 'Five hundred years after the Duke of Chou died, Confucius was born. Since Confucius' time, another five hundred years have passed. In the tradition of enlightened times, abiding by the standards of Yi,[11] following the examples of *Spring-Autumn* and based on the ideals of Shih, Shu, Li and Yueh,[12] I shall write my book! This is how I intend to write my book!'[13] He was in fact saying that he wanted to write his book to carry on the tradition of Confucius and serve his country in the Confucian manner.

Szema Chien seemed then destined to realize his father's and his own ambition and to lead a comfortable and rewarding life under the reign of one of the most ambitious emperors of China. But fate intervened. Torn between his desire for an official career, his contempt for his spineless colleagues and his unappreciated loyalty to his Emperor, Szema was to lead a life of disgrace and almost inhuman torment.

In 99 B.C., when Szema was forty-seven, Emperor Wu sent General Li Ling to help General Li Kwang-li fight the Huns. Li Ling penetrated deep into Hun territory and killed more than ten thousand enemy soldiers. But as the war wore on, Li Ling was outnumbered and surrounded. His supply of arrows, bows and other ammunition and food were almost exhausted and the great majority of the five thousand soldiers under him were killed or wounded. Being so far away from his base, he knew that he could expect no help from General Li Kwang-li, who, for all the troops under his command, had not yet met the Huns in a single battle. Li Ling decided to surrender, and as he later told the Chinese emissary who went to the Huns to make peace with them, hoped to find an opportunity later to return to China.

When the news of his surrender reached Court, the officials who, when they first heard of Li Ling's victory over the Huns, toasted and congratulated the Emperor, now said that Li Ling was a traitor. The Emperor, being an expansionist, was of course furious at this setback. Now, Li Ling happened to be one of Szema Chien's acquaintances. Szema Chien did not have to speak up for him; at least, not at that very moment. However, when the Emperor asked for his opinion, Szema Chien said that 'Li Ling is a good son to his parents, faithful to his friends and has, often at the risk of his life, answered his country's call to duty. His conduct is like that of an outstanding leader of his nation. Now just because he is once unfortunate in his mission, all the officials who know how to look after themselves and protect their families are quick to point out his shortcomings and attack him. This s very regrettable!' He also said that Li Ling's exploits were as great as those of many famous generals of old, and that he was sure Li Ling was only waiting for a chance to serve his country once again.

Unfortunately for him the Emperor, seeing that General Li Kwang-li had not yet won a battle over the Huns, suspected that Szema Chien was in fact trying to attack General Li Kwang-li and indirectly blaming the Emperor himself for the failure of the expedition in appointing an incompetent commander. The Emperor was very angry and ordered Szema Chien's castration. According to the then prevailing law, Szema Chien could have paid a certain amount of money and be spared the humiliation, but he was poor, and had few friends to speak for him, since he devoted so much of his time to his books. He was at first imprisoned, and it was not until the following year that he was castrated. This was because Emperor Wu, too, retained some hopes that Li Ling might have been compelled to surrender and he did not want, perhaps, to act before he was sure. But after waiting a year for Li Ling to escape and return to China, the Emperor became impatient and sent General Kungsun Ou and a contingent of troops to the Huns to try to bring Li Ling back. Kungsun Ou could not get in touch with Li Ling, however. On his return he told the Emperor that he had learned from a captured prisoner that Li Ling had been teaching the Huns the arts of war to help them later to fight the Chinese. Emperor Wu was enraged and ordered that Li Ling's mother, younger brother, wife and children should be executed and Szema Chien at the same time castrated. When eventually Emperor Wu sent an emissary to the Huns and discovered that it had been Li Hsu, not Li Ling, who had taught the Huns how to fight, it was too late. Li Ling's family had already been killed and Szema Chien had suffered the greatest humiliation.

During his imprisonment, Szema Chien was in a mental torment. He felt that it was a great injustice to punish him simply because he had spoken up for a patriotic and brave general who had met with a temporary setback, and in spite of the loyal services he himself had rendered to the country. The fact that none of his friends offered to pay the money needed to avoid his castration, nor even spoke up for him, must have also greatly saddened him. He considered committing suicide, but felt that this would only make him more of a laughing-stock: 'People would only think that I was at my wits' end and committed suicide because I could not escape the punishment.' With time on his hands, he thought of the book which he had promised his father to write and with which he himself had hoped to carry on the tradition of Confucianism. His inward struggles must have been painful and unceasing. It is naturally impossible to say how long he took to come to a decision, but when he finally made his choice, he resolved to finish writing his book, even at the price of being castrated. Some years later, he wrote in a letter, 'I submitted to castration without showing anger. I thought that if I could finish the book, I would be willing to store it away in the mountain caves and wait for someone who understands me and is willing to publish it to come along. Should one day the book be read in the cities and towns, I shall be amply rewarded. In fact, even if I should be chopped to pieces, I will not regret it. But this will be understood by people of intelligence only and need not be told to ordinary folk.'[14]

But his feelings are perhaps best expressed in his *The Life of Chu Yuan*. For Chu Yuan, whom Szema Chien greatly admired, was also punished because of his loyalty to his king. It is not inconceivable that Szema Chien was also writing about himself in the following passages:

Chu Yuan was grieved that the King was so undiscerning, and that false witness could so darken counsel, crooked deceits injure justice and the upright be rejected. Full of sorrow and gloomy thoughts he composed the *Li Sao*. . . .

Chu Yuan was a man of undeviating righteousness who devoted all his loyalty and all his knowledge to the service of his prince; yet he was traduced by false witness. Well might he be called 'afflicted' He was faithful, yet was disbelieved; loyal, and yet calumniated. Is it any wonder that he should have felt wronged? It was the sense of wrong that inspired Chu Yuan's composition of the *Li Sao*. . . .

Chu Yuan's style is concise, his wording subtle, his mind pure, his actions noble. He can write of small things in a way that suggest great ones, or use simple themes to express complex ideas. Because his mind was pure, his subjects breathe a natural sweetness. Because his actions were noble, he preferred death to compliance. He withdrew himself from the muck and mire. He sloughed off the impurities of life to soar away out of reach of the dust and turmoil Refusing to accept the foulness of this world, he emerged shining and unspotted from its mud. Such a mind may, without hyperbole be said to rival the sun and moon in brightness.[15]

In fact, in his preface to the *Historical Record*, Szema Chien did compare the awful fate that had befallen him to that suffered by King Wen of the Chou Dynasty, Confucius, Chu Yuan, Tso Chiu-ming, Suntse and others—all of whom produced books of importance because of their various trials and tribulations. Nevertheless, he was, after being castrated, a changed person in every sense.

In 96 B.C., when he was fifty years old, Szema Chien was released from jail and appointed *Chung Shu Ling*, or confidential secretary to the Emperor, and official liaison between the Emperor and the Prime Minister. This was a very important post. When Jen An, Governor of Yi-chow, wrote asking him to recommend talented people to the Emperor for government service, Szema Chien replied, 'The gravest tragedy lies in avarice, the greatest sorrow arises when one's heart is broken, the worst conduct is that which brings shame on one's ancestors and the most awful fate which can befall a man is to be castrated. A castrated person is a nobody. This has long been so. . . . Even a mediocre person cannot stand a eunuch, not to mention the talented ones. Even though there is no one of any capability at Court, it is nevertheless not for a castrated person to recommend to the Emperor the talented and worthy people of the country. . . . I am not different from a eunuch. How can I present myself to those worthy people who do not know me? Therefore, I must follow the prevailing custom and go along with the others. . . .'[16] No, Szema Chien was no longer ambitious to pursue an official career. He also realized that although Emperor Wu might respect his literary talent, the Emperor also needed someone who, while having free access to the palace, could not cause trouble with any of his women. This of course rubbed salt into his already wounded pride. As his bitterness towards the Emperor persisted and grew, he lived more and more for the book that he was writing. He said of his life in this period that 'my inside twists and turns painfully many times a day. At home, I am at a loss as to what to do; outside, I have no idea where I am going. Every time that I think of the great humiliation that I have suffered, my clothes are soaked through with sweat.'[17]

At the age of fifty-five he finally succeeded in completing the *Historical Record*. It took him altogether eighteen years. A few years later he died.[18]

Szema Chien was bitter about his fate. In a letter he wrote about his family, he said, 'My ancestors did not help found the Royal House. They were in charge of historical records, astrology and the calendar, not very different from the work of fortune-tellers. They were the playthings of the Emperors, kept by prostitutes and actors and looked down upon by the common people.'[19] But he was a strong-willed man. He did not out of despair commit suicide as Chu Yuan did, but expressed his anger at the Emperors in his book. Writing about Kao Tsu, the first Emperor of the Han Dynasty, he mentioned the Emperor's drunkenness and licentious nature. He wrote of his vulgarity in passing water into the hat of a Confucian scholar in public. He also dwelt on Kao Tsu's meanness: when after gaining a certain measure of success Kao Tsu made a fool of his father by asking in front of everybody, 'What do you think of my accomplishment, a bit better than Second Brother whom you used to prefer to me, huh?' In the same manner, Szema Chien wrote in the *Annals of Hsiang Yu* that when Kao Tsu was once hotly pursued by the troops of Hsiang Yu he three times pushed his son and daughter out of the carriage in which they were riding in order to get away faster; in another instance, when Hsiang Yu captured and threatened to cook his father alive, Kao Tsu was represented as not a bit upset, but asked that he be given a bowl of the broth. Undoubtedly these touches make the *Annals* more readable. One wonders what Szema Chien wrote in the *Annals of Emperor Wu*, which was banned and destroyed immediately after the *Historical Record* was made public.[20] Perhaps he tried to point out the errors committed by Emperor Wu and to show that he was a victim of the capricious nature of the Emperor. He certainly could not have foreseen that this was to happen and still less, that Emperor Hsun, just because he thought Szema Chien's writing about the Royal House unduly abusive, would decide to ban his offspring from entering government service.

3. *THE* HISTORICAL RECORD

Historical Record is the first book which covers the entire history of China, starting from the reign of the legendary Emperor Huang-ti down to the fourth year of Tai Tse[21] (101 B.C.), or the thirty-ninth year of the reign of Emperor Wu of the Han Dynasty, totalling 2,597 years. It consists of 130 chapters,[22] of which 112 are *Pen Chi* or annals of all the dynasties preceding the Han Dynasty and the emperors and empresses of the Han Dynasty itself; *Shih Chia* or chronicles of the rulers of some of the states of the Spring-Autumn and Warring States Periods and famous prime ministers and generals of these two periods and the Chou and Han Dynasties; and *Lieh Chuan* or biographies of philosophers, scholars, merchants, farmers, astrologers, comics, assassins, prostitutes, good and bad officials. In other words, about ninety per cent of the book is devoted to presenting Chinese history through the lives and activities of leading personages of the various dynasties. Of the remaining eighteen chapters, eight are called *Shu* and deal with the changes through these 2,500-odd years in ceremony, law, music, calendar, astronomy, sacrificial rites, water conservation and weights and measures, and the other ten chapters are called *Nien Piao*, which are lists of important events in Chinese history and names of prominent officials under the reigns of the various emperors of the Han Dynasty. It is through these last-mentioned eighteen chapters, and to a lesser extent the annals of the dynasties preceding the Han Dynasty, that Szema Chien provided the necessary background or the tapestry of Chinese history in various periods against which the persons mentioned elsewhere play their important parts. We may say, therefore, that to Szema Chien, history is written by the acts of man. Considering the fact that *Spring-Autumn* and *Kuo Yu*, two history books written respectively in the Spring-Autumn and Warring States Periods, declared Heaven's will and natural phenomena to be deciding factors in the development of history, Szema Chien's emphasis on the importance of human effort is a striking advance in the understanding of the nature of the history of man. Indeed, so greatly admired was the *Historical Record* by Chinese historians that every history book written in later dynasties tried to a great extent to copy its method of presentation.

Because of this emphasis on the lives and activities of the prominent persons in Chinese history, the *Historical Record* became also a literary masterpiece. For Szema Chien's scholarship enabled him to grasp the significance of historical events. His extensive travels enabled him to write from personal experience about areas where important events occurred. He paid great attention to describing the different personalities of the leading figures through their actions. Because of this mastery of the art of prose writing, his narrations of events are always lucid and gripping and his descriptions invariably vivid and true to life. Chinese prose writers, including the 'Eight Prose Masters of the Tang and the Sung Dynasties', were greatly influenced by Szema Chien and tried to write like him. What is more, Chinese novels such as *Tung Chou Lieh Kuo Chih* (*Story of the Various States of the East Chou Dynasty*), *Hsi Han Tung Shu Yen Yi* (*Popular Stories of Hsi Han*) and many Chinese operas such as *Pa Wang Pieh Chi*, *Chiang Hsiang Ho* and *Wen Chao Kuan* are based on parts of some of the chapters of the *Historical Record*. The influence of the book on Chinese literature is as great as, if not greater than, its influence on Chinese, history books. This is perhaps not too common a phenomenon.

I quote here a passage from *The Annals of Hsiang Yu* which is considered to be one of the best chapters in the *Historical Record*.

(Hsiang Yu was made King Hsiang. He then prepared to invade the State of Ch'in. However, while he was fighting to save the State of Chao, King Huai sent the Duke of Pei to invade Ch'in. By this time the Duke had already conquered Ch'in and sent troops to guard Han Ku Pass[23] which towered over the principal road leading to Ch'in. Hsiang Yu's armies marching on to Ch'in were stopped by the Pass. Upon hearing the news that the Duke had captured the capital of Ch'in, Hsiang Yu flew into a rage. He stormed the Pass, advanced to the west of Hsi River[24] and with 400,000 troops made camp in Hung Meng.[25] He further received word from Tsao Wu-shang, one of the Duke's military aides, that the Duke wanted to be King of Kung Chung and seize all the treasures. Hsiang Yu was furious, and urged on by Fan Cheng, decided to attack the Duke, who with his 100,000 troops, was stationed in Pa Shang.[26] Hsiang Po, an uncle of Hsiang Yu, heard of this and went at night to Pa Shang. He had wanted only to take Chang Liang, a friend who had once saved his life, away from there. But Chang Liang, who was a close aide of the Duke, would not leave without first informing him. Upon hearing the news the Duke was frightened. Against Hsiang Yu he could not hope to win. He persuaded Hsiang Po to believe in his loyalty to Hsiang Yu and promised to call on the latter in the morning. Hsiang Po in turn persuaded Hsiang Yu to treat the Duke well when the latter came to visit him.)

The next morning the Duke of Pei came with a retinue of more than 100 men to call on King Hsiang.

'Your Excellency[27] and I have both tried our utmost to defeat the armies of Ch'in,' he said. 'While Your Excellency waged wars in the areas north of the Yellow River, I fought in the south. I did not expect to be the first one to storm the Han Ku Pass and conquer Ch'in, or to have the pleasure of meeting Your Excellency here again. It is unthinkable that people would sink so low as to spread malicious rumours and try to estrange Your Excellency's feelings towards me.'

'Tsao Wu-shang, your military aide, told me of the rumours,' said King Hsiang thoughtlessly, 'otherwise, I would not have thought of them.'

Hsiang Yu then asked the Duke to stay on and have a drink with him. (When the dishes were laid out) Hsiang Yu and Hsiang Po sat on the west side facing east, Fan Cheng sat facing south, the Duke of Pei facing north and Chang Liang also sat with the others, facing west. While drinking, Fan Cheng looked inquiringly at Hsiang Yu several times and thrice raised the semi-circular jade decoration he was wearing, signalling to Hsiang Yu to kill the Duke of Pei. But Hsiang Yu remained silent and made no move. Fan Cheng lost his patience and went out. He summoned Hsiang Chuan, a cousin of Hsiang Yu's, and told him, 'His Majesty[28] is too kind-hearted. You go in and pay your respects and then ask to be allowed to dance the sword dance. You should then look for a chance to strike and kill the Duke of Pei. Otherwise, all of you will later be captured by him.'

Hsiang Chuan went in to pay his respects and said, 'Your Majesty, there is nothing in the way of entertainment here in the camp. May I beg to be allowed to dance a sword dance to entertain you while you are drinking with the Duke of Pei?'

'Yes.'

Hsiang Chuan drew out his sword and started dancing. Hsiang Po, too, drew out his sword and joined him in the dance. He managed to keep dancing between the Duke and Hsiang Chuan, and the latter was prevented from hitting the Duke.

Chang Liang saw through it all. Desperate, he came out to find Fan Kwai.

'How is it going?' Fan asked.

'Terrible,' Chang answered. 'Hsiang Chuan is dancing with his naked sword and looking for a chance to strike the Duke.'

'Good Heavens! I'll go in and fight!'

So saying, he drew out his sword and, carrying a shield in his other hand, moved towards the tent. The guards tried to stop him from entering. Fan Kwai hit them and knocked them down with his shield, and entered. He stood by the flaps of the tent facing Hsiang Yu and looked at him so furiously that his eyes appeared to have burst from their sockets and popped out. Every hair on his head seemed to be quivering with anger.

King Hsiang saw Fan Kwai and half raised himself from his squatting position,[29] his hand on his sword. 'What are you doing here?' he asked.

Chang Liang, who had followed Fan Kwai in, answered, 'He is Fan Kwai, body-guard of the Duke.'

'Remarkable! Let him have a vessel of wine!'

A huge vessel of wine was poured for Fan Kwai. He bowed to thank the King and finished the wine in one gulp.

'Let him have a leg of pork!'

Fan Kwai put the shield down, put the uncooked leg of pork on one of his shoulders, cut small pieces from it with his sword and ate them.

'Well done! Could you drink some more?'

'I am not afraid to die! What is another vessel of wine?' Fan Kwai answered. 'Now, the King of Ch'in was a tyrant. He has killed numerous people and was always anxious to torture people. That was why everyone rose in revolt against him! King Huai's agreement with all his commanders is, "He who defeats the armies of Ch'in and enters first into Han Yang, her capital, shall be the King of Ch'in." Now the Duke of Pei is the one who has accomplished this task. He has not taken even a feather as his own, but closed the palaces of Ch'in and led his armies back to Pa Shang to await Your Excellency's arrival. He has also sent troops to guard the Han Ku Pass to prevent bands of bandits from going through and to guard against any emergency. Your Excellency has not rewarded him for fighting so hard and achieving so great a victory, but you seem to believe in rumours and want to kill him. To take such an action would be to follow in the footsteps of the annihilated State of Ch'in!'

King Hsiang could not immediately think of an answer and said simply, 'Sit down.'

After a while the Duke got up and pretended to go to relieve himself and took Fan Kwai with him. . . .

Outside, he asked, 'Shouldn't I say good-bye? What shall I do?'

'Let's forget the formalities,' Fan said. 'We are at the mercy of King Hsiang, just as if we were pieces of fish and meat on his chopping-block waiting for his knife to come down. Why say good-bye to him?'

The Duke decided to leave. (He called for Chang Liang and asked him to stay behind to thank the King for him.)

'What presents have you brought with you?' asked Chang Liang.

'I have brought a pair of white jade *pi*[30] for King Hsiang and a pair of jade wine vessels for Fan Cheng. But the King was angry and I didn't dare mention the presents. Please present them for me.'

'Yes, sir.'

The Duke decided to take only Fan Kwai, Hsia-hou Yin, Chi Chiang and Chi Hsin with him, and leave the others and his carriage and horses behind. By the main road they had to travel forty *li* before they reached their own camp. But he decided to take a short cut which ran from the foot of Li Mountain[31] through Tse Yang[32] to Pa Shang. He and the four others were to take only their swords and shields and go on foot.

'By taking this short cut we will have only twenty *li* to go,' he said to Chang Liang. 'Go back when you think we have reached our destination.'

Chang Liang waited. When he went in he said, 'The Duke of Pei cannot hold his wine and is thus prevented from taking leave of you. He has asked me to present to Your Excellency a pair of jade *pi* and to present to General Fan a pair of jade vessels.'

'Where is the Duke?' asked King Hsiang.

'He is fearful that he will not be able to please Your Excellency. He has left. By this time he should have arrived at his headquarters.'

The King took the present and put it beside him. Fan Cheng put the pair of jade vessels on the ground, and smashed them with his sword. 'God! How could one accomplish anything with a nincompoop?' he said angrily. 'The Duke of Pei will one day try to seize the country from the King. We are in for trouble. We are in for trouble!'

When the Duke of Pei arrived back in his camp he immediately ordered the execution of Tsao Wu-shang.

After a few days, King Hsiang marched westward to Han Yang. He executed Tse Ying, the King of Ch'in who had surrendered, and set fire to the palaces of Ch'in. The fires raged for three months. He then prepared to go home, taking with him all the captured treasures. Someone said to him, 'This place is easy to defend and the land is fertile. You could conquer the whole country if you use it as your base and set up your capital here.' The King saw that the palaces had all been burnt down and what was more he was anxious to go home. 'One has to go home when one becomes rich and powerful,' said the King, 'otherwise, it is like walking in the dark with beautiful clothes on. No one would see it.' The man said, 'It has been said that the people of Tsu are in fact only monkeys with men's hats on their heads (pretending to be men). It is true.' Upon hearing this, the King ordered the man to be boiled alive.

CHAPTER V

The Poetry of the Han Dynasty

1. *THE LINEAGE OF* FU

EMPEROR WU of the Han Dynasty was one of the most remarkable sovereigns[1] to rule China. Taking advantage of the prosperity of the country, he expanded his kingdom, opened the 'silk road' through Chinese Turkestan to Persia, and brought to China still greater prosperity and influence, and a consciousness of another civilization on the far side of the great Gobi Desert. Because of his love of literature, he ordered that folk songs should be collected and recorded, and he encouraged the development of *fu*. The majority of the 220 folk songs collected by his order have unfortunately been lost, but because of his encouragement, the composing and singing of folk songs became so popular that we are today still able to enjoy some of the folk songs of the Han Dynasty as collected in *Yueh Fu Shih Chi*.[2] But more important for the development of Chinese poetry is that these folk songs are the forerunners of the 'five-word' and 'seven-word' poems which became the principal poetic forms of China. Although not everyone considers that *fu* possesses great literary value, as a literary form it nevertheless lasted more than one thousand years. Emperor Wu may be said, therefore, to have contributed not inconsiderably to Chinese literature.

He himself was a poet. A short song which he is said to have composed when he was waiting for the spirit of Lady Lee, his beloved concubine, to appear after her death is quite famous.

> Is it really you, dear,
> Or—is it not you?
> Craning my neck, I stand here

And look, look for you.
Why is it that, mincing your steps,
You don't seem to come near me, here?

This song was written in the style of *Tsu Tse*, which was still very popular in the Han Dynasty.

It was indeed the rich rhetoric and the technique of describing a subject in great detail from every angle in the exaggerated terms of *Tsu Tse* which contributed greatly to the development of *fu*, which is a kind of poetic prose created in the Han Dynasty. There is, for instance, such a passage in *Chao Hun*:

High halls and deep chambers, with railings and tiered balconies;
Stepped terraces, storied pavilions, whose tops look on the high mountains;
Lattice doors with scarlet interstices, and carving on the square lintels;
Draughtless rooms for winter; galleries cool in summer;
Streams and gullies wind in and out, purling prettily;
A warm breeze bends the melilotus and sets the tall orchids swaying.
Crossing the hall into the apartments, the ceilings and floors are vermilion,
The chambers of polished stone, with kingfisher hangings on jasper hooks;
Bedspreads of kingfisher seeded with pearls, all dazzling in brightness;
Arras of fine silk covers the walls; damask canopies stretch overhead,
Braids and ribbons, brocades and satins, fastened with rings of precious stone.[3]

But *fu* is less ornate than *Tsu Tse*. Its requirements place less emphasis on personal emotions than on scenery, buildings and other objects, and in giving reasons for things happening. To trace its lineage, one has to turn to Hsuntse's *fu*.

Hsuntse was one of the great Confucians during the Warring States Period. He was also a poet. It was he who first called his pieces of writing *fu*, such as *The Fu of the Cloud*, *The Fu of Li*. His purpose in writing all five of his *fu* was to explain his philosophical thought, and the literary value of these is not considered significant. It is the literary form in which they were written which deserves our attention. For it was taken over by the writers of the Han Dynasty to serve, as it were, as an old vessel in which to put new wine. And this, indeed, was Hsuntse's unintended contribution to the growth of *fu*.

Here is a short passage from his *Fu of Li*.

'Here is an important something. It is not silk, not cotton. It has, nevertheless, orderly strands. It is not the sun, nor the moon. And yet it enlightens everyone in the country. Follow it, and the living will enjoy long life and the dead be properly buried; cities will become defensible and armies strengthened. When one accepts it wholeheartedly one becomes King. When one accepts it most of the time, one will still become a Po (or leader of nobles). But when one ignores it, one is doomed to lose one's fief. I am too ignorant to know what it is and therefore beg Your Majesty to tell me.' The King said, 'Isn't it graceful and not affected; easy to know and yet profound; and respected by the superior man but ignored by the common people? Isn't it that which when one's emotions are restrained by it, one behaves like a gentleman, otherwise like a beast? And that which when an individual reverses it, he becomes a sage; when the ruler of a state observes it, he will rule over the country? Profound and yet simple, easy to follow and yet of great importance, it must be *Li*, or the principle of social order.'

This is very similar to the *fu* of the Han Dynasty. The question and answer form, too, was almost universally adopted by the writers of *fu* in the Han Dynasty, of whom Chia Yu was perhaps one of the first. But it was Mei Sheng's[4] *Chi Fa* (*Seven Considerations*) which represented a step forward in the development of *fu*. For it was the first *fu* to have a moralistic overtone and the first to use seven paragraphs to develop a theme, a device which was much copied by the writers of later periods. Here is a short passage from *Seven Considerations*:

Deep in the hazel tree forest, by the big bog, where mists hang heavily and lights are dim, rhinoceros and tigers gather and feed. The hunters fearlessly advance, their bodies bare, and they are determined to bag their prey. We see their knives flying forward, flashing white in the semi-darkness; their spears and lances pierce and plunge down into the animals. When the hunt is over, gold and clothes are given as rewards.

Szema Hsiang-ju's *fu* became the model for his contemporaries and successors. He fused the rhetoric and descriptive techniques of *Tsu Tse*, the 'question and answer' form of Hsuntse, and the moralistic flavour of Mei Sheng. The *fu* as a literary form gained great popularity not only because it met the requirements of the times better than the purely poetic form of *Tsu Tse*, but because during the prosperous times under

Emperor Wu, writers could afford to devote much time to writing, and were in a mood to appreciate long and flowery phrases and poems.

But the most important factor which brought about the flowering of *fu* was perhaps the personality of Emperor Wu. He was ambitious, aggressive, capricious, literary, musical and had a deep sense of history. He waged a series of wars to expand his realm and increase his influence. He brought about even greater prosperity for his people. He built himself sumptuous palaces and often indulged in hunting. His consciousness of history led him to become the first Chinese emperor to institute *nien hao*, a designation of an Emperor's reign, for easy reference. He imitated emperors of the past in visiting famous mountains and great rivers to hold sacrificial rites and pray for the blessing of the gods, and collected and recorded folk songs. His love of music led him to appoint Court musicians who composed new musical scores and to order officials to write lyrics on special occasions. His love of literature made him send a special cart to invite Mei Sheng, a famous poet, to Court immediately after he ascended the throne. After reading Szema Hsiang-ju's *Tse Hsu Fu*, he was so moved that he said, 'What a pity we were not born at the same time!' Upon learning that Szema Hsiang-ju was in fact still alive, he immediately sent for him and appointed him an official of the Court so that he could have the poet's companionship. In addition to Szema Hsiang-ju, he also appointed as officials Tung Fang Shuo,[5] Yen Chi[6] and others solely because they, too, wrote good *fu*. These officials did almost nothing but write *fu* while others at Court wrote them as well from time to time to please the Emperor. This of course gave great incentive to the *literati* to follow the fashion. It was one of the surer ways to fame and official position. Later, Chang Heng[7] in his *Lun Kung Chi Su* (*Memoir on the Selection of Officials by Examination*) mentioned that everyone who elected to be examined in his skill at writing *fu* invariably passed the national civil service examination and was, at least, given a salary. When this happened, there was simply no way of stopping anyone from writing *fu*. And *fu* became the most popular form of literary activity of the day.

2. THE LIFE OF SZEMA HSIANG-JU

Szema Hsiang-ju (179–117 B.C.) was a romantic rogue. The best-known event in his life is perhaps his seduction of the widowed

daughter of a rich family by playing love songs on a *chin* and his elope-
ment with her when he had nothing to live on. Few would dare or
could accomplish such a feat, but of course, Szema Hsiang-ju had the
reputation of being a famous writer to help him when he attempted to
court the widow. It is difficult to believe that a good writer always has
to be unconventional, as many people seem to think, but in Szema
Hsiang-ju's case we do find a romantic and unconventional man.

It is said that he was first named Chien Tse, or Little Poppy, but he
changed his name to Hsiang-ju when he grew up and read of the
exploits of Lin Hsiang-ju, a Prime Minister of the State of Chao during
the Warring States Period, who several times saved his sovereign from
humiliation and who renounced his pride to conciliate a famous general
in order to defend the state against Chin. But China had by this time
been united for more than half a century and the country was in one
of its most prosperous periods and the strongest power in Asia. The
qualities the writer so admired in Lin Hsiang-ju would not, therefore,
seem to be what were most required in an official of the period. He
bought himself an official position and eventually became *Wu chi
chang shih*, or an assistant official in charge of the care of horses for the
cavalry. He was not happy for he felt that his knowledge was not put
to good use and his talents were unrecognized. On the other hand,
Emperor Ching, who was then reigning, did not think much of *fu*,
in which Szema Hsiang-ju excelled. This unhappy situation lasted for
some years until Prince Hsiao of Liang came with his retinue of poets,
such as Chou Yang and Mei Sheng, to the capital to have an audience
with the Emperor, when Szema Hsiang-ju met them and was attracted
to them by their talent and love of literature. He resigned from his post
on the pretext of illness and went to live in Liang.[8] For several years
he was happy there, having for friends famous men of letters. In this
period, he wrote *Tse Hsu Fu* allegedly to persuade the Prince to give
up hunting. But having devoted more than three-quarters of the piece
to describing the hunting-ground of Tsu, Yun Meng, the great varieties
of animals and birds to be found there, and the splendour of the retinue
of the King of Tsu, the result was exactly the opposite. Anyway, soon
afterwards the Prince died.

The group of poets and writers no longer had any sponsor, and dis-
persed from Liang. Szema Hsiang-ju returned to his native Chengtu
in Szechuan, but was too poor to support himself. Wang Chi, one of
his friends, was then Magistrate of Ling Chun.[9] He heard of Szema

Hsiang-ju's destitution and asked the writer to stay with him. Szema Hsiang-ju went and lived in a house just outside the outer wall of the city but he must have been rather disillusioned. Not only could he not expect to reach the illustrious position of his namesake, but with all his scholarship and talent he was now reduced to poverty and had to depend on a friend for a living. As is not uncommon with a man in his situation, he irrationally took it out on Wang Chi. Wang went daily to call on him to see if all was well with him, but after the first few days Szema Hsiang-ju refused to see him, saying that he was ill. When one morning all the rich families in the district, having heard that one of the friends of the Magistrate had come to visit him, gave a banquet in his honour, Szema Hsiang-ju let them wait until noon and then sent word saying that he was too unwell to come. Wang Chi was greatly embarrassed, and for fear of offending the leading families went personally to persuade him to join the party. When at last Szema Hsiang-ju went, all the people who were present—more than a hundred —were greatly impressed by his scholarship and personality.

It was, perhaps, at the banquet that Szema Hsiang-ju learned of the existence of the beautiful, recently widowed daughter of the very rich Cho family, who liked music. The young woman, Wen Chun, came also to hear of the young and talented friend of the Magistrate. She looked out for him and often saw him drive past in a carriage, elegant and handsome. In the meantime, Szema Hsiang-ju played up to Wang Chi and secured an invitation to the house of Cho Wang-sun. At dinner, noticing that Wen Chun was lurking behind a door, he played on a *chin* a love song expressing his longing for her. That night, he managed to send a message to her, and she, having fallen in love with him, came to him upon receiving the message. They eloped to Chengtu. Cho Wang-sun was furious with his daughter and decided not to give her any money. In Chengtu the young lovers, after the first flush of joy, were forced to face the stark fact that they had no means of supporting themselves. Soon, Wen Chun had had enough of the difficulties of making ends meet, and became angrier and angrier with her parents for not caring about her happiness. She and Hsiang-ju went back to Ling Chun and sold their carriage and horses to buy a small inn there. Wen Chun herself sold and served wine to the customers behind a stove in the shop, and Hsiang-ju, putting on an apron, washed dishes and other utensils with their employees. For a daughter of a rich family in the district to sell and serve wine in a small inn and her husband to work as a labourer was something which was unheard of, and it naturally created a scandal. Cho Wang-sun, feeling himself publicly humiliated, stayed at home and did not receive any visitors. But as time went on, he was forced to submit, and gave his daughter one hundred servants, a million cash and a great variety of presents as dowry, whereupon Wen Chun and Hsiang-ju closed the inn and went back to Chengtu. They built themselves a mansion and bought acres of farm land and settled down to lead the peaceful and comfortable life of the rich.

Wen Chun must have been a loving wife who spoilt her husband, for during this period he not only apparently lost interest in seeking an official career, and did not write a *fu*, but he also developed diabetes. Perhaps good food, good wine in plenty and a sedentary life may have helped ruin his health.

Szema Hsiang-ju rusticated for many years until one day Emperor Wu, who had acceded to the throne in 149 B.C., happened to read his *Tse Hsu Fu*. Upon learning that the poet was living in Chengtu, he immediately sent for him. Szema Hsiang-ju must have been more than happy at the unexpected turn of events. He was now in his forties and it must have seemed to him that his long-buried ambition might yet be realized. From the day he arrived at Court, he tried his best to please the Emperor. When the Emperor praised him, upon seeing him, for his great skill in describing the hunting scene in *Tse Hsu Fu*, he said, 'That is nothing. It describes the hunt of only a prince. I beg to be permitted to write for Your Majesty a *fu* on the hunt of an Emperor.'

He subsequently presented the Emperor with *Shang Lin Fu*, which described in exaggerated and grandiose terms the vastness of the hunting-ground, the splendour of the hunting-lodge, the pomp of the Emperor's retinue and listed every known or legendary animal, bird and plant. The result was a decorous *fu*, literally glittering with sequences of ornate and obscure words. Vain as a young girl who thrives on flattery, the Emperor was rapturous over it. He made Szema Hsiang-ju a *Lang*, or official in the Imperial Secretariat.

Some years later Emperor Wu sent Tang Meng as his emissary to contact Yeh Lang and Peh Chung,[10] two small states of minority tribes, and ask them to recognize the suzerainty of China. Tang Meng went to Pa and Shu[11] counties in Szechuan Province and took 1,000 soldiers with him. The Governors of the two counties recruited more than ten thousand people to transport the soldiers and their supplies. In the course of the expedition the leader of the recruits was executed because of some small offence, and the people of Pa and Shu were greatly disturbed. When Emperor Wu heard of this he sent Szema Hsiang-ju to the two counties to reprimand Tang Meng and others who were connected with the execution. It is not clear whether the Emperor decided to send Szema Hsiang-ju because he thought that as a native son of one of the counties, the latter could more easily pacify the people there, or because Szema Hsiang-ju himself, his ambition still unrealized, asked for the assignment. Whatever the reason, Szema Hsiang-ju went, and issued a 'Declaration to the People of Pa and Shu' which, as he expected, placated the people. In the meantime, Emperor Wu received information that the rulers of Chun and Cho,[12] two states formed by other minority tribes in the south-west, wanted to become vassals of China, provided that they were given enough presents. So when Szema Hsiang-ju returned to the capital, the Emperor sent him as his emissary to negotiate the necessary agreements with these rulers. The Emperor also ordered him to collect money and treasures in Pa and Shu counties as presents for these rulers.

Szema Hsiang-ju was warmly welcomed when he went back to Shu. The Governor and his subordinates came outside the walls of the county seat to greet him and magistrates carrying bows and arrows walked in front of the carriages of his party to clear the way for them. To the people of Shu the great respect shown to Szema Hsiang-ju by the Governor and other officials gave substance to the great honour the Emperor bestowed on him, and proud of their native son, they were happy to bathe in reflected glory. Rich families all went to call on him and presented him with gifts. Cho Wang-sun, his erstwhile reluctant father-in-law, was also made to feel that he had not done right by his daughter, and decided to give her more money so that she would have an equal share of his fortune with her brothers. Szema Hsiang-ju then went to visit many of the minority tribes in the south-west of China, as a result of which the rulers of Chun, Cho, Jan, Mang, Sze and Yi[13] all asked to become vassal states of China. This was, presumably, the proudest moment of Szema Hsiang-ju's life, which is not to say that he was not happy at Court. In fact, it seems that he got along quite well with the Emperor. Perhaps his stammering had something to do with it. For we have seen that Szema Chien was castrated simply because he spoke up too readily for Li Ling. If it had been Szema Hsiang-ju, he simply would not have said anything—it would have been too much trouble. But more important, perhaps, was Szema Hsiang-ju's determination to please the Emperor. When he learned of the Emperor's infatuation with the idea of immortality, for instance, he wrote *Ta Jen Fu* about the joys of being an immortal and presented it to the Emperor.

It is perhaps also worth mentioning that his *Chang Meng Fu* was written at the request of Empress Chen. She was for a time the favourite of the Emperor, but because of her uncontrollable jealousy, was rejected by him and assigned rooms at Chang Meng Palace. She heard of Szema Hsiang-ju's talent in writing *fu* and presented him with 100 catties, or about 130 lb. of gold ingots, and asked him to write about her loneliness and longing for the Emperor. Szema Hsiang-ju complied and wrote *Chang Meng Fu*, the length of which was less than 1,000 words. It is perhaps the highest fee a Chinese writer ever commanded. But, considering the fact that Emperor Wu was so moved by it that he summoned Empress Chen back to his palace to live together again as man and wife, the gold was indeed well spent.

When he was sixty-one years old, Szema Hsiang-ju died while *Hsiao wen yuan ling*, or Master of the Literary Academy.

3. FU *BY SZEMA HSIANG-JU AND OTHERS*

According to Pan Ku, in his 'Record of Arts and Letters' in the *History of Han Dynasty*, Szema Hsiang-ju wrote twenty-nine *fu*. There are, however, only six of his *fu* extant, namely, *Tse Hsu Fu* (*Mr Non-being*), *Shang Lin Fu* (*The Imperial Hunting Reserve*), *Ta Jen Fu* (*The Immortals*), *Chang Meng Fu* (*The Chang Meng Palace*), *Mei Jen Fu* (*The Beauty*) and *Ai Erh Shih* (*Lamentations for Erh Shih*). Besides these, we know the titles of three others: *Li Fu* (*The Pear*), *Yu Chui Fu* (*The Fish Paste*) and *Tse Tung Shan Fu* (*The Tse Tung Mountain*). The most famous of all his *fu* are *Tse Hsu Fu* and *Shang Lin Fu*, which also represent the best and the most typical of the *fu* of the Han Dynasty.

I mentioned earlier that *fu* tends to be a highfalutin poetic prose, describing or explaining its theme by listing exhaustively anything that has anything remotely to do with it. Now let us consider, for instance, *Tse Hsu Fu*, which describes a hunt held by the King of the State of Tsu. It starts by saying that Tsu sent Mr Non-being as an emissary to Chi where he was taken to a hunt by the King of Chi. They did not bag any animals. When Mr Non-being returned from the hunt, he met a Mr Non-existent and told him that he was happy in spite of the poor result because the hunting trip had given him an opportunity to boast to the King of the grandeur of Yun Meng, one of the royal hunting reserves of Tsu. At the request of Mr Non-existent, he went on to describe the beautiful scenery and great variety of animals, plants, etc., in Yun Meng, and the King's rare horses, carved jade carriage and glittering entourage, the beauty and skill of the King's wife and concubines, the excellent weapons and spectacular skill of the hunters, the great amount of animals and game shot or killed, the happiness of the hunting party when they returned by boat and the comfort and ease enjoyed by the King after the hunt. Mr Non-existent remonstrated with Mr Non-being about this, saying that he should have talked about the achievements of the King of Tsu, not boasted about Yun Meng or the King of Tsu's wasteful indulgence in hunting.

Here is a paragraph of *Tse Hsu Fu* which describes Yun Meng.

There is a mountain in Yun Meng, an area of nine hundred square *li*. Only winding, tortuous and sinuous paths lead up to the steep and lofty heights, the ridges of which are craggy and jagged, the peaks twist and turn into the blue sky, shutting off half the moon and sun. Where the mountain becomes undulating foothills, there are rivers and streams. The earth of Yun Meng is multi-coloured: deep red, cobalt, ochre, chalky, creamy, alabaster, white lead, jade green, gold and silver. Intermixed and mingled, these colours glisten and glitter as the shiny scales of a dragon under the sun. The stones there include agate, red as roses; crocoite, yellow as the gold of Kun Wu; and basalt jasper, porcelain jasper, opal jasper and riband jasper. To the east, there are melilotus gardens. There are asarums, orchids, valerians, herbs, hemlock parsleys, calamus, selineas, deer parsleys, silkworm thorns and plantains. To the south, there are plateaux and swamps, swelling, falling, alternately flat and depressed; they expand to the edge of the Yangtse, to the foot of Wu Mountain. High where the land is dry, there are indigo plants, oats, wool grass, hill buckwheat, creeping figs, nut grass, sedges. Where the land is low and damp, there grow henbanes, rushes, salt plants, grains, Indian lotus, bottle gourds, cottage thatches, taro and numerous other plants. To the west, there are springs gushing like waves up into a big pond of crystal clear water. Lotus and water caltrop flourish all over the pond, concealing beneath them boulders and white sand. In the pond, there are great turtles, iguanas, tortoises and terrapins. To the north, there are forests of giant trees. There are elms, cedars, silky spice bushes, camphor trees, cassia trees, pepper shrubs, magnolia trees, yellow bark, wild pear trees, purple willows, Japanese quince trees, date-plum trees, chestnut trees and fragrant orange and pumelo trees. Up on the trees there are Yen Tse, peacocks, phoenixes and gibbons; under the trees, in the forests, there are white tigers, black leopards, cheetahs, wolves and wild dogs.

In English, some of the fascination one derives from a series of often beautiful, sometimes obscure words in its original Chinese version is lost. But if one could imagine the alluring imageries, the accumulation of extravagant words in the original created in the mind of the reader, then one may have an idea of the attraction an ambitious, powerful and young Emperor found in this form of literature, just as some people are now attracted by loud-coloured ties, sequined dresses and gaudy-jewelled necklaces.

One of the pitfalls of writing *fu* is that inevitably everyone tries to outshine everyone else by listing greater and greater numbers of animals, vegetables, minerals, emotions, astronomical phenomena, philosophical ideas, etc., irrespective of any other consideration. Even Szema Hsiang-ju, the best of the *fu* writers, committed the error of mentioning the appearance of falling stars and a rainbow at the same time. The fact that writers of *fu* were thus driven to know more about the meanings of greater numbers of words, and became, like Szema Hsiang-ju and Yang Hsiung, philologists, is of small comfort, when one is conscious that even the best *fu* has become difficult to understand, let alone appreciate. Tsao Chih, one of the famous poets of the Three Kingdoms Period (A.D. 220–280), is right when he said, 'The *fu* by Yang Hsiung and Szema Hsiang-ju are lofty in purpose and profound in meaning. However, one must be a learned scholar before one can read and understand them. This is because one is not only less talented than they are, but the words and terms they used are very obscure.'

Perhaps Szema Hsiang-ju was also conscious of this shortcoming. For his *Ta Jen Fu* and *Chang Meng Fu* were composed in the style of Tsu Tse and are easier to appreciate. I quote here a short passage of *Chang Meng Fu* which allegedly won back for Empress Chen the favour of Emperor Wu.

When dusk came and I had lost hope of your coming,
Only the empty hall saw how deep my sorrow was,
At night, I begged the moon to shine on me,
To help me in my cavernous room to pass the lonely hours.
I played on a *chin* a different tune,
Hoping to arrest, to forget my longing for you.

My distress was not reduced but I was reduced to sobs,
Standing up, raising my foot, I didn't know where to go.
I covered my face with my long sleeves,
Thinking of the errors I made.
Now that I had no chance of seeing you,
Feebly, I thought I'd take myself to bed.
I rolled the fragrant herbs into a pillow,
And spread flags, orchids and valerians as a sheet,
I lay down, suddenly dropped off to sleep and thought
That you were here by my side.
Abruptly I awoke and found that you were not here,
It was as if I had lost my soul,
And many cocks crowed in sympathy with my despair.
I rose to gaze at the moon
And looked at the constellations in the sky;
To the east, Aldebaran had appeared
But in the courtyard, the faint moonlight lingered
Like the light frost of the last month of autumn.
Oh, long as one whole year the night hovered,
And I, burdened with misery, dreaded to face another;
Trembling, I stood to await the dawn
And yet, from afar, the dawn was slow to come.

Mei Jen Fu is also different from the other *fu* which Szema Hsiang-ju
wrote. Because of its rather erotic nature, many people thought that it
was not written by him. Unfortunately for them there is no evidence
to prove that Pan Ku was wrong in attributing its authorship to Szema
Hsiang-ju. In fact, if we think of his behaviour with Wen Chun, it
seems quite probable that he did write it. Here is a short passage from
Mei Jen Fu.

It was a magnificent and stately house, and immersed in a poetic
quiet, it was not unlike the abode of the fairies. It was daytime and
the doors of the house were half closed. I went in and walked into a
hall. Waves of fragrant scent washed over me when I came to it and

I saw embroidered screens had been set up and a young girl was sitting gracefully there, alone. She was exceedingly beautiful, like a rare flower, elegant and radiantly attractive. Seeing that I hesitated to enter, she said, smiling, 'From which country do you come? It must be a remote place, far away from here!' She then ordered excellent wines to be brought in and showed me a *chin* with fine tone. I played on it the Songs of Valley Orchid and White Snow. Afterwards, she sang me a song:

> I live alone and have no one to look after me,
> And yet, dreams have only brought me sorrow.
> Why is it, my charming prince, that you come so late?
> The day is almost gone and my beauty faded.
> Giving myself to you,
> I hope that we'll forever be together.

She was so close to me that her hairpin tore at my cap, and her long gauze sleeves fell on my dress. And then it was evening. Grey cumulus clouds gathered and darkened the sky, the wind started to howl mournfully and white snowflakes, like feathers, lightly floated down. In the room that we were then in we could not hear a sound outside, and everything seemed to be holding its breath, waiting. We set out the bedding made of precious and rare materials and put under the coverlet a golden brazier in which fragrant incense was smouldering. Over and around the bed an embroidered curtain hung cosily down and on it, a sheet was spread over the mattress and a pillow with inlays of horn was put at one end of it. She then let her dress drop, took off her underclothes and her white body, small and yet well developed, came to light. She leaned over to embrace me, her body smooth and soft as silk. . . .

These three types of Szema Hsiang-ju's *fu* represent the kinds to which writers of the Han Dynasty devoted their lives. In point of fact, *fu* which were written in the style of *Tsu Tse* should be called *Sao Ti*[14] poems, and be distinguished from the ornate *fu* of the Han Dynasty. There were famous *Sao Ti* poems such as Tung Fang Shuo's *Chi Chien* (*Seven Remonstrances*), Yen Chi's *Ai Shih Ming* (*Alas That My Lot Was Not Cast!*), Wang Pao's *Chiu Huai* (*The Nine Regrets*), Liu Hsiang's *Chiu Tan* (*The Nine Laments*), Wang Yi's *Chiu Sze* (*The Nine Long-*

ings) and others. But they were only symbols of the continuation of a poetic form which fewer and fewer people practised.

The typical or orthodox *fu* flourished in the reigns of the Emperors Wu, Hsuan, Yuan and Cheng (140–6 B.C.). According to Pan Ku,[15] more than one thousand *fu* were selected and presented to Emperor Cheng from all those which had been written during that period. Taking the Han Dynasty as a whole, the Chinese agree that Szema Hsiang-ju, Yang Hsiung (53 B.C.–A.D. 18), Pan Ku (A.D. 32–92) and Chang Heng (A.D. 78–139) were the greatest of the writers of *fu*. But, in varying degrees, the other three writers all imitated the style and format of Szema Hsiang-ju's *fu*.

Yang Hsiung said in his letters to Huan Tan, commenting on *fu*, that 'When one has read and understood one thousand *fu*, one can write *fu*. There is a saying: practice can produce miracles. Those who are talented cannot do better than those who persevere in practising.' Perhaps he was right to a certain extent. In any case, the four *fu* which he wrote: *Kan Chuan* (*Sweet Spring*), which is about sacrificial rites, *Yu Lieh* (*Hunting by Arrow*), *Chang Yang* (*Chang Yang Palace*) and *Ho Tung* (*Districts East of the Yellow River*), which are all about hunting, are all imitations of Szema Hsiang-ju's writing. In fact, Pan Ku said in his *Biography of Yang Hsiung*, 'Yang Hsiung was of the opinion that of all the classics, *Yi* or the *Book of Changes* was the greatest: he therefore wrote *Tai Hsien*; that *The Analects* was the best of personal commentaries; he therefore wrote *Fa Yen*; that Chang Chi was the best lexicologist; he therefore wrote *Shun Chuan*; that *Li Sao* was the most profound of the *fu*; he therefore wrote *Kuang Sao* trying to explain its meanings; and that Szema Hsiang-ju's *fu* were the most beautifully written; he therefore wrote four *fu*. In writing all these books and *fu*, he tried to imitate those he thought were the best of their kind.' Practice may perhaps produce perfection, but Yang Hsiung perhaps confused imitation with practice in writing his *fu*. He was indeed a rather bookish fellow, which explains why he was disappointed when he learned that writing *fu* was not a good way to dissuade one's sovereign from indulging in wasteful pursuits. In his autobiography, he wrote, 'Emperor Wu used to try to find ways to become an immortal and Szema Hsiang-ju wrote *Ta Jen Fu* to persuade him not to waste time on this pursuit. The effect was the opposite. The Emperor found his appetite whetted by the descriptions of the lives of the immortals and wanted to become an immortal even more badly. It is plain, therefore, that *fu* is ineffective as a means of persuasion. . . . I resolve not to write another *fu*.'

Pan Ku was a famous historian. His *History of Han Dynasty* is considered to be of almost equal standing with the *Historical Record*. In writing *fu*, however, he also imitated the style of Szema Hsiang-ju. In his *Liang Tu Fu (Two Capitals)*, which is his most famous *fu*, he even used in one part, i.e. *Western Capital*, the same formula as appears in *Tse Hsu Fu*: 'In front of it . . . at the back. . . . In the eastern suburb. . . . In the western suburb. . . . In the centre. . . . The palaces are. . . .'

Chang Heng was a scientist famous for his design of an armillary sphere. *Liang Ching Fu (Two Capitals)*, which took him ten years to write, is the best known of his *fu*. But it is also an imitation, even the title is that of Pan Ku's. Chang Heng's contribution to the development of *fu*, however, lies in his other pieces, such as *Kuei Tien (Return Home)*, *Tu Lou (Skeleton)* and *Sze Hsien (Thoughts on Tao)*, which are much shorter and in simple language express his feelings. These *fu* may be said to be the forerunners of the shorter *fu* of the Wei and Chin Dynasties which so well expressed the personalities and emotions of the authors in plain and yet descriptive phrases, as exemplified by Tao Chien's *Kwei Chu Lai Tse (Oh, I am going Home)*.

However, *fu* as represented by Szema Hsiang-ju's works may be said to have had its day soon after Chang Heng's time. Tso Sze's *San Tu Fu (Three Capitals)* was supposed to have been so popular that the price of paper went up in Loyang because of the great numbers of people who wanted to buy paper to copy it. *Fu* was nevertheless on the decline. In the Northern-Southern Dynasties, the term was still in use, but it referred actually mostly to poems, and in the Tang and Sung Dynasties, the term either referred to *lu fu*, a formalized paper for examinations which made hardly any sense, or to a kind of prose which is unrhymed, such as Su Tung-po's *Cheh Pih Fu (Red Cliff Fu)*.

Here I quote Tao Chien's *Oh, I am going Home*, which is perhaps one of the best.

OH, I AM GOING HOME

Oh, I am going home! My farm and garden are overgrown with weeds, why shouldn't I be going home? I myself let my mind be the serf of my body, why then regret and mourn over it?

What is done cannot be undone, yet my future is for myself to decide. I really have not gone so far astray that I cannot see that I have made a mistake.

The boat sways lightly and a breeze softly ruffles my clothes. I ask how far it is still from home and fret over the dimness of dawn.

When I see the door and roofs of my house, I run towards it with excitement. My servants bid me welcome and my young children greet me by the door.

The path to the house may look deserted, but pine trees and chrysanthemums there remain. I lead my youngest child in by the hand and there on the table is a pot of wine!

I pour myself a cup of wine and am happy to see the hanging branches of trees in the courtyard. Leaning upon the southern window to look at the surroundings, I find that it is easy to be comfortable even in a small room.

My garden becomes more interesting after my daily explorations and I would not think of opening the garden door. Carrying a cane, I saunter and rest in the garden and, from time to time, raise my head to gaze at the sky above.

Clouds aimlessly drift out of their mountain recesses and tired birds are returning to their nests. When darkness finally gathers, I yet linger by the lone pines before going into the house.

Oh, to come back to my own home! From now on, I shall stop seeing people of position. For the world and I are not made for one another, what shall I go around and look for?

I shall be content with talking with my kinsmen and depend on music and books to comfort myself. When spring comes, farmers will tell me that they will be busy on the western farm.

While I shall ride in a covered wagon and drive over undulating mounds; or take a small boat and look for quiet corners along mountain streams.

Leaves on trees will be thick and mountain springs flow. Envying every living thing its season of growth, I shall feel sad about what I have gone through in my life.

But, enough! How long shall I keep my mortal form in this world? Why should I not do what I like? Why burden myself with worldly pursuits?

I do not wish to seek wealth or position and the abode of gods cannot be reached. I shall go out alone one fine morning, and planting my cane, start to clear the weeds and till the ground.

Or I shall climb up the Tungkao and yodel or compose poems by a clear stream. So will I adjust myself to the changes of life and, without a question in my heart, accept Heaven's will to the day I die.

CHAPTER VI

The Poetry of Six Dynasties

1. YUEH FU[1] *AND THE EVOLUTION OF THE 'FIVE-WORD POEM'*

THE advent of the 'five-word poem', or poems with five words to the line, is one of the most important developments in Chinese poetry, for with the refinements that came with the acceptance by the poets of Shen Yueh's *Sze Sheng Pu* or Theory of Four Tones[2] and Chou Yu's *Sze Sheng Chieh Yun* or Rhymes of Four Tones, five-word poems became one of the two principal poetic forms of China. But more important than this perhaps is the fact that the five-word poem was a more flexible and therefore more expressive poetic form than the four-word poem which preceded it. Chung Yung,[3] the famous Chinese critic of poetry, said, 'Four-word poems expressed a great deal in a short stanza. One may learn much of the techniques of writing four-word poems from studying those collected in the *Book of Poetry* and from *Tsu Tse*. Nevertheless, one may find that this form of poetry is perhaps not best suited to express fully one's emotions, and that after a long poem has been written in this form, one's feelings are only half expressed. Therefore, few people try to write the four-word poem. On the other hand, the five-word poem is the most popular poetic form. . . . Isn't it because it is the best form in which to narrate an event, create an image, express feelings, and describe an object?' This, of course, could be true. However, I suspect that the fact that there are more masterpieces written in this form of poetry than in the seven-word poem, the other principal form of Chinese poetry, had something to do with the great importance the Chinese subsequently attached to the emergence of the five-word poems.

The first five-word poem ever recorded was a folk song written during the reign of Emperor Chen (32–7 B.C.) of the Han Dynasty, and recorded in the 'Record of Astromancy' in the *History of Han Dynasty*.

> Crooked paths spoil fertile fields,
> Just as good men are confused by gossip;
> But passerines will nest on their top branches.
> They are used to admiration,
> But now people only pity them.

Folk songs of the Han Dynasty passed on to us are said to be divisible according to their musical score, namely *Hsiang Ho* Songs, *Ching Shang* Songs and Miscellaneous Songs, but as there exist few, if any, musical arrangements of the Han Dynasty, this grouping is purely academic. Nevertheless, it is worth mentioning that there are a few songs, such as *Chan Chen Nan* and *Shang Ya*, which are believed to have been written according to the music imported from Pei Ti, or the Northern Barbarians.

It is impossible to say when *Yueh Fu*, the folk songs of the Han Dynasty, other than the one quoted above, were written, except that the great majority were dated after the reign of Emperor Ai (6–1 B.C.). Before he ascended to the throne, Emperor Ai realized how popular love songs were, and noticed the fierce competition which raged between the relations of the royal family and the imperial household itself for the services of famous folk-song singers. He found the situation disgusting, and primarily because he did not like music, he ordered that folk songs should be excluded from imperial patronage after he succeeded to the throne, and dismissed about half of the eight hundred-odd officials in the Office of Music, who were in charge of matters relating to folk songs. Although this had little effect on the people's love of folk songs, records of folk songs of the previous periods, including almost all of the 220 folk songs collected by the order of Emperor Wu, were lost.

Judging by folk songs collected in *Yueh Fu Shih Chi*, it is probable that the shorter ones are of the earliest period. The style of *Kiang Nan Ko Tsai Lien* (*Collecting Lotus Flowers in Kiang Nan*), for instance, calls to mind the earliest Chinese songs inscribed on the oracle bones:

> It is pleasant to collect lotus flowers in Kiang Nan,
> One is happy to see the luxuriant lotus leaves
> And the fishes darting in between the leaves:
> There are fishes to the east of the lotus leaves,
> There are fishes to the west of the lotus leaves,
> There are fishes to the south of the lotus leaves,
> There are fishes to the north of the lotus leaves.

But the subject-matter of these folk songs was varied. For although emperors of the Han Dynasty might have expanded their realm and increased the wealth and influence of the country after long periods of wars, when the wealth was not distributed, what the people experienced were the horrors of war and the subsequent suffering. Their folk songs reflected all their emotions. *Chan Chen Nan (Fighting South of the Ramparts)* and *Shih Wu Tsung Chun Cheng (I Joined the Army at Fifteen)* are the best songs of war.

I JOINED THE ARMY AT FIFTEEN

> At fifteen I went with the army,
> At fourscore I came home.
> On the way I met a man from the village,
> I asked him who there was at home.
> 'That over there is your house,
> All covered over with trees and bushes.'
> Rabbits had run in at the dog-hole,
> Pheasants flew down from the beams of the roof;
> In the courtyard was growing some wild grain;
> And by the well, some wild mallows,
> I'll boil the grain and make porridge,
> I'll pluck the mallows and make soup.
> Soup and porridge are both cooked,
> But there is no one to eat them with.
> I went out and looked towards the east,
> While tears fell and wetted my clothes. [4]

Chu Tung Men (Out at the Eastern Gate) and *Ku Erh Hsing (The Orphan)* are among the best folk songs, which depicted the social turmoil and suffering of the people.

OUT AT THE EASTERN GATE

I went out at the Eastern Gate
Determined not to return.
But I came back home
Yet again, and seized with grief I almost cried:
There was not a peck of rice left in the bin,
There was not a piece of clothing hanging on the pegs.
Again taking my sword, I walked towards the Eastern Gate.

My wife and child clutched at my coat and wept:
'Others may crave solely riches and fame,
I am content to share porridge with you.
We may rely on the blessings of Heaven high above
And count on the help of this child.'
'Stop it! I must go!
I have already tarried too long—
When one is old and things are difficult
One cannot just stay at home and sit.'

Love songs abounded. *Peacock Flew South-eastward, Gathering Wild Herbs upon a Mountain* and *Shang Ya* are the more famous ones.

GATHERING WILD HERBS UPON A MOUNTAIN

She went up the mountain to pluck wild herbs;
She came down the mountain and met her former husband.
She knelt down and asked her former husband,
'What do you find your new wife like?'
'My new wife, although her talk is clever,
Cannot charm me as my old wife could.
In beauty of face there is not much to choose,
But in usefulness they are not at all alike.
My new wife comes in from the road to meet me;
My old wife always came down from her tower.
My new wife weaves fancy silks;
My old wife was good at plain weaving.
Of fancy silk one can weave a strip a day;
Of plain weaving, more than fifty feet.
Putting her silks by the side of your weaving
I see that the new will not compare with the old.'[5]

But, as stated above, it is impossible to say when these folk songs were written. Judging from the technique and wording employed, there is no doubt that they were written over a long period. Somewhere along the line the new five-word to the line poetic form took the fancy of the *literati*, and was gradually developed until it reached the height of its evolution as represented by *Nineteen Old Poems*, some poems written allegedly by Li Ling and Su Wu, and others by Tsao Chih, Yuan Chi, Tao Chien and Hsieh Tiao.

There has long been disagreement as to who was the first among the *literati* to compose the five-word poem. Hsu Ling[6] thought Mei Sheng was the first, while Siao Tung[7] and Chung Yung were of the opinion that Li Ling[8] was the first. Only recently were Chinese scholars agreed that it was not until Pan Ku wrote *Poems on History* that the basic poetic form of the five-word poem was established. They feel that had Mei Sheng been the poet who wrote eight of the *Nineteen Old Poems* as Hsu Ling thought, the art of writing five-word poems would have been so advanced that poets of the same or slightly later periods, including Szema Hsiang-ju and Yang Hsiung, would have written some of them. For when a new form of poetry emerged, it invariably attracted many famous poets of the day, as was the case with the emergence of *fu* in the Han Dynasty, and the new-style poetry of the Tang Dynasty, and of *tse* in the Sung Dynasty. But none of these poets wrote any five-word poems. This applies to Li Ling, too. Liu Hsieh[9] said of the three five-word poems ascribed to Li Ling, 'Until the reign of Emperor Cheng of the Han Dynasty, more than three hundred poems were selected and then recorded from those written by the best poets of the previous periods. None of these are five-word poems. That is why people doubt that poems ascribed to Li Ling and Pan Chao were really written by them.'[10] Poems ascribed to Su Wu were not even mentioned in Chung Yung's *Shih Pin* (*Criteria of Poetry*) and Liu Hsieh's *Wen Hsin Tiao Lung* (*The Carved Dragon of the Literary Mind*) and are considered therefore to have been written and improved upon by some anonymous poets of still later periods.

Pan Ku's five-word poems, while they are strictly five words to a line, are rather weak in creating poetic imagery. It was not until poets such as Chang Heng, Chin Chia and Tsai Yung began to write them that the five-word poem as a poetic form was fully developed, during or before the Chien An[11] period of the Han Dynasty. I say during or before this period purposely, for *Nineteen Old Poems* were written by anonymous poets at about this time and they are considered to be

among the best of the five-word poems. Shen Teh-chien,[12] a critic in
the Ching Dynasty, said of them, 'They are not necessarily the work of
one person, or of one period. They express the feelings of exiles and
jilted women, of friends long separated and of people stranded away
from home, of birth, death and of things new and old. They may or
may not use metaphor, or repeat the lines, and even though they
contain no new or unique idea or attempt difficult phrasing, none of
the poems written in the Western Han Dynasty[13] is as good as these
nineteen poems.'[14] Here are two from this collection:

I drive my chariot up to the Eastern Gate;
From afar I see the graveyard north of the Wall.
The white aspens how they murmur, murmur;
Pines and cypresses flank the broad paths.
Beneath lie men who died long ago;
Black, black is the long night that holds them.
Deep down beneath the Yellow Springs,
Thousand of years they lie without waking.

In infinite succession light and darkness shift,
And years vanish like the morning dew.
Man's life is like a sojourning,
His longevity lacks the firmness of stone and metal,
For ever it has been that mourners in their turn were mourned,
Saint and Sage—all alike are trapped.
Seeking by food to obtain immortality
Many have been the dupe of strange drugs.
Better far to drink good wine
And clothe our bodies in robes of satin and silk.[15]

*

A visitor came a long way
To bring me a piece of silk from you;
We are separated by thousands of miles
And yet your feelings towards me remain true.
I embroider a pair of Mandarin ducks on the piece of silk
And make with it a double blanket;
When I cover myself with it and think of you,
I know that our destinies are one—
For just as glue is mixed with ink,
No one can take us apart again.

Poems ascribed to Li Ling and Su Wu were written at about the same period by anonymous poets. Here are two of the poems, attributed to Li Ling and Su Wu respectively:

> The good time will never come back again;
> In a moment our parting will be over.
> Beside the crossroads we faltered, uneasily;
> In the open fields we paused, hand in hand.
> The clouds above are floating across the sky;
> Swiftly, swiftly passing, or blending together.
> The waves in the wind lose their fixed place
> And are rolled away each to a corner of Heaven.
> From now onwards long must be our parting,
> So let us stop again for a little while.
> I wish I could ride on the wings of the morning wind
> And go with you right to your journey's end.[16]

*

> I was twenty and you were fifteen when we married,
> Since then, our love has never been tinged with doubt.
> 'Only tonight, can we be happy and merry,
> Let us enjoy ourselves while there is still time.'
> But I cannot forget the long distance I have to travel,
> And, restless, I got up to see the time:
> The stars and planets have all faded away,
> And it is time for me to leave.
> I am to serve at the front,
> And I don't know when I shall see you again,
> Holding your hands, I can but deeply sigh
> And tears come of themselves at this parting:
> 'Try to love the flowers of spring
> And remember the happy times we had together;
> Alive, I shall return to you,
> Dead, I will be longing for you.'

In the late Han Dynasty, in the reigns of Emperors Huan, Ling and Hsien (A.D. 147–190), a series of conflicts arising from the intrigues of the relatives of the royal family and the eunuchs to seize the government in the names of the Emperors, and of friction between cliques of officials, resulted in misrule and neglect of the welfare of the people. Coupled with this there were successive floods and drought, and hundreds of thousands of people died in famines and in exile, so that at last almost a million people rose against the government, and a rebel army, the so-called 'Yellow Turbans', was formed. There followed the appearance of Tung Cho and Tsao Tsao, who, with their own soldiers, took over successively the rule of the country, in the names of Emperors Ling and Hsien. By then, the country was in a turmoil. Regional military leaders refused to obey them and wars were incessantly waged for personal gains and brought greater suffering to the people. In A.D. 220, Tsao Pi, Tsao Tsao's son, overthrew the Han Dynasty and established his state of Wei, and Liu Pei and Sun Chuen set up their states of Shu and Wu in south-west and southern China respectively. Thus China entered the Three Kingdoms Period. We read in Chinese history books of many instances of the cruelties which occurred in the wars waged during this period, such as 'within two hundred *li*, every house was ravaged and ruined, not to mention chickens and dogs', and 'hundreds of thousands of people were driven into and drowned in the River Sze. Their bodies stopped the flow of the river.'

During this period, however, because Tsao Tsao and his sons Tsao Pi and Tsao Chih were themselves great poets, the technique and form of the five-word poems advanced further. Generally speaking, their poems and those written by other poets of the same period were still under the influence of Yueh Fu songs or folk songs, in that they reflected the reality of their time. But even in Tsao Tsao's poems, there was a touch of sadness about the transience of life. In the poems of the others who were not aggressive, self-made military heroes, this was more apparent. In a sense, they were the forerunners of the escapism to be found in the behaviour and poems of the poets of the Chin Dynasty (A.D. 265–419) which followed. Of these poets, Tsao Chih (A.D. 192–232) was the best. It was he who extended the technique of writing five-word poems to cover almost every subject under the sun, and the wordings of the verses became polished and stylish. Because of the jealousy and suspicion of his brother, who was Emperor Wen of Wei, his life was a harassed and miserable one. A series of seven poems written for Chao, Prince of Paima, expressed some of his frustrations, and are considered to be among his best poems. Here are two of them:

Even the sky and the earth cannot help moving and evolving
And yet my myriad thoughts are tied in knots;
Around what do my thoughts revolve?
Separated and estranged from me are my loved ones.
I had hoped that harmoniously we would work together
But things changed and my hopes were shattered.
White horned owls hoot in front of your carriages,
Jackals and wolves prowl the main routes;
For lies have obscured what is right and wrong
And calumnies have alienated me from my dear ones.
I want to hold on to the days of old, but there is no way,
Holding back the reins of my horse, I hesitate to move.

*

I hesitate to move but here I cannot stay,
For endless and limitless is my longing for you.
The autumn wind is becoming chilly
And cicadas shrill by my side.
How desolate is the vast plain—
With the sun fast setting in the west!
Birds are returning to their nests up in the tall trees, rapidly
  flapping their wings,
And a stray animal is running, searching for its companions,
  too anxious to eat the food it carries.
Looking at them, I am assailed by sorrow
And thinking back, I can only heave a sigh.

Not long after the establishment of the State of Wei, the power of
the government was taken over by the Szema family. In addition to the
suffering which came with continuous wars, scholars and poets were
always kept under surveillance by the Szema family, who suspected and
feared anyone who might come to the aid of the Emperor. Ho Yen and
Hsia-hou Hsien and every one of their clans were summarily executed
simply because Szema Yi suspected them. In such circumstances, men
of letters were forced into adopting various subterfuges and indulging
in fanciful eccentricities. Of these eccentric scholars, the 'Seven
Worthies of the Bamboo Grove',[17] and especially Yuan Chi and Hsi
Kang (A.D. 223–63), were the best known. It is said that Yuan Chi
would look only at people he liked. Those he didn't like, he would
avoid looking at by moving his pupils and showing them only the
whites of his eyes. He could be compelled to sit with a visitor, but he

would not utter a sound all day long. And when Szema Chao, Prince of Chin, approached him, wishing to ask for the hand of Yuan Chi's daughter on behalf of his son, who later became Emperor Wu of the Chin Dynasty, he found Yuan Chi continuously drunk for sixty days and had to drop the proposal. Yuan nevertheless devoted what energy he had to writing five-word poems and brought this poetic form one step nearer perfection. Here is one of his *Yung Huai Poems* (*Poems of My Heart*):

> Being sleepless at midnight,
> I rise to play the lute.
> The moon is visible through the curtains
> And a gentle breeze sways the cord of my robe.
> A lonely wild-goose cries in the wilderness
> And is echoed by a bird in the woods.
> As it circles, it gazes
> At me, alone, imbued with sadness.[18]

About a hundred years after the time of the 'Seven Worthies of the Bamboo Grove', there appeared a poet whose work was to outstrip all the other five-word poems by comparison. This was Tao Chien. Of him, Su Tung-po of the Sung Dynasty said, 'I don't like any poet in particular, but I like Tao Chien's poems. They appear to be plain, but convey a great variety of mood. They are unadorned, yet rich in meaning, and not even poems written by Tsao Chih, Liu Kun, Pao Chao, Hsieh Tiao, Li Po and Tu Fu can compare with them.'

2. THE LIFE OF TAO CHIEN

Tao Chien (also known as Tao Yuan-ming) was born in A.D. 372 and died in 427. He was best known for always being himself no matter where he was or whom he was with, and his poetry reflected his natural ease. Su Tung-po said that 'when he wanted to be an official, he thought nothing of asking for an appointment; when he wanted to resign, he did not pretend that to resign from an official position was something to be admired; when he was hungry, he went around to beg for food; when he had enough to eat, he had chicken and millet for his guests. People have long thought highly of him because he was always true to himself.'[19]

There is a streak of romanticism in the make-up of the Chinese character, but until quite recently Confucianism saw to it that we did not show it in public. We like to admire, therefore, and perhaps envy, those who dare to be themselves and yet do not make a show of it.

To be one's true self in Tao Chien's time was more difficult than in other times. Soon after Emperor Wu of the Chin Dynasty brought to an end the chaos of the preceding centuries and reunited China in A.D. 280, war again broke out, waged by the members of the royal family against Emperor Hui, and lasted for more than ten years. In the end, China's strength was so sapped and she became so weak that Emperors Huan and Mien were captured by foreign invaders. In A.D. 318 Emperor Yuan established his capital in Chienkang, the present Nanking, leaving the north of the Yangtse River almost entirely to the foreign tribes, and the East Chin Dynasty was founded. But other wars were to follow, started by Wang Tun, Huan Wen and others.

In the meantime Liu Yuan of the Huns had already established a new state called Han in A.D. 304 with its capital in Ping Yang, or the present Lung Fen district in Shansi Province. Four other tribes, namely Tungus, Chieh, Ti and Chiang, also established states on the soil of China. From 304 to 439 they fought with each other and with the armies of the Chin Dynasty, and successively established sixteen states, adding humiliation to the suffering of the Chinese people, while in the south Liu Yu forced Emperor Kung of the Chin Dynasty to abdicate in 420 and himself became Emperor Wu of the Liu Sung Dynasty. Tao Chien was then forty-nine years old.

During this time Confucianism greatly declined. In the reign of Emperor Fei of Wei (circa A.D. 250), of more than four hundred officials at Court fewer than ten could write anything about Confucianism. This was perhaps because Confucianism is a positive and systematic doctrine about life and government, and it invariably suffers in popularity when China is in a chaotic or transitional period, and the lives of the common people are being sacrificed. By the same token, the theories of Laotse and Chuangtse, which preach inactivity, the levelling of all things, and especially in *Chuangtse*, the sameness of life and death, gain great currency during times of tumult. This was what happened in the two centuries before Tao Chien's time, and persisted until A.D. 589 when China was reunited under Yang Chien. But what is more important from the point of view of the development of

Chinese literature was the ascendancy of Buddhism during this time. It is most difficult to pinpoint the time when Buddhism was introduced into China. But in the eighth year of the reign of Emperor Ming of the Han Dynasty (A.D. 66) the Emperor in a decree mentioned that Ying, Prince of Tse, respected the teachings of Laotse and liked those of Buddha. Later Emperor Huan, who reigned from 147 to 167, set up altars for both Laotse and Buddha in his palace. It must be pointed out that the Mahayana Buddhism, which was introduced to China at this time, was often being confused with Taoism, a degenerate religious form of Laotse's teachings, primarily because Buddhist sutras had not been accurately translated into Chinese, so that even Buddhist missionaries did not really know the difference between these two religions.

It was not until some time after the Chin Dynasty was established when more Buddhist sutras had been translated by Kumarajiva and others and learned Buddhist monks such as Tao An and Huei Yuan began to appear, that Buddhism established her own identity as a religion and began to be accepted by Chinese scholars. In East Chin Period, it was already quite common for Chinese scholars to befriend Buddhist monks. No doubt the attraction and the rapid development of Buddhism in China during this time was due at least partly to its promise of a future life, which satisfied the need of the people to whom the transience of life had been made only too plain by the ruthless killings in continuous war.

In fact, human lives did not seem to mean much. We see that most of the famous scholars and poets during the two centuries before Tao Chien's time died unnatural deaths. These included Kung Yung, Mi Heng and Yang Hsiu of the Chien An Period of the Han Dynasty (A.D. 196–220); Hsi Kang of the early Chin Dynasty; and Chang Hua, Shih Chung, Lu Chi, Lu Yun and Pan Yueh of the Tai Kang Period (A.D. 280–300), and Liu Kun and Kuo Po of the Yung Chia Period (A.D. 307–312) of the Chin Dynasty. After Tao Chien's time, Hsieh Ling-yun, Hsieh Tiao and Pao Chao met with the same fate.

In the circumstances, it really took a man of courage to be true to himself. But perhaps Tao's family heritage had something to do with his character. His great-grandfather was a distinguished scholar and official who was known for a unique eccentricity: he would move a pile of bricks from one place to another in the morning and move them back in the afternoon just to keep himself occupied. His maternal grandfather was a general who according to Tao Chien himself 'did not act just to conform with society, and was not boastful in his speech. He never showed his pleasure or anger. He liked to drink and kept his manners even when he was drunk. When he was happy he would be lost in thought, as though no one were with him.' Tao Chien's grandfather was the governor of a county. So, people say, was his father, but there is some doubt about it. Anyway, it was said that when Tao was young he accepted a minor official job because 'his parents were old and his family was poor'. It seems obvious that if his father had been governor of a county he must have been a man who did not care too much about an official career and did not know how to handle money or provide for his old age or his family—traits which Tao Chien apparently inherited, together with those of his maternal grandfather.

For we see that Tao Chien soon resigned from the minor official position and went back to his home in the present Chiukiang district in Kiangsi Province to till the few acres of land his family had. Although his life is one of the better documented of the Chinese poets, it is impossible to say if the hardship had anything to do with the death of his first wife, who was the mother of Ah Hsu, his eldest son. As a result of this manual labour, however, he became afflicted with an illness which made him weak and easily tired. At twenty-eight he again became a minor official for a time. When he was thirty-five, he was again too poor to support himself and his uncle helped to get him appointed magistrate of Peng Tseh, about 100 *li* from his home. It is said that when he took up the job, being fond of wine, he ordered that all the fields belonging to the local government should be planted with glutinous rice, from which wine could be made, and said, 'I should be content to be drunk all the time.' It was only because his wife protested against this scheme that he allowed half of the acreage to be planted with another kind of rice.

But he was not happy in his duties and wanted to resign again. According to one version, he left his post when the Assistant Governor came and his secretary told Tao Chien that he should have his gown girdled before meeting him. 'I cannot scrape and bow for the sake of five bushels of rice,' he said. In his preface to *Oh, I am going Home*, he wrote, 'Not long after I was appointed [Magistrate of Peng Tseh] I often thought of resigning. Why? Because I was used to being myself and could not force myself to do things I did not want to do. Although hunger and cold had long been like wolves at my door, to go against my nature would only make me gravely ill. I was often reminded that people strive and work solely to keep themselves fed. But I was nevertheless grieved, for I had been forgetting my life-long ambition. . . . I had hoped to perform my duties for one year and then pack my things and depart. Not long afterwards, however, my younger sister died in Wuchang, and I could no longer wait. I resigned from the magistracy. From mid-autumn to winter, I was Magistrate of Peng Tseh for eighty-odd days.' He resigned and refused thereafter to become an official again. For, as he himself said after he had laid down the burdens of a magistrate's office, 'Things are not exactly as I wish them to be.'

I quoted *Oh, I am going Home* in the previous chapter. Here, however, is one passage from it which described his frame of mind at the time:

But enough! How long shall I keep my mortal form in this world? Why should I not do what I like? Why burden myself with worldly pursuits?

I do not wish to seek wealth or position and the abode of gods cannot be reached. I shall go out alone one fine morning, and planting my cane, start to clear the weeds and till the ground.

Or I shall climb up the Tungkao and yodel or compose poems by a clear stream. So will I adjust myself to the changes of life and, without a question in my heart, accept Heaven's will to the day I die.

This, indeed, was Tao Chien's proclamation of personal intention. He was only thirty-four, but he stood by it for twenty-two years, in spite of the fact that he was often poor and sometimes had to go without food, and that his house was once burnt down by fire and he had to move his family back to Shan King, another town in the same district where his forebears had lived.

He declined the summons of Emperor An to be a secretary in the Imperial Secretariat. Thus he lived among the peasants, leading a simple, humble and independent life until he died at fifty-six.

But his peace was perhaps not easily won. For judging by the poems he wrote, he was in his youth not without ambition. There is, for instance, this stanza:

I remember that when I was young and strong,
I was contented even though nothing happened to please me;
My fervent ambition transcended the bounds of the four seas,
Just as for strong-winged birds, its goal was far-away places.

And this:

> When I was young I was strong and vigorous,
> I visited many places, with only my sword,
> Who shall say that I have not been to far-away places?
> From Chang Yi to Yuchow I went!

His poem about Ching Ko, who attempted to assassinate the first Emperor of the Chin Dynasty, also shows that he was not yet ready to forget the affairs of the country:

> It was a pity that he forgot how to use his sword
> And a singularly great task was left unaccomplished;
> Although he passed away long ago,
> People still think of him after all these years.

It was later that we find sadness creeping into his poems:

> Days and months continuously abandon me
> And I am left with ambitions unrealized;
> Thinking of that makes me grieve,
> When dawn comes, I have still not slept.

But once he had made peace with himself, he was content with the simple life he led. He was notable for not indulging in self-pity as other poets did. Nor did he try to escape into day-dreaming and want to become immortal. He seemed to be content with his lot, and his poems reflect this spirit, being natural and simple.

In the twenty-two years after he resigned from his last official position, he did not really become a hermit as so many people have suggested. He had many friends and he somehow became quite well known. This can be seen from the fact that the Lotus Society, a famous, exclusive Buddhist society, which many famous poets, including Hsia Ling-yun, tried to join but were refused membership, asked him to become a member. They were even prepared to break their rules on abstention from alcoholic drinks if Tao Chien would join them. Tao went along but when he was on the verge of putting his name down as a member, he 'knitted his brows and stole away'. Some people said it was the tolling of a bell which so saddened him that he decided not to join the Society. Whatever the reason, he was not a man to lead a ecluded life. This is further shown by the fact that when he died, Yen Yen-chih, one of the two currently popular poets, wrote a memorial essay in his honour. If Tao had befriended Yen he must have known many other poets of his day. But Tao Chien did not (during his lifetime) know the prestige that his poetry was to enjoy after his death. It was not until a hundred years after he died that Prince Chao Ming of the Liang Dynasty collected and published his complete works, including a biography and a memoir of him, in eight volumes. Many other editions of his works followed in later dynasties. But in his own day and during the periods immediately after his death, he was not considered to be a first-class poet, because his poems were very different from those ornamental poems which were in great vogue at the time. Chung Yung, the famous critic of poetry of the Chi Dynasty (? A.D. 52) considered him a second-rate poet. It was not until the Tang Dynasty that his poems gained great acclaim from famous poets and Wang Wei, Meng Hao-jan and other poets started to imitate the style and mood of his poems.

Yet, not to have been burdened with the distinction of being the foremost poet of his time probably suited him just as well. Once, he refused to receive the Governor of the County, saying that he was sick. But when one of his friends, conspiring with the Governor, intercepted him when he was on his way to visit Lu Mountain and asked him to join a wine party in a pavilion by the roadside, he consented, and did not mind when the Governor joined them later. In fact, he must have drunk and talked a great deal with the Governor, for later, when the Governor noticed that Tao Chien was wearing no shoes, he ordered his assistant to have a pair made for him. When the assistant asked for the measurements Tao just stuck his foot out and asked the man to measure it. Whether or not he was shoeless on purpose was never established. In any case, he was not at all embarrassed, for when the party was finally over and the Governor asked him to visit the Government House, he consented.

'Where is your sedan chair?' the Governor asked.

'I have a kind of foot ailment,' he answered, 'and go about in a bamboo litter. It serves me well.'

He went and visited the Governor, riding in the bamboo litter, carried by one of his students and two sons, and was perfectly at ease amidst the sedan chairs of the others and in the splendour of the Governor's residence. From then on the Governor often sent him rice and wine as presents. Tao accepted them, but did not go to visit the Governor again, although he was always happy to meet him by chance and have a drink with him.

Tao, because of his fondness for wine, would go to any party where wine was served, no matter whether he knew the host or not. It was also said that once when his friends were brewing wine, he offered the use of his linen turban as a strainer in order that he should have wine to drink. His fondness for wine was perhaps his only weakness.

I sometimes wonder if writers have taken too much for granted his contentment with life. For except for one poem written before that time, it was only after he had decided to give up his official career that we find him often writing about drinking in his poems. It is also said that Tao would fondle his stringless *chin* (seven-stringed lute) after a feast. When asked why he did this, he said, 'If one can appreciate the happiness to be had from a *chin*, one does not have to depend on the sound from its strings.'

Whatever his reasons for drinking, he did seem to enjoy it. He drank by himself, he drank with others, and he drank when he moved his family back to his ancestral home. He drank when he was irked by his sons, when it rained, when the harvest was in—in fact, he drank on any occasion, or no occasion at all. In the preface to his twenty poems entitled *Drinking*, he said, 'I have few pleasures in living in retirement and recently the nights have become longer. I have been drinking almost nightly when I could lay my hands on good wine. Drinking alone, with only my shadow as company, I easily became drunk and afterwards I often wrote a few lines to amuse myself, and these accumulated, I have neither tried to judge nor to group them, but have asked my friends to copy them as a pastime.'

Somehow, wine-drinking fitted into the image he left behind of himself. It is perhaps best to let him describe himself. In his *Biography of Mr Wu Liu (Five Willows)*, he was in fact speaking about himself:

No one knows where Mr Wu Liu came from, or his real name and surname, but because there are five willows by his house, he is known by that name.

He is quiet and seldom speaks. He does not care for money or fame. He likes to read books but is not over-zealous to search for their hidden meaning. If he feels that he has grasped the real meaning of a passage, he is so happy that he forgets his food. He is fond of wine but being poor, cannot always afford it. His friends and relatives know about this, and they sometimes ask him to go over for a drink. He always finishes all the wine there is, intending to get drunk. And when he is drunk, he retires not caring if he remains the night or returns home. The four walls of his house are bare and do not adequately shelter him from wind and sunshine. He wears a short flax-cloth jacket in tatters and often has nothing to eat or drink. But he does not care. He often writes to amuse himself and to indicate his ambitions in life, but forgets all about worldly success or failure; and like that he will die.

It cannot be denied that he was remarkably candid and lovable.

3. *THE POEMS OF TAO CHIEN*

Tao Chien wrote about 150 poems. Of these, more than a quarter are 'four-word' poems. If we were to divide his life into three periods, i.e. the period before he gave up his official career (372–405) at the age of thirty-four; the period after he resigned from his last official position to the time when the Chin Dynasty was overthrown (405–420) when he was forty-nine years old; and from then on until his death at fifty-six, we could say quite definitely that twenty-eight of the poems were written in the first period, forty-eight in the second, and thirty-eight in the third, leaving some forty to fifty poems undatable. Generally speaking, the five entitled *Return to the Farm* were written in the first period; twenty poems entitled *Drinking* during the second period; and nine poems entitled *After the Style of Old Poems*, and twelve miscellaneous poems, one poem entitled *Begging for Food*, three elegies of himself and the first of his thirteen poems under the heading *Reading the Book of Hills and Seas* were written in the third period. These are his most famous poems.

ELEGY FOR MYSELF

Where there is life, death there must be;
To die young does not mean life has been cut short.
Last night we were both human beings,
This morning I am among the spirits.
Where will my soul disperse?

Here in the hollowed piece of wood only my withered body lies.
My young children cry for their father
And my good friends weep over me.
But I no longer know gain and loss
Neither do I feel right or wrong.
When thousands of years have gone by,
Who will recall my glory or shame?
I regret only that while I was alive
I never drank as much as my heart desired!

DRINKING

I built my hut in a zone of human habitation,
Yet near me there sounds no noise of horse or coach.
Would you know how that is possible?
A heart that is distant creates a wilderness round it.
I pluck chrysanthemums under the eastern hedge,
Then gaze long at the distant summer hills.
The mountain air is fresh at the dusk of day;
The flying birds two by two return.
In these things there lies a deep meaning;
Yet when we would express it, words suddenly fail us.[20]

READING THE BOOK OF HILLS AND SEAS

In the month of June the grass grows high
And round my cottage thick-leaved branches sway.
There is not a bird but delights in the place where it rests;
And I too—love my thatched cottage.
I have done my ploughing;
I have sown my seed.
Again I have time to sit and read my books.
In the narrow lane there are no deep ruts;
Often my friends' carriages turn back.
In high spirits I pour out my spring wine
And pluck the lettuce growing in my garden.
A gentle rain comes stealing up from the east
And a sweet wind bears it company.
My thoughts float idly over the story of the King of Chou,
My eyes wander over the pictures of Hills and Seas.
At a single glance I survey the whole Universe.
He will never be happy, whom such pleasures fail to please![21]

AFTER THE STYLE OF OLD POEMS

The tower stands one hundred feet high
Overlooking everything to the horizon.
At dusk clouds fall and shroud it,
In the morning, birds gather and perch on it.
Standing on its top, one sees the mountains and rivers
And the great plain is a wild expanse.
Those who pursued careers and fame
Have long fought over this land;
Once they are dead though
They go to their burial ground.
Their graves range high and low.
Over them, pines and cypresses are chopped down.
There is no one to claim the ruined houses
And where indeed have the wandering ghosts gone?
Although glory and splendour are attractive,
To what a pitiful state have they reduced human lives!

RETURN TO THE FARM

I

When I was young, I had not the taste of the vulgar crowd,
For by nature, I loved only the hills and mountains;
Unwittingly, I let myself be trapped into worldly affairs
And thirty years had gone by when I found myself again.
Just as caged birds long for their ancient woods
And fishes in the house pond think of their former waters,
So I, remembering my own self, returned to my garden and field
And reclaimed some land on the edge of the Southern Moor.
My cottage stands on ground of about two acres
With eight or nine rooms;
At the back, birches and willows shelter the eaves;
In front of the hall, peach trees and plum trees grow.
Hazy are the distant hamlets of men,
And the smoke meandering over their houses rises;
A dog barks somewhere in the quiet lanes
And atop a mulberry tree, a cock lazily crows.
In my house, there is no other sound to distract me
And with no one to disturb me I have plenty of leisure.
Long was I fenced in by worldly ties
Now I've returned to nature and my **true self.**

2

In the country, few people come to bother me,
And carriages and horses seldom come to these quiet lanes.
Even in daytime, I close my doors,
And alone in the house, forget the outside world.
At times I chance to meet my neighbours on a lonely hill,
Each of us making our way through the tall grass.
When we meet we talk of nothing
Except how much the mulberry and hemp are growing day by day
And each day my field is cleared a little more.
My constant fear is that frost and sleet will come
And ruin my crops together with the grass and weeds.

3

At the foot of the Southern Hill, I've sown some beans,
But weeds flourish and few beans sprout.
I rise at dawn to clear away the weeds
And return under the moonlight, a hoe on my shoulder.
On the path narrow and overgrown with grass,
My clothes become damp with evening dew;
My dampened clothes would not worry me
If only I could have my wish.

Tao Chien also wrote two essays, *Peach Colony* and *Biography of Mr Wu Liu*, one memorial to himself, three *fu*: *Oh, I am going Home*, *On Scholars whose Ambitions are Thwarted* and *Hsien Ching Fu* (*Feelings at Leisure Moments*). The last-named *fu* was like a love poem, and was considered by Prince Chao Ming to be a 'blemish on white jade'. Scholars who admired Tao Chien tried to explain it away by saying that this *fu* had some symbolic value. It is difficult to see what that was, but it is certainly a good *fu*, and one that will help us to understand better this side of Tao Chien's personality, which has always been ignored or misunderstood by Chinese scholars.

FEELINGS AT LEISURE MOMENTS

You who are blessed, incomparable, unsurpassed,
So carelessly perfect in beauty and grace,
So chaste and ethereal in thought and demeanour,
        In all your ways.

You were sitting, unaware of not being alone,
Pensively fingering the strings—the while
Your white arms and silk sleeves trail the *chin*, and on
    Your lips a smile.

The melody stopped and you glanced at the view
Of lengthening evening shadows on the plains,
You could not have known, for you never know
    A man in chains.

O happy one, if I could tell you all my longing,
The envious thought of all things that you own,
The humblest objects close to you that belong
    To you alone.

I would be the rouge that kisses your lips,
The collar that brushes your fragrant hair,
The girdle that embraces your gentle waist,
Your shoes that follow your steps everywhere.
I would be the fan that wafts your whispers,
Your shadows that follow in your every move,
The candles that shine upon your beauteous face,
The bird you feed and which returns your love—
    Then I would live!

Yet were I any of these things, I would fear
To be the forgotten dove, the castaway fan,
The shadows in darkness, the candles at dawn—
    I live in vain![22]

CHAPTER VII

The Poetry of the Tang Dynasty

1. *THE EVOLUTION OF 'NEW-STYLE' POETRY*

IN A.D. 386, Toba Kuei of Hsien Pei or the Tungus tribe established his state of North Wei with its capital in Ping Chen, the present Ta Tung district in Shansi Province, and gradually occupied a large area of Chinese territory, including the present Hopei, Shantung, Shansi and Kansu Provinces, the northern part of the present Kiangsu, Honan and Shensi Provinces and the western part of the present Liaoning Province. This, and the establishment of the state of Liu Sung in southern China in the year 420, was called the Northern-Southern Dynasties Period, and China remained divided for 169 years until Yang Chien reunited it and established the Sui Dynasty in 589.

During this time the Northern Dynasties continuously imitated and followed the literary vogues of the Southern Dynasties, and the assimilation of the Tungus and four other tribes by the Chinese was so natural and thorough that when the Sui Dynasty reunited China, there was no cry of racial discrimination from the five foreign tribes. Thus, in talking about the evolution of Chinese literature during this period, it is principally the literary activities of southern China which are relevant.

But the Northern-Southern Dynasties was nevertheless a period of great change. In the south, the government was never really stabilized. In the sixty years of the Liu Sung Dynasty, there was a succession of eight emperors before the dynasty was overthrown by Hsiao Tao-chen. Hsiao's Chi Dynasty lasted only twenty-four years, but there were seven successive emperors, and it, too, was overthrown by Hsiao Yen, who thereafter established the Liang Dynasty. The Liang Dynasty lasted for fifty-five years, but the four emperors did not really rule over their realm. Emperor Yuan, the third emperor, was forced by one of his generals to move his capital from what is now Nanking to Kiang-ling in Hupei Province and had to make concessions to North Wei. Hsiao Cha, his brother, even surrendered to Wei. And then Chen Pa-hsien occupied Kiang-ling and an area around it, called himself emperor, and established the Chen Dynasty, so that from 555–587 there were two states in the south. Meantime, the state of North Wei had split into Eastern and Western Wei in 534, and these were over-thrown in 550 and 557 respectively. Two new states, Northern Chi and Northern Chou, came into being, and from 555 on, there were four states in China until 589 when the Sui Dynasty reunited it.

It was during this uncertain period that Buddhism came to flower in China. The fact that the Chinese people, weary of combatant life, were receptive to a faith which promised them future life after death as consolation, was certainly an important factor in the spread of Buddhism in China. But the almost fanatical zeal of the Buddhists in propagating their faith was an equally important factor. After an in-cubation period of about three hundred years, Buddhism had not only gained freedom from confusion with Taoism, but also become re-spectable and Buddhist monks gained acceptance by men of letters in the Chin Dynasty. In the Chin Dynasty, Fa Hsien, a Chinese monk, made a pilgrimage to India in search of Buddhist sutras. He went by land in 399 and returned by sea in 416, spending a total of about fifteen years there. His *Fo Kuo Chi* (*Record of the Buddhist Countries*) is still one of the most valuable books on Sino-Indian communications and Indian history.

In the Northern-Southern Dynasties Period there were in Lo-yang alone, capital of Wei, nearly one thousand Buddhist temples. In the South, many famous poets, including Hsieh Ling-yun (385–433), Yen Yen-chih (354–456) and Shen Yueh (441–513), became Buddhists. Emperor Wu of the Liang Dynasty went twice to Tung Tai Temple to practise physical mortification, and Liu Hsieh (470?–530?) became a Buddhist monk.

But it was not all smooth sailing for Buddhism. One difficulty perhaps came with the rapid increase of numbers of people converted to the Buddhist faith in an era of chaos. Buddhist monks interfered in politics and Buddhist nuns became concubines of princes. In the Liu Sung Dynasty, several hundred nuns became concubines of Prince Wu Shan.

In the Liang Dynasty, 'There are more than five hundred Buddhist monks and nuns. . . . Every monk has a servant, every nun, a maid. Every maid is clothed in silk.'[1] And there was an allegation that 'monks are pretentious, hypocritical and treacherous. They are lustful and disorderly and practise abortion to kill off their offspring.'[2] The steady growth of Buddhism aroused sporadic antagonistic reactions. These were often based either on Confucianism or on patriotic grounds. One of the more fanciful assertions was that Sakyamuni (Buddha) was begot by Laotse, and that Buddhism and Taoism were in fact one and the same religion. Therefore, the Chinese did not have to believe in Buddhism, which was Taoism adjusted to the needs of India. At the same time, Buddhist monks asserted that Laotse was in fact a Bodhisat who came to China to preach Buddhism, and it was better for the people to be converted to Buddhism as Taoism was but a degenerate form of Buddhism. The most serious attack on Buddhism was launched by Fan Cheng, who wrote *Shen Mieh Lun* (*On the Non-existence of the Soul*), which denied the independent existence of the soul after death. It was lucky for him that Emperor Wu of the Liang Dynasty, a Buddhist, did not treat him as a heretic and punish him.

In spite of the misbehaviour of some Buddhists and the opposition of some important Confucians and officials, Buddhism nevertheless continued to spread and gain in popularity. And because of this, more Buddhist sutras were accurately translated. According to *Kai Yuan Shih Chiao Lu* (*Accounts of Buddhism in the Kai Yuan Period*), from 318–589, there were ninety-six famous Chinese and Indian translators who rendered 1,087 sutras in 3,437 volumes into Chinese, which was no mean achievement.

However, even Kumarajiva, the most famous of all the translators, said of his work that 'Buddhist sutras in Sanskrit lose their beauty when translated into Chinese. Although one can manage to convey the general idea of the sutras, they are never the same. It is like giving food to others which one has first chewed in one's own mouth. It is not only tasteless, but nauseating.'[3] The difficulty of translating Buddhist sutras into Chinese was twofold: first, Sanskrit is alphabetical and Chinese is ideographic and monosyllabic; secondly, the literary form of the sutras combined prose and rhymed verses, a practice unknown in China. It was possible to convey the meaning, but impossible to retain the sonorous quality of the original, let alone the tonal harmony of the verses. Huei Chiao said in his *Biographies of Great Buddhist Monks*,

'Since Buddhism was introduced to the East, many people have tried to translate the meanings of the sutras, but few tried also to convey their tonal beauty. This is because Sanskrit is polyphonic and Chinese is monophonic. The Chinese language when read in a polyphonic manner is apt to sound hurried and abrupt. And to chant Sanskrit verses in monophonic Chinese lengthens the verses so greatly that the rhymes are lost.' In order that translated Buddhist sutras should be pleasing to the ear when the prose was intoned and moving when the verses were chanted, Chinese had to be adapted to the polyphonic sounds of Sanskrit and greater attention paid to *fan chieh*, or spelling phonetically by joining the initial of a word, usually a consonant, to the ending, usually a vowel, of another word. As a result of this, the tones of each monophonic Chinese sound were more accurately defined and the theory of the four tonal differences of the Chinese language, i.e. *ping* or 'soft' tone and three other *tseh* or 'abrupt' tone, was established. About this, Professor Chen Yin-keh said:

The *ju* or abrupt tone of the Chinese language was easier to define. The *ping*, *shang* and *chu* tones were, however, defined in emulation of the three tones which were based on the ancient Indian work (known in Chinese translation as *Sheng Ming Lun* (*Theory of Phonetics*)) and used in the Chi and Liang Dynasties to intone the prose part of the Buddhist sutras. This is how the Theory of Four Tones of the Chinese language came to be defined. When the tones used in intoning the prose part of Buddhist sutras were adopted in the writing of the ornamental style of Chinese prose, the Theory of Four Tones gained universal acceptance. On the twentieth day of the second month in the seventh year of Yung Ming (A.D. 489), Tse Liang, Prince of Ching Ling, called a conference of Buddhist monks at his palace in the capital to differentiate and define the tones of the Chinese language for reading Buddhist sutras and chanting the verses contained therein. This was a most important occasion.[4]

At the same time as the general acceptance of the Theory of Four Tones, a practical guide to the 'eight pitfalls' to be avoided in writing five-word poems was also proposed and accepted. Shen Yueh is generally considered to be the initiator of this guide. The 'eight pitfalls' can also be summed up as the rules concerning the tones and rhymes of the words in a five-word poem. The first pitfall, for instance, is called '*ping-tou*' or 'flat-top', which means the first characters of the first and second lines must not be of the same tone.

During this period, folk songs such as *Wu Shen Songs* and *Hsi Chu Songs*, which are generally short and to the point, also gained great popularity in the South. They are principally love songs, such as the following:

> I heard that my love was going to Yangchow,
> And I went with him to Kiang Tsin Bay;
> I wished that the bamboo poles and rudder would break,
> So that my love will have to come back.

★

> The night is long and I cannot sleep,
> How brightly the full moon shines;
> I think of the way you called for me,
> And I silently say yes.

The folk songs of the Northern Dynasties were very different. They usually reflected the nomadic custom and living conditions of the people in the North. The most famous of these are perhaps the *Ballad of Mu Lan* and the *Chih Leh Song*. The *Ballad* is about a girl who went to war in her father's place, while the *Chih Leh Song* gives in a few lines the local flavour of the nomadic people, a subject which is rare in Chinese poetry. Here is the *Chih Leh Song*.

> In Chih Leh River,
> By the Yin-shan Mountain,
> The sky is like the dome of a tent—
> Round, it covers the whole prairie.
>
> The sky is grey and fathomless,
> The prairie is a wide expanse—
> Where the wind blows and bends down the grass,
> There you see the oxen and sheep.

Under these influences the poets of this period experimented and tried to create a 'new-style' poetry, and paid more attention to the difference of tones and the balance of tonal harmony. Slowly, in the hands of Hsieh Tiao (464–499), Shen Yueh (441–513), Yin Hen, Yu

Hsin (513–581), and others, 'stop-short' poems, which consisted of four lines of five or seven words with rhyming at the end of the first, second and fourth lines, were developed.

Lu shih or 'regular' poems, a more complicated poetic form, also came into being. In its established form, this consisted of eight lines of five or seven words, each two lines of which formed a couplet and the middle two couplets had to be real couplets, i.e. all the words must be balanced in one line against corresponding words in the other line, both in meaning and tone. Rhyming occurred at the end of the first and each even-number line in soft tone and the tone of each word had first to conform to a few sets of patterns such as the following:

1. / / o o o / /
2. o o / / o o / (rhyme)
3. / / o o o / /
4. o o / / / o o (rhyme)
5. o o / / o o /
6. / / o o / / o (rhyme)
7. / / o o o / /
8. o o / / / o o (rhyme)

The 'o' stands for 'soft tone', and '/' stands for 'hard' tones.

Here is a poem by Hsieh Tiao (although in translation these values are of course lost).

> The green grass is now rich as silk,
> Around the trees, too, red flowers are in bloom;
> Though it is true that you will not come back,
> Should you return, these flowers will have faded.

In contrast to these efforts at experimentation, the 'palace style' poems dominated the scene. Started by Emperor Chien Wen of the Liang Dynasty, this type of poetry sought a formal beauty by relying on decorous and colourful phrases and tonal harmony, and was entirely lacking in spontaneity. That the themes of these poems were sex, women and even homosexuals, was perhaps a reflection of the corrupt lives the emperors and high officials of that period led.

Thus Chinese poetry slowly changed. In 589, Yang Chien reunited China and established the Sui Dynasty. But in his son's time, China was again divided and occupied by powerful warriors. It was not until

618, when Lee Yen again united China and established the Tang Dynasty, that the situation in China was finally stabilized. In the one hundred and fifty-odd years following the founding of the Tang Dynasty, Lee Yen and successive emperors—Tai Tsung, Kao Tsung and Hsien Tsung—continually took positive measures to expand the economic power of the country, and encourage education and literature, and thereby laid the foundation for military expansion. The Tang Empire, with territory stretching north to Outer Mongolia, north-east to Korea, south to Indo-China, west to Chinese Turkestan and east to the sea, was stronger than those of the Chin and Han Dynasties. This great expansion brought about greater and closer contact between China and other countries in Asia. The volume of international trade expanded with the great increase of economic activity and better transportation facilities along the Yangtse River and the Grand Canal, which had been dug in the latter part of the Sui Dynasty. Religious activity also flourished. Apart from Confucianism, Taoism and Buddhism, which were practised in China before that period, Mohammedanism, Manicheism and Zoroastrianism were also introduced to China, and mosques and temples were built.

Many scholars and Buddhist monks from Japan, Sin-lo, Po-chi,[5] Kao-chang[6] and Turfan[7] also came to China to study. Indian culture was further brought into China and slowly assimilated, exerting thereby a great influence on the development of Chinese literature and philosophy. Chinese music, painting, sculpture and architecture all greatly advanced under the impact of closer contact with the cultures of these other countries.

In these circumstances poetry flourished greatly and became the principal literary activity of the Tang Dynasty. This came about chiefly because almost all the emperors loved poetry. They themselves wrote poems and encouraged others to do so. The writing of poems became one of the subjects of examination through which candidates could gain official positions. Furthermore, well-known poets, notably Po Chu-yi (772–846) and Yuan Chen (779–831) were appointed officials without having to take part in the examinations. Inevitably, students were tempted to devote the greater part of their time to writing poems and their different backgrounds greatly enriched and expanded the themes of poetry.

But in the early years of the Tang Dynasty, most poets were still under the influence of 'palace-style' poetry, seeking the beauty of form.

It was through the efforts of the 'Four Principal Poets of the Early Tang Dynasty', Wang Po (650–676), Lu Chao-lin (650–690?), Yang Chuen (650?–700?) and Lo-pin Wang (650?–684?); and Shen Chien-chi (650–715?) and Sung Chih-wen (650–712) that *lu shih* became firmly established and 'stop-short' poems highly developed. There were also poets such as Wang Chi (590?–644), Wang Fan-chih (no dates) and Chen Tse-ang (656–698) who emphasized the contents of poems and advocated the return to the vigorous and simple style of the poetry of the Han and Wei Dynasties. Chen Tse-ang's *Upon the Yuchow Terrace* is one of his better-known poems.

> Before me, there is no trace of the ancients,
> Nor of future generations is there any sign;
> Thinking of the sky and earth, unchanged, everlasting—
> Grieved, I let my tears fall!

It was not until the first half of the eighth century that Tang poetry came into its own. The poets of this period can be said to have belonged to two schools, namely, the Wang Wei and the Tsen Tsan. Wang Wei (699–759), and the other poets of his school, including Meng Hao-jan (689–740), Chu Kuang-hsi (707–760?) and others, wrote mainly five-word poems, which were restrained and tender. Wang Wei is especially famous for his descriptive technique. Su Tung-po, a famous poet of the Sung Dynasty (960–1276), said of Wang Wei's poems that 'there is painting in his poetry and poetry in his painting'. The fact that Wang was also a painter might perhaps have had something to do with the excellence of his technique. His twenty poems collected in *Wang Chuan Chi* are the best examples of his rather impressionistic style of painting a picture with words. Here are two:

> In the lonely hills, I see not one person
> Yet hear voices floating up to me;
> Into the thick forest, the reflected sunshine comes
> And falls on the green moss.

★

> Alone, I sit in the dense bamboo grove
> Playing the lute and making a long-drawn call.
> Nobody knows I rest deep inside the grove,
> Only the moon seeks me out with her beams.

There are other good ones not in the book. For instance, the following:

> Moodily the river flows,
> In the dusk, birds fly and circle
> O'er a ruined rampart by a decrepit ferry,
> While the setting sun embraces the autumn hills.

It has been said that the restraint and calm shown in his poems were the result of his conversion to the Buddhist faith. For in his *Yueh Fu*, too, there is a tender sadness:

> The morning shower in Weichen has settled the dust,
> The hostel walls are green with the reflection of the rain-washed willows;
> May I persuade you to take another cup of wine?
> For west of the Yangkuan Pass—
> You will find no old friend!

Tsen Tsan (715–770) and other poets of his school, including Kao Shih (700?–765), Wang Chang-ling and Wang Chih-huan, wrote mainly seven-word poems with great gusto and display of passion. Many of them were about war, and the lives and longing of the soldiers on the north-western frontier, with its bitter cold and unbearable heat. These poems reflected the lives of the poets who were sent to the frontiers to wage war against foreign tribes in order to guard the frontiers or to expand the territory of the Empire. Tsen Tsan, for instance, was sent successively to An Hsi and Kuan Hsi, or the present-day Sinkiang and Kansu Provinces. His aggressive spirit and patriotism showed themselves in his poems. One thing unique about him was that he was almost the only poet in Chinese history to write poems in praise of war. His *Lun Tai Song* was one:

On top of the walls of Lun Tai in the evening
Someone was blowing a bugle
And on the northern side of the walls
The Pleiades began to fade from the sky.

The general, his *mao*[8] in hand, was going to the west on an expedition,
Before dawn, the grand army marched, surrounded by the music of pipes,
From all sides rolled the drums like the waves of Snow Sea,
And the shouts of the men shook the Yin-shan Mountain.

Everyone has read the records in history books
But the present exploits are greater than those of old!

His *Snow Song*, written when a friend of his was going home, is among his best poems:

The north wind swept over and broke the dried grass stalks,
And in this foreign place, it began snowing, even though it was still August.
Suddenly there was snow on the branches and boughs of thousands of trees,
As if after a night of sweet spring breeze, pear blossoms had profusely bloomed.
Through the curtains the snowflakes flew into the tents, wetting the walls,
Fox-fur jackets were not warm enough
Nor silk quilts thick enough,
The general could not draw his bow of horn,
Only the guards had still to put on their freezing armour.
Thousands of feet of ice pillars piled confusedly over the Han Hai[9]
And the greycast clouds hung frozen for miles.
At headquarters, a banquet was given for you who were going home
And to entertain you, Hu Chin,[10] Pi Pa[11] and the flute of the Kiang people
   were played.
In the evening, snow fell thicker and faster outside the general's tent
And the frozen red flag stood stiff in the wind;
Out of the East gate of Lun Tai I came to see you off.
The snow had now covered the road over the Tien Shan Mountains.
I lost sight of you when the curve in the road hid you,
Leaving on the snow only prints of your horse's hooves.

In Wang Chang-ling's and Wang Chih-huan's poems, we see more clearly the influence of the folk song. Incidentally, their 'stop-short' poems were considered to be among the best of the Tang Dynasty.

IN THE ARMY by Wang Chang-ling

In the great desert
A sandstorm has shrouded and darkened the sun,
And a red flag, half furled, leads columns of troops out of a pass.
For North of River Tiao, the previous night,
Our forces up front were in battle
And already they've reported: We've captured Turfan!

GOING OUT OF THE FRONTIER by Wang Chih-huan

The Yellow River stretches to the horizon and is lost in the clouds.
In a lonely outpost amidst a great range of steep mountains
Why play the song of willows on your flute?
The spring wind will never come here through the Yu-meng Pass.

Good though the poets of these two schools were, the greatest poets of the Tang Dynasty were by common consent Li Po and Tu Fu. After them, Han Yu (768–824) and Po Chu-yi (772–846), among others, are considered good poets, but they could not reach the standard set by the two masters. Han Yu, incidentally, in trying to create something new, used many allusions and recondite phrases. This style, generally speaking, became the vogue with the poets of the Sung Dynasty, and down to the early years of this century it remained the model for those who wrote classical Chinese poems.

2. THE LIVES OF LI PO AND TU FU

Li Po (701–762) and Tu Fu (712–770) were the two greatest poets of the Tang Dynasty. They lived in the same period and were friends, but it is difficult to think of two poets more different from each other in background, temperament and experience. We know Tu Fu, a native of Hsiangyang, was from a Confucian family. His grandfather, Tu Shen-yen, was one of the famous poets of the early Tang Dynasty; his father, Tu Hsien, was a minor official. For the last thousand years or so, there has been controversy about when and where Li Po was born, which it would be too tedious to go into here. Generally speaking, it has been accepted that his ancestors were banished to Sui Yeh, the modern Yen Chi in Sinkiang Province[12] at the end of the Sui Dynasty (589–618). Li Po himself was born there and when he was about five years old, his father took his family and returned to live in Chang Ming, about a hundred miles north-east of Chengtu, the capital of Szechuan Province. Most probably his father stayed in Chang Ming for the rest of his life and possibly became a trader. With such a background, Li Po nevertheless claimed to be one of the ninth-generation descendants of King Wu Chao of the state of Liang[13] whom the royal family of the Tang Dynasty also claimed as ancestor. He was thus claiming to be one of the cousins of the Emperor and seems to have been so accepted. On the other hand, Tu Fu's maternal grandmother was the daughter of one of the grandsons of Emperor Tai Tsung, but few people seemed to have noticed his relationship with the royal family. For although Tu Fu would go to great lengths to beg the Emperor to give him a job, he was usually a conventional Confucian, honest, reserved and patriotic. Li Po was not inhibited by conventions. In his youth he was infatuated by the idea of *hsieh*—one who would go to any length to help the widowed, the orphaned, the old and the weak. It was said that he killed several people in fulfilling the functions of a *hsieh*. This was unimaginable of Tu Fu, who was a gentleman always prepared to sacrifice himself to speak up for his friends, but not to the extent of endangering the lives of others.

The legends about the way they met their deaths reflect their different personalities. Li Po was said to have died one night when he was drunk in a-boat and tried to grasp the moon, which was reflected in the water. Another more elaborate legend was that he was summoned back to Heaven when he was having supper in the boat. Suddenly, on the water in the moonlight there appeared dolphins which stood on their tails and two 'children of immortality', carrying banners in their hands, to welcome Li Po back to the celestial palace, which he reached by riding on the back of a dolphin. The legend about Tu Fu's death was entirely different. He was said to have been without food for ten days when the Magistrate of Lei-yang presented him with some white wine and dried meat. That night, Tu Fu died of drinking too much wine and eating too much dried meat after fasting so long.

But there is no denying that Li Po was a genius. He may have been a boastful, dissipated, irresponsible and untruthful drunkard, as some people said, but to dwell on this would be to miss the significance of Li Po as a poet. Li Yang-ping, in whose house Li Po died, said in his preface to the *Collection of Tsao Tang*:

Since the Three Dynasties, in the one thousand years after the appearance of the *Book of Poetry* and *Li Sao*, there has been only Li Po whose achievement is comparable to those of Chu Yuan and Sung Yu and surpasses those of Yang Hsiung and Szema Hsiang-ju. Therefore, princes and dukes admire his poems, other poets set him up as their model and try to imitate his style, just like so many crows bowing before the beauty of a phoenix. Li Chang-yung said Chen Tse-ang tried to stop the decadent trend in poetry writing and the quality of poetry changed for the better. As a matter of fact, the poetry of our Tang Dynasty had still retained the 'palace-style' of the Liang and Chi Dynasties and it was because of Li Po's efforts that this was entirely changed and given up. Now, every collection of the past and contemporary poets is ignored and only that of Li Po is admired and accepted everywhere in the country. Can it not be said that Li Po's efforts are comparable to those of the Creator?

It is obvious that to his contemporaries Li Po was considered to be the best and thus became the most popular poet. Here it is necessary to point out that in poetry the Chinese prize most highly two qualities: *haofang*, or romantic abandonment, which immediately finds a response in the reader; and *wenyueh*, or an artistic restraint, capable of evoking seemingly endless imagery in the mind of the reader. To our mind, Li Po may not have followed all the rules of writing poetry, but his poems came nearest to achieving these two qualities.

How he did this was indeed a puzzle to his contemporaries. Fei Ching said,[14] 'Was he endowed with the vital essence of Heaven and Earth? If not, why was he so different from the ordinary people? Some said that he was the Spirit of Tai Po (Venus), who was banished to the Earth, and that was why he was named Tai Po[15] and Ho Chih-chang called him an immortal banished from Heaven. Is not this true?'

In fact, not only was there a legend while he was alive that his mother dreamed about the Spirit of Tai Po the night he was born, but in a poem Li Po said of himself, 'Immortals caressed my head. Plaiting my hair, I was blessed with longevity,' although he was, of course, merely boasting.

I am tempted to think that Li Po's genius and his way of living can be partly explained by the assumption that his mother was a native of Sui Yeh. Children born of parents of different races are said as a rule to be more clever. Until Li Po's father brought his family back from Sui Yeh to Szechuan, the family had been in exile for more than a hundred years. There are records of great numbers of criminals being banished to the Western Regions, but it stands to reason that the great majority, if not all of them, were men. It would have been nothing unusual if the descendants of these men had married local girls after they had lived in Sui Yeh for some time. In fact, Li Po's father might have been a man of mixed blood himself. It has been said that he resumed the surname Li only after he came back to Szechuan, and then, in spite of that, he was still called *Ke* by the people in Chang Ming, meaning that he was a man who came from another part of the country. Perhaps his appearance was already different from that of others. According to the Regional Record of Szechuan, there was in Ching-Lien-on-the-River of the Ping Wu District, Lung An County, a *man po tu*, or foreign-woman ferry, where, legend has it, Li Po's mother used to wash clothes. It would seem that Li Po was by blood more a native of Sui Yeh than Chinese. This seems to fit in with other descriptions of him.

He was said to be tall, strongly built, with a pair of glaring eyes and a mouth as big as a tiger—for a Chinese these were rather unusual features, even allowing for exaggeration.

The atmosphere at Li Po's home must have been quite different from that of Chinese families, and it must have been quite difficult to recognize China as his native country. Perhaps that was why, in his youth, he did not study the Confucian classics at all. He said he studied Liu Chia,[16] rare books, books of eclectics and literature, and that he liked to learn swordsmanship and the secrets of becoming an immortal. And in one of his poems he was openly contemptuous of Confucius: 'I am like the madman of Tsu who sang the song of the Phoenix in ridicule of Confucius.'[17] On the other hand, presumably because there are in Taoism no strict rules of behaviour but there is a promise to the faithful that they shall be immortal, we see Li Po making friends with Taoist masters such as Szema Chen-cheng and Wu Yun and studying Taoism under Hu Tse-yang and receiving *lu*, or a diploma of Taoism, from Kao Tien-shih. He was indeed an incurable romantic to dream of becoming an immortal. His belief in the idea of *hsieh* did not seem to have been a passing infatuation either. He had a sworn brother who dressed himself in the attire of a *hsieh* and Tsui Tsung-chih in a poem wrote that Li Po had a dagger concealed in his sleeves. All this seemed to be the expression of the temperament of a man who was warm-hearted, straightforward and who had a clear-cut sense of justice—in short, that of a frontiersman, a hero of a Western film. And just like some of the legendary people in the Westerns, he was good-naturedly boastful. When, at nineteen, he secured an interview with Su Ting, who was then demoted from Minister of Education and Examination to be Governor of Yichow, he showed Su Ting some of his compositions. Nine years later he was to boast that Su Ting thought he could become as good a poet as Szema Hsiang-ju, a native of Szechuan, who was probably his idol.

Speaking of his life from his twentieth year to around his twenty-fourth, a period when he lived as a recluse with Tung Yen Tse, he said he did not once go to a town and hundreds of rare birds came to feed from his hand. The local governor was moved to suggest sending him and his companion to the capital as persons of unusual talent to take part in a special Civil Service examination. Naturally he had to say that they refused. Li Po was perhaps at his most boastful when he commented on the fact that Ho Chih-chang, after having talked with him and seen his poems, made this remark: 'You are an immortal banished from heaven!' Li Po said simply, 'Ho was only telling the truth.'

I suspect that his physique, his boastful eloquence and, of course, his extraordinary talent in writing poems must have been the reasons which prompted Hsu Yu-shih, one-time Prime Minister of Emperor Hsuan Tsung, to let him marry his granddaughter. For Li Po was but twenty-six then; it was only two years after he had left Szechuan to tour the country and try to make a name for himself. He had visited Tung Ting Lake, Hsiang Yang, Nanking, Yangchow and other places, and came to An-lu ostensibly to visit Yun Meng which Szema Hsiang-ju wrote about in *Tse Hsu Fu*. In An-lu, he found himself married. But soon, perhaps because of doubts about himself, he was, as he said in a poem to his wife, 'Every day drunk as an owl.' Nevertheless, he wrote several letters to the Governors of An-chow and Chin-chow asking for a job, but without success.

It was said that part of the reason for his lack of success was his casualness when he went to see Han Chao-tsung, Governor of Chin-chow. He did not bother to bow but just raised his hands in greeting. Later, Li Po in his letter to Han Chao-tsung apologized for his behaviour. He was forgiven, but was not given a job. After a few years in An-lu, Li Po was apparently bored with the life he was leading and set out once again to visit Lo-yang. For a time he lived on Sung Mountain with Yuan Tan-chiu as a recluse again. Later he visited Tai-yuan with a Commissioner Yuan and then went to live in Jen-chen in Shantung Province, where he made friends with five scholars and went drinking and singing on Chu Lai Mountain. Some people said they lived as recluses there and were thus known as the 'Six Recluses of the Bamboo Stream'. But soon he started on a tour again. He visited Meng Hao-jan in Hsiang Yang, met Wang Chang-ling in Pa-ling and again visited Lo-yang. About 740 he returned to Jen-chen and in 742 he brought his family to Hui-chi in the south and stayed with Wu Yun, a famous Taoist. Li Po was then forty-one years old. He had not held a job all his life and did not know how to make money, nor did he seem to care about it. He said that once in Yangchow, he spent 300,000 cash. At first he might have been spending his wife's money, but later he seems to have been depending on the help of his friends and relations. Still, he managed to make himself a name as a poet. For soon afterward Wu Yun was summoned to the capital where, with the help of Princess Yu-chen, the younger sister of the Emperor, he persuaded Emperor Hsuan Tsung to summon Li Po to the capital. According to one version, when Li Po arrived at the capital, Emperor Hsuan Tsung, having heard of his fame as a poet, sent for him. He received the poet in a residential hall and, greatly taken by his bright and easy demeanour, forgot the protocol and asked the poet to make himself at home. Upon which Li Po stretched one foot out to Kao Li-shih, the powerful eunuch, and said, 'Take off my boot!' Kao was so taken by surprise that he did so.

What was more probable was that when Li Po arrived at the capital he was ordered to join the other distinguished poets and men of letters in the Han Lin Academy, and await the pleasure of the Emperor. It is impossible to say how long he was simply ignored. But one day he met Ho Chih-chang (659–745), secretary to the Crown Prince at Tse Chi Temple, and so impressed the latter with his personality and talent that Ho took off a golden tortoise which he had been wearing on his belt and bought wine with it so that they might make merry together. Later, Ho spoke to the Emperor about Li Po, and praised him to the skies. The Emperor became curious about the poet and sent for him.

Here it is necessary to mention that in the Tang Dynasty, Laotse and Taoism were greatly respected and encouraged by the Emperors. This might have been due to the fact that Laotse was said to have the same surname, Li, as the royal house. Whatever the reason, Laotse was proclaimed in the early Tang Dynasty by Emperor Hsuan Yuan. In the twentieth year of Kai Yuan (732), Emperor Hsuan Tsung ordered that a temple for Emperor Hsuan Yuan and a Taoist school be set up in the capitals Chang-an and Lo-yang, and in every county in the country.

In 741, persons who were brought up in Taoism were allowed to take part in examinations for selecting officials, in which they were tested in Taoist and not Confucian texts. In 742, Chuangtse, Liehtse and two other ancient scholars of the Taoist school were each honoured with the exalted title of Chen-jen, literally meaning 'immortal person'. From this and the fact that Emperor Hsuan Tsung received a Taoist diploma from Szema Chen-cheng, it can be seen that whoever was well-versed in Taoism or the technique of Taoists would receive special consideration from the Emperor. In fact, in the *History of Tang Dynasty*, there is a passage in which Szema Chen-cheng says to someone who pretends to be a Taoist hermit in Chungnan Mountain near Chang-an and contrives to make himself known and be summoned to

Court, that Chungnan Mountain is the short-cut to becoming an official.

In Li Po's case it is interesting to note that Ho Chih-chang had asked to be relieved from his post so that he might devote his time to studying Taoism. It may not be unjust to say that part of the attraction Ho and perhaps subsequently the Emperor found in Li Po was due to his knowledge of Taoism and its techniques, which also might have been part of the reason for Emperor Hsuan Tsung treating the poet indulgently. For there are many anecdotes or legends about Li Po's relationship with the Emperor which, if true, were strictly unconventional. One of them said he once submitted to the Emperor a *sung* or eulogy praising the exploits and accomplishments of the Tang Empire. The Emperor was so pleased that he asked Li Po to have a meal at the palace and personally served him with his food. Another was that Li Po was once dining with some aristocrats when the Emperor sent for him to frame a military order. He was still somewhat drunk when he arrived at the palace, but dashed off the order, properly worded, without making a rough copy. Still another had it that Emperor Hsuan Tsung was one day admiring the peonies with Yang Kwei-fei, his favourite concubine, in the imperial gardens and felt that a few new lyrics were called for. He sent for Li Po, who came and as usual was drunk. The Emperor ordered the eunuchs to splash water on his face to bring him round. When he came to, Li Po immediately wrote three poems which are now famous, called *Ching Ping Tiao* (*A Song of Pure Happiness*).

But happy and proud though he must have been, Li Po was not appointed to a position with any responsibility or power. And soon he was drinking around with Ho Chih-chang and other friends whom Tu Fu later on in one of his poems referred to as the 'Eight Immortals of the Wine'. In the same poem, Tu Fu said that Li Po was sometimes drunk in a boat. 'When the Emperor's summons came, he refused to go ashore, but said that he was an Immortal of Wine.' Not long afterwards, however, Li Po asked to be released from his work and to be allowed to go home. There were many different reasons given for his leaving the capital. One had it that Kao Li-shih could not forget the humiliation he suffered at the hands of Li Po and persuaded Yang Kwei-fei to stop the Emperor from appointing Li Po to any official position. Another was that Chang Chi, a son-in-law of the Emperor, was jealous of Li Po and changed the Emperor's feelings towards him, so that there was no hope of any appointment for the latter. Still another version had it that the Emperor himself was afraid that Li Po, being often drunk, would be indiscreet about affairs in the palace. Perhaps all these were true. When he left the capital Li Po was forty-three years of age.

It was in that year, 744, that Li Po first met Tu Fu in Lo-yang. Tu Fu was thirty, and apart from having sat and failed a Civil Service examination in 735, when he visited what is now Kiangsu, Chekiang, Shantung and Hopei Provinces, he had not tried to get a job.

When they met Li Po was already a famous poet, while Tu Fu was comparatively unknown. It was no wonder that Tu Fu was greatly taken with him. More important, Li Po's boastful eloquence, apparent insouciance and unrestrained romantic imagination seem to have hypnotized Tu Fu. In his first poem Tu Fu wrote of his impatience with the treachery and pettiness he had found in others during the previous two years in Lo-yang, and ended it by saying that he was going with Li Po to Honan to study Taoism. Although Tu Fu had to attend the funeral of his grandmother in August of that year, he went nevertheless immediately afterward to Honan. As the Confucian rites required a long mourning period, Tu Fu's hasty departure from home due to his eagerness to meet Li Po was, to say the least, unusual for a man of convention like him. In the modern Kaifeng, Tu Fu met Li Po and Kao Shih and they spent some time together drinking, hunting and discussing poetry and the affairs of the country. Later, Tu Fu and Li Po left for Wang Wu Mountain, hoping to study Taoism under Hua Kai Chun, a Taoist master. But on the way they learned that Hua had died and dejectedly returned to Kaifeng. From there they went to Chichow, the present Chinan, in Shantung. Li Po then went on to study under and received a *lu* or diploma of Taoism from Kao Tien-shih. Tu Fu seemed to have momentarily lost interest in the subject, and went to visit Li Yung. The following autumn Tu Fu met Li Po again in Yenchow, the present Chih Yang district in Shangtung Province. There they visited Tung, a Taoist priest, and Yuan, a recluse, and they became good friends. Tu Fu in one of his poems said of their life in this period, 'I also am a visitor in Tung Men/My feelings towards you are like those of a brother/When drunk we sleep under the same blanket through the autumn nights/In the daytime, we walk arm in arm.' Tu Fu felt it a pity that Li Po should continue to waste his talent: 'To waste so much time drinking wine and in song/For what purpose is your unconventional behaviour?' That winter they parted. Tu Fu went back to Lo-yang and Li Po went to the South. The latter saw Tu Fu off in Shih Meng and wrote two poems expressing his hope of seeing him again. But as fate willed it they never met again.

Tu Fu returned to Lo-yang and then went on to Chang-an. Once away from the influence of Li Po, and living in the country's seat of power, Tu Fu forgot about Taoism and returned to the traditions of Confucianism in which he was brought up. From then on he was dominated by an ambition to get himself appointed to a government post and serve the country. He made friends with Wang Wei, Tsen Tsan and others. The next year Emperor Hsuan Tsung declared that anyone who had mastered one of the Confucian classics could come to the capital and take a special Civil Service examination. Tu Fu sat the examination, but because Lee Lin-fu, the Prime Minister, wanted to show that he had all along been able to select all the talented people for government service, Tu Fu and others were prevented from passing the examination. Lee then reported to the Emperor, congratulating him that not a talented person in the country was not properly employed! Tu Fu was poor, and this failure left him destitute. None of his friends and relatives seemed able to help him. He said of his life, 'In the morning, I knocked on the doors of the rich/At dusk, I followed in the dust kicked up by sturdy horses/All I got was half-cups of drinks and cold dishes/Everywhere I went, I tried to suppress my misery and pain.'

In 750, probably in desperation, he presented his *Fu of the Eagle* to the Emperor. In the attached memorandum he wrote of himself, 'I am forty years old. . . . My clothes are tattered and torn, and I have to depend on others for food.' The Emperor did not answer. The following year he again presented a *fu* to the Emperor, this one called the *Fu of Three Great Rituals*, and once more in his memorandum said, 'I now have to sell herbs in the market and live on my friends' help.' This time the Emperor ordered him to wait for a summons to the Chi Hsien Academy, or Academy of Worthies.

That autumn it rained continually. Outside the inn where Tu Fu was staying water gathered in puddles for such a long time that small fishes were said to breed in them. Inside the inn it was so damp that green mould grew under his bed. Tu Fu became sick and later suffered bouts of malaria. In 752 he was ordered to sit again for an examination. His name was then included in a list of candidates who were to be appointed when vacancies occurred. But nothing happened. For the next two years he lived on grain, which was sold to the poor in Chang-an by the government at reduced prices. He again presented a *fu* to the Emperor, and receiving no news decided to take his family to live in Feng-hsien, the present Pu-chen District in Shensi Province.

In 755, when he was forty-three years old, he was for the first time in his life appointed to an official post, that of an assistant to the Magistrate of Ho Si District in Yunnan. But it was really too far away for him to go, and he declined the post. Luckily for him he was made an adjutant in the Capital Garrison Forces in charge of armour, weapons and so forth. This was really not much of an appointment, but he was happy enough to receive a salary. Not that this was enough to meet his needs and those of his family, for when he went back to Feng-hsien to visit them, he found that his youngest son had died of starvation.

In November of the same year An Lu-shan (703–757) rose in rebellion against the Tang Dynasty in Fan Yang, the present Peiping. Within a month he had captured Lo-yang, and in January 756 he called himself Emperor of Great Yen and sent his troops westwards. In June, Tungkuan Pass was captured by Tsui Chien-Ku, one of his generals, and Emperor Hsuan Tsung fled from Chang-an to Chengtu. In the same month, An Lu-shan captured Chang-an. In July, Crown Prince Heng ascended the throne in Ling-wu in Kansu Province, and styled himself Shu Tsung. He offered to Hsuan Tsung the title of Tai Shan Huang, which means literally the Most Reverent Emperor, but was, in fact, an empty title. However, Emperor Hsuan Tsung continued to issue orders. He ordered the Crown Prince to be the Commander-in-Chief of all the armies, and his three other sons to take over command of three districts. But only Ling, Prince Yung, went to Kiang Ling as ordered. However, he had no sooner arrived than he decided to declare himself emperor, and led his troops down the Yangtse River hoping to capture Nanking.

At that time Li Po, who in the past years had been visiting friends in the present Anhuei and Kiangsu Provinces, was living in Lu Shan Mountain in the present Kiangsi Province. Prince Yung had long heard of Li Po and summoned him to join the secretariat. From the poems he wrote at this period, Li Po seemed quite happy to join in the rebellion, although when Prince Yung was defeated in March 757 and Li Po was captured and put in jail in Chinkiang, he said that he had been forced to join Prince Yung. That year, Tsui Huan and Sung Juo-sze, who tried

Li Po, spoke up for him, hoping to clear his name. When Sung was sent to Honan to fight the troops of An Lu-shen, he released Li Po, appointed him a member of his staff, and sent a memorandum to Emperor Shu Tsung recommending Li Po for a higher position. The Emperor did not reply, but in the next year ordered that Li Po be banished to Yeh Lang, the present Tungtse district in Kweichow Province.

In the meantime, Tu Fu had fled from Chang-an to Feng Hsien, and went on to Po-shui and Fuchow, the modern Fu district in Shensi Province. In July 756 he heard that Emperor Shu Tsung had acceded to the throne in Ling-wu and decided to join the Emperor. On the way he was captured by rebel troops and sent to Chang-an. It was ironic that because Tu Fu had not had a high position or made a name for himself, he was spared any humiliation, while other poets, such as Chang Yueh and Ko Shu-han, were taken to Lo-yang, which had become An Lu-shan's capital, and forced or persuaded to surrender. Wang Wei, Chu Kuang-hsi and others were imprisoned in Chang-an.

Tu Fu was free to move about in Chang-an, but as the city was occupied by the rebels, he was daily reminded of the tragedy which had so suddenly befallen the country, and was worried about his family. In the following January, An Lu-shan was killed by his son, and a month later Emperor Shu Tsung moved his headquarters to Feng-hsiang in Shensi Province. The situation seemed to improve somewhat, and Tu Fu was the more anxious to go to Feng-hsiang. In April he risked his life in crossing the enemy lines and on arrival at Feng-hsiang was appointed *tso shih yi*, or censor. This was, of course, a much better post than the one he had held before. But almost immediately after he became censor, Fang Kuan, the Prime Minister, was defeated in battle in Chen-tao and Emperor Shu Tsung released him from the premiership.

Had Tu Fu bided his time and found out why the Emperor was in such a hurry to get rid of Fang Kuan he would have spared himself a great deal of trouble. Not knowing that several ministers had spoken ill of Fang Kuan to the Emperor and that Fang Kuan was suspected of receiving bribes, Tu Fu dashed off a memorandum to Emperor Shu Tsung, practically begging him not to demote Fang Kuan simply because the latter had made a small mistake. The Emperor was furious, and ordered Tu Fu to be arrested and tried for insubordination. One of the ministers who was to try him spoke up for the poet and said that Tu Fu was only trying to do his duty. The Emperor was not appeased, but became angry with the minister as well. At last, Chang Hao, the new Prime Minister, also spoke up for Tu Fu and the latter escaped punishment. Nevertheless, he was relieved of his post and went back to Fuchow in August.

In October, General Kuo Tse-yi recaptured Lo-yang and Emperor Shu Tsung returned to Chang-an at the end of the same month. Tu Fu came back to the capital also, and was reappointed censor. His financial worries having been relieved, he hoped to accomplish something for the country. But in June of the following year the Emperor, who apparently had neither forgotten or forgiven him, demoted him and made him an assistant to the Governor of Huachow in Shensi. The following year there was famine in Shensi, and because of the invasion of Nan-chao many people were recruited into the army or ordered to do auxiliary work. Moved by the tragedy, Tu Fu wrote his great poems *Three Bailiffs* and *Three Departures*.[18] Now he found it increasingly difficult to support his family, and grew more and more discouraged about the setback to his career. He decided to resign, and went back to Chinchow, the present Tien-shui District in Kansu Province, to live with one of his nephews. There he had plenty of time to think about his brothers and friends. On learning that Li Po was being banished to Yeh Lang and hearing many rumours that Li had died on the way, he dreamt of Li Po for three consecutive nights and wrote two most moving poems about his dreams.

In November of that year, when Li Po arrived in Wu Shan on his way to Yeh Lang, Emperor Shu Tsung proclaimed an amnesty, hoping thereby to relieve the great drought, and Li was pardoned. Tu Fu, on hearing the good news, wrote to Li Po, sending him a poem of congratulation, but the latter did not seem in the mood to reply. Soon afterwards, Tu Fu took his family and went to Tungku, the modern Cheng District in Kansu, where he gathered kindling and chestnuts to support his family, but several of his children died of starvation. In December he went south to Chengtu where, with the help of his relatives and friends, he built himself a thatched cottage.

His life in the ensuing years was comparatively uneventful. This was because his friend Yen Wu was appointed Military Governor of Szechuan and Tu Fu became his secretary. Judging by the poems he wrote, he was no longer the ambitious young man of earlier days, nor was he the poet who had shown his great sympathy for the suffering of the people only a few years before. He was resigned to his fate, and led a simple, peaceful life in exile. He was then more than fifty years of age.

In 762, Li Po died in Tan Tu in Anhwei Province. Tu Fu did not seem to hear of his friend's death but he did write one poem defending him against attack by some unknown poets. Tu Fu also noticed that in the two most popular anthologies of poetry, not one of his poems was included, and wrote six poems to express his ideas of poetry. It must have been at this period that he devoted more time to poetry writing. In 765 Yen Wu died, and Tu Fu drifted about eastern Szechuan for three years. In 768 Szechuan was in a state of turmoil. Tu Fu went down the Yangtse Gorges to Yuehchow in Hunan, living most of the time in a boat. In the summer of 770 he went farther south, hoping to visit his maternal uncle Tsui Wei in Chunchow. According to the legend quoted at the beginning of this section, he died when he arrived in Lei-yang. Another version had it that he did not see Tsui Wei, but turned north again when he arrived in Lei-yang, and died in his boat on his way to Yuehchow that winter.

It was not until 813 that Tu Tse-yeh, his grandson, brought his remains back to Yen-shih for burial near the tomb of Tu Shen-yen, the poet of the early Tang Dynasty. Li Po's remains, too, were not finally buried until Fan Chuan-cheng visited Tan Tu about forty years after he died, and discovered that Li's two granddaughters were married to poor peasants and still could not afford to bury their grandfather in Green Mountain as he had wished. Fan, an admirer of Li Po, paid for the interment in Green Mountain.

3. THE POEMS OF LI PO, TU FU AND OTHERS

The poems of Li Po and Tu Fu reflect the differences in their personalities and their views of life and of the world. Li Po is known as the 'Immortal of Poetry' and Tu Fu the 'Sage of Poetry'. I think this sums them up pretty well. Li Po was a genius who put down his feelings in short poems of twenty or twenty-eight words, probably without much premeditation. He also excelled in writing songs, paying little attention to tones and rhyming, but pouring out his emotions. A few of his poems are restrained in tone, but these are exceptions.

Tu Fu, on the other hand, was a technician. He was not very good at writing 'stop-short' poems but excelled in 'regular' poems. Because of their many requirements, these are more difficult to write. Nevertheless, it is a poetic form suited to a less spontaneous and more deliberate expression of emotions. Tu Fu used this poetic form to express his deep feelings in perfect balance of lines. Perhaps Tu Fu knew that his talent did not lie in writing poems which were 'like lotus flowers standing in a pool of clear water, naturally captivating and needing no artificial trimming', which was Li Po's ideal. Instead, Tu Fu aimed at perfection of form, and continually experimented with variations within the rules of different types of poetry. He himself said of his way of writing poems that 'after correcting my newly-written poems, I hummed them over and over again', and 'I have to rewrite my poems again and again until I am sure that they will be impressive'. This painstaking care led to the gradual build-up of his reputation so that not long after his death people began to argue as to who was the greater of the two poets. Considering the fact that Li Po in his lifetime was already considered to be the greatest among his contemporaries, Tu Fu had gone up in the world in a short time indeed.

Apart from the intrinsic artistic achievement of Tu Fu's poems, there were two factors which contributed to his comparatively rapid rise in esteem. To begin with, his technical perfection, unlike Li Po's genius, was something which any ambitious poet could emulate. Secondly, Tu Fu's poems were more reflections of his time than those of Li Po, depicting often the suffering of the people. This in the time following the rebellion of An Lu-shan, when the Tang Dynasty was on the decline, was especially praiseworthy in the eyes of poets who were sensitive, patriotic and worried about the affairs of the country. It was indeed these two features which most of the latter-day Tang poets tried to imitate. Briefly, Han Yu (768–824), Meng Chiao (751–814), Chia Tao (777–841) and others tried to achieve new variations of the different forms within their prerequisites, and Po Chu-yi (772–846), Yuan Chen (779–831), Chang Chi (765?–830?) and others strove to reflect and comment on the times in which they lived. The following are some poems by Li Po,[19] Tu Fu and others.

A SONG OF PURE HAPPINESS by Li Po

I

Her robe is a cloud, her face a flower;
Her balcony, glimmering with the bright spring dew,
Is either the tip of earth's Jade Mountain
Or a moon-edged roof of paradise.

2

There's a perfume stealing moist from a shaft of red blossom,
And a mist, through the heart, from the magical Hill of Wu—
The palaces of China have never known such beauty—
Not even Flying Swallow with all her glittering garments.

3

Lovely now together, his lady and his flowers
Lighten for ever the Emperor's eye.
As he listens to the sighing of the far spring wind
Where she leans on a railing in the Aloe Pavilion.

IN THE QUIET NIGHT by Li Po

So bright a gleam on the foot of my bed—
Could there have been a frost already?
Lifting myself to look, I found that it was moonlight.
Sinking back again, I thought suddenly of home.

THROUGH THE YANGTSE GORGES by Li Po

From the walls of Po-ti high in the coloured dawn
To Kiang-ling by nightfall is three hundred miles,
Yet monkeys are still calling on both banks behind me
To my boat these ten thousand mountains away.

DRINKING ALONE WITH THE MOON by Li Po

From a pot of wine among the flowers
I drank alone. There was no one with me—
Till, raising my cup, I asked the bright moon
To bring me my shadow and make us three.
Alas, the moon was unable to drink
And my shadow tagged me vacantly;
But still for a while I had these friends
To cheer me through the end of spring . . .
I sang. The moon encouraged me.
I danced. My shadow tumbled after.
As long as I knew, we were boon companions.
And then I was drunk, and we lost one another.
. . . Shall goodwill ever be secure?
I watched the long road of the River of Stars.

HARD ROADS IN SHU (written to music) by Li Po

Oh, but it is high and very dangerous!
Such travelling is harder than scaling the blue sky.
... Until two rulers of this region
Pushed their way through in the misty ages,
Forty-eight thousand years had passed
With nobody arriving across the Ch'in border.
And the Great White Mountain, westward, still has only a bird's path
Up to the summit of O-mei Peak—
Which was broken once by an earthquake and there were brave men lost,
Just finishing the stone rungs of their ladder towards heaven.
... High, as on a tall flag, six dragons drive the sun,
While the river, far below, lashes its twisted course.
Such height would be hard going for even a yellow crane,
So pity the poor monkeys who have only paws to use.
The Mountain of Green Clay is formed of many circles—
Each hundred steps, we have to turn nine turns among its mounds.
Panting, we brush Orion and pass the Well Star,
Then, holding our chests with our hands and sinking to the ground with a
    groan,
We wonder if this westward trail will never have an end.
The formidable path ahead grows darker, darker still,
With nothing heard but the call of birds hemmed in by the ancient forest,
Male birds smoothly wheeling, following the females;
And there come to us the melancholy voices of the cuckoos
Out on the empty mountain, under the lonely moon—
Such travelling is harder than scaling the blue sky.
Even to hear of it turns the cheek pale,
With the highest crag barely a foot below heaven.
Dry pines hang, head down, from the face of the cliffs,
And a thousand plunging cataracts outroar one another
And send through ten thousand valleys a thunder of spinning stones.
With all this danger upon danger,
Why do people come here who live at a safe distance?
... Though Dagger-Tower Pass be firm and grim,
And while one man guards it
Ten thousand cannot force it,
What if he be not loyal,
But a wolf towards his fellows?
... There are ravenous tigers to fear in the day
And venomous reptiles in the night
With their teeth and their fangs ready

To cut people down like hemp.
. . . Though the City of Silk be delectable, I would rather turn home quickly.
Such travelling is harder than scaling the blue sky . . .
But I still face westward with a dreary moan.

THE BAILIFF OF SHIH-HAO by Tu Fu[20]

I came to Shih-hao village and stayed that eve.
A bailiff came to press-gang in the night.
The old man, hearing this, climbed o'er the wall,
And the old woman saw the bailiff at the door.
Oh, why was the bailiff's voice so terrible,
And why the woman's plaint so soft and low?
'I have three sons all at the Nieh-cheng post.
And one just wrote a letter home to say
The other two had in the battle died.
Let those who live live on as best they can,
For those who died are dead for evermore.
Now in the house there's only grandson left;
For him his mother still remains—without
A decent petticoat to go about.
Although my strength is ebbing, weak and low,
I'll go with you, bailiff, at the front to serve.
For I can cook breakfast for the army, and
I'll march and hurry to the Ho-yang Front.'
—So spake the woman, and in the night the voice
Became so low it broke into a whimper.
And in the morning ere I resumed my way,
I said good-bye to her old man alone.

THE RETURN by Tu Fu

Peaks of scarlet cloud shine in the west;
The sun sets beneath the earth.
Sparrows twitter by the country gate,
I come home a stranger from a thousand miles.
My wife is surprised, she thought I was dead.
Restraining herself, she wipes away her tears.
I was dust in the storm of the world.
Only chance sent me back alive.
Neighbours come to the country gate,
Exclaiming and shedding a few tears.
We light a candle in the dense evening,
And face each other as though in a dream.

A MEETING by Tu Fu[21]

We were often separated
Like the Dipper and the Morning Star.
What night is tonight?
We are together in the candlelight.

How long does youth last?
Now we are all grey-haired.
Half of our friends are dead,
And both of us were surprised when we met.

Who would know that after twenty years
I would call upon you in your hall?
You were not married when we last parted,
And now you have sons and daughters,
Who come courteously to greet their father's friend,
And ask me where I come from.

While we are thus greeting each other,
Your sons and daughters begin to prepare the wine.
They gather the spring spinach on this rainy night,
And prepare for the feast with new-made ale.

You said: It is a heavenly chance that we meet.
With a single breath we drank ten pots of wine.
I am not drunk, even though I have drunk all this wine.
I commend you for your courteous friendship.
Tomorrow there will be mountains between us,
Nor you nor I knows what will come.

HEAVY TAXES by Po Chu-yi[22]

Yesterday I went to the yamen to pay my taxes,
And peeped through the store-house gates.
The cloth and silk were piled as high as hills,
And gauzes and cotton mounted up like clouds.
They were fine tributes
To be offered to the sovereign,
But they were really the warmth stripped from my back
To buy them temporal favours,
That they might enter the golden royal house
And become dust through the ages.

SONG OF A MODEST WOMAN by Chang Chi[23]

My lord, you know that I am married and have a husband,
Yet you still give me this pair of crystal pearls.
I am moved by your lingering passion;
I conceal the pearls in my coat of red silk.
There in the high towers adjoining the palace,
My husband holds the gold sword of a king's guard;
I know your heart shines like the sun and moon,
But you must know that I have sworn constancy whether I live or die.
I return your crystal pearls, while tears fall from my eyes,
Regretting that we did not meet when I was unmarried.

A LETTER HOME by Li Shang-yin[24]

You ask when I shall return; there is no knowing.
Night rain on Pa-shan floods the autumn pools.
Some day we shall trim the wick beneath the west window.
I'll tell you what it was like—Pa-shan—the night rain falling.

ON RETURNING TO PENG-CHEN by Han Yu

An expedition is being staged again,
When will there be peace!
Who is the planner of this policy—
    Is he not making a wrong move?

Two years ago there was drought
In Kuan-chung. Many people died of starvation;
Last year, there was flood
In Tung-chuen, again many people were drowned.

CHAPTER VIII

The Prose of the Tang and Sung Dynasties

1. THE EVOLUTION OF PROSE

THE prose of the Han Dynasty was noted for its clarity and unornamented style. Toward the end of that dynasty, however, when the
country was thrown into a turmoil by natural calamities and continual
wars, literature acquired the artifices which perhaps reflected the frustration of the writers and the times. The tendency towards balanced and
parallel construction of sentences became very noticeable. Later, Lu
Chi's *Wen Fu* (*On Literature*) and Tao Chien's *Feelings at Leisure
Moments* were to consist entirely of such sentence constructions. In the
Northern-Southern Dynasties the growth of Buddhism and establishment of the Theory of Four Tones also contributed to bring about a
new style of prose. In *The History of the Southern Dynasties* it was
recorded that 'Shen Yueh, Hsieh Tiao, Wang Yung and others used
kung and *shang* and the four tones as rhymes. They said that there were
four pitfalls in using the Theory of Four Tones which must be avoided,
so that in a line of five words every word should be of different tone,
and in two lines *chiao* and *cheng* should not be the same. This rule must
not be changed. This prose style was called the Yung Ming Style.' Also
in the same book Shen Yueh was quoted as saying that 'One must
make *kung* and *yu*[1] interchangeable and mix high tones with low ones.
In a line, no word should be of the same tone, and the arrangement of
words of sharp and soft tones in two sentences should be different. Only
when this is clearly understood may one start to talk about writing.'

This emphasis on tonal harmony and rhyming, coupled with the
trend toward balanced and parallel sentence construction in given lines,
and the use of classical allusions, came to be called *pien-ti wen*. With all

its requirements, it was highly artificial and restricted the free flow of thought. But in order to pursue beauty of form writers were willing to sacrifice content in their writing.

Chung Yung, in his *Shih Pin* (*Criteria of Poetry*), wrote about this, saying that over-restriction in literary compositions injured the natural beauty of thought. Although Liu Hsieh in his *Wen Hsin Tiao Lung* (*Carved Dragon of the Literary Mind*) accepted the function of tonal harmony in writing, he also stressed that beauty of form should not be achieved at the expense of content. But the popularity of the literary style of *pien-ti wen* was not to be stopped by these two great critics. In the end, as Lee O was to put it, 'numerous compositions were written which dealt only with the phenomenon of the rising of the moon. The pieces piled on top of the writers' desks and filled their bookcases, and were nothing but descriptions of the wind and the cloud.'[2]

Nevertheless, the greater consciousness of beauty of form in creative writing brought into sharp focus the difference between literature and other kinds of writing, such as philosophical, moral and historical, which had heretofore been lumped together and considered to be a part of literature. It is true that literary commentaries existed before the Northern-Southern Dynasties, such as Wang Yi's *Comments on Tsu Tse*, Wang Chung's *Lun Heng*, Tsao Pi's *Tien Lun Lun Wen*, Lu Chi's *On Literature*, but these were piecemeal commentaries on some of the aspects of literature. It was in the Northern-Southern Dynasties that 'literature' as such was defined and the difference between it and other kinds of writing became more definitely established. Liu Hsieh said, 'It has often been said that there are two kinds of writing, namely *wen* and *pi*, meaning that the writing which pays no attention to rhyming is *pi* while that which is rhymed is *wen*. Actually, the latter is that which expresses the opinion of the author—it should take into account the ideas contained in the *Book of Poetry* and the *Book of History*. The separation of *wen* from *pi* is a recent innovation.'[3] Emperor Yuan of the Liang Dynasty was more explicit: '*Wen* must have beautiful and pleasing wording and phrases, melodious tones and emotional power.'[4] This clear and definite understanding of the nature of literature, although somewhat biased, led for a time to the prevalence of *wen*, or pure literature, over *pi*, or practical writing. For the first time in Chinese history, the writings of Confucius, Laotse, etc., were not considered strictly as 'literature' any longer, and were not included in Prince Chao Ming's *Selected Literary Masterpieces*.

Out of the better understanding of the separate identity of literature
there also sprang books on literary criticism. The two most famous are
Liu Hsieh's *Carved Dragon of the Literary Mind* and Chung Yung's
Criteria of Poetry. Liu stated in his book that content and form in literature were both important, and that single-minded pursuit of formal
beauty could prove to be harmful. While a few literary critics thought
that it was solely the talent of the author which decided the development of various types of literature, Liu was the first to point out that,
although talent was important, it was principally social and natural environment which influenced the development and achievement of an
author. He was also the first to say that literary critics must equip themselves first with scholarship and an objective attitude before they could
criticize the work of others fairly. He further suggested that in evalu-
ating a literary work, the standard of style, rhetoric, originality, point
of view, content and tones might serve as the criteria of judgment.

Chung Yung listed more than one hundred poets from the Han
Dynasty to the Chi and Liang Dynasties, and divided them into three
categories. He also traced the influence on them of other poets, and
gave *feng* poems, *little ya* poems, two kinds of poems in the *Book of
Poetry*, and *tsu tse* as the three sources from which came the five-word
poems. His ideas on the writing of poetry can be summed up as
follows: poems must be natural and avoid using allusions; natural and
simple rhythms and tonal harmony are what poets should strive for;
over-emphasis on the rules of tonal values can be harmful; poems
should not be used to explain philosophical ideas to the detriment of
poetic standards; poetry must be closely related to the times, and the
personal experience of the poet.

These ideas may seem to be common sense. But as the Theory of
Four Tones and its resultant requirements were like colours given to
children who had previously only been playing with pencils, poets of
the day were like so many children infatuated with the possibilities, and
did not listen to the critics' advice. Moreover, the emperors of the
Southern Dynasties were all lovers of literature, and many of them
took a fancy to this form of composition. Perhaps, too, in the absence
of something more worth while to capture their attention in the political
chaos of the period, writers found an outlet in the pursuit of the exotic.

When China was reunited under Emperor Wen of the Sui Dynasty,
the popularity of *pien-ti wen* declined. Emperor Wen even went so far
as to punish a governor simply because his memorandum was written

in the style of *pien-ti wen*. Lee O, a censor, in a memorandum to the Emperor urging him to issue a decree forbidding the writing of *pien-ti wen*, blamed this literary form for the chaotic situation of the country during the Northern-Southern Dynasties, and reasserted the importance of Confucianism in helping the government to rule the country. He said, 'It has been said that the ancient sage-kings always controlled what the people saw and heard, tempered their urges and desires, controlled their improper inclinations and showed them the way of moderation and harmony.' He went on to say that:

The *Book of Poetry*, *Book of History*, *Book of Rites* and *Book of Changes* were what taught the people to be moral and just. Thus, in every family filial piety and kindness reigned. The relationship between father and son was correct and throughout the country everyone behaved with propriety and restraint. This was the cardinal rule in ordering the lives of the people. . . . In later dynasties, the customs and educational standards of the people deteriorated. The first three emperors of the Wei Dynasty loved literature, ignored the principles of government and indulged in the pursuit of petty techniques of writing. This created the vogue for writing flowery pieces. Down to the Chi and Liang Dynasties the situation worsened. The people, irrespective of their rank and wealth, devoted their time to studying and writing poems and other literary works. They became irreverent about the great teachings of the past, partial to the strange and exotic theories and looked for what was euphuistic and insignificant. They tried to outdo each other in the search for a clever rhyme or a single clever word, and their compositions had to do with only the rising of the moon and the weather. . . . The people judged each other and the government selected civil servants by their ability to write this type of composition. Encouraged by the reward of official positions, the people further abandoned themselves to this pursuit. . . . They forgot the rules and models set up by the great sages and thought that what was useless was useful. The result was that the more they dwelt on the intricacies of flowery writing, the more chaotic the country became.[5]

But Emperor Wen's efforts proved futile. Even famous works of the Tang Dynasty, such as Wang Po's *Teng Wang Ko Hsu* (*The Teng Wang Pavilion*), Lo-pin Wang's *Tou Wu Chao Hsi* (*Declaration against Wu*

Chao) and the writings of Chang Shuo and Su Ting, the two most famous writers of Emperor Hsuan Tsung's reign, were all in the style of *pien-ti wen*. At the same time many writers, including Chen Tse-ang, Hsiao Ying-shih, Liang Shu, Tuku Chi, Li Hua and Liu Mien, came out against *pien-ti wen* and wanted to revert to the prose style of the Han Dynasty or even earlier periods. Liu Mien particularly emphasized Confucianism as the guide and standard for literature. In his opinion, 'literary works should be based on the teachings of olden times, for the trends of literature decidedly influence the order of society and the customs of the people. . . . Since Chu Yuan and Sung Yu's time, literary writers have laid stress solely on what was strange and transient and ignored their social responsibilities. This was at variance with the practice of earlier writers. Therefore, although literary works might possess the descriptive power of the writing of Yang Hsiung and Szema Hsiang-ju, the vigour of that of Tsao Chih and Liu Cheng and the beauty and flowery phrases of that of Pan Yueh and Lu Chi, they serve no practical purpose and are only excellent in craftsmanship. No true person would care to engage in such pursuits.' He also said, 'After the reigns of Kings Chen and Kang of the Chou Dynasty, *sung* poems were no longer composed, and poets wrote of their emotions in exaggerated terms. The function of literature and education became divorced. Those not equipped with sufficient scholarship would not know how to express the moral principle in their writing, while others who understood the meaning of moral principles disdained expressing them. It was seldom that people who were blessed with the understanding of moral principles also had the literary talent to express themselves.' He further said that, 'In order to change the literary style of *pien-ti wen*, the social custom must first be changed. For the decadence in literature and social custom spring from the same cause. To change social custom it is necessary to change the ideas of the people, so that they would adopt a new code of behaviour without actually being conscious of it. The only way to accomplish this is to respect and elevate the status of Confucian classics and to demote that of literary writers.'[6] In short, Liu Mien contended that literary work had no intrinsic value, but must be based on the Confucian orthodoxy. This theory was later adopted by Han Yu in his effort to reform the prose style. Han Yu called the new prose style which he and his supporters tried to create *ku wen*, or classical prose, because he claimed that it was based on the prose of the Han Dynasty and earlier periods, although what they aimed at was a lucid, unornamented and crisp prose, suitable for discursive, narrative and descriptive purposes. Their concerted efforts came to be known as the Classical Prose Movement.

If we take the emphasis on *wen* or the separate identity of literature in the Northern-Southern Dynasties as a reaction against the situation in the previous periods when literary and practical works (*wen* and *pi*) were considered to be one and the same kind of writing, then Han Yu's assertion that Confucian principles should be the basis for literary writing may be considered as the synthesis of the previous two phases of the development of the idea of literature. Thus, the significance of the Classical Prose Movement does not lie in creating a new prose style alone. It represented, in the eyes of Confucian scholars, an advancement of the literary theory. But literature was reduced to a secondary position, and the *literati* tended to treat their creative work, especially novels, short stories and dramas, deprecatingly. In spite of this, it must be pointed out that the Classical Prose Movement in shedding the restrictions *pien-ti wen* imposed on the writing of prose, helped to bring about the flourishing of the short stories of the Tang Dynasty (*chuan chi hsiao shuo*).

Su Tung-po, the great poet of the Sung Dynasty, speaking about the achievements of Han Yu, talked of his great contribution in 'saving prose from the decadence of the previous eight dynasties'. It is understandable that Su, an admirer of Han, should have praised him so highly. However, there were in fact some good lyrical pieces written in the Northern-Southern Dynasties even when *pien-ti wen* was in great vogue. To this day, *pien-ti wen* is not entirely dead. On formal occasions, some messages of greeting are still written in this style.

Here I quote *At the Orchid Pavilion* by Wang Hsi-chih (321–379), which although not strictly of the style of *pien-ti wen* has the parallel sentence construction, and is considered one of the best pieces of lyrical prose.

This is the Ninth Year of Yungho [A.D. 353], *kueichou* in the cycle. We met in late spring at the Orchid Pavilion in Shanyin to celebrate the Water Festival.

All the scholar friends are gathered, and there is a goodly mixture of old and young. In the background lie high peaks and deep forests, while a clear, gurgling brook catches the light to the right and to the left. We then arrange ourselves, sitting on its bank, drinking in succession from the goblet as it floats down the stream. No music is provided, but with drinking and with song, our hearts are gay and at ease. It is a clear spring day with a mild, caressing breeze. The vast universe, throbbing with life, lies spread before us, entertaining the eye and pleasing the spirit and all the senses. It is perfect.

Now when men come together, they let their thoughts travel to the past and the present. Some enjoy a quiet conversation indoors and others play about outdoors, occupied with what they love. The forms of amusement differ according to temperaments, but when each has found what he wants he is happy and never feels old. Then as time passes on and one is tired of his pursuits, it seems that what fascinated him not so long ago has become a mere memory. What a thought! Besides, whether individually we live a long life or not, we all return to nothingness. The ancients regarded death as the great question. Is it not sad to think of it?

I often thought that the people of the past lived and felt exactly as we of today. Whenever I read their writings I felt this way and was seized with its pathos. It is small comfort to say that life and death are different phases of the same thing and that a long span of life or a short one does not matter. Alas! The people of the future will look upon us as we look upon those who have gone before us. Hence I have recorded here those present and what they said. Ages may pass and times may change, but the human sentiments will be the same. I know that future readers who set their eyes upon these words will be affected in the same way.[7]

2. *THE LIFE OF HAN YU*

The greatest achievement of Han Yu (768–824) was the part he played in creating the classical prose style. He was the leader of a group of poets who, after Tu Fu's death, carried on his work of searching for perfection of poetic form. But his fame in leading the reform of the prose style overshadowed his fame as a poet. Su Tung-po, in his *Memorial of Han Yu* for inscription on a tablet in his Memorial Temple in Chao-chow, wrote: 'For an individual to be the teacher of future generations and to have what he says followed by all the people in the country, he must be one who understands the reasons for the changes of heaven and earth. . . . After the East Han Dynasty, Tao was ignored and literature deteriorated. Even in Cheng Kuan and Kai Yuan, these two great periods of the Tang Dynasty, this situation was not corrected. But Han Yu was able easily to bring about a change, and everyone in the country followed him. Tao (moral principles) and literature thus regained their former exalted status and health. . . . Wasn't Han Yu the one person who understood the reasons for the changes of heaven and earth?'

But in spite of what Su said, it was not easy for Han Yu to start the Classical Prose Movement. Lee Han in his preface to *The Collected Works of Master Chang Li* (Han Yu's literary name) said, 'People were at first surprised by his new style and then ridiculed and attacked him. But he only became more confident. In the end people changed their minds and followed his example.'

There is no doubt that Han Yu was a self-confident man. In his letter to Feng Hsu about his writing, he said that what he himself liked in his writings seemed exactly the opposite of the taste of other people, but although 'I don't know what value writing in the classical style can have at present, I am willing to wait for those who understand. When Yang Hsiung wrote his *Tai Hsien* almost everybody laughed at him. But his words were, "It doesn't matter if the whole world doesn't know me. But if there is going to be another Yang Hsiung in future generations, he will love it." '

He did not care what other people thought of his writing, but the success of the movement was due more to his ability to win over and influence people than his undoubtedly great talent. In the *Old History of the Tang Dynasty*, it is said that 'Han Yu was loyal to his friends and his friendship was not dependent on what official positions his friends held. When he was young he befriended Meng Chiao and Chang Chi, who were then unknown and held no official position. Whenever he had a chance Han Yu would recommend them to the ministers he met. . . . Han Yu was also willing to help and encourage young men, many of whom stayed with him. There were times when he was without food for breakfast because of it, but he did not mind.' And in *Chuan Tang Shih Hua* (*Miscellaneous Jottings about Poets and Poetry of the Tang Dynasty*) it is recorded that when Han Yu first met and was impressed by Chia Tao's talent, he persuaded the latter, who was then a Buddhist monk some thirty years of age, to give up his faith and take the National Civil Service Examination. Chia Tao became a *chin-shih*, or scholar of the first rank. Judging from these two quotations it seems that Han Yu was a warm-hearted person who was always willing to help and encourage his friends. His ability to persuade Chia Tao to give up his faith is an amazing testimonial to his eloquence which, no doubt, he put to good use, especially when he talked to his students at the Royal Academy of Literature, where he was several times a teacher, about the necessity of prose reform.

There was another aspect of his attitude towards his friends which made him a leader of men. Once when someone asked Han Yu about the methods of writing in the classical style, he replied by saying that it would be best for him to ask Liu Tsung-yuan (773–819), whose prose was the best among Han's supporters. The man sent Han Yu's letter to Liu and sought his advice. Liu said in reply, 'Han Yu's ability is several times that of mine. . . . He likes to praise the ability of others, but he is too modest. He thinks that he must hide from others his talent before he can praise them.' In view of the fact that Han Yu thought not a little of his own gifts to be able to recommend others was a rare quality.

Han Yu passed the National Civil Service Examination in Chang-an when he was twenty-five years old, but was not appointed to any official post. In the subsequent three or four years his friends were Hsiao Tsun and Li Kuan, the son and nephew of Hsiao Ying-shih and Li Hua, who were both known for their opposition to *pien-ti wen*. He also became the follower of Tuku Chi and Liang Shu, two other scholars who did not like the restrictions which this form of writing imposed upon the writer. Apparently it was during this period that Han Yu became convinced of the necessity of reforming the style of prose. But as he said in connection with the problem of learning to write good prose in the classical style, 'One must continue to cultivate oneself, to follow the path of kindness and justice [Confucianism] and immerse oneself in the *Book of Poetry* and the *Book of History* before one can hope to write good prose.' He also said that 'The whole purpose of learning to master the techniques of the writing of the ancients is to know the teachings of olden times.'[8] In other words, he felt that the purpose of reforming the prose style was the better to propound Confucianism. This was his cause. With this end in view, Han Yu was able to launch the Classical Prose Movement and make it a success.

Han Yu's faith in Confucianism extended further than the literary movement. When he was the Vice-Minister of the Ministry of Justice, he wrote *On the Origin of Tao*, in which he went so far as to say that Taoist priests and Buddhist monks should be ordered to give up their faiths, that Taoist classics and Buddhist sutras should be burned, and that the temples of these two religions should be used to give shelter to the common people. This strong belief in Confucianism nearly led to his death. In 819, Emperor Hsuan Tsung, on hearing that a finger joint of the Buddha was kept in a tower in Fa Ming Temple in Feng-hsing, sent an emissary to have the relic brought to the palace for three days. When this was done all the people in the capital, from the princes down, crowded the streets to get a glimpse of the relic, causing near-riots. Han Yu was greatly disturbed and wrote a memorial to the Emperor, saying that Buddhism was but one of the ways of the barbarians and that if the Emperor did not do something to correct the idea that he believed in Buddhism, then the morals and customs of the people would be damaged. This was utterly naïve of him, for, after all, it was the Emperor who had had the relic brought to the palace. The Emperor was furious and ordered that Han Yu be executed. Luckily for him Fei Tu, under whom Han Yu had served when he was putting down a rebellion in Huai Si,[9] was then the Prime Minister. Fei spoke up for him, and with the help of other ministers persuaded the Emperor to change his mind. Han Yu was demoted to be Governor of Chao-chow, a district in the present Kwangtung Province, which was then considered to be an outlandish place.

Han Yu's character was complex. Although heretofore he had always lived up to the Confucian code of behaviour, upon his arrival at Chao-chow, he wrote to the Emperor a memorial of fulsome praise in an effort to get himself moved from Chao-chow. In his petition he thanked the Emperor for his kindness, and urged him to have special musical scores composed and to hold sacrificial rites on the summit of Tai Mountain and report to the gods the accomplishments of his reign. This was tantamount to saying that the Emperor was one of the truly great ones, for only great emperors could take these steps. In April 819, less than two months after his arrival in Chao-chow, he wrote *A Warning to Alligators*, ostensibly to chase away alligators which had been damaging crops and devouring pigs and cattle in the district. In it he did not forget to praise the Emperor once again. It was alleged that after he dropped his composition, together with a lamb and a pig, into the river as his offerings, the alligators moved sixty *li* away to the sea. Whatever effect this might have had, in October of the same year, Han Yu found himself transferred as Governor to Yuan-chow in Kiangsi Province. There he again sent a memorial to the Emperor, saying that there had appeared in the sky north-west of Yuan-chow dazzling multi-coloured clouds, which were an omen of peace in the country. This seemed rather unnecessary and proved to be untrue, for the following year Emperor Hsuan Tsung was killed by some eunuchs and Emperor Mu Tsang ascended the throne. In September, Han Yu was recalled to the capital and appointed Chancellor of the Royal Academy of Literature. Altogether he was in banishment for about a year and a half.

Some scholars think that Han Yu abased himself during this period. But perhaps his behaviour may be explained by modern psychological methods. His ability to look out for himself—if it was that—may have had its roots in his childhood. For Han Yu was orphaned when he was three years old, his three elder brothers died during his childhood, and he was brought up by one of his sisters-in-law. When his sister-in-law died, he mourned her for one year, a mourning period second only in length to that required to mourn one's parent. His childhood playmate and nephew, Shih Erh Lang, also died young. This might have hardened his attitude to the world. In any case, his behaviour at this time was considered distasteful by scholars. In all fairness to him, we must remember that the demotion was the greatest setback in Han Yu's official career, and he was then fifty-one years of age. Unwilling to sink into oblivion, he did everything he could to win the Emperor's favour again.

When he arrived back in the capital he was welcomed at the Academy. The following year he was promoted to be Vice-Minister in the Ministry of War. In the same year Wang Ting-chow, military Governor of Cheng-chow, the present Cheng-ting District in Hopei Province, rebelled against the Emperor. After a military campaign failed to put down the rebellion the Emperor somehow thought Han Yu could pacify the rebels. He was sent to Cheng-chow but orders soon followed that he was, for safety's sake, to stop at the border and check the situation before entering the area. At this juncture Han Yu seemed to recover from the moral torpor of his banishment, and wrote back to the Emperor, 'Ordering me to stop shows Your Majesty's kindness, but my duty is to die if necessary. I cannot consider my own safety in carrying out Your Majesty's orders!' He went into Cheng-chow and managed to persuade Wang Ting-chow to surrender. Upon his return to the capital he was promoted to be Vice-Minister of the Ministry of Examinations and Appointments. This post he held, with only a short break in 823, until he died early in the winter of 824 at the age of fifty-six.

3. THE CLASSICAL PROSE MOVEMENT

The Classical Prose Movement, which aimed at creating a clear, un-ornamented prose style as the vehicle of Tao, flourished under the dynamic leadership of Han Yu. He attracted and won the support of Liu Tsung-yuan, and many other scholars, and they continuously experimented and improved the new prose style he advocated. Han Yu even wrote the *Biography of Mr Brush*, a short story. Short story writers in adopting the classical prose style were all, consciously or not, supporters of Han Yu. But even in Han Yu's time, Fan Tsung-shih's prose was so involved in construction that it was difficult to read and understand. With the passing of Han Yu and Liu Tsung-yuan, some of their followers took to writing 'difficult prose', which was extremely hard to decipher, let alone understand. The result was that *pien-ti wen* was revived in the late Tang Dynasty and became prevalent in the early Sung Dynasty under the leadership of Yang Yi (994–1020) and others. But with the peace and prosperity brought by the new dynasty Confucianism again gained importance in the minds of some other scholars, among them Mu Hsiu (979–1032) and Shih Chieh (1005–1045). They all re-emphasized the ideas of Han Yu, principally that literature should be the vehicle for the propagation of Confucian teachings, and even compared Han Yu himself to Confucius. But even Mu Hsiu mentioned that at that time 'one who dares to talk about classical prose is treated as though he were talking nonsense. All the others attack him, scandalize him and deal with him as if he were a stupid fool who would not follow the fashion for fame and didn't know how to go after wealth and rank. None of his seniors would praise him, nor would any of his generation support him. If he did not believe in himself and had no strong will-power or great confidence in what he was doing, he would lose hope and doubt himself. He would also repent and change his mind. And then he would surely change his prose style to follow that of others.'[10]

But things gradually changed. Ouyang Hsiu (1007–1072) said:

When I was a child I obtained a copy of the *Complete Works of*

Master Chang Li of the Tang Dynasty. . . . At that time the prose style of Yang Yi and Liu Yun, which was called contemporary style, was in vogue. Every scholar tried to master that style. For only essays written in contemporary style were considered suitable for Civil Service examinations, and were capable of securing fame and position for the writers. No one paid any attention to the writing of Han Yu. . . . When I was seventeen I took part in an examination held in my native county and failed. I thus had a chance to re-read Han Yu's writing and I thought, 'This is the best style one can ever hope to write.' . . . Seven years later, having passed the final Civil Service examination, I became a *chin shih* and was appointed an official in Loyang. I met Yun Shih-lu (1001–1046) and others there, and we started writing in the style of classical prose. I took out my copy of the *Complete Works of Master Chang Li* and consulted other editions of this work to fill in what had been left out in this edition, and to correct any errors in it. Later on, scholars in the country gradually came to study classical prose, and Han Yu's writing was accepted in the entire country. This happened some thirty years ago. Nowadays, everyone studies the writing style of Han Yu. It is indeed a great phenomenon.[11]

From this it can be seen that the second and final phase of the Classical Prose Movement was launched by Ouyang Hsiu and completed in his lifetime. And it was only natural that Su Tung-po should compare him to Han Yu. For it was after the joint efforts of Ouyang Hsiu and his disciples in pushing through this reform of the prose-style that the style of classical prose was completely and firmly established as the model of Chinese style for the next nine centuries. In the Literary Revolution of 1919 this prose style came to be called *wen yen* or literary Chinese, as opposed to spoken or vernacular Chinese, which the leaders of the Revolution advocated. Since then classical prose as a style of writing has gradually been replaced by vernacular Chinese, or *pai hua wen*, although it is still being written.

Needless to say, in his effort to popularize classical prose Ouyang Hsiu received strong support from famous scholars—almost all his disciples—of his time, notably Su Shun, Su Tung-po, Su Cheh, Wang An-shih and Tseng Kung. In the Ming Dynasty, Mao Kun (1512–1601) collected the prose of these six scholars and that of Han Yu and Liu Tsung-yuan in a book called *The Masterpieces of Eight Prose Masters of the Tang and Sung Dynasties.* Ever since then these eight have been known as the 'Prose Masters of the Tang and Sung Dynasties'.

Here are Han Yu's *Prayer to Shih Erh Lang* and the first part of Su Tung-po's *Red Cliff Fu.*

PRAYER TO SHIH ERH LANG by Han Yu

On the twenty-sixth day of the fifth month of the nineteenth year of Cheng Yuan [803], seven days after learning of your death, Yu, your uncle, is able to restrain his grief long enough to send you sacrificial foods in season by Chien-chung, and to say a prayer for you, Shih Erh Lang.

Alas! I was orphaned when I was a small boy. I never knew my father, and depended entirely on my elder brother and sister-in-law, Huei and Cheng. A few years later, Huei died in the south, and you and I were still children. We followed Cheng back to Hoyang to bury Huei and then went to live in Kiangnan. We were then both fatherless, and in common difficulty lived together and never parted even for a day. I had three elder brothers but they all died before their time, so that to carry on the family line there was only you in your generation and me in mine. Cheng, with her arms around you, said, pointing to me, 'You are what's left of the two generations of the Han family!' You were younger than I was, and would not have remembered it. And although I remember it, I did not realize then how sad her words were.

I came to the capital when I was nineteen and visited you four years later. Another four years passed before I went to Hoyang to see to the family cemetery and met you bringing the remains of your mother to be buried there. Two years later, when I was assistant to Governor Tung in Pienchow, you came to visit me, and stayed with me for a year before you left for home, intending to bring your family back to live in Pienchow with me. But the next year the Governor passed away, and I left Pienchow and you could not come. When I became assistant to the Military Governor in Hsuchow the same year I sent for you, but no sooner had the bearer of the invitation left than I was relieved of my post. Again, you could not come to me. I then thought that even if you had come east you would still be living away from our home town and this could not go on forever. To find a permanent solution you had to go back to the west. I was thinking of building a house in Hoyang and sending for you. Alas! How was I to know that you would die suddenly and leave me!

You and I were still young. I thought that although we were separated temporarily from one another, we would have plenty of time to be together later. That was why I left you to come to the capital to find an official position with a monthly salary of a few *tou* of rice. Had I known what was to happen, even if I were offered the position of a Prime Minister or Duke, I would not have left. Last year, when Meng Tung-yeh went to Li-yang, I asked him to take a letter to you in which I said, 'I am not yet forty years old, but my vision has become blurred and my hair grey, and some of my teeth are shaky. Remembering that my father and elder brothers, although strong and healthy, died before their time, I am not sure how long I will live. I cannot come to you and you will not come to me. I am afraid that should something happen to me, you will be seized with great sorrow.' How could I know that it would be you, the younger of the two of us, who would die first!

Alas! Could your death be true? Is this but a dream? Could there be a mistake in the message I received? If you are really dead, then my elder brother, in spite of his great virtue, is now without an heir, and in spite of the purity of your heart, the brightness of your mind, you have not benefited from your heritage. That the young and strong should die and the old and weak should remain alive cannot be true! All this must be a dream! There must have been a mistake! But how is it that Tung-yeh's letter and Kan-lang's message are by my side? Alas! It is true that you have died! My elder brother, despite his great virtue, has lost his heir and you, his worthy and deserving son, who should have made his family prosperous, have not benefited from his great virtue. What is the way of Heaven? What is the will of God? And what is the reason of human life? And fate?

What do I care? Since this year, my grey hair has turned white, and some of my shaky teeth have fallen. My health is becoming worse, and my spirit weakens. Why should I not follow you and die? If, after death, one is still capable of knowing, then we shall be seeing each other, and you and I will not have parted for long. But if one perishes with death, then I shall not be mourning you for long, but shall take my grief to the grave with me. Your son is only ten years old, and mine, five. To think that the young and strong should have perished . . . can one expect the boys to live to be grown-ups? Alas! My grief is such! Alas! Such is my grief!

Last year you wrote me saying that you had contracted beri-beri and were sometimes greatly bothered by it. I replied saying that many people in Kiangnan were often sick with this disease and that it was nothing to worry about. Alas! Did you die of it, or of some other disease? Your last letter was dated the seventeenth day of the sixth month. But Tung-yeh said you died on the second of the sixth month, and Kan-lang in his message did not mention which day you died. Tung-yeh's servant did not ask the date, just as Kan-lang did not know that he should mention it in his message, so that when Tung-yeh in writing his letter to me asked about it, his servant simply mentioned any date which came to his mind. This must be what happened.

I have now asked Chien-chung to pay my respects to you on my behalf and to console and comfort your son and your wet nurse. If they have enough to support themselves until the required mourning period is over, Chien-chung will wait, and bring them over to me at that time. Otherwise, he will bring them over immediately. The other servants are asked to remain until the mourning period is over and then they will be free to do as they wish. If I can manage it, I will bring your remains back to Hoyang and rebury them in our family cemetery.

Alas! I did not know when you were fatally ill or the date you died. When you were alive, I could not have you come to live with me and support you. When you were dying, I was not there to comfort you. When you were embalmed, I was not by your coffin, and when you were buried, I was absent from your grave. I have conducted myself against the will of God so as to cause your untimely death! And I have been unfilial (to the memory of my parents) and unkind to you so that we could not help each other in our lifetime, or accompany each other in death. When you were alive, your shadow was not beside me, and when you died, your spirit did not enter my dreams. All this is my fault. How can I blame anyone for it? Only my grief is like the sky, limitless and endless! From now on, I shall have no aspirations in this world. I shall seek a few plots of land by the Yi Yin River and spend the rest of my life there. I want only to teach your son and mine, hoping that they will grow up safely, and see that your daughter and mine are married. Alas! I run out of words, but my grief has no end. Do you realize this, or can you not realize this? Alas! My grief is such!

RED CLIFF FU (first part) by Su Tung-po

One evening in the second half of the seventh month in the year Jen-hsu [1081], I went boating with a friend to the Red Cliff. A gentle breeze came softly up the river, hardly ruffling the surface of the water. I invited my friend to drinks, and humming the melody of the song *Bright Moon*, we were moved to singing the lyrics of *The Elegant Maiden*, part of the song. After a while, the moon rose over the eastern hills and loitered between the Dipper and the Cowherd. Over the river, a white mist had fallen, linking and merging into one the glittering river and the moonlit sky. In a small boat, we glided over the great expanse of the moonlit misty whiteness. It was as if we were up in the air and carried by the wind, without knowing where we were going. But we felt free as if we had left the world behind, and become immortals. We drank some more wine and were quite happy. Beating time on the side of the boat, I sang:

> Oars of cassia and sculls of the fragrant Lan
> Strike at the gleaming surface,
> Follow the stream of light;
> My heart wanders in the gloaming,
> Thinking of the Fair One far away.

My friend was a good flute player. He tried to accompany the words with his flute. The melody was strange and sad, evoking longing and regret, soft and plaintive with diminuendos that seemed to linger and then softly disappear into the thin air. It was so sad that a widow in a lone boat began to weep, and even the great fish hiding deep down in the waters must have been moved.

I was overcome by the music. 'Why is it so sad?' I asked.

> 'The moon is bright and stars are few
> Southward the ravens wing their flight.'

'You know these lines were written by Tsao Meng-teh,' he said.

'And on this stretch of river, west toward Hsia-kou and east to Wu-chang, where the verdant hills seem entwined with the river—was it not there that Meng-teh was defeated by Chou Yu? When Tsao Meng-teh captured Chingchow, took Kiangling by storm and sailed down the river eastward, his warships stretched stem to stern for a thousand *li* and the flags and banners of his great fleet filled the wide sky. He stood facing the river and poured himself a few cups of new wine, and sat across a long spear to write poems. He was really a hero of his generation, but where is he today?

'Tonight, you and I are carefree as two fishermen or woodcutters who happen to come to the river, with only fishes and shrimps in the river and deer in the woods for companions. We are sitting in a tiny boat, enjoying a short and happy moment over a cup of wine. We are but short-lived ephemerides in the everlasting universe and grains of corn in the vast ocean. Regretting the evanescence of my life, I envy the timeless flow of this great river. How I long to fly up to heaven, supported by two angels, and ascend to the moon to live forever there! But I know that this can never be. I therefore have expressed my sorrow with the sad melody.'

'Look at this water and this moon,' I said. 'The water flows continuously by, and yet it is always here. The moon waxes and wanes, but it always remains the same. If you look at the changes that take place in the universe, there is nothing in it that lasts more than a fraction of a second. But if you look at the unchanging aspects of things, then you realize that both things and ourselves are immortal. Why should you envy this river? Besides, everything in this life has its proper owner; there is no use trying to take what does not properly belong to us. But this clear breeze over the river and the bright moon over the mountain tops are the sounds and sights to be enjoyed by everyone, free and eternal. They are the boundless treasures of the Creator and what you and I can both enjoy.'

Upon hearing this, my friend smiled. We washed the cups and filled them with wine again. When we had finished eating we stretched ourselves out and fell asleep, without clearing the dishes away, unaware that dawn was breaking in the east.

CHAPTER IX

Short Stories of the Tang Dynasty

1. 'SMALL TALK'

ONE of the most striking features in the development of Chinese literature is that for more than two thousand years from the reign of King Pan Keng of the Yin Dynasty, or the beginning of recorded Chinese history, up to about the end of the eighth century A.D., there was no fiction in the sense we know it today. There was hardly even any mythology. For the stories to be found in *Shan Hai Ching* (*Book of Hills and Seas*), in *Huainantse, Liehtse, Mu Tientse Chuan*, etc., which had apparently been edited and rewritten by scholars of later dynasties, are only fragmentary sketches of myths and are short and bald in style. The following is one such story from *Huainantse*:

> In ancient times, Kung Kung (God of Water) contended with Chuan Hsu (God of Fire) for supremacy. In a rage, Kung Kung crushed Puchou Mountain, breaking the pillars of the sky and the foundation of earth. The sky tilted north-westward and the sun, moon, stars and planets were shifted towards that direction. There was a gap in the south-east of the earth, and flood water and dust gathered there.

Nevertheless, the heroes in these stories acquired human characteristics as time wore on, or human beings were endowed with god-like powers. In the section entitled 'Southern Regions of the Great Wilderness' in the *Book of Hills and Seas*, for instance, it is said that 'Hsi Ho was the wife of Emperor Tsun who gave birth to ten suns'. In another piece in the same book called 'The Western Region within the Seas' it is said that 'within the seas, there was Kunlun Mountain. It was the lower capital of God and the home of the deities. Only Yi could climb up to the summit of it.' In *Huainantse*, these two short pieces of mythology were combined to become the myth-history of Emperor Yao's time:

In the time of Emperor Yao, there were ten suns in the sky, scorching crops and destroying plants and trees. The people had nothing to eat, and wolves, buzzards, wild boars, huge serpents and other monsters preyed on them. Yao ordered Yi . . . to shoot down the ten suns and kill the wolves, cut into half the huge serpents in Tungting and capture the wild boars in Shanglin. All the people rejoiced and made Yao their Emperor.

Elsewhere in the book Yi was described as a god-like person. It is said that he was given an elixir by the 'Queen Mother of the West', who ruled over Kunlun Mountain, but Chang O, Yi's wife, found out and stole the elixir from him. After swallowing it, she ascended to the moon and became the Goddess of the Moon.

And yet, in Chu Yuan's *Tsu Tse*, Yi is again presented as a nobleman who revolted against King Tai Kang of the Shang Dynasty. The late development of fiction may be due to the fact that the Chinese as a people are a down-to-earth sort, who perhaps are not as imaginative as other peoples. *Hsiao shuo*, as fiction is called in Chinese, was first referred to by Chuangtse in speaking of 'winning honour and renown by means of *hsiao shuo*', the two words meaning literally 'small talk', or talk of little consequence. Confucius did not think much of *hsiao shuo* either. 'Even though there can be remarkable achievements in this insignificant craft, there is the danger of a person becoming too engrossed in it. Therefore, a gentleman does not engage in writing such work.' This became the traditional attitude of men of letters. In the Han Dynasty, Pan Ku gave only a list of *hsiao shuo* written before his time in the 'Record of Art and Literature' in his *History of the Han Dynasty*, which he disdainfully attached to the end of his book. According to him, there were fifteen collections of *hsiao shuo* in 1,380 volumes. None of these is extant today. Judging by his comments and fragments of some of these works quoted in the *Tai Ping Imperial Encyclopaedia* edited in the Sung Dynasty, these were either works attributed to some people of earlier periods or records of historical events. But as Lu Hsun said in his *Brief History of Chinese Fiction*, they were in fact either imitations of earlier philosophers' work, or erroneous historical records. In the Han Dynasty, then, the term *hsiao shuo* did not refer even to tales or stories.

In the Wei and Chin Dynasties (220–419), China was passing through a period of wars and natural disasters. This, together with the introduction of Buddhism with its rich lore, combined to fire the imagination of writers, and a host of ghost stories and stories about the supernatural came to be written.

It is interesting to note that while deities were invariably depicted as fierce monsters in the *Book of Hills and Seas* and other ancient books, they became entirely human in the tales of this period. The Queen Mother of the West, for instance, was there described as a 'creature wearing a tiara, with tiger's teeth and leopard's tail, who inhabits a cave'. But in the *Private Life of Emperor Hu of the Han Dynasty*[1] she was described as a beautiful woman:

> The Queen Mother of the West ascended to one of the great halls and sat down facing east. In her gold coat with bright designs, she looked glowingly happy and dignified. At her waist there was a long belt and a sword, over her Tai-hua style knotted hair she had a tiara of Tai-cheng, and on her feet there were black slippers embroidered with phoenixes. She appeared to be in her thirties, of medium height, and her natural beauty, elegance and magnificence were unsurpassed. She was a true goddess!

Ghosts, too, were treated as though they were real and had human qualities. In *Lieh Yi Chuan* (*Strange Stories*) there is a story which goes like this:

> When Tsung Tingpo of Nanyang was young, he once went walking at night and met a ghost.
> 'Who is it?' he asked.
> 'A ghost,' the ghost replied. 'And you?'
> 'Me too,' Tingpo lied.
> 'Where are you going?'
> 'Wanshih town.'
> 'Me too,' said the ghost.
> They walked together for a few *li* and the ghost said, 'It's stupid

for us both to walk, when we can carry each other by turn.'

'That's a good idea,' said Tingpo.

So the ghost carriéd Tingpo on his back first. After a while, the ghost said, 'You are very heavy for a ghost. Are you really one?'

'I only died recently,' Tingpo replied. 'That is why I am somewhat heavy.'

Tingpo then carried the ghost on his back and hardly felt his weight at all. After carrying each other by turn three times, Tingpo said, 'As I have just died, could you tell me what we ghosts are afraid of most?'

'Human saliva,' replied the ghost.

When they were approaching the town, Tingpo began to carry the ghost on his back and gripped him very tight. The ghost cried and shouted and struggled to free himself, but Tingpo held him even tighter. When he came to the centre of the town he flung the ghost down on the ground, and it changed into a goat. Tingpo spat on it to prevent it from changing into something else. He then sold the goat for fifteen hundred cash.

Buddhist influence on the rise of story-telling can be seen in the collection of tales published in the Northern-Southern Dynasties. Many of these collections, such as *Yuan Hun Chi* (*Accounts of Avenging Spirits*) by Yen Chih-tui[2] and *Ming Hsiang Chi* (*Records of Mysterious Manifestations*) by Wang Yen,[3] are tales based on Buddhist lore. There is such a story in the last-named book, now collected in *Gems of Buddhist Literature*.[4]

Emperor Ming of the Han Dynasty once dreamt of a god nearly twenty feet in height, with a golden body and a halo over his head. He asked his Ministers about the meaning of the dream. Someone said, 'In the west there is a deity called Buddha, who seems to resemble the god Your Majesty dreamt about. Perhaps it was Buddha Your Majesty dreamt of.' The Emperor decided to send emissaries to India to obtain Buddhist sutras and pictures. When these were brought back and exhibited in China, everyone from the Emperor, princes and peers down to the common people paid homage to them and was surprised to learn that human spirits were immortal.

Earlier, when Tsai Ying, the emissary, returned with Kasyapa Matanga and other Buddhist monks from the west, and presented the picture of Buddha painted by the King of Udhyana to the Emperor, the Emperor saw that Buddha was indeed the god he had dreamt about. Treasuring the picture, he ordered artists to make copies. These were kept in Chingliang Tower in the Southern Palace, and at the imperial sepulchre at the Kaoyang Gate. He also ordered that a mural painting depicting a scene of thousands of horses and carriages going around a pagoda, which was mentioned in the biographies of Buddha, be executed at White Horse Temple.

Besides this kind of tale, there were stories which were found in Buddhist sutras, but which were changed into Chinese scenes and characters and passed off by writers, consciously or unconsciously, as Chinese stories. For instance, 'A Scholar of Yanghsien', collected in the *Sequel to Tales of Chi Hsieh*,[5] tells of the meeting of a man with a scholar who produced a girl out of his mouth, who in turn produced a young man from her mouth when the scholar went to sleep. When the girl fell asleep, the young man also produced from his mouth another young girl to play with him. Later, when the first girl began to stir, the young man swallowed the second girl and waited. The first young girl woke and came over and swallowed the young man when she saw the scholar was awakening. Finally, the scholar swallowed the young girl and took leave of the man who had witnessed the incredible happenings, leaving him a copper tray as a souvenir. A similar Buddhist story can be found in Samyukta-avadana-sutra, which had been translated into Chinese in the Three Kingdoms Period by Kang Seng-hui.

The practice of writing stories to propagate Buddhism and of adapting Buddhist stories for the purpose of story-telling grew with the passing of time, and culminated in the great romantic novel of China, *Monkey*, which I shall describe in more detail in Chapter XIII.

In the Northern-Southern Dynasties, collections of anecdotes about the behaviour and temperament of men of letters were also very popular. The most famous of these collections was the *Shih Shuo Hsin Yu (New Anecdotes)* by Liu Yi-ching (403–444), because its style is crisp and it describes men of letters vividly:

Wang Tse-yu lived in Shanyin. One night there was heavy snow. Wang awoke, opened the window and saw snow everywhere. He ordered wine. . . . Suddenly, he thought of Tai An-tao, who was then living in Yen, and decided to visit him. He immediately got into a small boat and left. When he arrived at Yen the next day, and approached Tai's house, he suddenly decided to go back to his home. Asked why he did not go in to see Tai, Wang said, 'I came on an impulsive urge. When the urge is spent, why should I see Tai?'

There are many parables in ancient books, including *Mencius, Chuangtse, Liehtse, Hanfeitse, Chankuotseh*, etc., which are as a rule rather direct and to the point. Here is one from *Liehtse*:

> There was a man in Chi who wanted desperately to have gold. Early one morning he dressed himself properly and went to the market where he made straight for the goldsmith, grabbed some gold from his shop, and went out. He was arrested and an official asked him, 'There were many people around. How did you think you could get away with it?'
> 'I saw only the gold,' the man said. 'I did not see any people.'

The first collection of jokes was probably *Hsiao Lin* (*A Treasury of Jokes*) by Hantan Chun of the Han Dynasty. Later there were other books, among them *Hsiao Shuo* by Yin Yun (471–529) and *Book of Laughter* by Hou Po of the Sui Dynasty. Here is one from *A Treasury of Jokes*.

> Chia was one night suddenly taken sick. He ordered one of his students to drill a wooden block for fire to light a lamp. When it was dark, Chia became impatient and kept asking the student to hurry up.
> 'You are unreasonable,' the student said. 'It is dark here. Why don't you bring a light to help me find the drill? Once I have found the drill it will be nothing for me to produce a fire!'

In the Tang Dynasty the short story, or *chuan chi hsiao shuo*, developed from brief, outline-like tales of previous periods into fuller pieces. In the early Tang Dynasty there were two well-known short stories: *The Ancient Mirror* by Wang Tu, and *White Monkey* by an unknown author. The first one was about a wonderful mirror which killed monsters before it disappeared. *White Monkey*, on the other hand, relates that the wife of Ouyang Heh, a general of the Liang Dynasty, was one night abducted by a white monkey. When her husband finally found her deep in the mountains, she was already pregnant by the monkey and later gave birth to a son who looked like a monkey.

During the reign of Empress Wu, Chang Tsu (660?–690?) wrote *Yu Hsien Chu* (*A Visit to a Fairy's Cave*). It told how the author spent a night with two girls when he was travelling on a mission to the north-west. This story had long been lost, but as the *History of Tang Dynasty* said of Chang Tsu's writings, 'Envoys from the Kingdoms of Silla and Japan were willing to pay gold for them.' The text was found in Japan, and returned to China, in the 1930s.

Short stories, however, did not flourish until some sixty years after Chang Tsu's time, when the Classical Prose Movement was at its height. This was because the style of classical prose offered the writers more freedom than *pien-ti wen* to express themselves. But from the fact that many famous writers of short stories, including Shen Chi-chi, Han Yu, Yuan Chen, Po Hsien-chien, Lee Kung-tso and others were involved directly or indirectly in winning acceptance of classical prose, it is just possible that they wrote these short stories in the classical style essentially to promote their cause.

However, at this time candidates for the Civil Service examination could submit short stories to officials in their effort to get official positions, as short stories were thought to be a good way of showing the candidate's knowledge and understanding of history and poetry and were a demonstration of a candidate's skill. This, incidentally, was the beginning of writers using their imagination and perhaps personal experience in their writing, instead of writing compositions which were based purely on ancient classics.

2. *SHORT STORIES OF THE TANG DYNASTY*

Judging by the thirty-odd most popular short stories and others collected in the best-known collections, such as *Hsien Kuai Lu* (*Accounts of Mysteries and Monsters*) by Niu Seng-ju (780–844), love seems to have been the most popular theme of Chinese short stories. Yuan Chen's *Ying-ying Chuan* is perhaps the most famous of all the love stories. It describes the love affair of Ying-ying and Chang Sen, which ends when Chang jilts Ying-ying after he has tried every means to satisfy his desire for her. The attraction of the story lies, I think, in the detailed description of Ying-ying's hesitation over accepting Chang's protestation of love: how she first lures him to meet her at night and then rebukes him for taking advantage of having helped her family to ask for her love, and yet she suddenly capitulates and goes at night to receive his love. Her letter to Chang Sen, when he has left for the capital after showing coolness towards her, is considered to be one of the greatest love letters ever written in Chinese. It adds greatly to the fascination of this story. Research scholars claim to have proved that this was an autobiographical story, and that Yuan Chen was the ingrate Chang Sen.

The heroines of two other well-known love stories, *Li Wa* and *Ho Hsiao-yu*, are prostitutes. In *Li Wa*, written by Po Hsien-chien, a young aristocrat is disowned by his family because of his love for Li Wa. A few years later she finds him almost dying from starvation, and gives up her career to care for him. With her help and encouragement he passes the Civil Service examination and becomes an official. Finally, the young man's father hears what Li Wa has done for his son, comes to visit them, and takes them back into the family circle. This story was based on *I Chih Hua* (*One Flower*), which was one of the better stories being told by story-tellers of the day. For public story-telling was very popular during the Tang Dynasty, and even emperors listened to them. According to Kuo Chih's *Biography of Kao Li-shih*, 'When Emperor Hsien Tsung lived in the Southern Palace, Kao Li-shih used to tell him stories to entertain him.' It is difficult to pinpoint the influence of story-telling on the development of the short story in the Tang Dynasty, but it must have given a few ideas to the *literati*.

Buddhist ideas influenced many writers of short stories. The most noteworthy were Lee Kung-tso's *The Governor of Nan-ko* and Shen Chi-chi's *Pillow*. The transience of life and meaninglessness of wealth and fame are the themes of these stories. *Pillow* relates the chance encounter at an inn in Han Tan of a young man Loo with an old man Lu who lends him a pillow to sleep on. In his sleep Loo dreams that he has passed the Civil Service examination and become an official. He experiences the ups and downs of an official career and is at last ennobled to become the Duke of Yen. Members of his family marry into powerful aristocratic families. At eighty he dies, leaving behind five sons and scores of grandsons. At the time of his death he wakes up from a dream, and finds that the millet which the innkeeper was preparing to serve him before he went to sleep is still not cooked.

The Governor of Nan-ko tells the story of Chunyu Fen, who in his dream marries the Princess of the Kingdom of Huai An and becomes Governor of Nan Ko. He governs the state successfully for twenty years and raises a family of five sons and daughters, all of whom marry well. The people in the state praise and honour him, as also does the King. In that year he leads an army to defend the kingdom against invaders, but is defeated. Soon afterwards his wife dies and he resigns from the governorship and goes to live in the capital. Having been twenty years Governor of a state, he has many friends, including foreigners, and in retirement keeps up his friendship with them. This, together with his fame as a great Governor, arouses the King's suspicion. The King asks him to go home, and Chunyu wakes up from his sleep. 'In a few moments of dreaming a lifetime is spanned.'

Some stories are purely adaptations of Indian legends. According to Tuan Chen-shih,[6] *The Story of Hsiao Tung-hsien*[7] was based on an Indian legend recorded in Hsien Chuan's[8] *Accounts of the Western Regions*. This tells of a Taoist priest who asks a man to look after the furnace in which he is practising experiments in alchemy. He tells the man that as he himself has to go somewhere else, the man must concentrate on guarding the furnace and be absolutely quiet no matter what happens. The man promises, but when he is faced with an illusion that in his next life his wife kills his son because he refuses to speak to her, he cries out because of shock. This destroys the 'philosopher's stone' which the Taoist priest is trying to make. Tuan Chen-shih said that 'because of errors in recording this story (Buddhist monk) became Taoist priest'. What is more surprising is that the same story was dressed up in different garb and became *Tu Tse-chun*, collected in Lee Fu-yen's *More Accounts of Mystery and Monsters*, and *The Story of Wei Chih-tun* collected in Fei Hsin's[9] *Chuan Chi*.

Towards the end of the Tang Dynasty short-story writing fell into decline. Hsueh Tiao's *The Story of Wu Shuang* was an inferior imitation of *Ho Hsiao-yu*, Huanfu Mei's *The Story of Fei Yen* was an imitation of *Ying-ying Chuan*. Short stories assembled in famous collections such as *Accounts of Mysteries and Monsters* by Niu Seng-ju[10] and *A Collection of Strange Stories* by Hsueh Yung-jo,[11] etc., are as a rule inferior to those which had appeared earlier. However, stories of adventure with heroes who are good at swordsmanship, acrobatics or of miraculous skill, not unlike *The Count of Monte Cristo*, *Robin Hood* and *The Three Musketeers* of the West, were very popular, and continued to be written through the centuries, remaining the most popular kind of stories being read today in Taiwan and in Hong Kong.

Many people consider short stories a more worthy contribution to literature than the Classical Prose Movement. Many operas are based on the short stories of this period, including *The Western Chamber*, *The Story of Han Tan*, *Millet Dream* and *Pillow*.

Here I would like to quote Yuan Chen's *Ying-ying Chuan* and Tu Kuang-ting's *The Curly-bearded Man*, which are considered to be the best of, respectively, the love stories and stories of adventure.

YING-YING CHUAN by Yuan Chen

During the reign of Cheng Yuan (785–801) there was a young man by the name of Chang who was gentle, handsome and high-principled. Sometimes when he went out with friends to play, or attend a banquet, even though the others were noisy and playful, and acted as if there was not much time left for them to enjoy themselves, Chang only sat quietly and did not join in the pursuit of girls. Therefore, when he was already twenty-three years old, he had still never had anything to do with girls. His friends asked him why he did not like girls, and he said, 'You people don't really like girls. That is why you act like wolves. I, on the other hand, really like them, but I have not yet met a girl I deeply like. I say that because when I see something beautiful, I cannot forget it. I am sure I will feel the same if I see a beautiful girl.' His friends thought him not unreasonable. Not long afterwards Chang went to visit Pu and stayed in Pu Chiu Shih, a Buddhist temple some ten miles to the east of the county seat. It happened that a widow named Tsui was on her way back to Chang-an, and also stayed there. Upon inquiry, Chang learned that the Widow Tsui was his maternal aunt once removed.

That year Fen Han died and Ting Wen-ya, his assistant, did not know how to control the army under his command. The soldiers ran riot and started to rob the people in Pu. The Tsui family had a lot of things and money, and many servants as well. Fleeing from the troops they did not know where to turn, and were greatly frightened by the uncertain times. It happened that Chang knew indirectly one of the generals of the army. He asked for and secured a contingent of troops to guard the Tsuis and saved them from the ravages of the rioting soldiers.

Some ten years later Tu Chueh was appointed by His Majesty Commander-in-Chief of the armies in Pu, and after he had taken disciplinary measures, peace returned to the district.

Mrs Tsui was very grateful to Chang for what he had done for her family, and gave a banquet in Chang's honour to thank him. 'Were it not for your help I should have lost my life,' she said, 'and my son and daughter also owe their lives to you. I want them to consider you as their elder brother, in order to show that we are appreciative of your help.'

She first ordered her son Huan-lang, a quiet youth in his teens, to salute Chang. Then she called for her daughter Ying-ying to come out. But the girl sent word to say that she was ill. Mrs Tsui was angry, and said, 'Brother Chang saved your life. Were it not for his help you might have been captured by the soldiers. You should not avoid seeing him.'

The girl again let some moments pass before she came out. She was in her ordinary clothes, wearing no make-up or jewels. The bangs of her hair hung low over her eyebrows and her face was rosy. She was strikingly beautiful and radiant. Chang was startled by her beauty and hastened to greet her. Ying-ying sat beside her mother, and because she was shy looked unhappy and miserable. Chang asked her age, and Mrs Tsui said, 'She was born in the seventh moon of Chia-tse [784]. Now it is Keng-chu [800]. She is seventeen.' Chang tried to talk to her, but she would not answer, and the banquet was soon over.

Chang had fallen in love with Ying-ying, and wanted to tell her how he felt about her, but there was no way. However, he knew that Ying-ying had a maid called Hung-niang and several times seized a chance to talk to her, and finally told her of his feelings for his young mistress. The maid was taken by surprise, her face turned scarlet and she ran away, and Chang was ashamed of himself. The next day he saw the maid again and apologized to her. The maid said, 'I dare not tell anyone of what you said yesterday. But you know the Tsui family. Why don't you ask for the hand of the young mistress on the strength of what you have done for them?'

'Ever since I was a child it has not been easy for me to mingle with people,' Chang said. 'Sometimes when I happened to sit with girls I did not even dare to look at them. Because of this I don't know how to deal with the situation. The other day at the banquet I nearly lost my senses and ever since then I have not been able to rest or eat. I may not last another ten days. Were I to ask a go-between to arrange the marriage, and to follow all the rules of an arranged marriage, it would take more than a few months, and I would be dead. What shall I do?'

'My young mistress is very virtuous. She would not even tolerate what she thinks is wrong behaviour from her elders,' Hung-niang said. 'It is difficult for me to help you. But she likes poetry. Often she would read and re-read good poems, and be deeply moved. Why don't you write love poems to her and try to win her heart that way? Failing that, I don't think there is anything else you can do.'

Chang was overjoyed. He immediately composed two love poems and gave them to Hung-niang. That night the maid came back and gave Chang a piece of coloured paper, saying that it was from her young mistress.

There was a poem written on it:

> *A Night of Bright Moonlight*
>
> By the Western Chamber,
> I wait for the moon to rise:
> The wind half-opens a door
> And shadows of flowers
> On top of the wall stir—
> He has come! I think at once.

Chang felt that he understood what the young girl was trying to say.

It was the fourth day of the second month.

On the night of the fifteenth day Chang put a ladder against the almond tree which stood by the wall of the Tsui family home, and climbed up it and jumped into the garden. He went to the Western Chamber and found the door half-open. Inside, Hung-niang was sleeping in bed. Chang went in and woke her.

'Why are you here?' she asked, aghast.

'Remember the piece of paper you gave me? Your young mistress asked me to come,' he lied.

Soon Hung-niang returned. 'She's coming, she's coming,' she said.

Chang could not believe what he heard or that he was to have his heart's desire.

When Ying-ying arrived she was in formal dress, and sombrely she began to scold Chang: 'You saved our lives and became our benefactor. It was because of this that my mother trusted you, and wanted me and my brother to treat you as our elder brother. How can you ask my illiterate maid to send me lewd poems? You started by helping us, and end up trying to take advantage of us. Is there any difference between the soldiers and you? If I were to do nothing about it I would be shielding you, which is wrong. But if I were to tell my mother I would be forgetting your kind help and that would not be right either. I could not trust my maid to tell you what I felt. That is why I wrote you a silly poem, for I had to talk to you and was afraid that you would not show up if I did it another way. Aren't you ashamed for having acted without propriety? I really hope you will come to your senses now and behave yourself.'

She left immediately, and Chang, for a long time, did not know what to think. He returned to his quarters and gave up any hope of winning her love.

Days passed, and one night Chang was sleeping in his chambers when suddenly he felt someone tugging at his clothes. He sat up in surprise and saw Hung-niang holding a blanket and pillow, standing in front of him. 'She's coming, she's coming,' she said. 'Don't go to sleep now.'

She put the pillow beside Chang's, laid the blanket over the one already on the bed, and left. Chang sat and waited for some time, not knowing if it was only a dream. Then Hung-niang brought Miss Tsui with her, and Chang saw that Ying-ying seemed to be in a state of bewitched passion which was too much for her to bear, and was entirely different from the demure girl he knew. It was the night of the eighth day of the month, a crescent moon shone brightly and its rays lit half the bed. Chang was lost in ecstasy and did not know that it was possible to enjoy such bliss in this mundane world. Soon, the bell of a temple struck, and it was near daybreak. Hung-niang urged them to part, and Ying-ying sobbed and tarried, but finally the maid took her away. All night Ying-ying had not uttered a word. Chang got up and could not but believe what had happened was but a dream. But when it was light he saw that there were traces of her make-up on his arms, and found her fragrance still lingering in his clothes. There were teardrops glistening on the bed-mat made of fragrant grass.

For more than ten days Chang did not hear from Ying-ying again. He began a poem: *Meeting a Beauty*, but before he could finish it Hung-niang came to his place by chance, and he gave it to her for her mistress. Ying-ying was moved, and they met again at Western Chamber. This went on for a month, and Chang often asked Ying-ying if her mother should find out what she would do. 'I can't help myself,' she replied. 'I don't care.'

Not long afterwards Chang planned to leave for Chang-an. He explained to Ying-ying why he had to leave, and she did not try to stop him, but felt utterly miserable. The night before he left she refused to meet him.

A few months later Chang went back to Pu and again resumed his affair with Ying-ying. She was a good writer of both prose and poetry. Chang asked many times to see her writings, but she refused, even when he showed her his writings. She would only look at them, but never wrote anything in reply, as was the custom between poets and writers. She was not given to expressing herself. She could express her ideas clearly, but she could not be bothered to hold conversation. She offered Chang love, but did not express it in words. Sometimes, lost in thought, she seemed not to recognize Chang, and seldom showed her happiness or anger. Once, Chang overheard her playing on a *chin* at night by herself, tunes full of longing and sadness. He asked her to play for him, and she stopped playing altogether. Chang became the more infatuated by her, because of her seemingly unfathomable ways.

Soon, Chang again had to leave to sit the National Civil Service Examination in Chang-an. The night before he left he dared not tell Ying-ying that he was going, but she seemed to know from his sadness. In a respectful manner and a soft voice she said slowly, 'I would not blame you if after you seduced me you decided to give me up. I should, of course, be grateful if you would end our affair by marrying me. In that case the love to which we have pledged our lives will be fulfilled, and you need not be sad about your departure. But you are unhappy. I remember you said that I was good at playing the *chin*. I was too timid to play for you. Now that you are going I will play for you. Perhaps you will feel better.'

She ordered that her instrument be cleaned and she played the Overture of the Rainbow-coloured Skirt and the Feather-like Blouse. After a few notes, however, the musical score was utterly mixed up with the dull, dreary sounds she was helplessly making on the strings. She stopped and threw away the *chin* and wept. After hesitating for a moment she ran away and did not return. The next morning Chang left, and the next year he failed the examination, and stayed on in Chang-an, the capital. He wrote to Ying-ying to comfort her, and she wrote back roughly as follows:[12]

I am delighted to receive your letter and touched by your loving remembrance. I am excited and happy to receive the box of hair ornaments and five inches of rouge. I appreciate these thoughtful gifts, but of what use are they to me in your absence? They bring you closer to me, only because of my longing for you. I am glad that you were well and able to pursue your studies at the capital, and I am only sorry for myself, shut up in this small town. But there is no use grieving about fate. I am prepared to take what it has in store for me. I miss you so much since your departure in autumn, and I try to appear happy and gay when there is company, but when I am alone, I cannot restrain my tears. I dreamed often of you and we were so happy together like old times, and then I woke up, clinging to the half-warm quilt with a sense of desolation. I feel that you are so far away from me.

A year has passed since you left. I am grateful beyond words that in a gay city like Chang-an you have not forgotten your old sweetheart entirely. But I shall always be true to my promise. We were formally introduced by my mother, but under the circumstances I lost my self-control and completely surrendered myself to you. You know that after our first night together I swore I would never love anyone but you, and we would be true to each other for life. That was our hope and our promise to each other. If you keep your promise, all is well, and I shall be the happiest woman in the world. But if you discard the old for the new and think of our love as a casual affair, I shall love you still, but shall go down to my grave with an eternal regret. It is all up to you and I have nothing further to say.

Take good care of yourself, please. I am sending you a jade ring, which I wore in my childhood, hoping it will serve as a souvenir of our love. Jade is a symbol of integrity, and the circle of the ring signifies continuity. I am also sending a strand of silk threads and a tear-stained bamboo tea roller. These are simple things but they carry the hope that your love will be as spotless as the jade and as continuous as the ring. The tears on the (spotted) bamboo and the skein of threads will be reminders of my love and my tangled feelings for you. My heart is near you, but my body is far away. If thinking would help, I would be hourly by your side. This letter carries with it my ardent longing and my desperate hope that we may meet again. Take good care of yourself, eat well, and don't worry about me.

Chang showed the letter to his friends, and Yang Chu-yuan and Yuan Chen of Honan wrote poems about his affair with Ying-ying. Many of Chang's friends would not believe that there was such a girl as Ying-ying, but Chang decided to end his affair with her. Yuan Chen was especially friendly with Chang and asked why he so decided. Chang said, 'When beautiful girls are born, Heaven wills that they shall either bring trouble to themselves or upon others. Were Ying-ying to meet a wealthy or powerful person and become his favourite, I wouldn't know what the consequences would be. King Hsin of the Yin Dynasty and King Yu of the Chou Dynasty were both the rulers of a big and strong country, and both lost the support of their people and were finally killed because of their love for a woman. Even now, they remain the laughing-stock of everybody. I have not cultivated my virtue to such an extent that I can withstand the evil influence of a beautiful woman. I therefore must stop myself.'

More than a year later Ying-ying was married to someone else, and Chang, too, was married. One day he happened to pass through the city where she lived, and went to call on her husband, saying that he was her elder brother, and asked to see her. Ying-ying refused to come out to meet him, and Chang was greatly hurt. When Ying-ying heard of it she sent him a short poem secretly:

> When I longed for you and was sick,
> Day and night, I did not come out of my room;
> I was not ashamed to meet other people,
> I was withering away because of you,
> And was ashamed for you.

A few days later she sent him another poem before he left the city:

Let's not mention again that you deserted me,
We were both really in love.
Give now your love of old,
To the one who is married to you.

And Chang never heard from her again.

THE CURLY-BEARDED MAN by Tu Kuang-ting

When Emperor Yang of the Sui Dynasty went to visit Yangchow, he ordered Councillor Yang Su to guard the capital during his absence. Yang was a conceited man. Having held high positions for a long time he felt that he now carried the highest authority and enjoyed the greatest prestige in the land. He led a life of luxury and acted as though he were no longer a subject of the Emperor. When Ministers came to report to him or visitors came to call, he sat on his couch to receive them, without bothering to get up. When he went about the house, beautiful maids attended him. In this way he took on for himself some of the prerogatives of the Emperor. When he grew older he became worse. He paid no attention to the affairs of state although the country was on the verge of collapse.

One day Lee Ching, who later became the Duke of Wei but then was a private citizen, asked for and was granted an interview with Yang Su, saying that he wanted to offer suggestions on government policies. When he arrived, Yang as usual remained seated, and did not get up to greet his guest. Lee went up to him, bowed and said, 'The empire is in great danger, and ambitious and bold men are trying to seize power. Your Excellency is one of the most important Ministers in the realm. You should try your best to recruit good and talented men to serve His Majesty, and not receive your visitors without getting up to greet them.'

Yang was surprised. He stood up to apologize to Lee and talked with him. He was greatly impressed by Lee's opinions, and accepted his memorandum.

While Lee explained his ideas to Yang a beautiful girl who stood in the front row of the attending maids holding a red whisk looked intently at him. When Lee was leaving the girl asked an officer at the door to ask Lee his name. Lee told the officer, who told the girl.

The next morning, just before dawn, Lee heard someone tapping at his door. He got up and opened it and saw someone in a purple overcoat and cap, holding a staff and a bag.

'Who are you?' Lee asked.

'I am the maid who held the red whisk at Councillor Yang's house.'

Lee hurriedly asked her to come in. She took off her cap and overcoat, and Lee saw that she was a beautiful girl of eighteen or nineteen, with a fair complexion, and dressed in bright-coloured clothes. She bowed to him, and in surprise, he bowed in return.

'I have served Councillor Yang for a long time and seen many people,' the girl said. 'But I have seen no one like you. Just as vines cannot stand by themselves but must have tall trees to cling to, I have come to you.'

'But Councillor Yang is the most powerful man in the capital,' Lee said. 'How will he react to this?'

'He is living on borrowed time. You don't have to worry about him. Many of the maids know that he is no longer a power to contend with, and have left him. He has not troubled himself about them. I have thought this over carefully. You need not worry.'

Lee asked what her name was.

'Chang,' she said. 'I am the eldest of my family.'

Lee saw that her complexion, manners, way of speech and intelligence were all that one could hope for in a girl, and was both delighted and worried by his unexpected guest, and did not know what to do. Many people kept peeping through the window of his room to look at her. After a few days there were rumours that a search was being made for her. But nothing came of it, and Lee and the girl put on their fine clothes and rode out of the capital toward Tai-yuan.

One day they arrived in Ling-shih and stopped over night at an inn. They laid out the bedding and were cooking a pot of meat over the fire. Chang was combing her long hair which fell almost to the ground, standing by the bed, and Lee was rubbing down their horses, when suddenly a man with a red curly beard came up to him, riding on an apparently crippled donkey. He sat down, threw a leather bag down on the ground, and taking a pillow, lay down on the bed and watched Chang comb her hair. Lee was very angry, but went on rubbing the horses, thinking of what to do. Chang stared long and hard at the stranger and then, holding her hair in one hand, she turned her back on the stranger and gestured to Lee to hold his temper. Hurriedly she pinned up her hair and curtseyed to the stranger and asked his name.

'Chang,' the stranger said.

'My name is Chang too,' she said. 'I must treat you as my elder cousin.' She bowed to him and asked him his position in his family.

'I am the third child of my family,' he said, 'and you?'

'I am the eldest.'

'Then you are the eldest of my younger cousins,' he said, laughing.

'Come and meet my elder cousin,' she called to Lee. Lee came over and bowed to the curly-bearded man and they all sat down by the fire.

'What are you cooking?' the man asked.

'Mutton. It should be ready now.'

'I am hungry.'

While Lee brought out the cakes he had bought the man took a dagger from his waist band, cut the mutton, and they ate together. Afterwards the man chopped up what was left of the mutton and gave it to his donkey. The beast finished it in no time at all.

'You look like a poor fellow,' said the curly-bearded man to Lee, 'how did you manage to marry such a marvellous girl?'

'I may be poor, but I am also ambitious. That is how I got to marry her. Of course, I wouldn't tell anyone this but you.' He told the curly-bearded man how the girl came to be his wife.

'Where are you going?' the curly-bearded man said.

'To Tai-yuan.'

'By the way, I have come uninvited. Have you any wine?'

Lee said there was a wineshop west of the inn, and fetched him a catty of wine.

'Will you share something with me to go with the wine?' the stranger said. So saying, he opened his leather pouch, and took a man's head and heart and liver from it. He returned the man's head to the pouch, but cut the heart and liver into pieces to eat with the wine. 'This man was no good. It took me ten years to get him. I am sorry it took me that long,' the curly-bearded man said. 'Judging from your appearance and manners you are destined to become a famous man. Do you know of anyone of great talent in Tai-yuan?'

'I know one man whom I would call great. The rest of my friends are of the calibre of generals and commanders only.'

'What is his name?'

'Lee, the same as mine.'

'How old is he?'

'Only twenty.'

'Who is he?'

'He is the son of the Garrison Commander of Tai-yuan.'

'He sounds like the man I am looking for. But I must see him to make sure. Can you arrange for me to meet him?'

'My friend Liu Wen-ching knows him well. I can ask him to arrange a meeting for you,' Lee said. 'What do you want to see him for?'

'An astrologer said that there was a strange phenomenon over Tai-yuan. He asked me to find out more about it. When will you arrive in Tai-yuan?'

Lee told him.

'Meet me at dawn the day after you arrive, at Feng-yang Bridge.' So saying, the man got on his donkey and rode away so swiftly that it seemed he had vanished from sight a moment later.

Lee and Chang were astonished and delighted. 'Such a stalwart fellow should not deceive us,' they said. 'We have nothing to fear.'

At the appointed time they met the stranger again in Tai-yuan, and were very happy to see him. Going to find Liu Wen-ching together, Lee said, 'A fortune-teller wants to meet Lee Shih-min. Will you send for him?'

Liu always valued Lee as a person, and sent a messenger to invite Lee Shih-min. When the latter came, he wore no coat or shoes, but had a fur cape. He exuded spirit and impressed the curly-bearded man with his appearance and manner. After drinking a few cups of wine with him the curly-bearded man took Lee aside and said, 'This man will be the next emperor!' When Lee told Liu this the latter was delighted and pleased that he had come.

When Lee Shih-min left the curly-bearded man said, 'I am almost certain, but my friend the Taoist priest will know for sure. Go back to the capital, and meet me one afternoon at the wineshop east of Mahang. If you see my donkey and another lean one outside it means that we are there. Go right up to the shop.'

On the prearranged day Lee and his wife went to the wineshop and saw the two donkeys outside. They went upstairs and found the curly-bearded man and the priest drinking. After drinking ten or twelve cups together the curly-bearded man said, 'In the cabinet downstairs there are a hundred thousand cash. Take them. Find a safe place for your wife to stay, and meet me again at Feng-yang Bridge in Tai-yuan.'

When Lee went to the bridge at the appointed time the curly-bearded man was there. They went together to see Liu and played chess until Lee Shih-min should arrive.

When Lee Shih-min came his appearance and manner astonished them all. He seemed to bring with him a spirit and an atmosphere which impressed them all. At the sight of him the priest turned pale and said, putting down his pawn, 'All is finished. There is nothing I can say!' Taking his leave he went outside and told the curly-bearded man, 'This is not your world. You had better go somewhere else. Don't lose heart!'

To Lee the curly-bearded man said, 'It will take you some time to ride to the capital. When you get there come with your wife to my humble home. I know you have no property. I want you to meet my wife. Please do not fail to come.' So saying, he sighed and left.

When Lee arrived in the capital he went with his wife to the curly-bearded man's home. A man opened the door, bowed and said, 'The master has been waiting for you.' They were led through inner doors, each more beautiful than the last. Forty maids were standing and waiting for orders in the courtyard, and twenty slaves led them to the east hall, where there were rare and precious antiques, fine caskets and cabinets, crowns and caps, mirrors and jewels and clothing. The opulence seemed not of this world. After they had washed they changed into rich and strange-seeming clothes, and met their host. The curly-bearded man was wearing a gauze turban and a fur cape, and looked very impressive. When they met his wife Lee and Chang were impressed by her beauty. Sitting down in the central hall they were entertained to a feast such as even princes had rarely enjoyed, while twenty girl musicians played heavenly music for them. After the food, wine was served. Then servants came from the eastern hall bearing twenty litters which were covered with embroidered spreads. Under the spreads were record books and keys.

'Take these, all my treasures,' said the curly-bearded man. 'There is no longer any need for me to stay in this world and fight for peace when a real king has been found. Your friend Lee Shih-min will become a great emperor, and restore peace to your country in a few years. You will serve him well, and attain high rank, and your wife will win fame and honour because of you. It took a woman of her talent to recognize your worth, and it takes a man like you to bring her honour. An able minister always finds a wise sovereign, for when the tiger roars, the wind blows, and when the dragon cries, clouds gather. Use my gifts to help the real sovereign accomplish great deeds. Ten years from now, several hundred miles south-east of China, strange events will take place, and I will realize my ambition. When that time comes drink to me towards the south-east.'

He told his servants to bow to Lee and his wife and said, 'From now on they are your master and mistress.'

The curly-bearded man and his wife then left with only one servant.

Lee and his wife went to live in the curly-bearded man's house, and he used his great wealth to help Lee Shih-min conquer the empire.

In the time of Chen Kuan, Lee became acting prime minister of the land. He learned from the tribesmen in the south that a thousand big ships and one hundred thousand soldiers had conquered the kingdom of Fuyu and killed the king, and restored peace to the kingdom. Lee knew that it was the curly-bearded man's doing. When he told his wife they both put on ceremonial robes and drank a toast to their friend in the south-east.

From this it can be seen that no man can become emperor simply because he wants to become one, great though he may be. How futile it is for an ordinary man to aspire to that position! He who thinks that by simply staging a rebellion he can become an emperor is like a praying mantis who throws himself at the turning wheel of a carriage.

CHAPTER X

The Poetry of the Sung Dynasty

1. *THE EMERGENCE OF* TSE

THE 'new-style' poetry of the Tang Dynasty reached the zenith of its development in the poems of Li Po and Tu Fu. But even Tu Fu must already have felt that the rules of the 'stop-short' and 'regular' poems restricted the scope of his talents. It may be argued that when he said, 'I will not rest until my verses astound and awe people', he meant that he was going to write the best poems possible within the rules. He did, very often, achieve his aim. Nevertheless, some of his poems showed the strain under which he had to work. A few of them did not make any sense at all without a long commentary. In the last of a set of poems entitled *Chiu Hsing* (*Autumn*), for instance, he wrote:

Hung-tou	*tou*	*yu*	*ying-wu*	*lieh*
Red beans	peck	remaining	parrots	grains

Pi-wu	*chi*	*lou*	*fen-fang*	*chih*
Green cola-nut trees	perching	kept	phoenix	branch

In these two lines subject became object and vice versa. Even in poetry one may not say, 'The book is writing me', instead of 'I am writing a book'. The meaning of these two lines is nevertheless fathomable: 'Parrots peck at the remaining grains of red beans, and a phoenix stays perched on a branch of a green cola-nut tree.'

In the last of his set of poems, entitled *Yung Huai Ku Chi* (*Reflections on Ancient Sites*), however, what he wrote is not only ungrammatical but totally indecipherable.

Shan	fen	ke	chi	yu	chou	cheh
Three	parts	divide	occupy	slowly	planned	tactics

Wan-ku	yun-hsaio	yi	yu-mao
Thousands of years	high in the sky	one	feather

This is a poem about Chu-keh Liang, who helped Liu Pei to establish the state of Shu, one of the kingdoms of the Three Kingdoms Period (A.D. 220–276). The first line presumably means that Chu-keh Liang slowly planned his tactics to divide the country into three parts and occupy one of them to form a kingdom. But what about the second line? One feather is high in the sky for thousands of years? One feather is for thousands of years highly praised? Warmly remembered? Greatly revered? What is one feather? Whose feather was it? Tu Fu might have meant the feathered fan Chu-keh Liang was supposed to have carried about with him all the time, but why talk about the fan and not the man?

The effort to overcome the rules became more pronounced in the group of poets headed by Han Yu. Yeh Hsien said, 'Han Yu brought great changes to the poetry of the Tang Dynasty. His poems are full of vitality, and their contents are magnificent. In fact, Han Yu was the leader of a new school of poetry to which belonged the great poets of the Sung Dynasty, including Su Shun-chin (1008–1048), Mei Yao-chen (1002–1060), Ouyang Hsiu, Su Tung-po, Wang An-shih (1021–1086) and Huang Ting-chien (1045–1105).'[1] But Han Yu in writing poems aimed primarily at overcoming the restrictions of the requirements. For as Chao Yi (1727–1814) said, 'In Chang Li's (Han Yu's) time, Li Po and Tu Fu had already come and gone, which meant that however hard one might try, it was simply impossible to open up new vistas in writing new-styled poetry. What one could do was to follow and explore the precarious path of using recondite phrases and risky-sounding rhymes which Tu Fu introduced. . . . But there are pitfalls. Because of his talent Tu Fu occasionally succeeded. Han Yu, on the other hand, made a point of using old metaphors and doubtful rhymes in writing his poems. They therefore often showed traces of awkwardness.'[2] In other words, even great poets like Tu Fu and Han Yu felt hampered by the rules of poetry writing. It was natural that some poets should begin to look for another poetic form in which to express themselves.

In the meantime, Chinese music had undergone great changes,

brought about by increased contact with foreign countries to the west. The people learned and gradually became infatuated with the music of these countries. According to *Tung Tien*,[3] 'Since the Chou (North Chou) (557–580) and Sui (589–617) Dynasties, the several hundred musical scores for pipes and strings have mostly been based on the music of Hsi Liang,[4] and musical scores for song-and-dance acts were based on the music of Kueitse.[5] The music of these two countries is popular with the people.' Folk songs, too, were very popular. 'Record of Music' in *Old History of the Tang Dynasty*[6] mentions that 'since the Kai Yuan Period (713–741), singers have been singing indiscriminately foreign songs and folk songs'. This probably produced a hybrid music, more expressive than that of earlier periods. It will be recalled that in the Tang Dynasty the 'stop-short' poems and some 'regular' poems were adapted by singers as lyrics for their songs. Many of these songs must have been of this kind. In doing so, singers found that not every note in the musical scores had a corresponding word to go with it. They prolonged the sound of some of the words to fit the music, which is also done by singers nowadays. But in the Tang Dynasty singers found it better to repeat, rather than prolong, the sounds of some words. This became a challenge to the poets. Instead of letting the singers repeat some of the words, and spoil the image or mood they wanted to create, they filled in words to every note of a musical score. This was known as the technique of *tien tse*. The result was *tse*, a poetic form consisting of lines of irregular metres. Similarly, the poor quality of the lyrics of popular folk songs must have prompted the poets to try their hand at writing for folk song singers too. Liu Yu-hsi (772–843), a poet, said in his *Preface to a Collection of Chu Chih Songs*, 'Youths in the streets join in singing *Chu Chih* songs. They play short flutes, strike drums at every beat of the melody and the singer raises his hands and dances. The man who can sing the greatest number of songs is considered the best among them. . . . Although the songs are to listen to, the mood of lyrics is not unlike that of Chi O.'[7] The crudeness of the lyrics in popular folk songs can also be seen in the texts which were discovered in Tun-huang. The thirty songs collected in *Yun Yao Chi* (*A Collection of Songs of the Cloud*),[8] although apparently revised by some school-teachers or men of letters, still retain a certain crudeness of expression.

So it was that poets of the Tang Dynasty, in looking for a new poetic form the better to express themselves, found it in *tse*. At first, *tse* was short and like the seven-word 'stop-short' poems in form. The contents were often exactly what the titles of the musical scores implied. For instance, Liu Yu-Hsi's *Lang Tao Sha* (*Waves Shift Sand*) is primarily about the sands of the Yellow River. However, there seemed to have been several musical scores to one title, so that *tse* written supposedly under the same title had different rhymes and rhythms, as exemplified by Huangfu Sung's *Tien Hsien Tse* and one collected in *Yun Yao Chi*.[8]

The first poet to write *tse* was formerly thought to be Li Po, but it has now been generally accepted that the *tse* which were attributed to him could not have been written in his time. It was not until the second half of the eighth century that poets started writing *tse*. The most famous of them were Chang Chih-ho (730–810), Tai Shu-lun (732–789) and Wei Ying-wu (736?–830?). But it was through the efforts of Liu Yu-hsi and Po Chu-yi that *tse* gradually gained its own identity as a new poetic form.

In his note on one of his *tse* Liu said, 'I write this in response to Lo-tien's *tse*, according to the musical score of *Remembering Kiang Nan*.' This, incidentally, was the first time on record that a poet mentioned specifically that he was filling in words to the notes of a musical score. Liu's and Po's *tse*, which were capable of evoking poetic imagery in the minds of their readers, gained, as it were, respectability for *tse* and paved the way for its further development.

In the late Tang Dynasty many poets were engaged in writing *tse* to the tunes of the greatly increased number of recognized musical scores. Huangfu Sung (dates unknown), Szekung Tu (837–908) and Emperor Chao Tsung (867–904) were the best known of such poets. But the most famous poet and the one with the greatest achievement during this period was Wen Ting-yun (812–870). Wen came of an aristocratic family, but he failed to make politics his career. Perhaps in despair, he spent his time in brothels and theatres, mingling with prostitutes and musicians. Having a knowledge of music he wrote poems to musical scores, principally about the lives of prostitutes, their despair, hopes and pursuit of love. There were two collections of his *tse*, but both were lost. In his sixty-odd *tse* which were collected in *Hua Chien Chi* (*Among Flowers*)[9] he used nineteen different musical scores, showing a proficiency which no contemporary poet equalled. Wen was extremely ugly, but his *tse* are famous for their knowledgeable descriptions of the complicated emotions of women, and for their rich and colourful phrases. He was probably a sensitive and sympathetic soul, and won the friendship of singers and prostitutes by his talent and understanding, in spite of his unprepossessing appearance. Here are some of his *tse*:

TO THE TUNE OF KENG LOU TSE

The stars have faded,
Music has stopped;
Beyond the curtains, at dawn,
    Orioles sing
    As the moon goes down.

Dew is heavy,
Willows are swept by the wind;
And all over the courtyard
Fallen flowers pile high.

Up on an empty terrace
By the railing I gaze
My longing and sorrow—
    They are those of yesterday.

Spring will soon be gone,
But unending is my thought of you;
Our love is, however, already like a dream.

Fragrance comes from a jade incense-burner,
Teardrops flow from red candles;
Why should candlelight shine
On me, lost in longing on an autumn night?

Eyebrows unpencilled,
Hair dishevelled,
The night is long and
The bed is cold!

On the cola-nut trees
Rain is falling
    at midnight
Does the rain know
    that parting is bitter?

Leaf after cola-nut leaf
Drop after rain drop
Fall on my empty steps until dawn!

TO THE TUNE OF DREAMING OF KIANG NAN

Morning toilet done,
She leans on a terrace and gazes at the river.
Thousands of boats have sailed by,
But on none was her lover.
The setting sun quivers on the everflowing water,
And heart-broken is she, the girl on Pai Ping Islet.

Wen's achievements in *tse* were greatly admired, and his style was copied by poets of later dynasties. He was, in fact, the leader of the 'Among Flowers' school of writers of *tse*. This was the name of a collection of *tse* written by poets of the 'Five Generations and Ten States' Period, principally of the state of Shu. The period from A.D. 901 to 959 was a completely chaotic era in Chinese history. In a little over fifty years there were five dynastic changes in China proper, while in other parts ten states were established consecutively. Foreign tribes also invaded China and Shih Ching-tang, Emperor of the Shih Chin Dynasty (936–946), even became an adopted son of the chief of Chi-tan. But in the states of Shu and South Tang the situation was relatively stable, and with the help of the talent and skill of immigrants from China proper, the natural resources of these two regions were explored and trade prospered. Furthermore, the rulers of these states were either themselves poets or encouraged the writing of *tse* and *tse* therefore flourished.

The 'Among Flowers' collection consisted of 500 *tse* written by eighteen poets in ten volumes, of which more than sixty were written by Wen Ting-yun. Judging by the fact that Wen's *tse* were placed first in the collection, his influence on other poets of the period was already acknowledged by men of letters of the day. But except perhaps for Wei Chuang (855–920), none of the other poets represented in the collection had anything new to offer in the writing of *tse*. Although Wei, like Wen, wrote mostly about sing-song girls and prostitutes, he avoided the repeated use of dazzling words in describing colours and jewels, which Wen relied on for effect, and achieved simplicity of style. Here is one of his *tse*.

TO THE TUNE OF NU KUAN TSE

Last night at midnight,
I distinctly saw you

And talked to you for a long time.
Your face was still like peach flowers
And you often frowned, brows slender as willow leaves.

You were shy and yet happy,
You wanted to leave and yet you lingered.
When I woke and found this a dream,
I was overcome by boundless sorrow.

But the greatest poet of *tse* during the 'Five Generations and Ten States' Period was by common consent Lee Yu (937–978), or Lee Hou-tsu, last Emperor of the state of South Tang. His father, Lee Ching (916–961), Emperor Yuan Tsung, was also a famous poet. It was said that Lee Ching once teased Feng Yen-yi (903–960), another poet who was his Prime Minister, about one of the latter's *tse*. Feng said diplomatically that one of the Emperor's *tse* was better. Lee Ching might have been jealous, but it showed the importance even emperors attached to *tse*.

Lee Yu's *tse* can be divided into two groups, those written before and those written after his surrender to the armies of Sung. He was perhaps not a capable ruler, for even as the armies of Sung were entering his capital he was in a Buddhist temple listening to a sermon. He did not know what had happened, and it took the loss of a kingdom and the humiliation of capture and exile to bring out his latent poetical talent. The *tse* written in the period after he surrendered to Sung are considered to be his best work. Unlike those which he wrote on love and the pleasures of life when he was Emperor, these expressed his love and longing for his native land, his memories of better times, and his regret and despair. These *tse* were so deeply touching that it is said that during the Japanese occupation of Chinese provinces along the seacoast and the three rivers in the Second World War, Chinese youths used to read Lee Yu's *tse* and weep. But for their author these *tse* brought an abrupt end to his life. For after Emperor Tai Tsung of the Sung Dynasty read them he ordered Lee Yu to be poisoned. Lee Yu was forty-two when he died.

Here are two of his most famous *tse*:

TO THE TUNE OF LANG TAO SHA

I

From behind the curtains came the patter of rain,
And spring is now coming to an end.

Silk coverlets couldn't keep me warm in the cold of dawn,
And yet, in my dream, forgetting that I was in exile,
I grabbed another moment of happiness.

Alone, I dare not stand on the terrace,
For it was easy to leave
But is extremely difficult now to visit
My country and all her mountains and rivers.
Spring passes, just as
    The water flows away
The flowers fall down;
O! To find Heaven in this world!

2

When will spring flowers stop blooming
    and the autumn moon cease to shine?
And how many things of the past does one really know?
For the spring wind again visited my little terrace last night
And in the moonlight, I dared not think of home.

Perhaps the carved railings and jade steps still stand
But the rosy cheeks will have faded.
How much sorrow can a man bear?
My sorrows are like a river of spring flood,
    ever flowing eastwards![10]

When Sung united China in 960 the government devoted its energy to rehabilitation. It was not until some fifty years later, when the economy of the country had recovered from the devastation of war, that literary activity revived. The *literati* turned their attention to prose writing, and brought the 'classical prose' movement to a successful conclusion. There was also greatly increased activity in the writing of *tse*. However, most of the poets, including Yen Shu (991–1055), Ouyang Hsiu, Yen Chi-tao, etc., seemed content to follow the examples set by Wen Ting-yun, Wei Chuang, Feng Yen-yi and Lee Yu, and continued to write short lyrical *tse*. Their *tse* so clearly lack individuality that sometimes it is difficult to tell who wrote which, particularly of those written by Feng Yen-yi and Ouyang Hsiu. The only exception perhaps was Fan Chung-yen (989–1052). Here is one of his better-known *tse*.

TO THE TUNE OF YU CHIA AO

Things change with autumn
On the frontiers. Wild geese are flying
Southward to Heng Yang. With the sounds of bugles
Come the weird noises of the borderland.

For amidst thousands of high mountains,
In the setting sun, there rises meandering
Smoke, in an isolated, walled outpost
With gates closed.

Drinking a glass of wine, one thinks of home
Thousands of miles away. How is one to return
When the enemy is not yet defeated?

A sad song
On a Kiang pipe someone is playing—
Frost has spread all over the ground
And sleep comes not to the men;
The General's hair has turned white
And the recruits weep.

There is one strange thing about the poets who wrote *tse* in this period. When their collected work was published their *tse* were never included. The result is that many of their *tse* were lost. One cannot say definitely what the reason was, but it probably was because *tse* were songs sung in brothels and inns. Also the principal theme was love. When the poets became famous they felt uncomfortable or embarrassed about their *tse*, thinking perhaps that the sentiments expressed in them would prejudice their social and political reputation. Thus Yen Chi-tao denied his father ever wrote about love between a man and a woman, in spite of the fact that many of Yen Shu's *tse* are about love. And supporters of Ouyang Hsiu even said that his love *tse* were written by his enemies to smear him. It is therefore not surprising that *tse* made great progress only when Liu Yung came on the scene, a man who had no political career to pursue, and who loved the company of courtesans.

2. *THE LIVES OF LIU YUNG AND SU TUNG-PO*

Liu Yung, or Liu San-pien, as he was originally named (990?–1050), was the first, if not the only, Chinese poet whose career was ruined by his literary fame. All his life he wrote only *tse*. In view of the fact that it was considered to be a lower form of poetry by the *literati* of the time, Liu Yung must have been an extremely self-confident man. Even in his youth he liked to make friends with sing-song girls and prostitutes. He was also a master musician, and because of his friendship with the girls he often wrote new songs for them, and whenever they found new songs he wrote lyrics for them. In his lifetime China was peaceful. The state of Chin, or the Tartars, was admittedly getting stronger and stronger up in the north, but there had as yet been no war. In these circumstances the people enjoyed themselves, and found new songs in the brothels. Before Liu Yung tried his hand at writing lyrics for them the comparatively uneducated musicians and other helpers in the inns and brothels supplied the material to meet the need. Their lyrics were as a rule vulgar and not very significant. Liu Yung, on the other hand, brought his literary talents to bear in writing lyrics. But, in evoking moods and creating images, he also used colloquial expressions. This innovation, together with his mastery of music, brought about a new type of *tse* which was longer, described in detail a mood or scene and was easily understood by the common people. This was called *man tse*, or leisurely *tse*, and differed from the shorter ones, or *hsiao ling*, which left to the imagination details of emotions and scenes. Liu Yung's *tse* thus became very popular and he himself notorious. It is difficult to say why this should have been. After all, famous scholars and ministers wrote *tse* of love and longing. It was also considered 'chic' for the *literati* to refer to each other by the lines of their *tse*. For instance, Chang Hsien (990–1078) was called 'The vice-minister who wrote "The Clouds part/The moon comes,/And flowers play with their Shadows" ', and Sung Chi (998–1061) was known as 'The minister who wrote "Spring runs riot with red blossoms on the branches of apricot trees" '.

Liu Yung wrote about the same thing, and of the sorrow and heartbreak of leave-taking. He consorted with courtesans, yes. But so did everyone else. The only difference was that he did so more intensely, as he had no official reputation at stake. But he was ostracized for it, almost all the *literati* of his day looking down on him. It was said that once, after he had been without a job for a long time, he went to see Yen Shu, who was then the Prime Minister and known for his willingness to help people of talent. He had intended to ask Yen for help, but when Yen saw him he asked, 'Do you write *tse*?' 'Yes,' Liu replied, 'just like Your Excellency.' 'Although I also write *tse*,' Yen said, 'I never wrote anything like "I'll just hold my sewing and sit with him".' Liu left in a huff.[11]

Even Su Tung-po (1036–1101), who was known for his broad-mindedness, was not entirely free from the prejudice against Liu Yung. It was said that when Su saw Chin Kuan (1049–1100), after they hadn't met for some time, he said to the latter, 'I hadn't thought that you would imitate the style of Liu Yung's *tse*.' 'I may be an ignoramus,' Chin said, 'but I wouldn't sink so low as that.' 'What about "At that moment,/My soul seemed to have left my body?" ' Su said. 'Isn't it like one of the phrases in Liu Yung's *tse*?' Chin could not reply.

Among the many popular *tse* Liu Yung wrote is this one:

> By accident, I've missed the chance
> To head the golden list of successful candidates.
> And so my talents are not recognized, for the moment,
> In this glorious time. What should I do?
> But if I lost my chance,
> Why shouldn't I enjoy myself?
> Why bother to talk about gain or loss?
> A talented writer of *tse*
> Is surely an unofficial minister?
> In the lanes and places of pleasure,
> There are still screens made out of paintings.
> What is more fortunate than
> To have sweethearts to visit there?
> Come! Let me embrace and hold you,
> And you. All my life I've
> Enjoyed romantic affairs.
> Youth lasts but a moment,
> How can I exchange fleeting fame
> For your smile, as you pour me wine,
> And tenderly sing me songs?

It is said that this *tse* lost him an official position. Emperor Jen Tsung came to hear of it, and when he went over the results of the National Civil Service Examination and found Liu's name among the successful candidates, he deleted it, and Liu was not selected. Afterwards, someone recommended him for an appointment to the Emperor. The Emperor asked, 'Isn't he the Liu San-pien who writes *tse*?' 'Yes,' said the man. 'Let him go on writing *tse*,' the Emperor dismissed the subject. Upon hearing this Liu humorously styled himself 'Liu Shan-pien, writer of *tse* by Imperial Order'.

But life was hard for a writer without a steady income from an official position, which was the only opening for a man of letters at the time. So, after some time, Liu changed his name from Shan-pien to Yung, and in 1034, when he was more than forty years of age, he passed the examination and later became an official in charge of frontier reclamation work. But he does not seem to have held the job for long, for when he died he was penniless. It was his girl friends, the sing-song girls and courtesans, who donated money to have him buried, and every spring they held memorial services for him. It thus seemed that he left no family behind. This was a sad ending for a great poet, but perhaps it was in accord with the time in which he was born. He devoted his life to writing *tse*, and even in his lifetime his fame spread abroad. Yeh Meng-teh's *Pi Shu Lu Hua* (*Records of a Summer Vacation*),[12] quotes an official of Hsi Hsia (a state which is now part of modern Kansu, Ninghsia and Suiyuan Provinces), who visited China, as saying that 'Wherever there is a well (where people gather), there are people singing Liu Yung's *tse*'. *Chien Tang Yi Shih* (*Reminiscences of Chien Tang*)[13] said that Tsung Liang, the ruler of Chin, read one of Liu Yung's *tse* about the prosperity of Chien Tang and decided to invade China.

In spite of the fact that the *literati* of the time tended to look down upon Liu Yung's *tse*, his influence on the technique of writing *tse* was undeniable. Many famous poets, among them Chin Kuan, Ho Chu (1052–1125) and Chou Pang-yen (1056–1121), were to varying extents influenced by him. Su Tung-po said, 'People say Liu Yung's *tse* are vulgar, but there are stanzas in them, such as "With autumn wind gradually becoming fierce/Desolate are the river and pass/Only the setting sun comes to my terrace", which are as good as the best of the poetry of the Tang Dynasty.'[14]

This was high praise indeed, but justified, for Liu Yung created *Man Tse*, and paved the way for greater achievements in *tse*.

But it was Su Tung-po who brought the art to perfection. Su Tung-po was a man of many talents. Writing *tse* was but a small measure of them, just like 'a peck of water in a great ocean'.[15] He lifted *tse* to the same poetic level as orthodox poetry and, putting the stamp of his own personality on it, expanded its range to include a multiplicity of subjects, such as history, philosophy, fields and farms, affairs of state and family, and the myriad feelings of life. He not only broke away from the sticky sentimentality of the past, but like Li Po, who refused to abide by the rules of 'new-style' poetry, refused to be completely bound by the musical scores to the tunes of which the *tse* were written. His *tse* thus gained a vitality and force of their own, and swept the reader along with their emotional and descriptive power. Some Chinese critics felt that it was a pity that some of Su's *tse* were not written to musical scores and thus were not singable. This, of course, is true, if viewed from the point of strict rules.

But Su Tung-po's talents seemed boundless. His paintings and calligraphy differed from the traditional painting and calligraphy of his time, and reached a high artistic level; they were admired and treasured. His prose style was also different and surpassed that of Ouyang Hsiu and other prose-masters of his time. He said that when he composed an essay it was like sailing on clouds and floating on water without any pre-set form. The only thing was to go on writing when there were things which must be put down, and to stop when there was no point in going on. Ouyang Hsiu said of Su's writings that they were like beautiful girls who insisted on removing all their make-up before they came out to meet the public. Indeed, whatever Su Tung-po wrote, it reflected exactly the individuality and the effervescent, insuppressible spirit of the author. It was said that even in his paper written for the National Civil Service Examination, the most important event in a scholar's life, Su took some liberties with history and invented a dialogue just to help express his ideas. In the time of Emperor Yao, he wrote, a man was about to be sentenced for a crime he had committed. 'Three times the Minister of Justice said "Let him be sentenced to death!" and three times the Emperor said "Let him be pardoned!" ' It happened that other incidents he quoted to substantiate his opinion about the importance of simplicity and leniency in ruling a country were all true, and traceable, and the judges, won over by Su's brilliance of style and content, were hesitant to question the source of Su's invention. An unwillingness to admit their ignorance of the existence of an ancient text from which the young candidate quoted the dialogue also helped Su to fox his judges, and he passed the examination. Some time later one of the judges asked him privately in which book the incident about Emperor Yao was recorded. Su admitted that he invented it. 'I thought that was what the Sage-Emperor would have done,' he said.

Su Tung-po's irrepressible spirit may have been inherited from his father, Su Shun (1009–1066), as also his sense of detachment from his official career. Although an extremely intelligent and self-possessed person, Su Shun only started to study seriously at the age of twenty-seven, in the year of Sung-Po's birth. An official career held no interest for him; he preferred to enjoy life as best he could.

Su Tung-po had very strong convictions. According to the *History of Sung Dynasty*, as a child of eight or ten he was taught by his mother, in his father's absence. One day Su read in the *History of the Later Han Dynasty* of the scholars who, at risk of persecution, torture and execution, tried to combat the corruption of the usurping eunuchs, who were ruling the country with their henchmen and protégés. Among these scholars was a young man, Fan Pang, who after repeated persecution was finally sentenced to death. He refused the local magistrate's offer of assistance in escaping, as it would mean that his old mother would become a fugitive from justice, and his mother concurred in this decision, saying, 'I had hoped for you a long life and a good name, but since you cannot have both I prefer that you should have a good name.' The young Su Tung-po, upon reading this, asked his mother, 'If I grew up to be a man like Fan Pang, would you approve?' 'If you can become a man like Fan Pang,' his mother replied, 'can I not be like his mother?'

His determination to stick to his convictions was in fact the cause of all his troubles. At least four times he asked to be sent away from the capital, almost every time to take up a lesser post. Part of the reason for this urge to leave the seat of power was admittedly to avoid headlong conflicts with his political opponents. It nevertheless remains true that he was not over-zealous in the pursuit of his political career.

In 1069 Emperor Shen Tsung gave Wang An-shih (1021–1086) full power to carry out his ideas of reform. Su was then thirty-three years old. He was against putting into effect too hastily any measures which Wang proposed to make, and which Su thought could do more harm than good. So, when he was put in charge of the National Civil Service Examinations that year, he asked all the candidates to write a commentary on 'How Emperor Wu of the Chin Dynasty conquered the state of Wu by assuming dictatorial powers, but Fu Chien was defeated in his campaign against Chin in spite of his dictatorial powers', and describe how 'Duke Huan of Chi trusted Kuan Chung implicitly and became the First Lord of the Reign in the Spring-Autumn Period, but King Kuai of Yen was ruined when he similarly trusted Tse-tse'. This, as everyone knew, referred to the Emperor's trust in Wang An-shih and his granting to Wang of dictatorial powers. But Su Tung-po did not stop at referring obliquely to Wang An-shih. He sent a memorandum to the Emperor, opposing the measures Wang put into practice. Wang was furious and tried, but failed, to involve him in trouble. Nevertheless, Su was demoted to be an assistant to the Governor of Hangchow. In the next ten years he was sent from one place to another, and in 1079 three censors alleged that in his poems Su Tung-po slandered the Emperor. He was imprisoned and tried. There was no evidence to prove the charge, however, and the Emperor, who had long known Su to be a man of great talent, decided, after the trial had gone on for some time, that Su should be spared further humiliation. He was appointed a lieutenant in an army training corps in Huangchow and at the same time forbidden to leave the area. Su's appointment was, of course, a nominal one. For the next six years he lived as a farmer. He converted a plot of land on the Eastern Slope into rice fields, and built his family a house which everyone thought was too small and simple. But Su was content. He called himself the Recluse of the Eastern Slope, or Tung-po for short.

This period of his life was perhaps the most important from the standpoint of his literary career. He managed to live and support his family without getting any salary from an official position. In his youth, when he read *Chuangtse*, he had said that, 'I used to have ideas but was unable to express them. Now this book expresses exactly how I felt.' Now, living in compulsory retirement, he must have found great comfort in *Chuangtse*, and come to acquire the calm detachment expressed in the poems of Tao Chien. In one of his *tse* he said that Tao Chien must have been the previous incarnation of the same soul which now resided in him. He wrote many of his best *tse* and traditional poems during these years. He also became more mature, and formed an optimistic yet detached view of life, which together with his warm and gregarious personality helped him to endure his later exile.

On the death of Emperor Shen Tsung in 1085 Su Tung-po was recalled to the capital and promoted to a post second in importance only to that of the Prime Minister. He could at this time have crushed all his opponents and made secure his political career; instead, he soon asked to be sent away again, and became Governor of Hangchow. The contrast with his opponents, who were all self-appointed and ruthless zealots trying to institute misguided reforms, contributed significantly to his fall from favour. In 1094 Chang Chun, his political opponent, became Prime Minister and Su was again accused of having slandered Emperor Shen Tsung, and ordered to live in Huichow, Kwangtung. Three years later, at the age of sixty, he was banished to Hainan Island, at that time a barbarous place. The story goes that he was sent there because while living in Huichow, Su described in a poem his beautiful nap in the spring breeze, listening to the temple bells at the back of his house. When Chang Chun read it he said, 'So! Su Tung-po is having a good time!' He thereupon ordered that Su be banished to Hainan. Perhaps Chang Chun thought that Su would die there; instead, Su's cheerful outlook helped him to enjoy life under any conditions. Even in Hainan people had heard of him, and he had countless admirers. So, although he was in great difficulties and homesick in his old age, he did not despair. During this period, in a letter to a friend, he wrote, 'I was driven out of a government house (where I have been staying) and have now built myself a small hut which barely gives me shelter. I have used up all the money I had. When one finds oneself in such straits anything can happen. You just expect it to happen and laugh at it.'

In this period, as in all his life, the moral support of his friends helped him. As well as almost all the famous scholars of his time, including Ouyang Hsiu, Huang Ting-chien, Chin Kuan and others, Su Tung-po also had as his friends, among others, Chen Chi-chang, who was a *hsieh*, and Tsan-liao-tse, a monk. Tsan-liao-tse, for one, insisted on going to Hainan with him, and was dissuaded from doing so only with difficulty. Tsan-liao-tse later sent an acolyte to Hainan to see Su, with a letter and presents. In reply, Su wrote, 'I have been here for over half a year and manage to get along. . . . Think of me as a monk who has been driven out of Lung-yin Temple and is now living in a small cottage, and having simple peasants' fare. I can live like this for the rest of my days. As for malaria, and other local diseases, aren't there diseases also in the North? . . . It is true there are no doctors here, but think how many people are annually murdered by doctors in the capital! I know you will laugh when you read this, and cease to worry about me.'

In 1100 the young Emperor Tseh Tsung died at the age of twenty-four and Emperor Hui Tsung ascended the throne. Su Tung-po and others who had been persecuted, demoted and banished under the reign of Tseh Tsung, were pardoned. Su was ordered successively to go and live in Lien-chow, the modern Ho-pu District in Kwangtung Province, and Yung-chow, the modern Ling-ling District in Hunan Province. Before he reached Yung-chow, he was given permission to live wherever he chose, and he started to go North. He was dined and entertained all the way until he arrived in Chang-chow, the modern Wu-chin District in Kiangsu Province, where he had a farm. It was June 1101. The next month an illness, which may have been amoebic dysentery which he contracted on the journey, worsened, and on 28 July 1101 he died at the age of sixty-five.

3. *THE POEMS OF LIU YUNG, SU TUNG-PO AND OTHERS*

The difference between Liu Yung's and Su Tung-po's *tse* can roughly be summed up by this anecdote:

When Su Tung-po was serving as an academician of the Han Lin Academy, there was in the Academy a secretary who sang quite well. One day Su asked the secretary, 'How are my *tse* compared with those of Liu Yung?' 'Liu's *tse* containing lines such as "Banks of Willows/A Wind Rises at Dawn/A Moon, Fading . . ." should only be sung by girls of seventeen or eighteen years old, using red ivory clappers to mark the beats, while your *tse*, sir, such as "East Flows the Great River", must be sung by burly fellows from Kuangsi, using huge iron clappers to mark the beat.' Upon hearing this Su burst out laughing.[16]

The style of Liu Yung's *tse* was restrained, and the mood sad and delicate, while Su Tung-po's *tse* were full of verve and gusto, and free and easy. But Su was also capable of expressing the myriad emotions of an evanescent life in as refined and elegant a manner as any other poet who thought Su's *tse* violated the rules of writing *tse*. Su Tung-po knew all the rules. Many instances are on record of his *tse* being sung and occasions when he revised some poems to render them suitable for singing. On the other hand, Liu Yung's *tse*, though singable and very popular, were considered by other poets to be crude and anaemic in content. But there were poets, notably Chou Pang-yen (1056–1121),

Chin Kuan and Ho Chu (1052–1125), who tried to coin new words and phrases and to find and use the right words to express themselves strictly in accordance with the requirements of writing *tse*. Chou Pang-yen contributed considerably to regulating musical scores, and the contrasting and balancing of tonal values of words. He also created many new musical scores. Because of his mastery of the technique of writing *tse* and his elegant wording and refined style, he was considered by some critics to have been the model for Chiang Kwei (1155?–1230?), Wu Wen-ying (dates unknown), Chang Yen (1248–1320?) and others to imitate. Generally speaking, their *tse* suffered from over-emphasis on form and dependence on allusions which, particularly in the works of Wu Wen-ying and Chang Yen, made their *tse* difficult even for other poets to understand and appreciate.

In 1126 the armies of the state of Chin invaded China, captured the capital and took Emperors Hui Tsung and Chin Tsung as prisoners. The following year Emperor Kao Tsung established his capital in modern Hangchow. The loss of the territory north of the Yangtse River, and the suffering and humiliation of the people, fired the patriotic feeling of poets, who also felt ashamed that China's ministers were trying to appease the Tartars. Many poets in this period ceased observing strictly the requirements of *tse* and took up the vigorous and free style of Su Tung-po's *tse*. Among them Yao Fei, Hsin Chi-chi, Lu Yu (1125–1209) and Liu Ke-chuan (1187–1269) were the best known and the achievement of Hsin Chi-chi was the greatest.

Many Chinese scholars now consider Hsin Chi-chi the greatest of the writers of *tse* of the South Sung Dynasty (1127–1276). But it was the poets who pursued formal beauty and observed the rules of *tse* who were considered to be representative of poetic orthodoxy and were most respected and imitated. For, following the peace treaty signed by Emperor Kao Tsung with the Tartars in 1141, the government and the people, living in the rich provinces south of the Yangtse, soon forgot their compatriots north of the river and ignoring the growth of another foreign state in the North, indulged in material comfort in the ensuing period of shameful peace and prosperity. In the hundred-odd years before the Mongolians swept down from the North and put China under foreign rule for the first time in her history, beauty of form became the primary objective of poets in writing *tse*.

Here are *tse* written by Liu Yung, Su Tung-po and some of the other poets mentioned above.

TO THE TUNE OF SHEN CHA TSE by Ouyang Hsiu

On the Yuan-yeh[17] of last year,
In the flower market, lights were bright as day;
When the moon was up to the top of the willow trees,
In the evening, I had a meeting with my man.

This year, on the night of Yuan-yeh,
The moon and the lights remain bright;
But I do not see the man I met last year
And the sleeves of my spring robe are wet with tears.

TO THE TUNE OF YU LIN LIN by Liu Yung

Amidst the sad shrilling of a few cicadas in the evening,
In the Pavilion of Leave-taking,
After a shower has stopped—
We sit and drink in misery,
Lingering over our parting,
As the boatman hurries us.
Holding hands, we look into each other's eyes
Brimming with tears, and our hearts are full.
I am sailing into a thousand miles
Of misty waves. Over the evening haze that hangs
Dark and heavy, the sky of Tsu looms in great expanse.

Ever since ancient times, lovers have grieved o'er partings,
That did not fall on such a desolate, gloomy autumn day.
Where shall I wake up from this drunken stupor?
—By a bank of willows
When the morning wind stirs under the fading moon.
In this year of long separation,
Happy occasions and beautiful scenery will not be for me;
And even if I should be deeply moved
To whom should I tell my feelings?

TO THE TUNE OF SHUI TIAO KO TOU by Su Tung-po

How often is there this bright, full moon?
Holding a cup, I ask the blue sky:
'In what year, is this night—
Up in the Celestial Palaces?'
I want to go back, riding on the wind,
But I am afraid that high in the crystal towers,
I cannot endure the cold.

Around the red pavilion;
Down to the silk-screened door,
The moon shines on the sleepless.
Surely, she is not malicious,
Yet why does the full moon shine—
When we are parted?
Imperfect is life:
Men part and meet, the moon waxes and wanes.
I only pray that we shall live long
And though a thousand miles apart, share the beauty of the moon.

TO THE TUNE OF HSI KIANG YUEH by Su Tung-po

Things in life happen as if in a dream
And yet how many times, one finds oneself
Again in autumn? Fallen leaves rustled last night
In the corridor. Over the brows, by the temples
One looks for signs of ageing.

When wine is cheap
There are few friends around;
When the moon is bright,
It is often shaded by clouds.
At this Mid-Autumn Festival
Who is to enjoy with me the lonely moon?
Holding a wine-cup, I look sadly northward.

TO THE TUNE OF TA SHA HSING by Chin Kuan

Terraces are lost in the fog,
And the moonlit mists—where is the ferry?
Peach Spring,[18] too, cannot be found.
How, in the lonely hostel, with its doors closed,
Is one to bear the chill of spring?
Amidst the calls of the cuckoo, the sun sets.

Songs of longing
And letters from home
Have formed this boundless sorrow.
The Chun River would do well to circle around
The Chun Hill. For whom should it flow
Down to Hsiao-hsiang?

TO THE TUNE OF HAO SHIH CHIN by Lee Ching-chao

Fallen flowers pile up on the ground
When the wind falls. Outside the curtains
Are heaps of red and mounds of snowy white.
Long will I remember that after apple-blossoms fade
Spring will soon be over.

The cups are empty
When songs have ceased and the party is over;
Only the oil lamp flickers.
Even in dreams, sorrow is with me.
How am I to stand also
The wail of the owl?

TO THE TUNE OF HO HSIN LANG by Hsin Chi-chi

O, how weak I have become!
I am sad that in my lifetime
My friends have scattered and died
And only a few of them now remain.

Now that my hair is white and long
Worldly affairs can laughingly be dismissed.
You ask what
Will make me happy?
I find the green hills charming,
Charming, too, they may well find me;
My feelings and appearance
Are roughly the same.

By the east window, I sit with a bottle of wine.
Perhaps Yuan-ming[19]
Having written his Ting-yun poem
Felt what I feel now?
Those who chase after fame in Kiangtso[20]
Would not understand the attraction of wine.
Turning around I shout from my heart.
With it, clouds seem to move and winds rise.
I don't regret not having met people of ancient times
But regret their not seeing how wild I am!
Only two or three people
Know how I feel.

CHAPTER XI

Libretti of the Yuan and Ming Dynasties

1. THE EMERGENCE OF CHU[1]

IT will be recalled that *tse*, the most popular poetic form of the Sung Dynasty, came into being when 'new-style' poetry of the Tang Dynasty became too stylized, and poets sought a new vehicle of expression in the songs of the people. *Chu* of the Yuan Dynasty (1277–1367) developed in the same manner. For writing *tse* had become so hard, laden as the form was with so many refinements and sophistications towards the end of the South Sung Dynasty (1127–1276) that only a small number of poets could be said to have mastered the difficult art. Poets felt that *tse* was no longer a poetic vehicle through which they could express their feelings freely. The common people felt that it had nothing to do with their lives any more, for it could no longer be sung, although it was from the songs of the people that *tse* began.

At this time foreign tribes encroached upon Chinese territory and occupied several parts of it. The Chitan tribe established the kingdom of Liao in north-west China. The Tartars, who allied themselves with the Chinese to defeat the Chitans, established the kingdom of Chin, and went on to capture and rule the territory north of the Yangtse River, while the Chinese Emperor and his court fled south of the river and set up the South Sung Dynasty. Together with the invaders came their songs, and the common people were the first to sing them. According to one source, even as early as the reign of Hsuen Ho[2] (1119), 'people in the streets of the capital often sang foreign songs. . . . The verses were extremely vulgar, but many of the *literati* also developed a taste for them.'[3] Inevitably, the *literati* tried to write their own verses to the tunes of foreign music. This came to be known as *chu*.

Chu in its earliest form was short, and there were no set rules as to form and rhyme. This form was called *hsiao ling*, or ditties, which was exactly what it was. In some of the best of them we can still detect the flavour of folk songs, which perhaps shows that from using the original verses of foreign songs to the *literati*'s composing better and more expressive verses for the tunes, there was an intermediate stage when ordinary people wrote their own crude verses to foreign music. I quote here two *hsiao ling* by Kuan Han-ching, one of the best writers of *chu*.

> It was quiet outside the gauze-green window
> And nearby, no one was to be seen;
> He knelt down anxiously—
> > Searching for a kiss.

> 'You ingrate!' I said, and turned away:
> Even though I scolded him
> I half resisted
> > And half yielded.

*

> Seeing him off,
> I wished he could have stayed;
> My longing for him is unceasing.
> I stand by the terrace, embraced
> By white flowers of the willows
> Gazing—
> > The stream meanders
> The hill closes in
> And he is not where I used to see him.

The best *hsiao ling* were written by Ma Chih-yuan, who excelled in creating word-images comparable to the best of the 'stop-short' poems of the Tang Dynasty. His *Tien Ching Sha* is by general consensus one of the finest short poems ever written in Chinese.

> Dead vines (entwine)
> Old trees (over which fly)
> Black crows;

> (By a) tiny bridge
> (Over a) little creek,
> (There is a) lone house;

(On an) unused path
(In the) autumn breeze
(An) emaciated horse (has halted).

(For) the sun is setting
In the West
(And) the heart-broken man
Has come to the end of the world.

I have followed the original order of the words in translating this poem, and except for the last stanza have tried to show by using brackets to exclude the words I have added that the original is a short poem of words dexterously arranged into a word-image. Altogether there are only twenty-eight Chinese words. Perhaps if the reader imagines that the stanzas are rhymed also, it is possible to appreciate this poem as the Chinese do.

Soon, however, *hsiao ling* was found to be inadequate to contain fully the poets' feelings, and *shuang tiao* or double tunes, which consist of verses written to two or three different tunes, came into being. Later these were further expanded to form *tao chu*, or a set of tunes. In a set of tunes all the tunes must be in the same key, and must have the same rhythm. In most cases there is also an epilogue to signify the end of a set of tunes. These three forms of musical lyric are called *san chu*,[4] or 'separate songs', as opposed to operas which are organic entities.

Here it must be pointed out that although *tse* and *chu* are both verses written to tunes of varying lengths, in *chu* poets are allowed to add to the prescribed number of words to make them better for singing. The extra words are called *chen* words, or 'fillers'. Furthermore, although every *chu* must have only one rhyme, words of three of the four tones of the Chinese language, that is, the soft, acute and grave tones, are considered to rhyme with each other, thereby allowing greater freedom to poets. The result is that *chu* is free from the restrictions of prescribed forms and limited rhymes. This explains why it is nearest to spoken language in Chinese rhymed verses.

Together with the development of these new forms of lyrics Chinese drama also came into being at this time. Although China was perhaps the slowest among ancient civilized nations to develop drama, she had nevertheless produced variety shows, such as song and dance acts, humorous story-telling, wrestling, puppet shows, shadow plays, etc. By the Sung Dynasty (960–1276) there were developed comical and satirical shows.[5] But apart from the fact that such shows were the first to employ five people and thereby encourage later poets to expand the structure of their poetic dramas, their importance was less than that of *kutse tse*, which was probably developed under the influence of *pien wen*,[6] using songs and linking narration to tell a story. For *kutse tse* was the first of a series of art forms which developed gradually into the Chinese opera, the only form of drama that China knew before Western plays were introduced at the beginning of this century.

The most famous of *kutse tse* is *Shang Tiao Tieh Luan Hua* by Chao Ling-shih, which is based on *Ying-ying Chuan*, one of the famous stories of the Tang Dynasty by Yuan Chen (see pp. 192–9). But as the songs of *kutse tse* were all sung to one and the same tune, it was gradually replaced by *chu kung tiao*, which consisted of a varying number of sets of songs, in each of which songs were sung to a number of tunes of the same *kung tiao* or, roughly, key, and each set of songs could be in different keys. *Kutse tse* were as a rule rather short, consisting of some twelve or fewer songs to the set, with narration, while *chu kung tiao* had no set rules as to length. They could have different numbers of sets of tunes and each set could have different numbers of songs. Thus, it was more flexible than *kutse tse*, and the songs were less monotonous and more pleasing to the ear. According to Wang Shuo's *Random Jottings in Pi Chi*, 'During the reigns of Hsi Feng and Yuan Yu, Kung San-chuan of Tse-chow first created *chu kung tiao*, and the *literati* of the day could all sing them.' It is a pity that we don't know more about Kung, but as he was mentioned in connection with other artists who made a living by telling stories, he must have been one of them. As a rule they were not scholars.

Three *chu kung tiao*[7] have come down to us, of which Tung Chieh-yuan's *Hsien So Hsi Hsiang* is complete, and seems to be the best. It also is based on Yuan Chen's *Ying-ying Chuan*, but instead of an abrupt, tragic and, to many people, unreasonable ending, it ends with the hero and the heroine getting married. The author also added to the story a few characters, the most successfully drawn of which is Hung-niang, the maid, who acts as go-between, and plays a big part in the romance. What impresses the Chinese most is the beauty of the verses.

We know only that Tung Chieh-yuan lived in the reign of Emperor Chang Tsung of the state of Chin (1190–1208), and nothing else about him, but his *chu kung tiao* was the only literary achievement of his country during her one hundred and twenty years' existence to have

gained wide recognition and been handed down to posterity. Here is a
passage from it.

(*To the tune of* Yu-yi Shen *in* Ta-shih *key*[8])

A candidate for official posts starts
On his journey to the Imperial Capital
And is being seen off outside the city;
For a short time has he lived with Ying-ying.
The desire for fame drives them apart.
He is going to seek a career,
But he feels sad, sighing,
Sighing, he does not take leave lightly.
He is rueful, desolate, and miserable.
Why should he leave
On a late autumn day?

The rain has stopped, towards evening
The wind is cuttingly cold,
Must there be the mournful screeching of cicadas
On the leafless willows?
When is he going to see her again,
After this day—today?

Wiping tears unceasingly, his sleeves are wet,
And heavy on his brow lies his sorrow;
How is he to leave?
What good is it to talk,
Of their life and love in the last six months,
Of the myriad feelings and things?
And to whom is he to talk from now on?

EPILOGUE

Don't think that a man's heart is hard as stone,
Don't you see that the leaves all over the valley
Are painted by the blood from the eyes
Of wayfarers . . . when their tears run dry?

(Chun-jui and Ying-ying can't tear themselves away from each other, and her
 mother
Says, 'However long you may linger, you will eventually have to part.')

(To the tune of Chu Tui Tse *in* Huang chung *key)*

Saddest it is to part
When each cries out for the other;
Dazed and benumbed from crying is Ying-ying,
Her tear-stained face looks blood-smeared.
To whom will she entrust
Her sentiments and love, all devouring?

Mrs Tsui says:
'It is getting dark. Tell him to hurry.'
Her heart is hard as nails,
Hung Niang helps Ying-ying to her fragrant carriage.
Chun-jui climbs on his horse,
'Bewitching darling, try to bear with this parting!'

EPILOGUE
The horse is on its way,
The carriage heads for home;
The horse gallops westward,
The carriage goes east.
Every moment, the lovers
Are further away from each other.

(To the tune of Shang Hua Shih *in* Hsien kung *key)*

Noisily cry the crows
Over the forest, in the setting sun,
Urging on the lean horse, he goes
On a path leading to the far horizon.
By the lonely river bank
Frost has covered the decaying grass.
A few trees stand near to a stretch of sand
By the stream. An old man is fishing
Near the bridge. There are cottages
In the flowers of rush groves.

EPILOGUE
To a hunchbacked willow tree
Is tied a fishing boat;
Over the eaves of a cottage,
Flies a flag on a bamboo pole.
A slight haze has fallen, hanging
Over two or three houses.
(Chung-jui goes into the village inn.)

It can be seen here that the author tried to present several people's points of view, with linking narration and dialogue. This was the evidence of *chu* becoming the libretti of Chinese opera. Gradually, the division of roles to be sung by different peoples became clearer, so that in the end music, dialogue, stage design and acting were complete, and became an organic entity.

It seemed inevitable that because of the affinity of *san chu* and *chu kung tiao* there should develop an art form which combined the merits of both. That *tsa chu* or Northern Drama, the first kind of Chinese opera, did come about, however, was due primarily to the conquest of China by the Mongols in 1279, and the establishment of the Yuan Dynasty and all which ensued from foreign rule. For the Mongols, being a nomadic people, ignored and destroyed the agricultural economy developed in China during the Tang and Sung Dynasties. They also disregarded Chinese culture and assigned Chinese in the south who were under the rule of the Emperors of the South Sung Dynasty to the lowest caste of the people.[9] This was the darkest hour in Chinese history. The people were not only conquered but had lost the standards by which they regulated their lives. Under Mongol rule no Civil Service examination was held from the reign of Kubla Khan on, and Chinese scholars were treated as equals of only prostitutes and beggars, perhaps because the Mongols wanted to destroy Confucianism. Deprived of their traditional way of making a living, not to mention gaining fame and position, the scholars turned to other ways to support their families. Those who had some knowledge of music turned to writing libretti, for there was a demand for entertainment. The Mongols had created a vast empire which embraced most of the Euro-Asian land mass. There was greatly improved inter-continental transportation, and with it an expanded volume of international trade. The resultant prosperity led the people to find entertainment and amusement in shows. Owners of entertainment establishments turned to scholars and musicians for help in producing shows, and so Northern Drama came into being.

Northern Drama in its standard form consists of:

(*a*) *Libretto*. Sets of *tao chu* or lyrics to various tunes in the same key. A set of lyrics together with dialogue and directions for acting, forms an act in an opera, which must have four acts. However, many authors used a subterfuge in the form of *chitse* to get away from this limitation. *Chitse* normally means 'introduction', but as used in Northern Drama it means simply an addition. It may consist of only one or two ditties, or it may be as long as an act. It may be at the beginning of an opera, or between acts.

(*b*) *Dialogue.* The Chinese of that period did not seem to care too much about dialogue. Tsang Mou-hsun said in his preface to *A Selection of Operas of Yuan Dynasty*, 'Dialogue was made up by singers as they sang in an opera. Much of it was therefore vulgar, or pedantic.' To a certain extent this is true. Nevertheless, there is excellent dialogue in Kuan Han-ching's *Tou O Yuan*, Wang Shih-fu's *Western Chamber*, etc.

(*c*) *Directions for acting.* These are called *ko* or 'acts'. There are many directions in an opera, written usually under the characters in the book, such as 'Act as if crying', 'Act like a drunkard', etc.

Apart from this there are also directions about make-up, including the kind of beard to be used, costume and props. The most impressive advance made in Northern Drama perhaps lay in the increase in the numbers of singer-actors. There were five different roles for men singers, ten for women singers, and many different roles for 'extras'. This was brought about by the comparatively complicated plots of the stories, and added to the dramatic effect. On the other hand, Northern Drama had a serious defect, which was that all the lyrics in an act, sometimes the entire libretto of an opera, were sung by the same singer. Only rarely in *chitse*, or at the end of an act, were other singers allowed to join in. What is strange is that no one seemed to mind, and no effort was made to change this during the long time that Northern Drama was in vogue.

According to *Lu Kwei Pu*, which is a book about the development of Chinese drama published in 1330, thirty-odd years after the Yuan Dynasty was overthrown, there were 458 titles of Northern Drama. Authors of operas listed in the book can be divided into two groups: those who died before the year 1300 and those who were still living in that year. The majority of the first group were natives of Ta Tu or Peking, and other northern regions, while those in the second group were mostly people who had migrated to or were natives of southern China, principally from Hangchow. Thus, whether it is because Northern Drama followed the Mongol conquerors to the south, or simply because the author of *Lu Kwei Pu* went to Hangchow and tended to select Northern Dramas written by authors in nearby districts, it would seem that Northern Drama had become popular in the south in the later period of the Yuan Dynasty, and exerted great influence in the development of *nan hsi* or Southern Drama.

In its earliest form, which was nothing but ditties strung loosely together to tell a story, Southern Drama had existed since the reign of Emperor Hui Tsung of the Sung Dynasty. We now have only some ditties from *Inspector Chen Lost His Wife in Meiling*, one of the five known titles of these dramas of the Sung Dynasty. Of the Southern Dramas of the Yuan Dynasty, there are now three such texts extant, i.e. *Little Sun Tu*, *Chang Hsieh Chuang-yuan* and *Huan-men Tse-ti Tsuo Li Sheng* (*Mistakes of the Son of an Official*). They are not of high artistic standard, but from them it can be seen that Southern Drama differs from Northern Drama in many ways. First, while Northern Drama is divided into acts, Southern Drama has only one act and an introduction. Secondly, while the lyrics of an act in Northern Drama are sung by only one person, in Southern Drama they can be sung by as many as necessary. Thirdly, in Northern Drama, the lyrics of each act must be written to tunes of the same key, and the rhyming must not be changed. There is no such restriction in Southern Drama.

When Northern Drama became popular in the south the writers of Southern Drama started to improve the style and content of their drama to compete. But it was not until some thirty years later during the last years of the Yuan Dynasty and the first years of the Ming Dynasty (1368–1643) that good Southern Dramas were produced. By that time the Southern Drama had become what is known as *chuan chi* and had any number of acts. The best of these written in this period were *Dog Killing*, *White Rabbit*, *Pray to the Moon*, *The Story of Pipa* and *The Story of Ching Cha*, of which the first three were either based on earlier popular stories or written by unknown authors, and the fourth was written by Kao Ming, a scholar. The last was written by Prince Ning Hsien of the Ming Dynasty. *The Story of Pipa* (a four-stringed musical instrument) is perhaps the best of the lot. It has forty-two acts and tells the story of the bride Chao Wu Niang who after her husband Tsai Po-chia went to the capital to sit the Civil Service examination, remained at home to take care of her parents-in-law. Po-chia passed the examination with top marks, married the daughter of the Premier, and stayed in the capital, forgetting all about his family at home. There was famine in his home town, and his parents died in spite of the efforts of Wu Niang to save them. Wu Niang buried her parents-in-law and, playing the *pipa* and begging for food all the way, went to the capital to look for her husband. She found him after some time and, with the consent of his second wife, stayed with him. When the Emperor heard of her filial piety and her love for her husband he was deeply moved, and sent Tsai Po-chia and his wife back to their home town to rebury his parents in the proper manner, and bestowed on them both honour and many gifts.

The Story of Pipa is famous for the skill with which the author described the emotions of the characters, and his use of easy-to-understand language. Here is a short passage from the twenty-ninth act, describing the last visit Wu Niang paid to the tomb of her father-in-law before she set out on her journey:

TAN[10]: Since he died, apart from the few moments in my dream,
    I have not been able to see him.
    Even if I tried to draw a picture of him, I could not succeed.
    I think of him and tears roll down my cheeks
    Before I write about him.
    How am I to write about the bitterness in his heart?
    How am I to draw the way he suffered from hunger.
    How am I to paint his expectant look—
    Brightly shining, gazing, looking for his son.
    I can only paint his dishevelled hair
    And his clothes, dirty and worn.
    No, no!
    And yet, if I paint a picture of a healthy man
    He would not be that father-in-law of mine.

    His soul must have wandered afar
    And I am alone, having no one to depend on.
    The journey is one of ten thousand miles
    And I am frightened.
    I shall now go to visit his tomb.

CHORUS: Everywhere I look there is sadness.
    Tears fill my eyes and drop to the ground.

The flowering of *chuan chi*, however, proved to be short-lived. The immediate reason was that the capital of the Ming Dynasty was soon moved from the present Nanking to Peking, where Northern Drama originated, and was still popular. Royal patronage of it added to its popularity, while *chuan chi*, for the lack of a definite way to sing the libretti, lapsed into confusion and finally died out. It was not until some two hundred years later, during the reign of Chia Ching (1522–1566) that it was revived. This was primarily due to the efforts of Wei Liang-fu. We do not know much about his life, but he was a great musician who devoted ten years to establishing new tunes and rules for the music of *kun chiang*, which were being sung in the Kun Shan District of Kiangsu Province. This was one of the four styles of singing the lyrics of *chuan chi*, and Wei instituted a harmony of sounds, based on his study of musical instruments. This proved to be so popular that from then on *chuan chi* was sung only in *kun chiang*. Because it was so popular, Northern Drama adapted several features of it for its own. It became much shorter, and was finally replaced by *chuan chi*.

A trend towards using allegory and parallel structures in lyrics started with Liang Tseng-yu's *Huan Sha*, or *Washing Gauze*, which was the first and best *chuan chi* to be written in *kun chiang*. Eventually, *chuan chi* became 'lacking not only in beauty of libretti, but also in true expression of emotion'.[11] Authors strove to satisfy the artificial standards which had been imposed on the music, and *chuan chi* became something quite different from the art form of the people from which it had originated. Had it not been for Tang Hsien-tsu (1550–1617), who broke away from the restraints which had been imposed upon the music of *chuan chi* and wrote operas in a new tradition, this form of expression would probably have spent its force by the late Ming Dynasty. As it was, we have Lee Yu, Yuan Ta-chen and others of the Ming Dynasty, and Hung Sheng, Kung Shang-jen, etc., of the Ching Dynasty (1644–1911) who wrote *chuan chi*, which are still being enjoyed today. Another author, Shen Ching, also contributed in no small measure to changing the trend in writing lyrics and freeing such writing from the rules which had been imposed upon it. Few of his works, however, have survived.

During the reign of Chien Lung (1735–1795), of the Ching Dynasty, *chuan chi* and *hua pu*, or local operas of various districts, became merged. The latter were easier to understand, the tunes more pleasing to the ear, and the subjects had more variety and were very popular. Those that originated in Huang Kang and Huang Po districts in Hupei Province and merged with those of Anhwei Province were brought to Peking in the early years of Hsien Feng (1851–1861). Cheng Chang-keng improved the tunes of this type of opera, or *pi huang* as it was called, based on the principles of *kun chiang*, and the operas became very popular in the capital. Later this type of opera acquired the accents of the Peking dialect and became known as *erh huang* or *ching hsi*, which means Peking opera. This is the main form of Chinese opera being sung today.

2. *KUAN HAN-CHING, WANG SHIH-FU AND THEIR WORKS*

Kuan Han-ching was probably born in 1224, the first year of the reign of King Ai Tsung of the state of Chin. When Chin was conquered by the Mongols he was about eleven years old. But unlike Pai Po, another famous writer of Northern Drama, who was only seven when Chin was lost, and later refused repeatedly to serve under the Mongols, Kuan did not seem to care too much about the affairs of the country. It is said that he once served as a clerk in the Royal Academy of Medicine, and later presented one of his Northern Dramas, *Yi Yun Fu Tang*, to the government. Perhaps too much should not be made of this, for after all the Mongols were at the height of their power, and the end of foreign rule was nowhere in sight.

Furthermore, Kuan was not from an official or scholar's family, which traditionally serves the country as a matter of duty. He came from, probably, a lower-middle class family which tends to regard a change of dynasty as natural as the change of seasons, or, as the saying goes, this kind of family 'just goes on paying taxes'. According to Tsang Mou-hsun's preface to *A Selection of Operas of the Yuan Dynasty*, Kuan would go to the theatre, put on his make-up and act, feeling that this was his life, and did not mind being found in the company of singers and actors, who were not accorded great respect in society. In *Pu Fu Lao (Never Say Too Old)*, one of his *tao chu*, he said that he was happy with the life he was leading: 'Even if you knocked out my teeth, struck askew my mouth, made me a cripple and broke my arms, you would not change me from what I am. Unless King Yen of Hell personally summons me, gods and ghosts come to fetch me, and my three souls are brought to hell, my seven spirits lost in purgatory, I will go on leading a gay life.'

Kuan's way of looking at life helped him greatly in his work. He knew what the ordinary people liked to listen to, what the requirements of the theatre were, and he based his writing on popular stories and legends known to the people, and presented them in a way which was acceptable to professionals as well. He must have been a highly successful actor-playwright in his time, too, for there is no record of his ever having taken another job. We know that he wrote more than sixty Northern Dramas, of which fourteen have been handed down to us. The great number of his dramas shows that he was constantly in demand, which enabled him to live the kind of life he liked.

According to Wu Mei's *Ku Chu Chu Tan* (*Random Thoughts on Chu*), Kuan Han-ching once saw a beautiful maid and tried very hard to have her for a concubine, but was frustrated by his wife. Helpless, he wrote a ditty to his wife:

> Her hair is black
> Her cheeks, rosy.
> It's a shame that she is a maid.
> Her manners are those of a girl from a rich family
> And are equal to those of Hung Niang.
> She always has a smile for me and talks elegantly.
> She is like a flower which understands me.
> If I should have her as mine,
> Will you be jealous?

His wife replied also by a poem:

> I hear you've been casting your eyes on a beauty,
> This is totally unlike King Kuan, your kin, and a brave man;
> Should you set up a separate household for her,
> I would certainly be terribly jealous.

Kuan had to give up.

The range of his dramas was wide, and his work touched upon many subjects. There are historical romances such as *Tan Tou Huei* (*Meeting Enemies Alone*); and dramas which deal with social problems such as *Chiu Feng Chen* (*Saving a Prostitute*); family relations, such as *Tou O Yuan* (*Injustice Suffered by Tou O*); and on trials, such as *The Execution of Lu Tsai Lang*. Kuan was equally good at writing tragedies, comedies and satires, and his lyrics were descriptive and always full of gusto. Wang Kuo-wei, the modern authority on Chinese drama, in his

History of the Drama of Sung and Yuan Dynasties said of him, 'Han-ching did not depend on anyone to create his great operas. His libretti have a host of vivid characters of different background, and every word he wrote was apt.'

Because of his great accomplishments and of the fact that according to all available evidence, he was the writer who established the final form of Northern Drama, Kuan Han-ching's contribution to the Chinese theatre has been compared to Shakespeare's to the English theatre. Whether Kuan's work was of the same quality is, of course, a matter of taste and judgment. Of Kuan's dramas, the best known are *The Injustice Suffered by Tou O, Meeting Enemies Alone* and *Saving a Prostitute*. The first-named is perhaps the most highly praised, and was said by Wang Kuo-wei to be one of the best tragedies in world literature. According to Professor Su Hsieh-lin of the National Normal College of Taiwan, it has been translated into French.

The Injustice Suffered by Tou O concerns a girl named Tou O who has been given by her father to a moneylender, Mother Tsai, to be her daughter-in-law in order to repay a loan and secure money for his trip to the capital to take part in the Civil Service examination. Not long afterwards Tou O's husband dies, and the two women, sustaining each other, live on. One day, Mother Tsai goes to collect her loan from Dr Lu. Lu, unable to repay her, lures her to a suburb and tries to kill her by putting a rope around her neck but, at the last moment, Mother Tsai is saved by Donkey Chang, senior and junior, a father-and-son team of scoundrels. Knowing that Mother Tsai is rich, the pair turn this good deed to their advantage and impose themselves on the Tsai household. Once installed, the younger Chang insists that Mother Tsai should marry his father, and Tou O should marry him. Tou O opposes the idea strongly, and the Changs are furious. They decide to do away with her, in order to get Mother Tsai's money when Mother Tsai is married to one of them. One day, when Mother Tsai is ill, and asks Tou O to prepare 'lamb's stomach soup', the younger Chang slips some poison into the soup, hoping to kill Mother Tsai and come into her money. But the older Chang drinks the soup by mistake and dies, whereupon the younger Chang accuses Tou O of murdering his father. The local magistrate, by using torture, forces Tou O to confess to her alleged crime. When she is to be executed she prays that her blood will spray a flag which is flying eight feet from the ground, instead of flowing to the ground, that it snows in June, and that there should be drought for three years in succession. All three wishes come true. In the end, Tou O's father, who after many years becomes an important official, returns to his home town and finds the culprit and clears her name.

Here are two passages from the libretto of this opera, both sung by Tou O. The first passage is sung after the discovery of the older Chang's death.

Tou O is telling Mother Tsai, who had wanted to marry the older Chang, not to cry unduly over his death.

Tou O *sings*: It's no use to grieve too much,
Life and death are part of transmigration.
When one is sick, only one knows
Whether it is due to wind, cold, heat or damp;
Or hunger, over-eating, overwork.
When a man dies,
Is there anything the living can do?
The span of one's life is not for us to decide.
You have known him only for a short while,
It is silly to talk of the family and our livelihood:
He did not give you lamb, wine or silk,
Or flowers, or money or wedding presents.
He worked with his hands for a living,
When he died, he had nothing to do with you!
Please forgive Tou O's impudence,
But are you not afraid of people's gossip?
Listen to me,
Treat this as your bad luck:
Give him a coffin
And a few pieces of cloth
And get him out of our house.
Send him to his own cemetery.
He is not the husband you married when you were young.

He is not my relative
And I have no tears for him.
Oh please do not act as if you were drunk
As if you were stunned
And sigh and grieve
And cry and wail.

The following passage is sung just before Tou O is put to death:

TOU O *sings*: Please, in consideration of the years that I have served you,
        Mother, give a bowl of cold porridge as offering
        And burn a few paper coins over my dead body.
        —Think of it as acts done for your dead son.

MOTHER TSAI *says*: Please don't worry, my daughter. I'll remember
what you said. Oh, God, why should this happen to me!

TOU O *sings*: Oh, dear Mama!
        Don't keep on crying and wailing,
        Don't be too deeply grieved
        Or harbour great resentment.
        All this was fated to be,
        There was nothing I could do to clear myself,
        Innocent though I am.

THE EXECUTIONER *shouts*: There, old woman, get back. It's almost
time. . . .

TOU O *sings*: It is not that I want to make untoward wishes
        But I have suffered great injustice.
        Were there no miracle for the world to see,
        How are people to know there is God?
        I pray not a drop of my blood will fall on the earth,
        But that it should spray the white flag
        That hangs from the pole eight feet above.
        So that everyone can see.

        You may think that the summer heat is hot
        That this is not the time for snow.
        Haven't you heard, though, that because of Chou Yen[12]
        Snow fell in June?
        If my grievance is like a billowing flame,
        It must snow in June, and cover the ground like cotton
            flowers,
        Covering my dead body
        So that I need no white carriage or white horse
        To take me out to the old fields and desolate hills.
        (*She kneels and says*)
        Sir! It is a great injustice to put me to death.

From now on, there will be drought for three consecutive
years here in Tsu-chow!

THE EXECUTIONER *says*: Be quiet! Whoever has heard of such a thing!

TOU O *sings*: You may think that God's will cannot be anticipated,
        That human misery is not to be pitied,
        But He does grant people's wishes,
        Do you not know there was no rain in Tung-hai
        Because a filial woman suffered an injustice?
        Now it's Shang-yan District's turn,
        Because no official here abides by the law
        And the people cannot make themselves heard.

Kuan led a successful life and lived to about the age of seventy-three years. There was a belief during the Ming Dynasty that Kuan Han-ching also wrote the last part of *The Western Chamber* after Wang Shih-fu died of exhaustion after writing the first four-fifths. This would have added to Kuan's laurels had it been true, for *The Western Chamber* is considered by some critics the best Northern Drama, and it was a love story, which Kuan could not list among his works. Unfortunately *Lu Kwei Pu*, the earliest book on Chinese drama, which was written in the Yuan Dynasty, asserts that Wang Shih-fu wrote *The Western Chamber*, based on Tung Chieh-yuan's *Hsien So Hsi Hsiang*, and did not mention Kuan.

Wang Shih-fu was, like Kuan Han-ching, a native of Ta Tu, and several years his junior. It is said that he wrote fourteen Northern Dramas, but of them only three complete ones remain. The most famous was *The Western Chamber*. It is not only the longest of all Northern Dramas of the Yuan Dynasty, consisting of five books of four acts each, but also the only one to have a closely knit plot. The first three books describe the meeting of Chang Sheng and Ying-ying, the gradual change in Ying-ying's attitude toward Chang Sheng after he rescues her family from a band of brigands, his subsequent illness, and his love for her, through to the consummation of their love with the help of Hung-niang, the maid. The fourth book is devoted to the discovery of the affair by Ying-ying's mother, and the lovers' separation. The last book describes how the lovers overcome the last hurdle of suspicion and finally marry each other. Except for the happy ending it has the same story as Yuan Chen's *Ying-ying Chuan*.

Here is a passage from Act 2, Book 4, of the drama, after Hung-niang finds out why Lady Tsui, Ying-ying's mother, has sent for her:

HUNG-NIANG: *Chieh chieh!*[13] It has been found out! The Old Lady has sent for me. What shall I do?

YING-YING: Please cover up for me!

HUNG-NIANG: Oh, heavens! You cover up for yourself. I'll simply tell her what you have done.

YING-YING *says to herself*: Clouds will come to hide the full moon, just as showers fall when flowers are in bloom.

HUNG-NIANG *sings*: I had thought that meeting him by night and coming back at dawn would lead to marriage between you which lasts forever.

It doesn't matter that you made love,
Although it caused me great concern.
You should have shuttled back and forth under the moon and stars,
Who would think that you always stay the night through?

The Old Lady is cunning,
Her temper is fiery,
However eloquent I am,
It will be of no use.

The Old Lady has guessed
The poor scholar is already a bridegroom,
And my Young Mistress is someone's wife.
And I am the shameless maid who was the go-between.
Recently, Young Mistress, you look happy.
Let us not talk about anything else,
But do put on the belt of your skirt,
Button up all the buttons
And see if you have gained or lost weight.
You look vivacious
And peculiarly alluring.

YING-YING: Hung-niang, be careful what you say.

LIBRETTI

HUNG-NIANG: When I go to the Old Lady's place, she will certainly scold me.
(Sings)
You shameless maid
I only asked you to chaperon Ying-ying
Who told you to lead her astray?
If she were to ask me this,
What shall I say?
—I shall tell her everything.
Chieh chieh, there are good reasons why you should be punished, but why should I be involved?
(Sings)
You made love behind the embroidered screen,
With him you tried every posture.
While I waited outside the window . . .
Did I even utter a cough?
And, of course, you didn't know the cold or damp,
That seeped through my shoes from the moss-covered stone.
Now, my tender flesh is to be struck by coarse sticks
Oh, for what have I acted as your go-between?
Chieh chieh, you wait here. I'll have to go over to the Old Lady's place now. If I succeed in covering up for you, you needn't feel too happy. If I fail, you needn't feel too sad.

From this it can be seen that the character of Hung-niang is quite vivid. Here is a dialogue between Hung-niang and Ying-ying from the introduction of Book 4, which takes place before Ying-ying again goes to meet Chang Sheng at a previously agreed time.

YING-YING: Hung-niang, lay out the bedding, I am going to sleep.

HUNG-NIANG: You are going to sleep! How are you going to deal with the young man?

YING-YING: Which young man?

HUNG-NIANG: Chieh chieh, don't you pretend. It would not be funny to cause his death. If you should fail to keep your word again, I shall tell the Mistress that you asked me to take a note to him and make a date with him.

244

YING-YING: You are indeed difficult! How embarrassing it is to go to him!

HUNG-NIANG: What is there to be embarrassed about? Once you are there just close your eyes. Come on, come on. The Mistress has gone to bed. You may have said you are embarrassed, but your feet start walking before you finish speaking.
(*They go, and Hung-niang knocks on Chang Sheng's door*)

CHANG SHENG: Who is it?

HUNG-NIANG: Your dear old mother reincarnated!

Many Chinese considered the verses in *The Western Chamber* to be too audacious and obscene, others considered them as nothing but pornography. But *The Western Chamber* has won many fervent supporters from the Ming Dynasty down to the present time. Chin Sheng-tan, the famous critic of the Ching Dynasty, considered it, together with *Chuangtse*, *Li Sao*, *The Historical Record*, *Poems* by Tu Fu, and *All Men Are Brothers*, one of the six books of genius in Chinese literature.

3. *THE LIFE OF TANG HSIEN-TSU AND HIS WORKS*

Tang Hsien-tsu (1550–1617) was a typical Chinese scholar, who had great talent and knowledge but who would not modify his opinions to suit anyone, and cared little about what people thought of him. He was rather good-looking, with a fair complexion and clear, bright eyes. According to himself,[14] someone once said of him that, judging from his physiognomy, he was destined to be poor and had no hope of gaining high official position. This turned out to be true. But it was due, at least partly, to his own behaviour. When he was twenty-one, he became *chu-jen* or a scholar of the second rank in his home town in the Ling-chuan District of Kiangsi Province. Seven years later Chang Chu-cheng was the Prime Minister, and wanted his son Tse-hsiu to pass the Civil Service examination together with famous scholars of the country. Chang heard of the fame of Tang Hsien-tsu and Shen Mou-hsueh and asked them to come to the capital to participate in the examination with his son. Shen went, and passed, together with the

Prime Minister's son, with honours, but Tang refused to go, and it was not until he was thirty-three that he finally passed the same examination, and was appointed a minor official in the ministry responsible for sacrificial rites at royal ancestral mausoleums. Presumably, the post was a boring one, and he sought refuge in books. It was said that he invariably studied until midnight, reading out loud the books he liked. When asked why he should bother to study any longer, he said that he liked to, and it had nothing to do with his having an official position. A few years later he was transferred to the Ministry of Appointments, and while he was there he sent a memorial to the Emperor saying that, because there were cliques in the government, no one dared to tell the Emperor what the real situation in the country was. After having sent in his memorandum he said in a letter to one of his friends, 'I have sent a memorial (about cliques in the government) on an impulse. I don't know how the authorities are going to deal with me.'

As it turned out the Emperor was furious, and demoted Tang to be an assistant to the Magistrate of the Hsu-wen District in Kwangtung Province. Later, Tang was promoted again, to be Magistrate of Shiu Chang District of Chekiang Province. There he adopted what he believed to be the method of administration in ancient times: he released all the prisoners and did not keep any records. It is difficult to say what the results were. Anyway, he resigned or was relieved of his post in 1597 and went back to his home town, where he lived for twenty years in Yu Ming Hall, a cottage so small that a pig-sty and a chicken coop had to be placed very near to his bedroom. He died in 1617 at the age of sixty-seven.

There is a collection of his poems and essays, but it is his *Four Dreams of Yu Ming Hall*, a collection of his four *chuan chi*, for which he is famous. *Mou Tan Ting (Peony Pavilion)* is considered by many people to be his best drama. In writing his dramas, Tang Hsien-tsu also showed his strong character. Many of his contemporaries told him that he must change the libretto of *Peony Pavilion* to conform to the prevailing rules of music and rhymes. He answered, 'I believe I know the intricacies of writing libretti. But sometimes I am too lazy to bother about the rules, and it did not seem to matter that the vocal cords of everyone in the country should be hurt singing the verses of *Peony Pavilion*.' Shen Teh-fu, among other critics of Tang's time, said of *Peony Pavilion*, 'Immediately after it was published everyone was talking about it and singing its libretto. The popularity of the opera was almost greater than that of *The Western Chamber*. It is a pity that Tang Hsien-tsu is not well-versed in music, and flagrantly ignores the rules of rhyming. Nevertheless, because of his great talent, the opera will certainly be handed down from generation to generation.'

The critics of that period were all propounders of the rules of music and rhyming, but they had nothing but praise for Tang's work, so much so that Lu Yu-shun took the trouble to alter some of the words in it to make them rhyme better. Tang was, however, not appreciative of Lu's effort. He compared his *Peony Pavilion* to Wang Wei's paintings. 'There was a man who was not happy with a painting of banana trees in winter painted by Wang Wei. He cut away the banana trees part of the painting and replaced it with a piece of paper on which there were plum trees. The painting may have conveyed the winter scene better, but it was not what Wang Wei painted.' No, he did not like Lu to meddle with his opera. In a letter to an opera singer he said, 'You must follow my original libretto and not that which Lu has altered. Even if you only add or take away one or two words to make it easier to sing, you will have greatly changed what I intended the work to be.'

The story of *Peony Pavilion* concerns Tu Pao, Governor of Nan-an County, who decided one day to employ a private tutor to teach his beautiful and talented young twenty-year-old daughter Li Niang. On the first day Chen Chui-liang, the tutor, taught her the first poem in the *Book of Poetry* which is a love song. Li Niang, aroused by the song, let herself be persuaded by her maid, Chun Hsiang, to take a walk in the garden after the lesson. Many flowers, among them peonies, were in full bloom, and birds were singing. Li Niang returned to her bedroom and, tired, fell asleep. She dreamed of meeting a handsome young man in the garden who gave her a branch of willow and compelled her to write poems in reply to those he had written to her. Later, he took her to the Peony Pavilion and made love to her. At the height of their passion a flower fell on her, and she woke suddenly, murmuring, 'Young man, where are you?' Just then her mother came in and heard her, and asked her who she was talking to, but Li Niang refused to say. From then on the dream was always on her mind. One day she went back to the garden and in the Peony Pavilion felt that she could almost relive the scene of her dream. But the young man was not there, and the flowers, too, were fading. It made her feel very sad, and she fell sick. Her illness dragged on for several months. One day Li Niang, horrified at the sight of her own emaciated image in the mirror, decided to paint a picture of herself as she was before she fell sick. When she finished the picture she was saddened by the thought that she had no one to send the painting to. Recalling her dream, she wrote on the painting, 'Should I one day become close to a talented young man it will be like leaning on a plum tree or a willow tree.'[15] On 15 August she died. She had asked to be buried under an old plum tree in the garden, and told her maid Chun Hsiang to leave her painting of herself by a rock. This would seem to be the end of the poor girl.

South of Ta-yu Mountain, however, there lived a poor but handsome scholar by the name of Liu Meng-mei (Willow dreaming of Plum), and three years after Li Niang died he received help from Miao Shun-pin, an Imperial Emissary, and went to the capital to sit the Civil Service examination. When he arrived in Nan-an he fell sick and Chen Chui-liang, who was asked by Li Niang's father on Tu Pao's promotion to Pacification Commander of Huai Yang to take charge of Li Niang's tomb, saw the young man, and took him to the temple in which Li Niang was interred. When he recovered, Liu Meng-mei saw Li Niang's painting. Reading the words inscribed on it, he believed that the artist must have had him in mind and fell in love with the girl in the painting. It so happened that Li Niang was allowed to come back to this world at that time to live out her allotted span of life. She saw the handsome young man who was in love with her painting, and recognized him as the one she had dreamt about. She managed to let him know her identity, and Meng-mei opened up her tomb. Li Niang, whose soul had already come back to earth from the nether world and entered her body, sat up and looked exactly as she did three years ago; in fact, prettier. The young couple decided to go to the capital, where few people knew them, so that Meng-mei could take the examination. After they had left, Chen Chui-liang discovered that Li Niang's tomb had been opened and went to Huai Yang to report to Tu Pao. When he arrived on the outskirts of the city, however, he was caught by Lee Chien, a pirate who had been ennobled by the state of Chin and laid siege to Huai Yang. Lee then sent Chen into the city with a message to Tu Pao, saying that Tu's wife and her maid had been killed by the soldiers and demanding that Tu surrender. Tu Pao, instead of surrendering, sent Chen Chui-liang after a few days to see Lee and ask the latter to surrender. Lee, who was on bad terms with the emissary of Chin, decided to accept Tu Pao's proposal. In the meantime, Liu Meng-mei took the examination but because of the rebellion of Lee Chien the results were withheld. Li Niang, hearing that her father was surrounded by Lee's forces, asked Meng-mei to go to Huai Yang to learn of Tu Pao's fate. By the time Meng-mei arrived in Huai Yang, Lee had already surrendered, and Tu Pao was preparing to leave for the capital after having been promoted Prime Minister. Meng-mei, therefore, hurriedly went to the Governor's house, saying that he was the new Prime Minister's son-in-law. Tu Pao could not believe his ears. He had Meng-mei arrested and sent to the capital where, after he himself had taken up his new post, he could deal with the young man in the proper manner. When they reached the capital the results of the examination were announced, the rebellion of Lee Chien having been put down, and Liu Meng-mei topped the list of successful candidates. While officials were searching for him to invite him to the banquet given by the Emperor in honour of successful candidates, Meng-mei was being tortured in the Prime Minister's house, Tu Pao refusing to believe that his daughter was alive. Fortunately for Meng-mei, the officials found him and saved him from further punishment. At last the Emperor heard of this strange affair and asked Tu Pao, Liu Meng-mei and Li Niang for a personal explanation. Li Niang was able to convince the Emperor that she had really been resurrected because of her love for Meng-mei and on the order of the Emperor the Tu family was reunited.

Peony Pavilion consists of fifty-five scenes and is one of the longest *chuan chi* of the Ming Dynasty. The characterization of Li Niang is very well done. Her constant love for her young man, which survived life and death, won the hearts of many women. This drama gave rise to many romantic legends. Shang Hsiao-ling, an actress of Hangchow, was said to have died of a broken heart after playing in *Peony Pavilion*, when she herself was jilted by her lover. A woman in Nieh-kiang in Szechuan Province was supposed to have become a fanatical admirer of Tang Hsien-tsu after reading *Peony Pavilion* and wrote to him proposing marriage. It was said that Tang wrote back declining the proposal on the grounds of old age. It is certainly true that a woman of Lou-kiang was so deeply moved by the drama that she died of grief over Li Niang's premature death. Tang Hsien-tsu himself wrote a poem in memory of her.

Here is a passage from the tenth scene of the opera, entitled *Ching Meng* (*Dream*).

Li Niang *sings*: Songs of orioles meet my ears
Whenever I wake and everywhere
Light of spring is there. In my room,
Deep in the inner small courtyard,
Sticks of incense have burned down.
Throwing away the coloured threads for my em-
broidery,
I wonder if this spring can be no different
From the spring of last year.

Whence spin with the wind
These gossamer webs to this quiet place?
Like silky threads woven by the spring.
I stop to rearrange my hair-pins
And unexpectedly see half my face
And my long and wavy hair in the mirror.
(*She walks*)
Stepping out of my room, I show myself to the
world. . . .
You see my blouse and petticoat in bright pink,
My hair-clasp of shining precious stones,
Would you know that I have always loved nature?
But it seems that no one cares about spring.
I don't expect birds would chirp so noisily
Simply because of my looks.
I'm afraid that flowers, too, would tremble and
Become sad. . . .

Oh, look, everywhere flowers of every colour have
blossomed.
They have been uncared for in a desolate garden;
What is the use of beautiful scenery, on a fine day?
In whose courtyard are people happily enjoying the
natural beauty?

CHORUS: There are magnificent carved pillars shaded with pearly
screens
And tall terraces that seem to have been lost in clouds;
Out there, over the misty waves, glide picturesque boats
Amidst soft breezes and a little rain.
—All this beauty I have unknowingly missed!

(Li Niang sleeps and dreams of Liu Meng-mei. Liu enters, holding a twig of willow in his hand)

LIU *(speaking to himself)*: I have followed Miss Tu all the way here. Where can she be? *(He turns around and sees Li Niang)* Oh, lady, lady! *(Li Niang awakens and sees him)*

LIU: Where did I not go to look for you? To think that you are right here!
(Li Niang darts a few glances at him but remains silent)

LIU: I have just broken a twig from a willow tree. You are talented and well-read. Would you care to write a poem about it?
(Li Niang appears flattered and happy. She barely stops herself from talking to him, and wonders why he has come to the garden)

LIU: Lady, my love for you is like madness.
(He sings)
> This is because you are beautiful as a flower
> And as time passes like a river of water
> I have looked everywhere for you in vain
> Not knowing that you, too, are filled with longing.

LIU: Let's go over there and talk.
(Li Niang smiles without moving, and Liu pulls at her sleeves and urges her to go with him)

LI NIANG *(in a soft voice)*: Where to?

LIU *sings*:
> Around this trellis of peonies,
> By the rockery with stones from Tai-hu.

LI NIANG: What for?

LIU *sings*:
> To loosen your collar buttons
> And take away the girdle of your clothes. . . .
(Li Niang appears embarrassed. Liu steps forward and tries to embrace her, but she pushes him away)

LI NIANG and LIU *sing together*:
> Where have we met before?
> For I seem to recognize you;
> But why is it that when we meet
> We can find no word to express our happiness?
(Liu lifts Li Niang from the ground and walks away with her in his arms)

CHAPTER XII

Short Stories of the Sung, Yuan and Ming Dynasties

1. THE EVOLUTION OF VERNACULAR SHORT STORIES

THERE seems little doubt that translated Buddhist sutras of great literary value such as *Buddha Charita*, *Vimalakirti-nirdesa*, *Surangama Sutra*, etc., called forth in Chinese writers a greater consciousness of the importance of the imagination in creative writing, as can be seen from the great difference between *Monkey*, where the imagination was given free rein, and *The Biography of Emperor Mu*, for instance, which was written before the influence of Buddhist literature was felt, and comprised the barest outlines of stories. In particular, Buddhist sutras which had both prose and verse in them had direct influence on the growth of fiction as a literary form.

To explain this, it must be recalled that, although Buddhism gained rapidly in popularity during the Northern-Southern Dynasties, the need further to propagate the faith was ceaselessly expounded by the converts, and Buddhist missionaries worked tirelessly to win new converts in the face of intermittent opposition and persecution. Apart from chanting the verses in Buddhist sutras correctly and harmoniously so as to attract the fancy of the people, missionaries explained the often obscure meanings of the sutras by illustrating them in anecdotes and stories with a moral. This process was begun by Huei Yuan, a monk of the East Chin Dynasty (317–420). Monks went to great lengths to arouse and hold the interest of their audience during sermons, and developed a story-telling style. Huei Chiao referred to this in his *Biographies of Great Buddhist Monks*, saying that 'when the monks talked about the transience of life, the people were seized by fear and trembled; when they described the scenes in Hell, the people burst into tears from shock; when they examined the causes of tragedy, the people felt they were witness to wrongdoing; when they preached the moral of their stories, the audience anticipated the punishments which were to follow; when they described happiness, the audience was comforted; when they portrayed sorrow, they whimpered and sobbed. Thus the people were moved and won over. They left their seats to kneel down and repent. And then everyone joined in intoning Buddhist sutras and felt happy.'

The efficacy of this technique became obvious, and was adopted by almost every Buddhist monk. As a result, Buddhist sutras became popular, and *pien wen* was evolved, combining straight narrative explanation of the texts of Buddhist sutras with rhymed verses, descriptive passages and allegories.[1]

It is difficult to say when *pien wen* as a literary form became established. But according to Kuo Chih's *Biography of Kao Li-shih*, 'After the abdication of Emperor Hsuen Tsung who ruled China from 712 to 756, Kao Li-shih the eunuch told him stories based on *pien*, hoping to distract him from his sorrows.' It is possible that *pien wen* were in existence before 756. We now know that they were being written in the tenth century. Nevertheless, before the 1920s, not even the Chinese knew that such a literary form existed, in spite of the fact that there were several references to it in standard works. That a literary form prevalent for almost two centuries should be completely overlooked is certainly a mystery. But part of the reason must be that *pien wen* in itself was of no great literary value. Another reason may be that in the Sung Dynasty telling stories based on Buddhist sutras had become one of the four main forms of popular story-telling, thus masking the individuality of *pien wen*, so that when Emperor Cheng Tsung (998–1022) prohibited Buddhist monks from singing and telling *pien wen* containing texts of Buddhist sutras, story-tellers took over and *pien wen* as a literary form was forgotten.

The discovery of *pien wen* was made in 1907 when Sir Aurel Stein went to Tun-huang in Kansu Province and discovered in the caves a treasure of ancient manuscripts, pictures and antiques. He persuaded the priest who was in charge of the cave to sell to him twenty-four cases of manuscripts and five cases of pictures on silk and other antiques. The following year Paul Pelliot, a French sinologist, having heard of Stein's haul, went to Tun-huang and also took away with him a large number of manuscripts and pictures. In 1910, the Chinese Government ordered the provincial government of Kansu to collect the remaining manuscripts and pictures from the caves and send them to Peking. These were mostly copies of Buddhist sutras. Some of the better manuscripts somehow found their way into private hands and were subsequently sold to the Japanese. Then Sir Aurel Stein went back to Tun-huang and bought from the priest his 'private collection', and there were no more treasures left in Tun-huang.

The treasures of Tun-huang became scattered between the British Museum in London, the Bibliothèque Nationale in Paris, the Museum of Calligraphy in Tokyo and the Peking Library in Peking. Chinese scholars such as Lo Chen-yu, Chen Yuan and Liu Fu did much pioneering research work on them, but it was not until the latter half of the 1920s that they agreed that what they had referred to variously as *fo chu*, or Buddhist songs, and *shu wen*, or popular texts, etc., were in fact *pien wen*. In recent years the introduction of microfilm helped to overcome the difficulties in research arising from the geographical distribution of the four libraries, but the research work is by no means finished. As far as can be judged by dated documents, the manuscripts found in Tun-huang were written between the latter part of the fourth century and the last years of the tenth century. There were some most interesting finds such as Wang Fan-chih's poems and Wei Chuang's *Chin Fu Yin*, a first-class long poem. There were ballads, popular narrative poems and songs. From the point of view of the development of Chinese literature, however, there is no doubt that the most important discovery was the collection of stories written in the literary form of *pien wen*. From these the development of Chinese fiction can be traced from the popularized versions of Buddhist sutras, which was what *pien wen* was, and thus, the influence of Buddhism on Chinese fiction was firmly established.

Pien wen means etymologically 'illustrative text'. *Pien* as used here means change, the opposite of *chang* which means constant. When the meaning of the unchangeable (basic) texts of Buddhist sutras needed to be explained to the uninitiated, different illustrative texts were developed. Pictures were also used for the same purpose, and these were called *pien hsien* or 'illustrative pictures'.

Pien wen was used for a time solely to explain the meanings of Buddhist sutras and to propagate Buddhism. It may be said that of the *pien wen* we now have *Wei Mo Chieh Ching Pien Wen* (*Illustrative Text of Vimalakirti-nirdesa sutra*) is the most important. It has been suggested that the inclusion of several colourful and sometimes action-packed paragraphs in the polished *pien-ti wen* style in *Wei Mo Chieh Ching Pien Wen* was so admired by novelists of later dynasties that in *All Men Are Brothers*, *Golden Lotus* and *Monkey*, for instance, novelists switched to the artificial *pien-ti wen* style to describe in one paragraph a beautiful girl, a battle or some extraordinary scenery. But the most popular *pien wen* is undoubtedly *Mu Lien Chiu Mu Pien Wen* (*Mu Lien (Maugalyāyana) Rescues His Mother*). So far as is known there are three versions of it, *Ta Mu Lien Ming Chien Chiu Mu* (*Great Mu Lien Rescues His Mother from Hell*), which is now in the British Museum; *Mu Lien Yuan Chi* (*The Story of Mu Lien*), which is at the Bibliothèque Nationale; and *Mu Lien Chu Mu Pien Wen* (*Mu Lien Rescues His Mother*), which is at the Peking Library. They all describe Mu Lien's journey through every place in Hell to find and rescue his mother. This is the first Chinese story to describe imaginary scenes in Hell, which may also account for the great interest in it. For we see that this story was already being widely told in the Tang Dynasty. In Wang Ting-pao's *Tang Chih Yen* (*Miscellaneous Anecdotes of the Tang²* *Dynasty*) it is said that Po Chu-yi, the famous poet, once laughed at Chang Ku, another poet, for writing a poem with many questions in it. Chang retorted, 'You seem to have written another version of *Mu Lien Pien Wen*. "Up in Heaven and down in Hell he searched/Nowhere could he find a trace of her." Aren't these two lines about Mu Lien's search for his mother?' He was referring to a couplet from Po's *Song of Everlasting Sorrow*.

Through the ages the popularity of this *pien wen* has remained unchanged. But even in its prime *pien wen* was too good a literary form to serve only religious purposes. Chao Lin of the Tang Dynasty said in his *Ying Hua Lu* that 'There was a Buddhist monk, Wen Shu, who openly gathered groups of people together and, under the pretext of preaching Buddhism, told nothing but vulgar and obscene stories. Persons worked up enthusiasm for his stories by talking about them and many ignorant men and idle women crowded into Wen Shu's temple to listen to him. . . . Prostitutes imitated his style of singing songs.' Chao might have been exaggerating when he said that the monk told obscene stories in a temple, but it may well have been that his stories were not entirely 'illustrative texts' of Buddhist sutras. Thus, it is not unreasonable to look on this Buddhist monk as the forerunner of the writers who adopted the *pien wen* style to tell popular stories.

Judging from the non–Buddhist *pien wen* we now have, it might well be that this form was first used to tell historical stories. Many of these, including *Shuntse Chih Hsiao Pien Wen* (*The Most Filial Hsuntse*), *Lieh Kuo Chih Pien Wen* (*The Story of Lieh Kuo*) and *Ming Fei Pien Wen* (*The Story of Ming Fei*) are historical stories. But the most interesting of these are perhaps *Chiu Hu Pien Wen* (*The Story of Chiu Hu*) and *Tai Tsung Ju Ming Chi* (*Emperor Tai Tsung's Experience in the Nether World*), although the texts we have are not complete. For in these two stories we see the embryo of *hua pen* or the text of story-tellers of the Sung Dynasty. Their style had veered away from the artificial and flowery *pien-ti wen* towards the vernacular language, and the way questions and answers were presented was almost exactly that of the story-tellers.

Here is a short passage from *Emperor Tai Tsung's Experience in the Nether World*:

The Judge was too embarrassed to give his name.

'Come nearer,' the Emperor said. 'You can tell me softly.'

'Tsui Tse-yu.'

'I will remember that.'

The Emperor had barely finished saying this when the Emissary urged him on and brought him to the front door of a court.

'Your Majesty,' said the Emissary, 'please wait a moment. I have to go in and report to the Judge.'

He went in and bowed to the Judge.

'Your Honour, in accordance with the order of the great King Yama, I have brought the living wraith of the Emperor Tai Tsung here to be tried by you,' he said. 'He is outside. I did not venture to bring him in.'

The Judge hastily stood up. . . .

(*Words missing here.*)

Tsui Tse-yu bowed and in the presence of the Emperor opened and read the letter. What he read so agitated him that he forgot all the etiquette of a subject in the presence of his ruler. . . .

The development of popular stories in the form of *pien wen* to vernacular stories in the form of *hua pen*, however, took some three hundred years. Kao Li-shih, the eunuch, told Emperor Hsien Tsung stories based on *pien wen* after the Emperor abdicated in 756, but it was after Emperor Jen Tsung of the Sung Dynasty who ruled China from 1023 to 1032 that story-telling flourished as a trade, and that *hua pen* became established. The fact that from 805 until the Tang Dynasty was overthrown in 907, there was a quick succession of emperors, and that from 907 to 960 five dynasties were established and overthrown may explain why the development of *hua pen* as a literary form took so long. However, some sixty years after the establishment of the Sung Dynasty (960–1279), after the country and the people had recuperated from the devastation of wars and built up their economy, story-telling, upon the demand of the prosperous citizens, became a flourishing trade.

According to Meng Yuan-lao's *Tung Ching Meng Hua Lu*[3] (*Reminiscences of the Eastern Capital*), story-tellers specialized in telling different types of stories: historical novels, romantic stories and comical stories. Story-telling became even more popular in the South Sung Dynasty (1127–1279). In *Reminiscences of Things that Happened in Wu Ling*,[4] it is said that toward the end of the South Sung Dynasty there were ninety-three famous story-tellers, of whom fifty-two specialized in romances and short stories, twenty-three in historical stories, seventeen in Buddhist stories and one in jokes. It would seem, therefore, that historical stories and romantic stories were from the very beginning the two most popular subjects of public story-telling. To describe the scenes vividly and achieve realistic characterization, story-tellers had to use the vernacular or spoken language. But they had to have prepared texts, too, for they could not rely solely on *ad lib* to hold the interest of their listeners. These texts were called *hua pen*. It is difficult to say whether they were written by the story-tellers themselves or by their guilds. What is certain is that these stories, written for the first time in the vernacular, read as well today as they did almost a thousand years ago.

2. POPULAR STORIES OF THE CAPITAL

It seems strange that *hua pen* was almost never mentioned by the *literati* of the time. But such was the contempt of orthodox scholars for popular stories that of all Chinese bibliographies only Tsien Tseng's *Yeh Shih Yuan Shu Mu*[5] listed twelve titles of short stories which were told by story-tellers of the Sung Dynasty, and listed them under the classification of drama. Because no one else mentioned *hua pen* stories, and those mentioned by Tsien Tseng were not available to him, Wang Kuo-wei, the modern Chinese authority on the development of Chinese drama, was misled into thinking that those listed by Tsien were dramas written in the South Sung Dynasty, in his *Hsi Chu Kao Yuan* (*On the Origin of Drama*).

It was not until 1915 when Miao Chuan-sun discovered and published in two volumes seven of the stories in *Ching Pen Tung Shu Hsiao Shuo* (*Popular Stories of the Capital*) that we knew what they were like. Miao mentioned that he had also discovered two other stories, but one, *Ting Chow San Kuai* (*Three Monsters of Ting Chow*), was far from complete, and the other, *Chin Chu Liang Huang Yin* (*The Debauchery of King Liang of Chin*), was too obscene to be included. We may never know how many stories there were originally in *Popular Stories of the Capital*, for the seven stories discovered by Miao were from the remains of Volumes 10 to 16 of the book. The two stories which Miao did not publish were later found in two other collections[6] of short stories discovered in the late 'twenties. These, except for *Three Monsters of Ting Chow*, were published in book form and entitled *Eight Hua Pen Stories of the Sung Dynasty* by the Ya Tung Book Company of Shanghai. They are: *The Jade Goddess, Ghosts of the West, The Stubborn Prime Minister, The Reunion of Feng Yu-mei, Pu Sha Mang, The Honest Clerk, A Miscarriage of Justice* and *The Debauchery of King Hai Ling of Chin*.[7]

This represents the bulk of *hua pen* stories of the Sung Dynasty. Other stories, including *The Note from a Monk* and *Three Pagodas of Western Lake* collected in *Ching Ping Shang Tang Hua Pen*; *Yang Sze Wen Met His Old Friend in Yen Shan* and *Old Chang, the Cucumber Farmer* collected in *Yu Shih Ming Yen* (*Stories to Enlighten Men*); and *Wan Hsin Niang* and *Tsui Ya Nieh* collected in *Ching Shih Tung Yen* (*Stories to Warn Men*), may also be considered as *hua pen* of the Sung Dynasty.[8] It is possible, however, that these stories were later edited by compilers of collections of stories, but as many of these stories referred to the years during the Sung Dynasty as 'of this Dynasty', they were considered by Feng Meng-lung, the greatest authority on popular stories in the Ming Dynasty, to have been written in the Sung Dynasty.

Several features of *hua pen* stories developed because story-telling was a trade. First, because of the necessity to attract and hold the interest of the few early arrivals and wait for a larger crowd to come before telling the main story, story-tellers recited one or two poems or told a short short-story as a curtain-raiser. In *The Jade Goddess*, for instance, poems are used as a preamble, while in *A Miscarriage of Justice* a short short-story was told first for the same purpose. These preambles may be similar in nature to the main story, or they may be different, and are referred to as 'triumphant preambles'. Lu Hsun, the modern Chinese writer, maintained that they were so called because many in the audience were soldiers. Others, however, thought that the name might have been that of a song often played as a prelude.

Another feature of *hua pen* stories was that the chapters always stopped at a crucial moment of the story, and ended with the words, 'If you want to know what happened, please come back and listen to the next chapter.' This, of course, was good business.

These two features, strange to say, were carried over to later novels when they no longer served any purpose. Another thing about *hua pen* stories is that one can almost imagine the atmosphere of story-telling by reading the texts. For there are sentences like, 'Now, why should I, a story-teller, talk about this poem on how spring vanishes?' or 'Today, I, too, will talk about a scholar who came to Ling-an to sit an examination', and 'Now, what was the name of this gentleman? His last name? And what was he going to do?' These showed the different ways in which a story-teller put his stories across to his listeners. In many Chinese novels the author often used sentences such as 'Now, why is this, reader? Well, I shall go on with the story and explain the reasons to you,' which could have been the influence of *hua pen*.

Except for *The Stubborn Prime Minister*, which attacks Wang An-shih, Prime Minister during the reign of Emperor Shen Tsung (1068–1085), the majority of the stories of the Sung Dynasty were romantic stories with ghosts as subjects. There seems no apparent reason why love stories should have been so closely linked with ghosts, but apparently audiences of that period liked them. There were detective stories and stories of mystery too.

I have translated here an edited version of *Chih Chen Chang Chu Kuan* (*The Honest Clerk*):

There is no reason why things happen, new and old,
Prosperity and misery soon come to naught.
Even when one accepts things as they come,
Is it better to feel detached?
My eyebrows grow white as snow,
Too soon the colour, too, fades from my cheeks;
Depressed and desolate, I look around me,
In the evening, the wind has risen and rustles in the woods.

Now, this poem was written by Wang Chu-hou of Hua-yang District, Chengtu County, in Szechuan. One day, when he was nearly sixty years old, he was deeply moved to see in the mirror that his hairs and beard had turned white. The fact is, every living thing must grow into maturity and then become old, and human beings are no exception. But while the colour of almost everything else changes from white to black, the colour of human hair changes from black to white. There was, however, a Liu Shih-chun who wrote a different poem on seeing his hairs turn white:

In my lifetime
I've had my share of fun
I drank and I loved.
Now, although my heart is still full of jest in spite of my age,
And on my cloth-cap I still wear flowers,
My hair has become white as frost,
My beard, white as snow.
I can't help feeling sad.

Some friends advise me to have it dyed,
Others say I should have it plucked.
But what good would this do?
I used to worry that I might die young,
Now that I have passed my prime,
I shall let my white hairs and beard be,
And add to the decorum of my old age.
Oh, let them turn white!

Well, in Kaifeng County, Pienchow, East Capital, there was a shop-keeper, sixty-odd years old, whose hair and beard had all turned snowy white. He was, however, not willing to act his age, and still longed for a woman, and lost all his property and almost his

life because of it. Now, what was the name of this shop-keeper?
What did he do? It is said:

> When will dust stop kicking up after horses' hoofs?
> Emotions in human hearts will sooner or later subside.

As I said, there was in Kaifeng County of Pienchow, an owner of a
thread shop by the name of Chang Sheh-lien. He was more than
sixty years old, and since his wife died, leaving him with no offspring, he had lived alone. He was worth more than one hundred
thousand strings of cash and employed two clerks to help him run
his shop.

One day Chang suddenly felt sad. Striking his breast, he sighed
heavily and said to his clerks, 'I am now over sixty years old and have
no family. What is the use of having one hundred thousand strings
of cash?'

'Why don't you marry again?' the clerks said. 'You may have a
son or daughter then to carry on the family line.'

Chang happily agreed, and sent for two go-betweens, Mrs Chang
and Mrs Lee. These two ladies:

> Opened their mouths, and made a match
> Said a word, and arranged a marriage.
> They cured the troubles of bachelors and spinsters,
> Made the loneliness of all who slept alone their business.
> They can make even the Weaving-maid love-lorn,
> And induced Chang-O to leave her palace in the moon.

Chang said to them, 'I have no son. I want you both, therefore, to
arrange a match for me.'

Mrs Chang was silent for a moment. Such an old man, she said
to herself. How am I to arrange a match for him? What am I to say
to him? She was still thinking these thoughts when Mrs Lee nudged
her. 'It is easy to arrange a match for you,' she said to Chang, the
shop-keeper. And the go-betweens started to leave.

'Wait a minute,' said Chang.

And because of what he was going to say:

> Although his road led to prosperity,
> He was made to suffer;
> There will be no burial place for his bones,
> And he became a wandering ghost.

The go-betweens said, 'What is it?'

'The bride must satisfy three conditions,' he said. 'First, she must be better-looking than the average woman. Second, she must come from a good family. Third, I am worth one hundred thousand strings of cash, and she must have the same amount of money.'

The two women almost laughed out loud, but said, 'These conditions can easily be met,' and left.

Once outside, Mrs Chang said, 'We shall make one hundred strings of cash or so if a match can be arranged. But he is aiming a bit high, isn't he? Any woman who satisfies these three conditions would marry a young man instead of this old one. Does he think that his white beard is made of sugar?'

'It so happens that I know of a woman, good-looking, and from a suitable family, too,' Mrs Lee replied.

'Which family is it?'

'Oh, a concubine of Wang Chao-hsuan [an official title which probably means Imperial Emissary for Pacification of Bandits]. She was at first very much a favourite of Wang, but she spoke too carelessly about something once, and Wang was offended. He has now decided to give her to anyone from a respectable family. This woman has many thousands of strings of cash of her own. The only thing is, she is too young.'

'We have not only to worry about the age of the old man, but also that of the young woman!' Mrs Chang said. 'I don't think merchant Chang would mind marrying a young wife. It is the woman who would object. If we take some twenty years off the age of the old man we should be able to arrange a match.'

'Tomorrow is a propitious day. Let's go to see Chang first thing in the morning and decide on the amount of gifts he is willing to provide. It should be no problem to persuade Wang Chao-hsuan.'

At the wedding ceremony Chang was happy to find a young and beautiful bride. But the bride was bitter at finding that the groom's brows and beard were already snowy white. . . .

After the first night Chang was happy and the bride unhappy. . . .

One day Chang said to his wife, 'I must go out today. I'm afraid you might feel a bit lonely.'

'Please come back as soon as you can,' she said half-heartedly.

After her husband left she thought to herself, 'I'm not bad-looking, and have no small dowry. It is not fair that I should be married to this old man whose beard has already turned white.' Her maid, who was standing next to her, said, 'Mistress, why do you not go out to the front of the house and look at the people on the street to amuse yourself?' She agreed.

Now the front of Chang's house was used as the shop to sell all kinds of thread and rouge. Along the two walls there were showcases and cupboards. In the middle at the back there was a curtain lined with purple silk. The maid came out, unhooked the curtain and let it down. The two clerks in the shop, one called Lee Ching, some fifty years old, and the other, Chang Shen, who was some thirty-odd years, saw her and asked, 'What are you doing?' 'The Mistress wants to look at the street scene,' she said. The clerks came forward and bowed to their Mistress standing on the other side of the curtain.

'How long have you been working for the Master?' the Mistress asked Lee Ching.

'Lee Ching has worked for the Master for more than thirty years.'

'Has he taken good care of you?'

'Everything that I eat and drink is provided by the Master.'

She then asked about Chang Shen.

Chang Shen said, 'My father served the Master for more than twenty years. I myself have served him for more than ten since my father died.'

'Has the Master been good to you?'

'Everything that my family enjoys, the food and the clothes, is given to us by the Master.'

'You wait here,' said the Mistress.

After a while she came out and gave something to Lee Ching. Lee used his long sleeves to cover his hands before taking the gift from her and, bowing, thanked her.

'I can't give him a gift without giving you something,' she said to Chang Shen. 'This is not worth much, but not entirely useless.'

Chang Shen received the gift as Lee did and thanked her.

The Mistress stood there for some moments and then went in. The two clerks also went back to attend to the business.

The fact was Lee Ching was given ten pieces of silver coins and Chang Shen ten pieces of gold coins. But they did not know the difference. . . .

That evening they entered the day's transactions in the account book, signed and handed the book to their master for checking.

It was Chang Shen's turn to keep watch in the shop that night. He sat in a small room with a small lamp. After a while he started to get ready for bed. Suddenly there was a knock on the door.

'Who is it?' he asked.

'Open the door quickly and I will tell you,' came the reply.

Chang Shen opened the door and a person rushed into the room and stood on the other side of the lamp. He was surprised to find that it was a woman. Hurriedly, he said, 'Lady, what do you want at this hour of the night?'

'I have not come for my own sake,' said the woman. 'The woman who gave you a gift asked me to come.'

'Oh, the Mistress gave me ten golden coins. She must have told you to take the coins back.'

'You don't understand. Mr Lee got ten silver coins. The Mistress has asked me to give you something else.' So saying, she lowered a bundle from her back and untied it. 'These suits are for you. The woman's dresses are for your mother.'

She turned to leave, but at the door she came back. 'I almost forgot an important matter!' she said and took from inside her sleeves a fifty-tael silver piece, threw it at him and left.

Chang Shen had received so many gifts apparently for no reason that thinking about it that night he could not go to sleep.

The next morning he opened the door of the shop and carried on with the business until Lee Ching arrived. He then went home and showed his mother the clothes and the money.

'Where did you get all this?' his mother asked.

Chang Shen told her.

'My son, why should the Mistress give you all these gifts?' his mother said. 'I am now more than sixty years old and since your father died I depend on you. Should anything happen to you, to whom should I turn? You are not going back to work tomorrow.'

Chang Shen was an easy-going man and a good son. He agreed.

The next day merchant Chang sent someone to inquire why Chang was absent from work.

'He has a chill,' said his mother. 'He will go back once he is well again.'

After a few days Lee Ching came and asked, 'Why has Chang Shen not shown up? There's no one to help me in the shop.' The old lady said her son was not well and had become worse.

Merchant Chang sent people several times to ask when Chang Shen would be coming back to work, but every time the old lady said her son was not yet recovered. At last the store-keeper decided that Chang Shen must be working for someone else.

Time flies. In the twinkling of an eye Chang Shen had stayed away from work for more than a month. Although he had received many gifts from his Mistress, he did not want to change the fifty-tael silver piece, nor could he sell the clothes. One day he asked his mother, 'You don't want me to go to work for the Master and I now have nothing to do. Where are we going to get money from for our daily expenses?'

Pointing to the beams of the house, his mother said, 'Do you see that?'

Chang Shen saw that it was a bundle. He took it down from the beam and handed it to his mother.

'Your father depended on this to bring you up,' she said, and untied the bundle and revealed a bamboo basket. 'You must first follow your father's footsteps and start selling rouge and thread.'

That day happened to be the Lantern Festival. Chang Shen said to his mother, 'There will be a lantern display at Tuan Gate. May I go and have a look?'

'My son, you have not been to Tuan Gate for a long time,' his mother said. 'Besides, you would have to pass the shop to go there. You might get into trouble.'

'Everyone I know has seen the display and said it is better than ever before,' Chang Shen said. 'I will return immediately after I have seen it and avoid passing the shop.'

'All right. But you must go with someone.'

' I will go with Second Brother Wang.'

'Good. The two of you must not drink and must come back together.'

So Chang Shen went with Second Brother Wang to see the lantern display. When they arrived at Tuan Gate the people who staged the best display were being awarded wine and some of the crowd were throwing coins at them. It was very noisy and crowded.

'We can't see much of the display here,' Wang said. 'Why should we jostle and be pushed around by the crowd? Let's go and see the floats.'

'Where?'

'Why, in the great courtyard of Wang Chao-hsuan's residence!'

So they went, but the crowd was as big there as at Tuan Gate, and Chang Shen was separated from his friend. 'What shall I do?' he thought. 'If I go home sooner than Wang it will be all right. Otherwise my mother will be worried.' He did not enjoy the display, but walked restlessly. After a while he recalled that at the shop where he worked they used to stage displays too and set off fireworks, and he walked there. When he came near he was greatly taken aback to see the door blocked up by two crossed bamboo poles, over which was a strip of leather nailed at one end to the door. An oil lamp was hanging at the other end of it, and its pale light shone on a notice stuck to the door.

Chang Shen went up to the door and read it. 'The High Court of Kaifeng County, in view of Chang Sheh-lien's offence. . . .'

Before he could finish reading it someone came from behind him and shouted, 'What are you doing there?'

Startled, Chang Shen hurriedly walked away.

The man gave chase and shouted, 'Who are you? Why are you reading the notice at night? What impudence!'

Chang began to run. After a few turns he came to a crossroad and started to go home. It was about ten o'clock and the moon was full and clear high up in the sky.

After a while someone came running up to him, calling, 'Mr Chang, someone wants to see you.'

Chang looked back and saw someone dressed like a waiter in an inn. 'It must be Second Brother Wang,' he thought. 'I might as well have a few drinks with him before going home.' He followed the waiter back to an inn, went upstairs and came to a room. The waiter lifted the curtain for him. 'In there,' he said.

Chang Shen went in and saw a woman in rumpled dress and with dishevelled hair. . . .

'It is I,' said the woman, 'Mr Chang.'

Chang Shen thought she looked familiar but could not place her. 'Don't you recognize me?' she said. 'I am your former Mistress.'

'Why are you here?'

'It's a long story.'

'But what happened?'

'I should not have trusted the go-betweens and married Chang, the shop-keeper. He was found to have been making counterfeit silver coins and they arrested him. There has been no news of him and our house and properties have been seized by the authorities. I have no place to go and in desperation have to turn to you for help. Please think of the past and let me stay in your home for a while.'

'This I cannot do,' said Chang Shen. 'My mother is very strict. Besides, what will people say? I am afraid you just cannot come and stay in my home.'

'I understand,' she said. 'Perhaps you are afraid that you would have to spend a lot of money on my account, but look . . .'.

She took from her dress a pearl necklace, consisting of one hundred and eight pea-sized pearls, glimmering under the light.

'How beautiful!' Chang Shen said. 'Never in my life have I seen anything like it!'

'Of all my jewellery, I have managed to keep only this from being confiscated,' she said. 'If you would let me stay in your house we can sell these pearls one by one and we would not have to worry about money.'

'If you really want to stay in my house I must first get my mother's permission.'

'I will come with you now. You can go in and ask her while I wait at the house opposite yours.'

They went to Chang Shen's home, and he went in and told his mother about his former Mistress. The old lady was kind-hearted, and said immediately, 'What a pity, what a pity! Where is she?'

'She is waiting outside.'

'Ask her to come in.'

The young woman came in, and told the old lady what she had told Chang Shen and concluded by saying, 'I have no one to turn to now. Please let me stay.'

'You are welcome to stay for a few days,' said the old lady. 'I am afraid that you will find things here not very comfortable. Perhaps you will think of some relatives you can go to after a few days.'

The young Mistress took from her dress a few pearls and handed them to the old lady. The latter saw the pearls glimmering under the lamplight and asked the young woman to stay in her home.

'We shall sell one of the pearls and start a rouge and thread business, using the bamboo basket as the trade sign in front of the shop,' the young woman said.

'We can get a lot of money without difficulty with one of these beautiful pearls,' Chang Shen said. 'Besides, there is the fifty-tael silver piece with which we can buy merchandise.'

When Chang Shen opened his shop all the clients who used to deal with his Master came to him, and people started to call him Young Merchant Chang. The young Mistress repeatedly tried to win his love, but Chang Shen resisted her advances and treated her as the wife of his old Master.

Soon, it was the Ching Ming Festival. Like everyone else in town Chang Shen went for an outing to Chin Ming Pong. He returned by nightfall and when he was approaching Victory Gate he heard someone call him, 'Chang Chu-kuan (clerk)!' Chang Shen was surprised at being so addressed. 'Everyone now calls me Young Merchant Chang,' he thought. 'Who could this be?'

He turned around and saw his old Master, dirty and dishevelled. On his face there were four words tattooed in gold. Chang Shen immediately took him to an inn. 'What happened?' he said.

'I shouldn't have married a woman who was released from the family of Wang Chao-hsuan,' said the old Master. 'On New Year's Day, your Mistress was standing behind the curtain looking at the street scene when she saw a messenger boy of the Wang family walk by. "What's new in the mansion?" she asked. "Nothing much, except two days ago Wang Chao-hsuan could not find a pearl necklace with a hundred and eight pearls, everyone in this household was punished for it." The messenger boy left and I noticed my wife looked upset and nervous. Soon afterwards more than twenty people came and took away all her jewels and my cash and sent me to the High Court, demanding that I return the necklace. I never saw any pearl necklace, and I said so. But I was tortured and put into prison. That day my wife hanged herself. Having no evidence, the Judge nevertheless sentenced me to a short term in prison. The strange thing is, until now, no one seems to know where the pearl necklace is.'

Chang Shen was frightened and puzzled. 'The young Mistress is in my house, and so is the necklace,' he thought. 'The trouble is we have already sold a few pearls.' Confused, he urged his old Master to have a few drinks and some food, and went home.

He was frightened when he arrived home and saw the young

Mistress. 'Please, Mistress,' he entreated, backing away from her. 'Have mercy on me!'

'What is this?' she demanded.

Chang told her about what the old Master said.

'Isn't this strange!' she said. 'You can see that my dress is real. Wouldn't you have noticed it if there was something wrong with me?' she added. 'He must have known that I am staying in your place and purposely told you this story hoping that you will turn me out!'

'What you said seems reasonable,' Chang Shen said.

A few days later someone called from outside the house, 'A visitor to see Young Merchant Chang.'

Chang Shen went and saw it was his old Master. 'I'll ask the young Mistress to come out and meet him,' he decided. 'Then I'll know definitely if she is a ghost.' He asked the old man in and secretly sent a maid to ask the young Mistress to come out and see him. The maid looked everywhere but could not find her.

Chang Shen knew then that the young Mistress was really a ghost and told his old Master all about it.

'Where is the necklace?' asked the old man.

Chang Shen went to his room and took the necklace and with the old man went with it to the residence of Wang Chao-hsuan. They returned the necklace to its rightful owner and paid for the few pearls which were sold. Wang Chao-hsuan, on his part, arranged to have the old man's record wiped out, and his properties returned. Old man Chang was able to reopen his shop and he asked the Taoist priest at Tien Chin Temple to conduct a memorial service for his young wife.

Now it is apparent that Chang Shen's young mistress was infatuated with him, and that was the reason why, as a ghost, she came back to try to lure him. Fortunately for Chang he was not tempted, otherwise he would have been harmed. Many are the people who are tempted by money and women. One would have difficulty nowadays in finding a person like Chang Shen in ten thousand people! There is a poem in praise of him:

> Everyone likes money and loves women,
> But money and women cannot change an honest man.
> Were youths all to behave like Chang Chu-kuan,
> Neither ghosts nor tricks could harm them.

3. FENG MENG-LUNG AND LING MENG-TSU AND THEIR THREE 'YEN'S' AND TWO 'PAI'S'

Story-telling as a trade seemed to lose much of its attraction during the Yuan Dynasty (1260–1368), owing to the prevalence of Northern Drama. But this is not to say that it died out during this period. In fact, story-tellers who specialized in historical stories slowly improved their art, so much so that the great Chinese novels of the Ming Dynasty (1368–1644), including *Three Kingdoms*, *All Men Are Brothers* and *Monkey*, were to a varying extent based on their texts. During the Chia Chin Period (1522–1566) of the Ming Dynasty, because of the popularity of novels, short stories also received attention from scholars, and collections of vernacular short stories or *hua pen* were published. Up to the reigns of Emperors Shen Tsung (1573–1620) and Hsi Tsung (1621–1627), *hua pen* were so popular that many imitations appeared, and created thereby another golden age of short stories.

The first scholar in the Ming Dynasty to collect *hua pen* stories of the Sung and Ming Dynasties was probably Hung Pien. We do not know how many vernacular stories he collected and published. In the late 1920s, fifteen of the stories published by him were discovered in Japan. Because these were published without a title, the publishers decided when they were reissued in 1929 in China to use the name of Hung Pien's studio as the title of the book. The volume became known as *Ching Ping Shang Tang Hua Pen*. In 1933 twelve more of the stories that Hung collected were discovered in China, so that altogether there are twenty-seven vernacular stories which are known to have been collected by Hung Pien. Judging from these, his collection seems to have been a motley one. Some were written in classical Chinese, others in verse, although the majority were in the vernacular. Nevertheless, *Ching Ping Shang Tang Hua Pen* is one of the important literary discoveries. From the crude and simple style of story-telling, we can see clearly how the story-tellers used to tell their stories.

The most important collections of *hua pen* stories are no doubt *Stories to Enlighten Men*, *Stories to Warn Men* and *Hsin Shih Heng Yen* (*Stories to Awaken Men*). The three are referred to as the 'Three *Yen*'s'. They were compiled by Feng Meng-lung.

We do not know much about Feng's life, except that he was a native of Wu District of Kiangsu Province, and that he was the

Magistrate of Shou Ning District during the reign of Emperor Tsung Cheng, the last Emperor of the Ming Dynasty, and that he committed suicide after the Ming Dynasty was overthrown. But we know a little more about his writing. He was a man of many talents. He edited *Ping Yao Chuan*, *Hsin Lieh Kuo Chih* and other novels. He wrote plays, including *Two Heroes* and *All is Well*. He compiled collections of anecdotes and published selections of folk songs. He also wrote poems and published a collection of them, of which a critic said, 'He likes to write jokes into his poems and does not follow strictly the rules of poetry-writing.' This was perhaps intentional, for Feng seems to have been an unconventional man. He tried to persuade, though to no avail, Shen Teh-fu to publish *Chin Ping Mei (Golden Lotus)*, the Chinese Decameron. He also said in his preface to *Shan Ko*, a collection of folk songs, that 'There may be insincere poems and essays, but all folk songs are true to life.' Apparently he did not care too much what the orthodox critics had to say about his poems. He only wanted to express what he felt in whatever form he liked.

Feng's greatest contribution to literature, however, was his collecting and editing of the three collections of vernacular stories of the Sung, Yuan and Ming Dynasties. In his preface to *Stories to Awaken Men*, Ho Yi Chu Shih said, 'Apart from the Six Classics of Confucianism and official history books, all writing can be considered as *hsiao shuo* (fiction). But some of the writings deal with theories and are difficult to understand. Other pieces pay too much attention to rhetoric and formal beauty and are too ornate. . . . The writings cannot hope to attract the attention of the ordinary people or to lift up their spirit. That is why following the publication of *Stories to Enlighten Men* and *Stories to Warn Men* this collection of forty stories is now brought out. . . . These three collections have different names, but their purpose is the same.' Of the purpose of these collections, Wu Ai Chu Shih in his preface to *Stories to Warn Men* said, 'I once saw a boy cut one of his fingers while cooking for me in place of my cook. He did not so much as make a noise about it. Surprised, I asked him if he felt any pain. He said, "I just came back from Hsien Miao Kuan Temple after listening to a story-teller tell the story of *Three Kingdoms*. He talked about how General Kuan Yun-chang talked and laughed as a doctor operated on his arm to scratch from his bone the poison from an enemy's arrow. Now if General Kuan did not feel anything when his arm was being opened up, why should I scream when I have only a cut?" Well, if a story about bravery could inspire a boy like this, then stories about filial piety, loyalty, faithfulness, good character and sensibility too can lead ordinary people to aspire to the same qualities. In comparison with those scholars who are studious but hypocritical, well-read but superficial, it is difficult to say whether it is the ordinary people or the scholars who have learned the real knowledge.' According to him, popular stories teach people to be good, just as Confucian classics aimed to do the same thing, only the influence of popular stories was more direct and lasting. This apparently was also Feng Meng-lung's opinion. Each of his three collections of *hua pen* stories consists of forty stories of Sung, Yuan and Ming. Six of the seven contained in *Popular Stories of the Capital* and discovered by Miao Chuan-sun are included in *Stories to Warn Men*. Another story, *Three Monsters of Ting Chow*, which Miao also discovered but did not publish, is included in the same book. Two other stories, *A Miscarriage of Justice* and *The Debauchery of King Liang of Chin* from *Popular Stories of the Capital*, are collected in *Stories to Warn Men*. There are other vernacular stories of the Sung Dynasty collected in these three collections, such as *The Note from a Monk, Old Chang the Cucumber Farmer*, etc. But the total number of Sung Dynasty stories collected comes to only about twenty, and since story-telling as a trade was not too popular in the Yuan Dynasty, it may safely be said that the bulk of the stories in these three collections are imitations of *hua pen* stories written in the Ming Dynasty.

The most famous of *hua pen* story-writers of the Ming Dynasty is Ling Meng-tsu (dates unknown). He was once assistant Magistrate of Shanghai and Judge of Hsuchow. And like Feng Meng-lung, he was a prolific author. He wrote more than twenty operas and books on poetry. Of his *hua pen* stories, he said in his preface to *Pai An Ching Chi Tsu Kek (First Collection of Amazing Stories)* that 'they are based on various miscellaneous notes which are interesting or concerned with strange happenings. I expanded them into these stories. They are half factual, half imagined. . . . The style of the stories may not be good, but every story has a moral. . . . It will be harmless to tell these stories, and the listener may learn a lesson or two from them.' His purpose, then, seemed moralistic. Yet there are several stories in his collection which rank with *Chin Ping Mei* in exhaustive description of sexual scenes. This was perhaps a sign of the 'sexual sophistication' of the Ming Dynasty. The collection proved so popular that Ling's publisher asked im to prepare another. He compiled the *Second Collection of Amazing Stories* perhaps in a hurry. For one of the stories in the first collection was included, and another was written by someone else. What is amazing is that one Northern Drama was included in this collection of vernacular stories, supposedly to make up the number of forty.

No one seems to know why the number forty was so important. But the fact is Feng Meng-lung's three collections of *hua pen* stories and Ling Meng-tsu's two collections of creative writing of his own each consisted of forty stories also. So altogether there were about two hundred short stories of the late Ming Dynasty. It was difficult and presumably expensive for the general public to buy all five collections and ultimately a selection of these two hundred stories was made by Pao Weng Lao Jen, entitled *Chin Ku Chi Kuan (Strange Stories of Past and Present)*, also consisting of forty stories, twenty-nine of which were from the 'Three *Yen's*', ten from Ling Meng-tsu's 'Two *Pai's*' and one from another book. This was so very popular that the 'Three *Yen's*' and 'Two *Pai's*' were forgotten by the people for three hundred years until they were rediscovered in the late 1920s.

Here is a passage from *The Pearl-sewn Shirt*, which has to do with the unhappy effects of illicit love. Chiang Hsing-ko, a travelling salesman, has been away from home for a long time. His wife, Fortune, is lonely, and comes to know a procuress, Dame Hsueh, who moves in to live with her, and introduces Chen Ta-lang, another travelling salesman, to her. They have an affair, and Fortune presents Chen Ta-lang with a pearl-sewn shirt which is an heirloom of the Chiang family. When Chen Ta-lang goes away he meets Chiang Hsing-ko by accident, and not knowing that he is the husband of Fortune, tells him about his affair and shows him the shirt. In a rage, Chiang goes home and divorces his wife, although he still loves her, and gets a band of men together and wrecks Dame Hsueh's house. Fortune tries to hang herself, but is rescued, and in time is given away as a concubine to Wu Chieh, a magistrate. But since Chiang still loves her, he presents her with a substantial dowry. He is later to be repaid for his kindness when he accidentally kills someone, and Fortune intervenes on his behalf, for Chiang is to appear before Magistrate Wu. The story is distinguished for its vivid description of Dame Hsueh, the procuress. Here is a passage in which she figures prominently.

On entering the city Chen Ta-lang made straight for the East

Alley off Market Street and pounded on Dame Hsueh's door. Dame Hsueh was in her little yard, her hair dishevelled, grading her pearls. When she heard the knocking on the door she wrapped up the pearls and asked, 'Who is it?' But as soon as she heard the words 'Chen of Hweichow' she hastened to open the door and invite him in. 'I'm not yet washed and so I don't presume to receive you formally,' she said. 'What noble errand is it, sir, that brings you out at this time of the morning?'

'I have come specially to see you,' replied Chen, 'and was afraid of missing you by coming later.'

'Perhaps you have some jewels or trinkets you want me to dispose of?' asked Dame Hsueh.

'I want to buy some jewels,' said Chen Ta-lang. 'But there is also a bigger deal I want you to undertake for me.'

'I'm afraid I'm not familiar with any trade other than this one,' said Dame Hsueh.

'Can we talk here?' asked Chen, whereupon Dame Hsueh bolted the front door and invited him to take a seat in a little private room.

'What are your instructions, sir?' she inquired.

Satisfied that there was no one else about, Ta-lang drew the silver from his sleeve, unwrapped it and placed it on the table. 'I can mention it, godmother, only when you have agreed to accept these hundred taels of silver,' he said.

Not knowing what was behind this, Dame Hsueh was reluctant to accept it. 'You must not despise it as too little,' said Chen, and he hurriedly brought out two gold bars as well, shining yellow, and placed these also on the table. 'Please accept these ten taels of gold in addition,' he said. 'If you will not accept them, godmother, I shall take it as a deliberate refusal to help me. Today it is I who seek your help, not you who seek mine. This big deal I mentioned is not something beyond your capacities. That is why I have come to you. And even if you are unable to bring it off, this money is still yours to keep. There is no question of my coming back to retrieve it and then never having anything further to do with you. There is no meanness of that kind about Chen Ta-lang.'

Tell me, members of the audience, when was there an old procuress who didn't covet money? How was Dame Hsueh to remain unmoved at the sight of all this silver and gold? At this point her whole face creased into smiles and she said, 'Please do not misunderstand me, sir. Never in my life have I taken a single cash from anyone unless all was clear and above-board. I shall accept your instructions now, and so for the time being I will take charge of this money; but if I fail to do what you wish, I shall return it to you.'

With these words she placed the gold with the silver in its packet and wrapped the whole lot up together; then calling out, 'This is very bold of me,' she went to secrete it in her bedroom. Hurrying out again, she said, 'I shall not presume to thank you yet, sir; but tell me now, what kind of business is this that I may be able to help you with?'

'There is a certain gem, a talisman,' replied Chen Ta-lang, 'which I am most anxious to procure. You have nothing like it here. It is only to be found in a particular household on Market Street. I beg of you, godmother, to go and borrow it for me.'

The old woman began to laugh. 'You're making fun of me again. I've lived in this alley for more than twenty years, but never have I heard of any talisman on Market Street. Tell me, sir, whose family does it belong to, this gem?'

'Who lives in the big double-storeyed house across the street from the pawnshop kept by my fellow-townsman, Manager Wang Three?' asked Ta-lang.

The old woman thought for a moment, then said, 'That house belongs to Chiang Hsing-ko, a man of this town. He himself has been away, travelling, for more than a year now. Only his wife is at home.'

'That is precisely the person from whom I wish to borrow this talisman I speak of,' said Ta-lang, and he drew his chair up close to the old woman and revealed to her his heart's desire, thus and thus.

But when he had finished speaking the old woman shook her head impatiently. 'This is a matter of the gravest difficulty,' she said. 'It is not yet four years since Chiang Hsing-ko married this wife of his. The two of them were like fish and water, never apart by a foot or an inch. Now that he has had to go away, the lady never descends her staircase, so great is her chastity. And since Hsing-ko has this peculiarity of being easily roused to anger, I have never yet crossed his threshold. I do not even know what the lady looks like, so how am I to undertake this business for you? As for what you have just given me—I have not the good fortune to be able to make use of it.'

At this Chen Ta-lang flung himself down on his knees, and when the old woman tried to get him to rise he clutched with both hands at her sleeves and pinned her to her chair so that she could not move. 'Godmother,' he began to mumble, 'Chen Ta-lang's life is in your hands. You must not fail to think out some cunning stratagem which will enable me to possess her and thus save my poor life. When this thing is done there will be another hundred taels of gold for your reward; but if you turn me down, there is nothing for me but to die this minute.'

The old woman was too terrified to think, and could only consent. 'All right, all right,' she said again and again, 'don't tear me to pieces. Please rise, sir, and I will tell you what I think.'

At last Chen rose to his feet, and said, hands folded respectfully before him, 'Please inform me at once, what is your cunning plan?'

'This affair must be allowed to run its natural course,' said Dame Hsueh. 'As long as it succeeds in the end, there must be no counting of months and years. If you are to set me a time limit, I can hardly undertake this for you.'

'Provided it really does succeed,' said Chen, 'what does it matter if I have to wait a day or two? But where is our stratagem to start?'

'Tomorrow, after breakfast,' began the old woman, 'not too early and not too late, I will meet you in Manager Wang's pawnshop. You, sir, must bring along a good quantity of silver, giving out that you have some business with me. There is of course some point to all this. If I can get these two feet of mine through the Chiang's doorway, then, sir, you are in luck. But you must hurry straight back to your lodgings. Don't loiter about in front of her doorway or people will see through our game and the whole plan will be ruined. If I can devise an opening of some kind I shall of course report to you.'

'I shall follow your instructions to the letter,' said Chen Ta-lang; and with a great shout of assent he joyously opened the door and left.[9]

CHAPTER XIII

The Novels of the Ming Dynasty

. THE EVOLUTION OF VERNACULAR NOVELS

WE have seen that short stories and historical stories were the two most popular kinds of story-telling in the Sung Dynasty. Historical stories from which Chinese novels developed may have been more popular than short stories. For Meng Yuan-lao mentioned in his *Tung Ching Meng Hua Lu* (*Reminiscences of the Eastern Capital*) that Ho Sze-chiu specialized in telling *The Story of the Three Kingdoms*, and Yin Chan-mai specialized in telling *The Story of Five Dynasties*.[1] This was in addition to the five persons whom Meng gave as famous for telling dramatized historical incidents. But since *The Three Kingdoms* and *The Five Dynasties* are themselves historical stories, this seems to show that because of greater demand for this type of story, story-tellers had to specialize in certain stories to satisfy the customers.

Of the extant historical stories, *The Story of Five Dynasties*, *The Story of the Hsuan Ho Period of the Sung Dynasty* and *The Story of San Tsang's Search for Buddhist Sutras* are generally considered to be those of the Sung Dynasty. *The Story of Five Dynasties* was originally in ten volumes, two for each dynasty, but only eight volumes now remain. Major events mentioned in it are based on official history books, but battle scenes and the personal characteristics of the characters are written in exaggerated, expansive or humorous terms. These eight volumes were discovered by Chao Yuan-chung at the end of the Ching Dynasty. Although they have little intrinsic value, they are important evidence in the study of historical stories as a form of popular literature.

Some Chinese scholars argue that *The Story of the Hsuan Ho Period of the Sung Dynasty* in four volumes is not the actual text of the historical story-tellers. Their reasons are that the whole book consists mostly of direct quotations from official history books, and, what is more important, there is at the end of the book this statement: 'That is why loyal officials and faithful subjects are saddened by past events and are only sorry that they cannot eat the flesh and sleep on the skins of the traitors,' which they believe shows that the book was written by the *literati*. There is no need to go into this argument here, but it is perhaps appropriate to say that the above quotation does not seem to exclude story-tellers. Loyalty is more often a characteristic of the common people than of the *literati*.

The importance of this story, from the viewpoint of the development of Chinese literature, lies in the part which deals with Sung Chiang and his band in the story called *Liang Shan Po*. For this is the story from which the famous Chinese novel *Shui Hu Chuan* (*All Men Are Brothers*) developed. Events such as Yang Chih selling his sword, Tsao Kai intercepting and holding the gifts sent to the capital, Sung Chiang killing Yen Po-hsi and seeing the Revelation Book which contains the names of the thirty-six persons who are later to become his partners, etc., which were later found in the famous novel, were mentioned in this story. Incidentally, these parts of the story are written in vernacular Chinese, and form the better portions of the whole book.

Here is a passage from the story. If readers wish they may compare it with *All Men Are Brothers*, which is readily available in English and see how the sketch is expanded in the later and more famous version.

One day in the fifth month of the second year of Hsuan Ho Period (1119–1125), Liang Shih-pao, Garrison Commander of Peking, sent Lieutenant Ma An-kuo and a party of soldiers to take ten thousand strings of gold beads to Kaifeng, the capital, together with many jewels and curios, as his birthday present to the Prime Minister Tsai. The birthday being the first day of the sixth month, Ma and his party were ordered to march as fast as they could. One day they came to an embankment near the Five Flower Barracks. As they had marched under the hot sun for some time, they decided to rest for a while in the shade of the willow trees and bamboo grove on both sides of the embankment. Soon afterwards, eight men carrying two pails of wine came and rested under the trees also.

'Is your wine for sale?' asked Lieutenant Ma.

'Yes,' said one of the men. 'This wine is smooth and has a beautiful bouquet. Would you want some to quench your thirst?'

The lieutenant was thirsty and tired. He bought two bottles and shared them with his party.

Once the men had drunk some wine, gold stars appeared before their eyes, and the sky and earth seemed to change places. They soon lost consciousness. The eight men took all the gifts and went away, leaving the two pails of wine behind.

About midnight Lieutenant Ma and his party gradually regained consciousness. They saw that the containers in which they had been carrying the gifts were gone, and only two empty wine pails were left behind. Ma ordered his men to pick up the pails and carry them to Nan-lo District where he told Yun Ta-liang, the Magistrate, what had happened. The Magistrate asked his clerk to find out to whom the pails belonged, so as to trace the whereabouts of the robbers. The clerk saw that on the bottom of the pails were written four words: 'Hua Family of the Sea of Wine.' Wang Ping, a detective, was assigned to find out where the Hua family lived.

One day he came to Five Flower Barracks and saw the flag of an inn on which the same four words were written. He went in and arrested a man by the name of Hua Yueh. Chang Ta-nien, the legal assistant to the Magistrate, took charge of the interrogation.

Hua Yueh said truthfully, 'Three days ago eight men came to my place at noontime. They said that they were going to pay tribute to the mountain god, and asked me to lend them two pails so that they could take some wine with them, and I did.'

'Do you know the names of the eight men?'

'The leader of the band is Tsao Kai, alias Iron Sky King, who lives in Shih Chieh Village, Yun Cheng District. The rest are Wu Chia-liang, Liu Tang, Chin Ming, Yuan Chin, Yuan Tung, Yuan Hsiao-chi and Yen Ching.'

Chang Ta-nien ordered Hua Yueh to sign a statement and wrote a memorandum to the Magistrate of Yun Cheng District for the arrest of Tsao Kai.

Sung Chiang, the confidential clerk of the district, saw the names and ran over to Shih Chieh Village at night to pass the news to Tsao Kai, and to tell him and his men to run away immediately. The next morning Sung Chiang sent another memorandum up to the

Magistrate, and Tung Ping was sent with thirty men to arrest Tsao Kai in the village. Did they succeed? It was indeed a case of

> Nets were not there when the birds took flight,
> Tigers were already gone when the traps were set.

The Story of San Tsang's Search for Buddhist Sutras is based on the life of the famous Chinese monk San Tsang, or Tripitaka, of the Tang Dynasty. It has seventeen chapters in three volumes. Many people attach great importance to the fact that there is a title given to each of the chapters. For this shows that it is the first of Chinese *chang hui hsiao shuo* or novels in chapters, to have so many chapters, each of which has a couplet for the title. But more important perhaps is that it is the first and remains one of the very few novels of romantic fantasy and imagination. This is no doubt due to the influence of Buddhist literature. For prior to the introduction of Buddhist literature to China, Chinese stories were merely outline sketches. Apart from the fact that this story has a Buddhist theme and is based on the actual journey of a Chinese monk from China overland to India, I suspect this story was also written by someone who, if not a Buddhist monk, was familiar with Buddhist literature. For along with the figure of San Tsang on his travels there is a monkey who looks like a scholar. This monkey has magical powers and writes poems, and has a striking similarity to Hanuman, the monkey in the Indian epic *Ramayana*. This could not have been a coincidence. The great magical powers possessed by the all-too-human monkey so fascinated the Chinese that this story or variations of it continued to be popular throughout the Sung, Yuan and Ming Dynasties, and was rendered into one of the great Chinese novels *Hsi Yu Chi* (*Monkey*) by Wu Cheng-en (1505–1580). It may be of interest to quote here a short passage from *The Story of San Tsang's Search for Buddhist Sutras*:

> One day at noon a scholar came from the east and bowed to the Buddhist monk. 'Greetings, greetings!' he said. 'Where are you going? Are you going to India in search of Buddhist sutras again?'
> The monk raised his hands and pressed his palms together in salutation. 'The people in the land of the East do not know the teachings of Buddha. I have been ordered by the Emperor to seek and bring back Buddhist sutras.'

'You twice tried to go to India for the same purpose in your previous incarnation, but died on the way. If you go to India again, you will certainly die.'

'How do you know?'

'I am no other than the King of eighty-four thousand bronze-headed, iron-foreheaded Monkeys in Purple Cloud Cave of Flower Fruit Mountain,' said the scholar. 'I have come to help you in your mission. For you have to pass through thirty-six countries, and many disasters and troubles will befall you.'

'In that case we were destined to meet. The people in the East will benefit from this,' said the monk. He then decided to call him Monkey the Novice.

In the Yuan Dynasty story-telling as a trade seemed to have lost its drawing power against the competition of the newly-developed Northern Drama. There are now extant five historical stories: *Chuan Hsiang Ping Hua Wu Chung* (*Story-tellers' Five Stories*), in fifteen volumes, published in the Chih-chih Period (1321–1323) of the Yuan Dynasty. These five stories are *King Wu's Expedition against Chou, Lo Yi's Invasion of Chi, Biography of the First Emperor of Chin, The Execution of General Han Hsin* and *The Story of the Three Kingdoms*. The style of these stories was crude, but the first two stories contain a lot of imaginary incidents wherein supernatural powers and gods are involved, and historical events are used merely as pegs on which to hang these incidents. The other three stories stick pretty closely to historical events, although legends and incidents fabricated by the unknown authors are also included.

The most important of these five stories so far as the influence on novels is concerned is undoubtedly *The Three Kingdoms*. For Lo Kuan-chung's *San Kuo Chih Yen Yi* (*The Three Kingdoms*) is based on it. But the story itself is the end-product of centuries of story-telling. As early as the Tang Dynasty, *The Story of the Three Kingdoms* was very popular. Su Tung-po, the great poet of the Sung Dynasty, said in his *Chih Lin* (*Miscellaneous Record*), 'Wang Pan once said that when the common people found that their children were too mischievous to have about them, they often gave them a few coins and sent them to listen to story-telling. If the story being told was *The Story of the Three Kingdoms*, the children would knit their brows or cry when they heard that Hsuan-teh suffered defeats, and shout and sing with happiness when they heard of Tsao Tsao losing a battle. It shows, therefore, that the ideas of a gentleman and a mean person do not change with the times.' According to Chung Tse-cheng's *Lu Kwei Pu* and Chu Chuen's *Tai Ho Cheng Yin Pu*,[2] there were more than ten different Northern Dramas based on *The Story of the Three Kingdoms*. There must have been an earlier version of this story other than the one published in the Yuan Dynasty, but none has so far been discovered. However, judging from the low standard of the Chinese and the crudeness of the style of telling in the version which is found in *Chuan Hsiang Ping Hua Wu Chung*, we should not expect too much from any earlier version. Here is a passage from this version.

Chang Fei therefore asked Hsuan-teh, 'Elder Brother, why are you annoyed?'

'I have been appointed an assistant to the Governor, with the ninth rank,' Liu Pei said. 'Generals Kuan and Chang and others fought and defeated five million yellow-turbaned bandits at the front just as I did. Now I have become an official but you two have not acquired any rank. That is why I am not happy.'

'Now, wait a minute! We travelled with you from Chang-an to Tingchow for ten days, and you were not unhappy,' said Chang Fei. 'Why is it that you are unhappy since you presented yourself to the Governor? He must have said something to you. Tell me about it.'

But Hsuan-teh refused to tell him anything.

Chang Fei walked away from Hsuan-teh saying, 'I must find out what happened.' He went to the stable at the back of the house, found the two attendants (who went with Hsuan-teh to the Governor's office) and asked them, but they would not tell him anything. Chang was furious.

That night, about ten o'clock, Chang Fei took a sharp knife and slipped out of the office of the Assistant to the Governor and went to the back of the Governor's residence. He climbed over the wall and into the rear garden where he saw a woman.

'Where are the Governor's quarters?' he asked. 'If you don't tell me I will kill you.'

The woman was terrified. Trembling, she said, 'The Governor sleeps in the rear hall.'

'Who are you?'

'A maid.'

'Lead me to the rear hall.'

The woman led him there and Chang Fei killed her. He also killed Yuan Chiao the Governor. Lady Yuan saw what happened and shouted, 'Killer! Thief!' and Chang Fei killed her also.

Throughout the Yuan Dynasty story-telling was in a decline, and as far as we know the art of writing and telling historical stories remained static until the end of the Yuan Dynasty when Lo Kuan-chung started to rewrite *The Story of the Three Kingdoms*.

2. *THE NOVELS OF THE MING DYNASTY*

The Ming Dynasty, especially in the last years, from the reign of Emperor Shih Tsung (1522–1566) to the twentieth year of Emperor Shen Tsung's reign (1593), is the golden age of the Chinese novel. It at last emerged from the comparatively crude style of *pien wen* and *hua pen*, and came into its own. The 'Four Great Amazing Novels', *The Three Kingdoms*, *Monkey*, *All Men Are Brothers* and *Golden Lotus*, were all written in this period. Except for *The Three Kingdoms* all were written in the seventy-odd years of the late Ming Dynasty. The glory of this period is comparable to that of the Spring-Autumn and Warring States Period when the development of Chinese philosophy was at its height.

There were many factors which helped to bring about this golden era of literary talent. The times were stable and prosperous, the great expansion of trade by sea routes and tremendous advances in the technique of printing all helped. But the most direct and important factor was the new idea of scholars regarding literature as a whole, including the novel and drama.

The new idea was based on the philosophy of Wang Yang-ming (1472–1528), who proclaimed that 'the most important criterion of knowledge is man's mind. If a man finds that what he reads is wrong, even though it was spoken by Confucius, he should not say that it is right.' This emphasis on independent judgment gradually developed and reached its height, in so far as application to literature was concerned, in the writings of Lee Cho-wu (1527–1602) and Yuan Chung-lang (1568–1610), his student. For it was Lee who stressed the importance of novels, drama and folklore, and broke the hold of the orthodox idea of literature that only classical, historical writing, poems and essays were worthy to be called literature, while dramas and novels were 'petty crafts'. Lee said, 'Good poems are not limited to those written in ancient times, nor are good essays necessarily only those written before the Chin Dynasty. The lyrical prose of the Six Dynasties, the "new-style" poems, the short stories of Tang Dynasty, the Northern Dramas and *The Western Chamber* and *All Men Are Brothers* . . . these also are the best literature of all times. One cannot judge the merits of literary works only by the fact that they were written during a certain period.'[3]

Because of Lee's influence, Yuan Chung-lang dared to say that only the folk songs of his time could be expected to be passed on to later generations. This was during the period when imitation of the style of essayists of the Chin and Han Dynasties was the vogue. Yuan's idea gained support from scholars such as his two brothers, Yuan Chung-tao and Yuan Tsung-tao, and Chiang Chin-chih, Tao Wan-lin, Huang Huei and Feng Meng-lung. Lee Cho-wu himself wrote a preface and commentary for *All Men Are Brothers*, and it was due to Yuan's praise of the manuscript of *Golden Lotus* that it became well known before it was published. To a great extent it was thanks to people like Lee, Yuan and other like-minded scholars that the golden period of Chinese novels was brought about.

A. The Historical Novel: *The Three Kingdoms*

Lo Kuan-chung is one of the most important novelists in Chinese literature. He wrote *The Three Kingdoms, The Romance of the Sui and Tang Dynasties* and *The Suppression of the Sorcerer's Revolt*. *All Men Are Brothers* was said to have been revised by him. He also wrote an opera, *The Meeting of the Dragon and the Tiger*. But the paucity of biographical literature is such that all we know about him is what Chia Chung-ming wrote about him.[4] 'Lo Kuan-chung was a native of Tai-yuan (in Shansi Province), also called Wanderer among the Lakes and Seas. He was a shy and reserved man. His opera is full of light and fresh verse. Although there was great disparity in our ages (Chia was much younger than Lo), he and I were good friends. But because there have been great upheavals in our time, we were seldom together. I last saw him in 1364, which was sixty-odd years ago. I do not know what happened to him.'

The biographical details on the dust jacket of a book nowadays give much more about an author than this. To think that Chia was Lo's good friend, and his book was about Lo and other dramatists! But at least we know that Lo lived some time between the last years of the Yuan Dynasty and the early years of the Ming Dynasty.

In his preface to *The Three Kingdoms* Yung Yi-tse said, 'In previous dynasties there were people who wrote stories based on unofficial history books for the use of blind story-tellers. Passages in such stories are often vulgar and facts were misrepresented. Scholars look upon such stories with contempt. Lo Kuan-chung of Tung-yuan has now written a novel, based on history starting from the first year of Chung-ping (A.D. 187) in the reign of Emperor Ling of the Han Dynasty to the first year of Tai-kang (280) in the reign of Emperor Wu of the Chin Dynasty, as recorded in *The Annals of the Three Kingdoms* by Chen Shou of Ping-yang. He calls the novel *The Three Kingdoms*. The language he uses is not difficult to understand, nor has the standard been lowered to cater to popular tastes. Furthermore, it is based on facts. This novel is not very different from a history book. The author obviously wants to acquaint his readers with history. In adopting the literary form of the novel he was apparently thinking of the folk songs collected in the *Book of Poetry*.'

The ideas expressed here must have been those of Lo Kuan-chung. Lo was therefore the first novelist to realize the influence a novel can exert on readers, and spent most of his life writing them. Apart from those quoted above, he is said to have written a huge novel called *The Romance of Seventeen Dynasties*. If this is true one must pause to consider the great ambition and tremendous confidence Lo must have had. But as his works were edited by other people, it is now almost impossible to tell what the original form of his novels was except, perhaps, *The Three Kingdoms*. For even though this was revised by Mao Tsung-kang of the Ching Dynasty, the revision was confined to (1) changing parts of the book to conform to historical facts, (2) changing the headings of each chapter into couplets, (3) editing poems and abolishing euphemistic comments of the characters, and (4) paying more attention to rhetoric.

Lo's *The Three Kingdoms* is vastly more vivid in characterization than the story-tellers' *Story of the Three Kingdoms*. A host of characters in the novel were widely known to the people, and their names became synonymous with the qualities and personalities they possessed. The relationship between the sworn brothers Liu Pei, Kuan Yu and Chang Fei has so long been admired by the Chinese that in Chinatown districts all over the world when three partners start a restaurant, they most probably will call it Tao Yuan, or The Peach Garden, which was the place where the three heroes swore their brotherhood.

Lo expanded the story, and put in much more detail. Also, he wrote into the novels incidents recorded in official history books, and actual poems, memoranda, etc., written by the principal characters. He also deleted unfounded legends. His chief weeding-out effort was the deletion of the superstitious tale which appeared in the introduction to *The Story of the Three Kingdoms*. This told how Han Hsin, Peng Yueh and Yin Pu, the three generals who helped to establish the Han Dynasty but were put to death by Han Kao Tsu, the first Emperor, appealed to God in Heaven for redress of the wrong they suffered. God was at a loss to know what to do, and sought Szema Chung-hsiang's advice. Szema suggested that the three generals should be reincarnated as Tsao Tsao, Liu Pei and Sun Chuan as a reprisal, to divide the territory of China among themselves and that Han Kao Tsu was to be reincarnated as Emperor Hsien. God was so happy with the suggestion that he decided Szema Chung-hsiang should reunite China and become an Emperor, too, after the country had been divided into three kingdoms for a number of years.

But Lo Kuan-chung's decision to stick as closely as possible to historical facts had its drawbacks. First of all, the great amount of factual data prevented him from giving free rein to his descriptive powers, so that in spite of his talent for characterization, the novel consists mainly of narrative and a few descriptive passages. Secondly, perhaps to simplify his effort in quoting from official record books, he could not use the vernacular language to express himself. Instead he used a compromise of half-vernacular and half-classical style. He may perhaps have purposely adopted this style, however, so that scholars of his time should not consider the work 'vulgar'.

The Three Kingdoms covers a period of ninety-three years, starting from the year 187 to the end of the Han Dynasty and early Chin Dynasty, which is to say a longer span than the actual existence of the three kingdoms of Wei, Shu and Wu. For the author went back to show how Liu Pei, Tsao Tsao and Sun Chuan rose to power in the reigns of Emperors Ling and Hsien of the Han Dynasty, when because of natural disasters and misrule, the country was in chaos. Also, although

Sun Hao, the ruler of Wu, was reduced to the rank of Marquis in 264, he maintained autonomy in the area he ruled over until 280, at which date the novel ends.

Two-thirds of the novel is devoted to telling how Tsao Tsao slowly came to power and ruled the country in the name of Emperor Hsien, how Liu Pei and his two sworn brothers were repeatedly defeated and chased from place to place by Tsao Tsao's forces, and how Sun Chuan built up his forces in the area south of the Yangtse River. It may sound strange to the reader, but Lo Kuan-chung presented Liu Pei as the legitimate heir to the throne of the Han Dynasty simply because Tsao Tsao had taken over the actual power to rule the country from Emperor Hsien and Liu Pei had the same surname, and claimed to be one of the remote cousins of the Emperor. In this he was extremely successful, so that when Liu Pei, himself depending on the goodwill of a cousin for a place to stay in and with the rank only of a Magistrate, went to visit Chu-keh Liang, an untried strategist, and asked him for help, it was described as though only a legendary sage-emperor of ancient times *could* have acted as Liu did. When he was again driven out of his base by Tsao Tsao and went to seek shelter in Sun Chuan's territory, the victory gained in the subsequent great battle of Red Cliff, which was waged chiefly by Sun Chuan's forces against those of Tsao Tsao, was credited to Chu-keh Liang, Liu's chief-of-staff, in spite of the fact that Kuan Yu, Liu Pei's sworn brother, intentionally let Tsao Tsao and the remnants of his forces escape the encirclement that was to bring the battle to a successful conclusion. What is more amazing is that to most Chinese readers *Three Kingdoms* loses its interest after Kuan Yu, acting against orders, is killed in battle by the forces of Sun Chuan. All this happened before the three kingdoms were formally set up in 220. It may be argued therefore that *Three Kingdoms* is a misnomer. But the book is also a testimony to Lo Kuan-chung's skill as a novelist.

Here is a passage from the novel:

After receiving instructions from Chou Yu, Lu Hsu went to see Kung Ming. Kung Ming welcomed him on board.

Lu Hsu said, 'I have been very busy with military affairs, or I should have called on you sooner.'

Kung Ming said, 'I, too, have not had the chance to congratulate the Commander-in-Chief yet.'

Lu Hsu said, 'On what?'

Kung Ming said, 'You need not be afraid. Tsai Mou and Cheng Yun are both dead and the state of Wu is safe. Why should I not congratulate you? Tsao Tsao was fooled for a while, but realizes his mistake now, but he will not admit it. I hear that he has put Mao Chieh and Yu Chin in charge of the naval forces. Somehow or other they will lead their naval forces to ruin.'

Lü Hsu digested this in silence. After a while he took leave of Kung Ming.

Kung Ming said, 'Chou Yu might be jealous of me, please don't tell him about this, or he might do me harm.'

Lu Hsu returned and told Chou Yu what had happened.

Chou Yu cried, 'This man must not be allowed to live! I am going to kill him!'

Lu Hsu said, 'If you kill Kung Ming, Tsao Tsao will laugh at you.'

Chou Yu said, 'I'll manage to have him killed in such a way that I cannot be blamed for his death.'

Lu Hsu said, 'What do you mean?'

Chou Yu said, 'You shall see.'

The next day Chou Yu gathered his men in the tent and sent for Kung Ming to discuss tactics. Kung Ming walked in, looking quite happy. After they were seated, Chou Yu asked Kung Ming, 'We will soon be fighting Tsao Tsao's army across a river. With what should we fight them?'

Kung Ming said, 'Across the river—of course, we will use bows and arrows.'

Chou Yu said, 'That is what I thought. But we are short of arrows now. We will need a hundred thousand arrows at least. Will you kindly take charge of the manufacture of arrows? You know this is a matter of great importance.'

Kung Ming said, 'Gladly. May I ask you, Commander-in-Chief, when is the earliest you will need the hundred thousand arrows?'

Chou Yu said, 'In ten days. Can I have them by then?'

Kung Ming said, 'Tsao Tsao's army will be here in less than ten days. If you wait so long you will be defeated.'

Chou Yu said, 'When can you give me the arrows then?'

Kung Ming said, 'I can give you a hundred thousand arrows in three days.'

'You know this is not a joking matter,' said Chou Yu.

'Would I dare joke with the Commander-in-Chief?' said Kung

Ming. 'If I do not deliver the arrows within three days you may punish me according to military law.'

Chou Yu was very happy, and had a contract drawn up and wine brought. 'I will reward you duly when this is accomplished,' he said.

Kung Ming said, 'I will start making the arrows tomorrow. Please send five hundred soldiers to the side of the river to carry away the arrows on the third day.' After several cups of wine he departed.

Lu Hsu said, 'Is this man serious?'

Chou Yu said, 'I did not force him to sign the contract, he will not escape if he does not deliver. I will tell my men not to supply him with any material. Nobody will blame me for punishing him if he fails to fulfil his half of the bargain. But go now and find out what he really has on his mind and come back and report to me.'

Lu Hsu went to see Kung Ming, who said, 'I told you not to tell Chou Yu, because he might want to harm me, but you would not believe me. Now I am in trouble. How can I deliver a hundred thousand arrows in three days? You must help me.'

Lu Hsu said, 'If you are in trouble you asked for it. How can I help you?'

Kung Ming said, 'Please lend me twenty ships with thirty men on each ship. The ships should have blue awnings and be decked with straw on both sides. I have a plan, and you shall have the arrows in three days. But Chou Yu must not know. If he knows my plan will miscarry.'

Lu Hsu promised and reported back to Chou Yu, but he did not mention the ships. He only said that Kung Ming did not need bamboo, feathers or glue for his arrows, but he would deliver them just the same. Chou Yu was surprised and said, 'We shall see how he does it!'

Lu Hsu got ready twenty fast ships with thirty men each and decked them out according to Kung Ming's instructions and waited for him. On the first day Kung Ming did not make any move, nor on the second day. But at dawn on the third day Kung Ming secretly sent for Lu Hsu. When he arrived on Kung Ming's ship he said, 'You have sent for me?'

Kung Ming said, 'I want you to come with me to fetch the arrows.'

Lu Hsu said, 'Where shall we go to fetch them?'

'You shall see,' Kung Ming said, and ordered the twenty ships, connected by ropes, to make for the northern bank.

A thick fog lay over the water and it was densest in the middle of the river, and they could not see the bank clearly. By the fifth watch the ships were near to Tsao Tsao's warships. Kung Ming ordered that the ships should spread out, with their bows towards the west and sterns towards the east, and that the men should beat the war drums on board.

Lu Hsu was surprised and said, 'What if Tsao Tsao sends his men to attack us?'

Kung Ming smiled and said, 'I do not think he will do that in this fog. All we have to do is drink and wait for the fog to disperse.'

In Tsao Tsao's camp, Mao Chieh and Yu Chin heard the drums and reported to him. Tsao Tsao said, 'The enemy's troops have arrived at the river in the fog. They must be trying to ambush us. We must not take any action. Order the naval forces to shoot at the ships.' He further ordered the commanders of his land forces to send three thousand men to the edge of the river to assist. When Mao Chieh and Yu Chin received their orders they immediately ordered their men to shoot their arrows at the ships for they were afraid that the enemy forces would land on shore. In a little while the land forces also arrived, and more than ten thousand men were shooting arrows in the direction of the ships. The arrows fell like rain. After a while Kung Ming ordered that the ships be turned around so that their bows were pointed towards the east and the sterns towards the west. As the drums rolled the bundles of straw on the twenty ships were filled with arrows. When it was almost dawn, Kung Ming ordered the men on the ships to call out all at once, 'Thank you for the arrows!' Before Tsao Tsao's men could report back the ships were already carried by the rapid currents more than twenty *li* away.

Kung Ming said to Lu Hsu, 'There are five or six thousand arrows on each ship. We have our hundred thousand arrows. Tomorrow we will use them to attack Tsao Tsao's men.'

Lu Hsu said, 'How did you know there was going to be such a thick fog today?'

Kung Ming said, 'If a general does not understand astronomy, terrain, meteorology, strategy or tactics he is a poor general indeed. I knew three days ago that there would be fog today. That is why I dared to promise to deliver the arrows today, although I knew that Chou Yu was trying to set a trap for me.'

Lu Hsu was deeply impressed. When the ships returned Chou

Yu's five hundred men were waiting on shore for the arrows. Kung Ming ordered them to take the arrows from the ship and carry them to the camp. There were indeed more than a hundred thousand arrows. Lu Hsu went to see Chou Yu and told him what happened. Chou Yu was astonished and sighed and said, 'Kung Ming is really very clever. He is a better general than I am!'

B. The Novel of Adventure: *All Men Are Brothers*

At the end of the Southern Sung Dynasty there were popular story-tellers' texts about Sung Chiang, the hero of *All Men Are Brothers* and the thirty-five members of his gang of bandits. Kung Sheng-yu, a scholar and artist of that time, wrote a *Tribute* to them and said in a prefatory note: 'There are popular stories about Sung Chiang which are not worthy of our attention, but accomplished artists such as Lee Sung drew pictures of the thirty-six men and scholars did not think any less of him. When I was young I too greatly admired the exploits of Sung Chiang and his men. I therefore like to express my admiration in this tribute.'[5] The reason for the scholars' admiration for this gang of bandits seemed to lie in the fact that Khitan and Golden Tartars were consecutively threatening the existence of the Sung Dynasty, and they were hoping that someone like Sung Chiang would rise to meet the threat and the aggression of the foreigners. Chou Mi said in his postscript to Kung Sheng-yu's *Tribute*, 'Sung Chiang and his men were all bandits. Why should Sheng-yu pay tribute to them and comment on them? Ta Shih Kung (Szema Chien) wrote about *Hsieh* (gallant knights) and was blamed for encouraging unruly elements, but he was the first author to include Chen Shen and Wu Kuang in *Lieh Chuan* (*Biographies of Famous Generals and Ministers*) and write about Hsiang Yu's life as though Hsiang were an Emperor. His reasons for doing so were profound and full of implications. The wise should realize what they are.' Now Chen Shen, Wu Kuang and Hsiang Yu were all rebels against the Chin Dynasty. In spite of the fact that Hsiang Yu was at one time the most powerful man in the country, these three rebels were all defeated. In saying that Kung Sheng-yu was doing what Szema Chien did before him, Chou Mi was saying that Sung Chiang and his men were not different from the emperors of previous dynasties, if they should be successful. Taking into consideration the fact that when Chou Mi wrote this, the Sung Dynasty had already fallen, it seems probable that he was thinking of success in repelling foreign invasion when he wrote it. This admittedly is a very roundabout way to express one's opinion, but when the Mongols had overrun the country, any suggestion of revolt could only be deviously hinted at.

The popular stories about Sung Chiang originated from the following passages in the *History of Sung Dynasty* in the *Annals of Emperor Hui Tsung* and the *Biography of Hou Mung*.

A gang of bandits in the area south of Huai River under the leadership of Sung Chiang attacked the garrison of Huaiyang. Troops were sent to suppress them, but the bandits thrust into the areas east of the capital and north of the Yangtse River, and penetrated into Huaichow. Governor Chang Shu-yeh was ordered to persuade them to surrender.

Hou Mung wrote a memorial to the Emperor saying, 'Sung Chiang and thirty-five other bandit leaders roamed the areas of Chi and Wei and tens of thousands of government troops did not dare to try to stop them. This shows that Sung Chiang is talented. . . . Why not pardon him and order him to fight Fang La to expiate his crime?'

This explains why in the *Story of the Hsuan Ho Period of the Sung Dynasty*, Sung Chiang was said to have been persuaded by Chang Shu-yeh to surrender, and later, after he and his men had suppressed the rebellion of Fang La, promoted to be a Military Governor.

How *All Men Are Brothers* came to be written is unfortunately a matter of speculation. The earliest edition of the novel is no longer extant. If we are to follow the majority opinion of Chinese scholars, the book was written by Shih Nai-an and edited by Lo Kuan-chung. Some people, however, agree with Chin Sheng-tan, a famous critic of the Ching Dynasty, who thought that Shih Nai-an wrote the first seventy chapters, and Lo Kuan-chung the last thirty. Chin omitted the last thirty chapters of the novel in an edition which was published, saying that what remained, together with the introduction, formed the text of an older edition which he had discovered. This is not the place to go more deeply into this controversy, but we shall assume that *All Men Are Brothers* was first written by Shih Nai-an.

We have no idea what the earliest edition was like, but it is probable that like *The Story of the Hsuan Ho Period of Sung* it was written in vernacular Chinese. The main structure of the novel, probably, was roughly the same, although more detail and description must have been added later. *All Men Are Brothers* became the first great Chinese novel to be written entirely in vernacular Chinese.

There have been many editions of the novel published in the last seven hundred odd years. Two of them are worth mentioning here. One is the hundred chapter edition, or Kuo Wu-tin edition. This was sponsored by Kuo Hsun, Marquis Wu Tin, and published during the reign of Emperor Shih Tsung (1522–1566) of the Ming Dynasty. We do not know the author of this edition. I say author, not editor, because this edition is so much better than the previous one in style and descriptive power that it can almost be said to be a new novel, based on previous editions. Hu Yin-lin, a critic of the early seventeenth century, said, 'It is impossible to describe the excellence of this edition, whether in explicitly narrating and describing the scenes of the story, or in showing the emotions and characterization by inference; whether in the flow of its prose or the beauty of its poems.' Because of its excellence many people maintain that it was written by Wang Tai-han, who was one of the foremost scholars of the day and wrote the preface to this edition. But this is only an intelligent guess.

According to Yang Ting-chien,[6] 'In the Kuo Wu-tin edition, the episode about Sung Chiang and Yen Po-hsi was moved to another place in the story. This is good. But in cutting out the chapters about the revolts of Wang Ching and Tien Hu from the earlier editions and adding chapters about the expedition against Khitan, the editor erred in following the technique of literary hacks to tighten the plot. Apparently he did not realize that great authors do not bother themselves only with the plot.'

Yang was editor of the 120-chapter edition of the novel, which, published some time during the reign of Tien Chi (1621–1627) or Chung Cheng (1628–1644), added to the Kuo Wu-tin edition edited chapters about the revolts of Wang Ching and Tien Hu. He was perhaps biased in his comments. Nevertheless, the most popular edition of the novel remains the one edited by Chin Sheng-tan. This is because the language used was further improved by Chin. In his time people were not very sympathetic to bandits, whom they knew all too well. By omitting the last thirty chapters and concentrating on the story of Sung Chiang, and ending with a dream in which all 108 men of Liang

Shan Po were captured and killed by Chang Shu-yeh, Chin's edition struck the fancy of the people and became so popular that all other editions of the novel have been forgotten during the past three hundred-odd years.

All Men Are Brothers is actually a series of episodes in which the 108 heroes of the novel are forced by circumstances to become bandits in Liang Shan Po. It is packed with action, like the present-day thriller or 'Western'. Except for Li Kuei, Lu Chih-shen and Wu Sung, the characters are not very well drawn. Many of them were obviously brought in to make up the number of thirty-six 'Tien Kang Stars' and seventy-two 'Ti Sha Stars'. Others are stereotyped characters, such as Wu Yung and Kungsun Shen. The character of Tsao Kai, the leader of the band, never comes alive. Even the popularity of Sung Chiang with every bandit of the same standing was never fully explained. In spite of its short-comings, however, including some geographical errors, the episodes have enthralled generations of readers. The Chinese like especially the chapters in which Wu Sung, Lu Chih-shen and Li Kuei figure, when these three straightforward and impulsive characters use sheer physical force to deal with situations.

Here is a passage from the book.

Thus Wu Sung invited the neighbours who lived on all four sides and there were also the old woman and his sister-in-law, six in all. Then Wu Sung drew out a bench and sat across the end of the table, and he called to the soldiers that they were to bar the front and the back doors, and a soldier came from the back and poured out the wine. Then Wu Sung gave a loud greeting to all and he said, 'Honourable Neighbours, you are not to blame this lowly one. I am but a coarse fellow, and I have invited a few of you anyhow.'

The neighbours answered him saying, 'We humble ones have not even invited the captain to a feast upon your return from foreign parts. On the contrary, we come hither to trouble you.'

But Wu Sung only laughed and said, 'These things I have prepared are not so good as they were. Do not laugh at them.'

As for the soldier, he did nothing but pour out wine. Yet even as they drank each one had a secret fear in him and in truth none knew what was to come. When the wine had been poured out thrice for each, Hu would have risen and he said, 'This humble one is somewhat busy.'

But Wu Sung shouted out, saying, 'You shall not go! Since you are come to this house, though you are busy yet must you sit awhile.'

At this Hu's heart seemed to him like a well in which seven buckets are drawn up and eight dropped down, and to himself he thought, 'If he invited us to drink wine with good intent, why does he treat us like this?' And so he could do naught but sit down again.

Then Wu Sung said, 'Bring the wine forth once more and pour it out!'

So the soldier came again and poured out four rounds of wine and this made seven rounds altogether and it seemed to the guests that by now they had sat through the length of a thousand feasts. Suddenly they heard Wu Sung shout to the soldiers, 'Take away the cups and the plates and we will wait awhile before we eat again.'

Then Wu Sung wiped the table clean and all the neighbours rose together, but Wu Sung stopped them with his two hands and said, 'It is just time for talk, and you are all here, Honourable Neighbours. Who is there among you who can write?'

The one surnamed Yao then replied, 'He who is surnamed Hu writes very well.'

So Wu Sung called out a greeting to that one and he said, 'I must trouble you, then', and he rolled up his two sleeves and he reached into his undergarments and brought his hand out with a jerk and out came a dagger. The four fingers of his right hand clasped the dagger handle and he held his thumb pointed to his breast. His two eyes he made big and round and fierce and he cried, 'Honourable Neighbours all! Upon him who has treated me ill I will revenge myself and him who has killed will I kill. All I ask of you is that you be just witnesses.'

Then they saw Wu Sung grasp his sister-in-law with his left hand and with his right he pointed at the old woman Wang. The four neighbours were so terrified they had not a word to say and they did not know what to do. They stared at each other and they did not dare to lift a voice. Then Wu Sung said on, 'Honourable Neighbours, you must not blame me. And you need not be afraid, for though I am a rude coarse fellow, yet am I not afraid to die. I know that him who treated me ill I must treat ill and upon him who took his revenge on me I must now take my revenge. But I shall not harm you. I must only trouble you, my Honourable Neighbours, to be witnesses. But if there is one among you who goes out too early, you are not to blame me if I change towards him, for I shall thrust my blade into him five or seven times. Even though I take his life it will be nothing to me.'

The neighbours stood there staring, their mouths ajar, and not one of them dared to move again. Then Wu Sung, looking at the old woman Wang, shouted out, 'Ha, you old pig and dog, hear me! This life of my brother's is all upon your body, and I shall ask you for it bit by bit!' And then he turned his face and seeing that woman he began to curse, saying, 'You adulteress, hear me! How did you take away my brother's life? Speak the truth and I will forgive you!'

That woman said, 'Brother-in-law, how without any reason you are! Your brother fell ill of a pain in his belly and he died, and what has it to do with me?'

But before she had finished speaking Wu Sung struck his knife upon the table and with his left hand he seized the knot of the woman's hair and with his right he grasped the clothing of her bosom and with his foot he kicked over the table and he lifted the woman clean across the table and threw her down before the tablet. Then he stamped on her with his two feet and with his right hand he took up his dagger and he pointed with it to the old woman Wang and he said, 'Old pig and dog, tell the truth!'

Now the old woman longed to run away but she could not and she could only say, 'Do not be so angry, Captain. I will tell you and there is an end of it.'

Then Wu Sung commanded the soldiers to bring out the ink and the paper and the pen and he placed them on the table set right again. And he pointed at Hu Chen Ching with his knife and he said, 'I must trouble you to listen to every sentence and write it down word for word.'

And Hu Chen Ching stammered and trembled and said, 'Hum— humble one will—will write. . . .'

Then Wu Sung mixed the water on the ink block and he stirred the ink and he took up the pen and opened the paper and he said, 'Old woman Wang, do you but speak the truth!'

But that old woman said, 'It has nothing to do with me . . . why do you bid me speak?'

Then Wu Sung said, 'Old pig and dog, I know all! Whom do you put it upon? If you do not speak I will first slice into pieces this adulteress, and then will I kill you, you old dog!'

And he took up his dagger and he smoothed it a time or two upon that woman's cheeks so that she cried out in haste, 'Brother-in-law, forgive me, pray! Let me rise and I will tell you all!'

Then Wu Sung reached down and he jerked her up and lifted her so that she knelt there before the tablet and he shouted out, 'Adulteress, speak quickly!'

Now that woman was so terrified that the souls and spirits were out of her and she could only speak the truth. She told the whole story from the day she let the curtain pole fall and it struck Hsi-men Ching to the day she went to make clothes for the old woman Wang when their desire was accomplished. Word by word she told it all and she told how Hsi-men Ching kicked Wu the Elder and why they prepared the poison and how the old woman Wang directed it all. And Wu Sung bade her speak a sentence and then he bade Hu Chen Ching to write the sentence down.

Then the old woman Wang cried to that woman, 'You biting insect, it was you who did the wrong first and how can I not say it? You have only made this old soul suffer bitterness!'

Yet the old woman Wang must confess it all, too, and all she said also Wu Sung commanded Hu Chen Ching to write down from first to last and it was all written there on the paper. Then he commanded the two women to make their marks on the paper with their fingers inked and he commanded the four neighbours to set their names down also, and he bade the soldiers bring a rope and he tied the old dog's hands behind her back. Then he rolled up the paper on which all was written and he thrust it into his bosom and he bade the soldiers bring out more wine. This wine he placed in a cup before Wu the Elder's tablet. Then he dragged the woman over to it and he forced her to kneel before the tablet and he shouted to the old dog and made her kneel there too. When they had knelt his tears flowed and he sighed and said, 'Elder Brother, your souls are not far from this place. Today has your younger brother avenged you, and I have wiped away my hatred as clean as snow!'

Then Wu Sung commanded a soldier to light the spirit money. Now that woman, seeing the outlook was evil for her, was about to scream, but Wu Sung seized her by the knot of her hair and he threw her down and he stood with a foot on each of her arms. He pulled open the garments of her bosom and quicker than speech he sank the dagger into her breast and twisted it. Then he pulled the dagger out and held it in his mouth and with both his hands he reached into her body and he pulled out her heart and liver and entrails and he placed them before the tablet.

Again came the sound of the dagger plunging in—chih-chah—and that woman's head was cut off clean and the blood poured over the ground. The four neighbours felt their eyes go askew and they were dazed with their terror and they covered their faces. But they saw how fierce Wu Sung was and they did not dare even to exhort him. They could but let him have his will.

Then Wu Sung bade the soldiers go upstairs and bring down a quilt and wrap the woman's head in it, and he wiped his dagger upon the quilt and thrust it into its sheath. Then he washed his hands and he called out and said, 'I have greatly troubled you, my Honourable Neighbours! But you are not to blame me for anything. Pray go upstairs and seat yourselves for a little while and wait until I come again.'

The four neighbours looked at each other but they did not dare to disobey him. They could but go up the stairs and sit down. And Wu Sung commanded the soldiers that they were to guard the old woman and take her upstairs too and shut the door on them all and he bade the two soldiers stand below on guard.

Then did Wu Sung take the woman's head wrapped as it was and he went in well-nigh one leap to the front of the medicine shop which was Hsi-men Ching's. . . .[7]

C. The Supernatural Novel: *Monkey*

In the Yuan Dynasty, many Northern Dramas, including Wu Changlin's *Hsi Yu Chi Tsa Chu*, were based on the story of *San Tsang's Search for Buddhist Sutras*. In the early 1930s a 1,200-word part of a chapter under the heading of *Wei Cheng Kills the Dragon King of River Ching in His Dream* in a book entitled *Hsi Yu Chi* was discovered in the *Yung Lo Encyclopaedia* edited early in the Ming Dynasty. This was a most interesting discovery, for it was written in the vernacular and the improved version of the same story can be found in Chapter 10 of Wu Cheng-en's famous *Monkey*. Obviously, this was part of an earlier version of the same book. Wu Cheng-en must have had this text and improved upon it to produce the novel for which he became famous, and which we now know. Here is a complete translation of the find.

To the south-west of Chang-an, there was a river called Ching. One day, in the thirteenth year of Cheng Kuan (639), two fishermen, by the name of Chang Hsiao and Lee Ting, were talking by the river bank.

'Inside the Western Gate of Chang-an there is a fortune-teller's shop called Shen Hsien Shan Jen. Every day I present a carp to the fortune-teller and he tells me where to spread my net. Following his advice, I have been catching fish every day,' said Chang Hsiao to Lee Ting.

'I must go and ask the fortune-teller tomorrow,' said Lee Ting.

They never suspected that while they were talking a Yaksha, patrolling the waters, overhead them. 'I must report to the Dragon King,' thought the Yaksha.

Now, the Dragon King was the Dragon of the River Ching. He was sitting in his Crystal Palace, facing the front door, when suddenly the Yaksha came and reported to him, 'There are two fishermen talking by the river bank, saying that inside the Western Gate of Chang-an there is a fortune-teller who knows what goes on in the river. They said that by following his advice, they will catch and kill every creature in the river.'

Upon hearing this the Dragon King was furious. He transformed himself into a scholar and went to Chang-an. There he saw a banner on which were written the words: 'Yuan Shou-chen, man with magic, awaits your pleasure.' The old Dragon went into the shop and sat down facing the fortune-teller. He asked hundreds of difficult questions and finally asked the fortune-teller when it would rain next.

'Tomorrow. The clouds will start to gather at seven in the morning and thunder start at eleven. Rain will begin to fall at three in the afternoon and stop at five.'

'How much will the rainfall be?'

'Three feet and three point eight four inches.'

The Dragon laughed. 'All may not be as you say.'

'If it does not rain tomorrow I am willing to pay you a fine of fifty taels of silver,' said the fortune-teller.

The Dragon said, 'All right. See you tomorrow.'

He took leave of the fortune-teller and went straight back to his Crystal Palace. Within a few minutes there came an Emissary in Yellow Cap who announced, 'By the Imperial Order of Jade Emperor, you, Dragon of the River Ching, Controller of Eight

Rivers, should start spreading clouds at seven in the morning tomorrow, start thunder at eleven, begin raining at three in the afternoon and stop at five.' The Emissary left soon afterwards.

The old Dragon said, 'I did not think the fortune-teller's preposterous prediction would come true. Well, when the time comes, I shall give a little less rain so as to collect the fine from him.'

The next day the Dragon King spread clouds at five in the morning and rained two feet of rain at seven.

On the third day the old Dragon again transformed himself into a scholar and went to see the fortune-teller.

'Your prediction was wrong. Pay me immediately the fifty taels of silver,' he said.

'I was not wrong, only you disobeyed the order from Heaven and gave less rain than ordered,' said the fortune-teller. 'You are not a human being but the dragon who gave out rain last night. You can deceive others, but not me.'

The old Dragon was furious. He reverted to his original form. And instantly the banks of the Yellow River were damaged and the three peaks of Hua Mountain trembled. The Dragon's fury terrorized every living creature in an area as large as ten thousand *li* away from Chang-an, and rain driven by the wind washed the sky. Everyone ran to seek shelter but Yuan Shou-chen did not move an inch. The Dragon wanted to move forward to harm him.

'I am not afraid to die,' said Yuan, 'you have gone against the order from Heaven and reduced the amount of sweet rain. You will soon be put to death. You cannot escape from being cut to pieces on the Kua Lung Platform.'

The Dragon was frightened and repented. He transformed himself again into the form of a scholar and knelt down. 'If this is the case,' he said, 'I wish you would explain to me the reasons' [*sic*].

'Tomorrow you will die. Wei Cheng, the Prime Minister, will come and pass sentence on you at eleven.'

'Help me!'

Yuan Shou-chen said, 'If you don't want to die, you must try to see the Emperor and ask him to talk to the Prime Minister on your behalf. Your life may yet be saved.'

The old Dragon thanked him and left for home.

This was indeed fantasy, mixing deities with human beings. In so far as endowing human beings with god-like powers is concerned, *Monkey* is not unlike the science fiction of today. It is what an imaginative child would like to read. The fascination of this type of story was in fact part of the reason why Wu Cheng-en came to write *Monkey*. He said in his preface to *Yu Ting Chih*:

I have liked to read strange and amazing stories ever since I was a child. I used to search for books of romance and unofficial histories in the bookstalls and, for fear of my father and teacher scolding me and taking the books away from me, hid myself in some out-of-the-way place to read them. This tendency grew up with me, and I read many more strange tales. When I was grown up I continued to search for this kind of book with the help of my friends, and my brain was filled almost entirely with strange and amazing tales. I used to like *chuan chi* written by Niu Chi-chang and Tuan Ko-ku and admired their skill in describing scenery and the personalities of the heroes. I had wanted to write one similar book, but owing to my laziness, never got down to it. Stories that I had stored in my mind were gradually forgotten, except for the thousand-odd tales which refused to be forgotten and which I have now jotted down in this book. I am quite amused by this, for it seems that strange tales have asked to be written, instead of my seeking to write these stories. . . .

Temperamentally, then, Wu Cheng-en was suited to write *Monkey*. But more important perhaps was the fact that he could not carve for himself a career as a government official. He was intelligent, talented and well-read. His poems were said to be as delicate and easy to read as those written by Chin Kuan, a famous poet of the Sung Dynasty. He also wrote plays. But he was never successful in the official examinations, and it was not until he was more than sixty years old that he was appointed an assistant to the Magistrate of Chang-hsin District, on the strength of his knowledge of one of the Confucian classics. He held this post for seven years and then resigned. Not long afterwards he died, in Huai-an, his home town. It is probable that it was during the seven years when he was in office and had a steady income that he began to write *Monkey*.

Monkey can be divided into three parts: (1) Chapters 1–7, which describe the background of Sun Wu-kung or the Monkey; (2) Chapters 8–12, in which the events leading to Hsien Chuang's (San Tsang's) search for Buddhist sutras are set down; (3) Chapters 13–100, which tell of Hsien Chuang's journey during which he found himself in eighty-one difficult situations, but was saved every time through the help of some deities and the efforts of Monkey. As far as can be judged, some of the events in the second part were based on *Tai Tsung's Experience in the Nether World*, a *hua pen* story of the Sung Dynasty, and the third part was based on *San Tsang's Search for Buddhist Sutras*. It is not known from which Chinese story the first part evolved, but perhaps the origin of *Monkey* can be found in Indian literature, as I mentioned earlier in this chapter.

Monkey, like *All Men Are Brothers*, consists of a series of action-packed episodes, but with Hsien Chuang's journey serving as the thread carrying all the episodes in *Monkey* (except for the first seven chapters). *Monkey* is a more tightly constructed novel than *All Men Are Brothers*. Because each and every one of the eighty-one difficult situations Hsien Chuang found himself in involved some kind of monster, endowed with peculiar magical powers imaginable to human beings, it is the more fascinating of the two novels.

Of the principal characters in the novel, Monkey is the best drawn. He is a mischievous, loyal and humorous personality. The greedy, gluttonous and lascivious Pigsy and the dependable, quiet Sandy come out rather well, too, but by comparison, Hsien Chuang's character is colourless and uninteresting. The Chinese like these four characters in the order mentioned. Even now, in Hong Kong, a film about an episode from the book, with Monkey as the hero, draws a full house for weeks on end.

Here is a passage from the novel which is perhaps the most hilarious.

Monkey was brought to the place of execution, where heavenly soldiers bound him to a pillar and began to hew him with axes, stab him with spears, slash him with swords. But all this had no effect whatever, and presently the Southern Pole-star sent for the spirits of the Fire Stars to come and set him alight; but they were quite unable to burn him. The thunder spirits hurled thunderbolts at him; but this had even less effect.

'I don't know where the Great Sage got this trick of inviolability,' said Mahabali to the Jade Emperor. 'Neither weapons nor thunderbolts have the least effect on him. What are we to do?'

'Yes, indeed,' said the Jade Emperor, 'with a fellow like that what line *can* one take?'

'It's not surprising,' said Lao Tzu. 'After all, he ate the peaches of Immortality, drank the wine of Heaven, and stole the Elixir of Long Life; five bowls full, some raw, some cooked, are all inside him. No doubt he has worked on them with Samadhi fire and fused them into a solid, that makes his whole body harder than diamond, so that he is very difficult to damage. The best thing would be to bring him to me. I'll put him in my Crucible of the Eight Trigrams and smelt him with alchemic fire. In a little while he will be reduced to ashes, and I shall recover my elixir, which will be left at the bottom of the crucible.'

So Monkey was handed over to Lao Tzu, and Erh-lang was rewarded with a hundred golden flowers, a hundred jars of heavenly wine, a hundred grains of elixir, along with a great store of jewels, pearls, brocades and embroideries, which he was asked to share with his brothers. He thanked the Emperor, and went back to the River of Libations.

When Lao Tzu got back to the Tushita Palace he untied Monkey's ropes, removed the blade that was stuck through his lute-bone, pushed him into the crucible, and told his servant to blow up a good fire. Now this crucible was in eight parts, each representing one of the eight trigrams. Monkey wriggled into the part corresponding to the trigram *sun*. Now *sun* is wind, and wind blows out fire; but wind raises smoke, and Monkey's eyes smarted and became red; a condition from which he never recovered, which is why he is sometimes called Fiery Eyes. Time passed, and at last the forty-ninth day came, and Lao Tzu's alchemical processes were complete. When he came to the crucible to take off the lid, Monkey was rubbing his eyes with both hands, so hard that the tears fell. When he heard the lid being moved he looked quickly up, and the light that came in hurt him so much that he could not bear it and jumped straight out of the crucible, uttering a piercing cry and kicking over the crucible as he jumped. He rushed out of the room pursued by Lao Tzu's servants, all of whom he tripped up, and when Lao Tzu clutched at him, he gave him such a push that he went head over heels. Then he took his cudgel from behind his ear and, armed once more, ran amok in Heaven, frightening the Nine Planets so much that they locked themselves in, and the kings of the Four Quarters vanished from the scene. This time Monkey hit out recklessly, not caring whom he struck or what he smashed. No one could stop him, and he would have broken up the Hall of Magic Mists, had not the divinity Wang Ling-kuan rushed forward with his great metal lash. 'Halt, cursed Monkey!' he cried. 'See who stands before you, and cease your mad pranks!' Monkey did not deign to parley with him, but raised his cudgel and struck. Ling-kuan faced him with his whip aloft. It was a great fight that the two of them had, in front of the Hall of Magic Mists, but neither gained the advantage. At last the thirty-six thunder dieties came to Ling-kuan's aid, and Monkey found himself beset on every side by swords, lances, spears, whips, axes, hooks, sickles. He thought it time to transform himself, and took on a form with three heads and six arms, and wielded six magic cudgels which he whirled like a spinning-wheel, dancing in their midst. The thunder deities dared not approach him.

The noise of the combat reached the Jade Emperor who in great consternation sent two messengers to the Western Region to see if Buddha could not come and help. When they had recounted Monkey's misdeeds and explained their mission, Buddha said to the Bodhisattvas who surrounded him, 'You stay quietly here in the Hall of Law, and don't relax your *yoga* postures. I've got to go and deal with this creature who is making trouble at the Taoist court.' But he called on his disciples Ananda and Kasyapa to follow him. Arriving in Heaven, they heard a fearful din and found Monkey beset by the thirty-six deities. Buddha ordered the deities to lower arms and go back to their camp, and called Monkey to him. Monkey changed into his true form and shouted angrily, 'What bonze are you that you ask for me in the middle of a battle?'

'I am the Buddha of the Western Paradise. I have heard of the trouble you have been giving in Heaven. Where do you come from, and how long ago did you get your Illumination, that you should dare behave like this?'

> Born of sky and earth, Immortal magically fused,
> From the Mountain of Flowers and Fruit an old monkey am I.
> In the cave of the Water-curtain I ply my home-trade;
> I found a friend and master, who taught me the Great Secret.
> I made myself perfect in many arts of Immortality,
> I learned transformations without bound or end.

I tired of the narrow scope afforded by the world of man,
Nothing could content me but to live in the Green Jade heaven.
Why should Heaven's halls have always one master?
In earthly dynasties king succeeds king.
The strong to the stronger must yield precedence and place,
Hero is he alone who vies with powers supreme.

So Monkey recited; at which Buddha burst out laughing. 'After all,' he said, 'you're only a monkey-spirit. How can you delude yourself into supposing that you can seize the Jade Emperor's throne? He has been perfecting himself for 1,750 kalpas, and every kalpa is 129,000 years. Just see how long it takes to achieve such wisdom as his! How can you, an animal who has only in this incarnation received half-human form, dare make such a boast? You exceed yourself, and will surely come to a bad end. Submit at once and talk no more of your nonsense. Otherwise I shall have to deal sharply with you, and there won't be much left of the longevity you crave.'

'He may have begun young,' said Monkey, 'but that is no reason why he should keep the throne forever. There is a proverb that says, "This year, the Jade Emperor's turn; next year, mine." Tell him to clear out and make room for me. That is all I ask. If he won't, I shall go on like this, and they will never have any peace.'

'What magic have you got?' asked Buddha, 'that would enable you to seize the blessed realms of Heaven?'

'Many,' said Monkey. 'Apart from my seventy-two transformations, I can somersault through the clouds a hundred and eight thousand leagues at a bound. Aren't I fit to be seated on the throne of Heaven?'

'I'll have a wager with you,' said Buddha. 'If you are really so clever jump off the palm of my right hand. If you succeed I'll tell the Jade Emperor to come and live with me in the Western Paradise, and you shall have his throne without more ado. But if you fail you shall go back to earth and do penance there for many a kalpa before you come to me again with your talk.'

'This Buddha,' Monkey thought to himself, 'is a perfect fool. I can jump a hundred and eight thousand leagues, while his palm cannot be as much as eight inches across. How could I fail to jump clear of it?'

'You're sure you are in a position to do this for me?' he asked.

'Of course I am,' said Buddha.

He stretched out his right hand, which looked about the size of a lotus leaf. Monkey put his cudgel behind his ear, and leapt with all his might. 'That's all right,' he said to himself. 'I'm right off it now.' He was whizzing so fast that he was almost invisible, and Buddha, watching him with the eye of wisdom, saw a mere whirligig shoot along.

Monkey came at last to five pink pillars sticking up into the air. 'This is the end of the World,' said Monkey to himself. 'All I have got to do is go back to Buddha and claim my forfeit. The Throne is mine.'

'Wait a minute,' he said presently, 'I'd better just leave a record of some kind, in case I have trouble with Buddha.' He plucked a hair and blew on it with magic breath, crying, 'Change!' It changed at once into a writing brush charged with heavy ink, and at the base of the central pillar he wrote, 'The Great Sage Equal of Heaven reached this place.' Then to mark his disrespect he relieved nature at the bottom of the first pillar, and somersaulted back to where he had come from. Standing on Buddha's palm, he said, 'Well, I've gone and come back. You can go and tell the Jade Emperor to hand over the Palaces of Heaven.'

'You stinking ape,' said Buddha, 'you've been on the palm of my hand all the time.'

'You're quite mistaken,' said Monkey. 'I got to the end of the World, where I saw five flesh-coloured pillars sticking up into the sky. I wrote something on one of them. I'll take you there and show you, if you like.'

'No need for that,' said Buddha. 'Just look down.' Monkey peered down with his fiery, steely eyes, and there at the base of the middle finger of Buddha's hand he saw written the words 'The Great Sage Equal of Heaven reached this place', and from the fork between the thumb and first finger came a smell of monkey's urine. It took him some time to get over his astonishment. At last he said, 'Impossible, impossible! I wrote that on the pillar sticking up into the sky. How did it get on to Buddha's finger? He's practising some magic upon me. Let me go back and look.' Dear Monkey! He crouched, and was just making ready to spring again when Buddha turned his head, and pushed Monkey out at the western gate of Heaven. As he did so he changed his five fingers into the Five Elements, Metal, Wood,

Water, Fire and Earth. They became the five-peaked mountain, named Wu Hsing Shan (Mountain of the Five Elements), which pressed upon him heavily enough to hold him tight. The thunder spirits, Ananda, and Kasyapa all pressed the palms of their hands together and shouted 'Bravo!'[8]

D. The Exposé Novel: *Golden Lotus*

Many people think that *Golden Lotus* is the best of the 'Four Great Amazing Books'. Their reasons are that while the other three are essentially the enlargement and embellishments of *hua pen* stories, *Golden Lotus* is the original creation of one author. Also, while *The Three Kingdoms* and *All Men Are Brothers* are stories of historical figures, and *Monkey* is fantasy, none have any connection with the times in which their authors lived. *Golden Lotus* is a reflection of the social conditions of the late Ming Dynasty through the description of a family's life. This novel, being the first one to describe the life of the people realistically, represents a great advance in Chinese novel writing.

In writing this enormous work with some ninety principal characters, the author used the barest outline of an episode in *All Men Are Brothers* and developed it from there. The episode is the one which has already been quoted in this chapter. In *Golden Lotus* the sister-in-law of Wu Sung is Golden Lotus, and her lover, Hsi-men Ching, is a *nouveau-riche* scoundrel of the Ching-ho District. He befriends local government officials in order to seek to influence them in civil and criminal cases. He amasses a great fortune and bribes a Censor Tsai to get him the rank of captain in the Imperial Guards. But most of the time Hsi-men is chasing women, using aphrodisiacs and indulging in debauchery. And it is through the description of Hsi-men Ching and his circle that the author exposes the decadence of his time.

Many people have long looked askance at the vivid descriptions of details of sexual acts which are found in so many passages of the novel. Others consider the novel nothing but pornography, and it is extremely difficult to get an unexpurgated copy of the book in Chinese. When the novel was translated into other languages the frank passages were either deleted or given in Latin. Within the context of the novel these passages are, I think, an integral part of the book.

Hsi-men Ching has, in addition to his wife, three concubines. He has nine friends who do nothing but play, gamble and drink with him, and act as go-betweens and procure women for him, flatter and build up his ego. When Hsi-men becomes infatuated with Golden Lotus he poisons her husband in order to possess her. When Wu Sung, her husband's young brother, seeks to avenge him but kills another person by mistake and is exiled to Mengchow, Hsi-men is sure that no one else will dare to oppose him. He makes love to Golden Lotus's maid Chun Mei, and has an affair with Li Ping-erh whom he also makes his concubine. These three women play large parts in Hsi-men Ching's life, which is not to say that he did not look at others. There is a lot of jealousy, gossip and competition among the women to win Hsi-men's favours. But Hsi-men is not easy to please. When he is feeling happy he calls his women 'strumpet', but when he is angry he has them stripped and thrashed with a leather whip-lash. He is, in fact, a spoiled sadistic sex maniac. Nevertheless, women cannot resist him. Golden Lotus would do anything for him and go to any length to win his love. She is barren, so when Ping-erh gives birth to a son Golden Lotus, feeling her position threatened, plays a cruel trick on her and has the child killed, and Ping-erh eventually dies of grief. In the end it is her insatiable desire which drives her to give Hsi-men an overdose of aphrodisiac which kills him suddenly. After Hsi-men has died, Golden Lotus and Chun Mei become the mistresses of Chen Ching-chi Hsi-men's son-in-law, and when another of Hsi-men's concubines gets to know of it they are driven out of the house. Golden Lotus goes to live with a Mrs Wang, a go-between, while waiting to get married again. But Wu Sung returns to Ching-ho, looks for Golden Lotus finds her and kills her. Chun Mei, on the other hand, is sold as concubine to an official named Chao, and after giving birth to a son is made his wife. However, she is not satisfied. She pretends that Chen Ching-chi is her brother, and takes him into her household and makes love to him. When the Golden Tartars invade China, Chao is killed and Chun Mei has an affair with his son by a previous marriage, and dies one night after excessive debauchery. As the Golden Tartars approach, Wu Yueh-niang, Hsi-men's widow, takes her son, who was born after his death, and flees to Tsinan. On the way they meet Monk Pu Ching who takes them to a monastery and reveals to them the law of cause and retribution, growth and decay, expansion and corruption which led to the downfall of Hsi-men's family. It is a shock, and the boy, deeply moved, decides to become a monk.

There is no doubt that the many frank passages in *Golden Lotus* helped to make it famous. But its success is due to more than these passages. The author described with consummate skill the thoughts of the people in a few sentences. Lu Hsun said in his *A Brief History of Chinese Fiction*, 'The author was thoroughly familiar with the life of his time. In describing the characters and the scenes he either uses a few clear and bold sentences or adopts the insinuating and subtle approach. He can be exhaustive and penetrating or suggestive and ironic. Sometimes, for the sake of contrast, he sets forth two sides of a story so that the emotional changes of the characters are everywhere clearly shown. No other novel of his time was comparable to it in this respect.'

In fact, even before it was published, *Golden Lotus* won great praise from scholars. Yuan Chung-lang, the master prose writer, saw it in manuscript form and was greatly impressed by it. He said only *All Men Are Brothers* was better. Feng Meng-lung, the famous editor of *hua pen* stories, was so enthusiastic about it that he encouraged book-sellers to pay a high price for the right to publish it.

Golden Lotus was first published in 1610. According to Shen Teh-fu the novel had a hundred chapters, but five chapters, Chapters 53-57 inclusive, were lost and someone replaced them with his own version and claimed that they were the original. In fact, while the rest of the book is written in the Shantung dialect, these five chapters are written in the Kiangsu dialect. Shen was content to record that '*Golden Lotus* is the work of a prominent scholar who lived during the Chia Ching period (1522-1566)'. If Shen, who was a contemporary of the author, did not know his identity, we should be satisfied that it was written by someone whose pen-name was Hsiao-hsiao Sen, of Lang Ling District of Shan-tung Province.

Here is a passage from the book.

One day, when the Moon Lady was having tea with Aunt Wu, she asked Tower of Jade to join them, but did not ask Picture of Grace. This made the woman very angry. She shouted at the Moon Lady and thumped the table upon which Hsi-men's tablet rested. At the third night-watch, she said she was going to hang herself. Her maid went to tell the Moon Lady, who was very much upset. She consulted her brother, and they sent for the old woman Li and told her to take Picture of Grace away. The old woman feared that the Moon Lady would not allow her to take her clothes and ornaments.

'My girl has been here and suffered from ill usage and backbiting, and you are not going to get rid of her so easily. She must have some money to wash away her shame.'

Uncle Wu, in view of his official standing, would not say anything either way, and after much haggling the Moon Lady let Picture of Grace go with clothes, ornaments, boxes, bed and furniture. She would not let the two maids go, though Picture of Grace tried to insist.

'No,' she said, 'certainly not. If you do take them I shall bring an accusation against you for procuring young maids to be whores.'

This frightened the old procuress. She said no more, but smiled and thanked the Moon Lady. Picture of Grace got into a sedan-chair and was carried to her old home.

Readers, singing-girls make their living by selling their charms. With them it is purely a business. In the morning they receive Chang the dissolute and in the evening Li the ne'er-do-well. At the front door they welcome the father, and by the back door they let in the son. They forget their old clients and love the new. It is their nature to keep their eyes open when there is any money about. Even if a man loves them with his whole heart and does everything in his power to make them true, their hearts can never be secured. They steal the very food from a man's mouth, and as soon as he is dead they quarrel and go away, back to their old business.

> I laugh at the flowers of the mist
> Which no one can keep for long.
> Each night they find a new bridegroom.
> Their jade-like arms are the pillow for a thousand men,
> Their ruby lips are enjoyed by ten thousand guests.
> Their seductions are many
> And their hearts are false.
> You may devise a host of schemes to hold them
> But you can never keep them
> From longing for their old haunts.

When Picture of Grace had gone the Moon Lady sobbed aloud, and the other ladies tried to console her. 'Sister,' Golden Lotus said, 'don't let it upset you so much. The proverb says that when a man marries a whore it is like trying to keep a seagull away from the water. When it cannot get into the water it still thinks about the eastern ocean. All this was his fault.'

While they were busied over this Ping An came and announced that His Excellency Tsai, the Salt Commissioner, had come. 'He is in the great hall,' the boy said. 'I told him that master had died. He asked when, and I said on the twenty-first day of the first month, and that we were now in the fifth week after his death. He asked me if the tablet had been set up and I told him it was in the inner court. He wishes to pay reverence to it.'

'Go and tell your brother-in-law to see him,' said the Moon Lady.

Ching-chi put on mourning clothes and went to receive Tsai. After a while the inner court was made ready and Tsai was invited to go there. He kowtowed before the tablet. The Moon Lady in return made reverence to him. He did not speak to her, except to invite her to retire. Then he said to Ching-chi: 'Your father was very kind to me, and today, on my way to the Eastern Capital, I stayed especially to thank him. I never dreamed that I should find him dead. What is the cause of his death?'

'Inflammation of the lungs,' Ching-chi told him.

'How very sad!' said Commissioner Tsai.

He called his servants, and they brought him two rolls of Hang-chou silk, a pair of woollen socks, four fish, and four jars of preserved food. 'These trifles,' he said, 'I offer to him who is dead.' Then he gave Ching-chi fifty taels of silver. 'Your father,' he said, 'was good enough to lend me this and now that I have been paid myself, I return the money to set the seal upon our friendship.' He asked Ping An to take the money.

'Your Excellency is over-conscientious,' Ching-chi said.

The Moon Lady told him to take Tsai to the outer court, but the Commissioner said that he could not stay and would drink only a cup of tea. The servant brought the tea and Tsai went away.

The Moon Lady was half pleased, half sad when she received these fifty taels of silver. She reflected that if Hsi-men Ching had been alive he would never have allowed such a nobleman to go away without staying for something to eat. He would have remained, she thought, and enjoyed the pleasures of the table for many an hour. Now he had gone. Though she still was rich, there was no man to entertain such guests.

When Ying Po-chueh heard that Picture of Grace had gone back to the bawdy-house, he went to tell Chang II. Chang took five taels of silver and went to spend the night with her. He was one year younger than Hsi-men Ching. His year animal was the Hare and he was thirty-two. Picture of Grace was thirty-four, but the old procuress told him she was twenty-eight and warned Ying Po-chueh not to let him know the truth. So Chang II paid three hundred taels and took Picture of Grace for his second wife.

Chu Shih-nien and Sun Kua-tsui took Wang III to Cassia's house and he attached himself to her again.

Then Ying Po-chueh, Li III and Huang IV borrowed five thousand taels from Eunuch Hsu, and another five thousand from Chang II, and began the business of purchasing antiquities for the authorities. Every day they went riding about on magnificent horses and calling at one brothel after another.

Chang II, now that Hsi-men Ching was dead, spent five thousand taels in bribing Cheng, one of the royal family in the Eastern Capital, so as to secure the appointment which Hsi-men Ching had held. He did much work upon his garden and rebuilt his house, and Po-chueh was there nearly every day. Po-chueh told him everything he knew about Hsi-men's household.

'His Fifth Lady,' he said, 'is as beautiful as a painting. She knows poems, songs, literature, philosophy, games, backgammon and chess. She can write very beautifully and play the lute exquisitely. She is not more than thirty years old and much more charming than any singing-girl.'

Chang II was greatly impressed and wondered what he could do to get her for himself.

'Is that the woman who was once the wife of Wu Ta the cakeseller?'

'Yes,' Po-chueh said. 'She has been in Hsi-men's household for five or six years. I don't know whether she would be inclined to consider another marriage.'

'Please find out for me,' Chang II said. 'If she has any such idea, let me know at once, and I will marry her.'

'I have a man still in that household,' Ying Po-chueh said. 'His name is Lai Chueh. I will tell him. If he can do anything in the matter I will certainly let you know. It would be much better for you to marry her than some singing-girl. When Hsi-men Ching married her he had considerable trouble, but things are never the same twice, and what will happen on this occasion I cannot say. But anyone who gets hold of a beauty like this will be a lucky fellow. You are a man of substance, and you certainly ought to have someone like her to enhance your standing. Otherwise all your wealth is wasted. I will tell Lai Chueh to find out what he can do for us. If there is the slightest whisper of the word marriage I will see what my sweet words and honeyed phrases can do to inflame that amorous heart. It may cost you a few hundred taels, but it will be worth it.'

Readers, all those who live upon others are people who seek power and money. In their time, Hsi-men Ching and Ying Po-chueh had been like blood brothers. They might have been glued together, so close was their affection. Day after day Po-chueh took his meals with Hsi-men, and was given clothes. Now, when his friend had only just died, almost before his body was cold, Po-chueh was planning to bring disgrace upon them. With friends it is only too possible to know the face and to know nothing about the heart, just as an artist may paint the outside of a tiger, but must leave the bones unseen.[9]

CHAPTER XIV

The Prose of the Ming and Ching Dynasties

1. THE EVOLUTION OF PROSE

'CLASSICAL' prose reached the height of its development in the Sung Dynasty. Under the rule of the Mongols in the Yuan Dynasty (1260–1368) all the best prose-writers, notably Yuan Hao-wen (1190–1257) and Yu Chi (1272–1348), did was to follow the path opened up by the pioneering masters, and for almost two hundred years after the founding of the Ming Dynasty in 1368 there was no change in the style of prose-writing. The overthrow of foreign rule and subsequent economic stability, and the compilation of the great encyclopaedia of Chinese thought, literature and science, i.e. *Yung Lo Encyclopaedia* during the reign of Emperor Chen-tsu, did not seem sufficient to spur Chinese scholars on to experimenting with prose, or to break out of the confinements of *pa ku wen* or 'eight-legged' prose.

Roughly speaking, *pa ku wen* was a composition with eight 'legs' or sections. The first section consists of two sentences and, not unlike news headlines, sums up the most important points of the composition. The second section is an expansion of the first. The third is the introduction of the main section. The fourth and fifth provide contrasting aspects of the topic, leading to the sixth section which is the body of the composition. The seventh section is the continuation of the sixth, and the eighth section is the conclusion. It may even be said to be a good guide to writing a short article. However, a writer's choice of subject matter was limited strictly to topics taken out of the context of a classic, and the length of a *pa ku wen* was limited to two or three hundred words.

As I have mentioned before, passing the Civil Service examination and getting an official post was the only way open to a scholar of making a living, so that when it was stipulated in the Ming Dynasty that papers for the examination must be written in the style of *pa ku wen*, scholars spent all their time learning the technique of writing it and imitating the prose styles of the prose masters of the Tang and Sung Dynasties, which were lucid and crisp. Later on it was essays written before the Han Dynasty which were considered the ultimate in prose-writing. Lee Meng-yang (1472–1529) and Ho Ching-ming (1483–1521), Lee Pan-lung (1514–1570) and Wang Shih-cheng (1526–1590), leaders of two literary groups[1] which held sway in the almost two hundred years from the establishment of the Ming Dynasty, were out-and-out imitators. Lee Meng-yang said, 'People learning calligraphy try to imitate the way famous calligraphers wrote characters. No one would think of criticizing them when the characters they wrote resembled those written by famous calligraphers. The same principle should hold true of writing essays and composing poems.'[2] Lee Pan-lung, too, believed that 'essays written later than the Western Han Dynasty and poems written subsequent to the Tien Po Period of the Tang Dynasty are all worthless'.[3] What they wanted was to learn the styles of the past masters, forgetting that the style cannot be separated from the content of an essay. The result was the essays they wrote 'contained so many difficult words with obscure meanings that few people could have the patience to finish reading them'.[4]

There were many scholars who felt that this emphasis on style was wrong, and spoke up against it. Among these were Tang Shun-chih (1507–1560) and Lee Cho-wu[5] (1527–1602). Tang said in a letter to the Magistrate of Lu-men District, commenting on literature:

There are two kinds of men. One has never taken a pen in hand and groaned in front of a piece of paper to write an essay, but writes down freely what he feels as if he were writing a letter to his family. His piece may not be well-reasoned and structurally sound, but it is devoid of pedantry and is therefore good writing. The other kind may devote all his energy to learning how to write and learn all the techniques of writing, but he only repeats clichés and has no original ideas. What he writes . . . cannot but be the worst kind of writing. . . . The reason that the standard of literature has deteriorated since the Han Dynasty is not that the technique of writing has become lost, but that men of letters have no original ideas and only imitate others. . . .

Lee Cho-wu was perhaps the more radical of the two scholars, and exerted greater influence on the development of prose in the late Ming Dynasty. He was a native of Chin-kiang in Fukien Province. After passing the provincial Civil Service examination he decided not to go to the capital to attend the national examination, and was later appointed a teacher in Hui District in Honan Province. After many years serving ᷉s a teacher in Nanking and Peking and in other minor posts, he eventually became the Governor of Yao-an County in Yunnan Province. After serving three years, he asked to be relieved of his post, but was refused. Unhappy at being forced to stay on he went to Chi-chu Mountain in Ta-li District and spent all his time studying Buddhist sutras, and acted as though he were no longer the Governor of the county. Finally, he was allowed to resign. He then went to stay with Keng Tse-yung in Huang-an. When Keng died he went to Lung Tan Lake in Ma-chen District (Hupei Province), where he became a Buddhist monk, but he continued writing books and commentaries on philosophy and literature. He was an independent thinker, and had many original ideas, and the courage to express them. He also encouraged others to think for themselves, and not be reliant on even the teachings of Confucius. 'Every person has a purpose in life and no one has to depend on Confucius to fulfil his destiny. If this were not the case how about those who were born before Confucius' time? They could not have been human beings!'[6]

About literature, Lee was definitely against imitating the poets and prose masters of the past. He insisted that 'good poems are not limited to those written in ancient times, nor are good essays necessarily only those written before the Chin Dynasty'.[7]

He also spent much time editing and writing commentaries on many dramas and novels, notably on *All Men Are Brothers* and *The Western Chamber*. The importance he attached to independent thinking, and the value he placed on novels as literature, greatly influenced Yuan Chung-lang (1568–1610) and his two brothers, who met Lee Cho-wu in 1590 when the latter was sixty-five years old. The Yuan brothers subsequently opened up a new field in prose-writing.

Lee Cho-wu's original ideas got him into trouble. When he was seventy-five he was arrested on a trumped-up charge, and ordered to go back to his home town thousands of miles away from where he was then living. While in jail he committed suicide by cutting his throat with a razor and died two days later. In his lifetime Lee was called a heretic, but perhaps it took a heretic to help Chinese prose break away from the restrictions of imitation which had prevailed for more than two hundred years.

2. THE KUNG-AN AND CHING-LING SCHOOLS AND THEIR INFLUENCE

The undercurrent of literary thinking in the Ming Dynasty which opposed the imitative style of writing, finally gathered momentum under the leadership of Yuan Chung-lang, and broke away at last from the past. A new vista for Chinese writers was opened up by Yuan leading to an intimate, personal style of writing, which appeals to Chinese writers even of today.

Yuan, influenced by Lee Cho-wu, was even more outspoken than Lee. He was convinced that literature changed with the times and that new styles of writing emerged because old styles had become inadequate.

Poetry and prose have in recent times deteriorated to a state of extreme poverty. . . . Everyone tries to copy, plagiarize and imitate, so that when someone uses even one word differently from the masters, he is accused of being a heretic [Yuan wrote]. In setting up the prose style of the Chin and Han Dynasties as the standard, people have not bothered to find out if the masters copied from the Six Classics.[8] They may try to emulate the poems of the Shen Tang Period, but they do not wonder whether the poets of that period had copied the styles of the poets of the Han and Wei Dynasties. The fact is there would have been no prose of the Chin and Han Dynasties if the prose masters of those periods copied closely the style of the Six Classics, and no poetry of the Shen Tang Period if the poets had followed only the style of the Han and Wei Dynasties. For times change and literary style cannot remain static. A new literary style develops to meet the needs of a writer in his time and it must be allowed to develop freely.[9]

He felt that the written language must be as close to the spoken language as possible. In this he agreed with his elder brother who said:

Speech is used to express one's feelings, and writing is used to record what is said. Even when the writing is lucid and concise, it may not express one's feelings as well as speech. To express one's true feeling by writing is therefore a most difficult task. That is why Confucius said, 'The purpose of writing essays is to express one's opinions clearly.' This indeed is the criterion by which to judge whether a piece of writing is good or not. The writing of the Tang, Yu and Three Dynasties[10] expressed thoroughly the ideas of their authors. Nowdays, people cannot immediately understand the meanings of the writing of ancient times, so they jump to the conclusion that ancient writing used difficult words with obscure meanings, and that therefore we should not use simple and easy-to-understand words. But language changes with time. How do we know that what we find difficult words today were not easy words spoken by the ordinary people in former times?[11]

Because of this Yuan Chung-lang's writing 'aims at breaking away from the rules and confinements set up by others. With tremendous talent and great confidence in himself he expresses freely what he wants to say, regardless of the praise and criticism of other people,'[12] said his brother Yuan Chung-tao. In his preface to *The Collected Works of Hsiao Hsiu*, Yuan Chung-lang himself said, 'The great majority of Hsiao Hsiu's poems and essays express his own feelings and inspiration. If he did not really feel it in his heart he would not write it. Sometimes, inspired by what he saw, he wrote thousands of words at a time, as quickly as water flows in the great river. He took people's breath away by it.'

To his mind, then, good writing was that which the author felt compelled to write, and expressed from a personal point of view in simple language, without reference to the rules and styles of the past. He was, therefore, more progressive than his elder brother Tsung-tao who could not entirely free himself from the influence of Po Chu-yi and Su Tung-po, although, of course, the writings of Po and Su were among the easiest to understand and appreciate.

The three brothers together placed emphasis on the importance of individuality, of using simple language and of adopting a personal attitude in writing prose. This won the support of many scholars and almost immediately gained the admiration and acceptance of literary practitioners. Because the Yuan brothers were natives of Kung-an

District in Hupei Province they and their supporters became known as the Kung-an School.

Yuan Chung-lang, like Lee Cho-wu, also attached great importance to novels, drama and folk song, which he considered to be the real expressions of the people. '*All Men Are Brothers* and *Golden Lotus*,' he said, 'are marvellous classics, equal in stature to the Six Classics, Li Sao and *The Historical Record*.'[13] This was completely contrary to the orthodox view which had only contempt for novels, particularly the two he mentioned, which were considered to be books of corrupting influence—*All Men Are Brothers* for inciting the people to become bandits, and *Golden Lotus* for encouraging people to be licentious.

The efforts of many scholars in later years in editing, collecting and publishing collections of folk songs, short stories and novels can be attributed to his influence.

As for the writing of the men of letters of his day, Yuan said, 'I feel that poems and essays written in our time will not be passed on to later generations. The only thing which might be admired by posterity are the ditties sung by women and children in the streets and lanes. They are the real people, untroubled by learning and restrictions, who express their feelings freely. They do not copy the songs of Han and Wei, or imitate the poems of the Shen Tang Period. Carried away by their emotions, they sing their ditties and others are moved by them.'[14]

However, Yuan's emphasis on individuality and originality gave rise, in the writing of some of his followers, to superficiality, vulgarity and an ignorance of the basic structure of a composition. Chung Hsing (1572–1624), who edited the *Complete Works of Yuan Chung-lang*, worked together with Tan Yuan-chun (?–1631) to try to rectify these short-comings by a more careful use of words, and by purposely changing the usual order of phrases to create a more studied style. Both Chung Hsing and Tan Yuan-chun were natives of Ching-ling District in Hupei Province, and they and their supporters were called the Ching-ling School. They supported every major tenet of Yuan's literary theory, except that to meet the criticism of superficiality, they wrote their pieces with more reserve.

It now seems amazing that to write what one is compelled to write, and to encourage original ideas and adopt a personal style of writing, could have aroused the great wrath of orthodox scholars in the late Ming and early Ching Dynasties. Chien Chien-yi (1582–1664) and Chu Yu-tsun (1629–1709), both great scholars, attacked the Kung-an and

Ching-ling Schools fiercely. They even went so far as to say that the poems written by poets of the Ching-ling School were the cause of the decline of the Ming Dynasty. The result was that at one time the literary works of the writers of these schools were banned.

But the trail to a more familiar and personal style in writing had already been blazed. Some thirty years after Yuan Chung-lang's time, *hsiao pin wen*, or the personal essay, had become so popular that Lu Yun-lung was able to edit his *A Selection of Hsiao Pin Wen by Sixteen Famous Authors*. Among other writers whose works were not included in the *Selection* the best known was Chang Tai, whom many critics thought was one of the best exponents of this form of writing.

In the Ching Dynasty, in spite of the efforts of orthodox scholars to discourage the writing of *hsiao pin wen*, and the apparent revival of 'classical' prose under the leadership of Fang Pao (1668–1749), Liu Ta-kwei (1697–1779), Yao Nai (1731–1815), Weng Chin (1757–1817), Chang Huei-yen (1761–1802) and others, *hsiao pin wen* flourished. Among the better-known writers of this form of writing were Chin Sheng-tan (*c*. 1609–1661), Shih Chen-lin (1693–*c*. 1779), Yuan Mei (1716–1797), Shen Fu (1763–*c*. 1808), Kung Ting-an (1792–1841) and Huang Tsun-hsien (1848–1905).

3. HSIAO PIN WEN

As *hsiao pin wen* is the expression of a writer's personal thoughts and his particular view of things, it is, at its best, full of pleasant surprises. Its subject matter and treatment are therefore of great variety, but 'serious' matters such as politics are as a rule not touched upon. Thus, *hsiao pin wen* is like the casual chat between friends in a teahouse, or perhaps the conversation between a boy and a girl in a boat cruising down a river. Most of the pieces are written in a calm mood, and find easy response in the reader.

Here are a few of the best pieces.

HARVEST MOON ON WEST LAKE by Chang Tai

There is nothing to see during the harvest moon on West Lake (Hangchow). All you can see are people who come out to see the moon. Briefly, there are five categories of these holiday-makers.

First, there are those who come out in the name of looking at the harvest moon, but never even take a look at it: the people who, expensively dressed, sit down at gorgeous dinners with music, in brightly illuminated boats or villas, in a confusion of light and noise. Secondly, those who do sit in the moonlight, but never look at it: ladies, daughters of high families, in boats and towers, also handsome boys (homosexuals) who sit in open spaces and giggle and chatter and look at other people. Thirdly, boat parties of famous courtesans and monks with time on their hands who enjoy a little sip and indulge in song and flute and string instruments. They are in the moonlight, too, and indeed look at the moon, but want people to see them looking at the moon. Fourthly, there are the young men, who neither ride, nor go into the boats, but after a drink and a good dinner, rush about in their rowdy dress and seek the crowd at Chaoching and Tuanchiao where it is thickest, shouting, singing songs of no known melody, and pretending to be drunk. They look at the moon, look at the people looking at the moon, and also look at those not looking at the moon, but actually see nothing. Lastly, there are those who hire a small boat, provided with a clay stove and a clean table and choice porcelain cups and pots, and who get into the boat with a few friends and their sweethearts; they hide under a tree or row out into the Inner Lake in order to escape from the crowd, and look at the moon without letting people see that they are looking at the moon, and even without consciously looking at it.

The local Hangchow people come out on the lake, if they do at all, between eleven in the morning and eight in the evening, as if they had a morbid fear of the moon. But on this night they all come out in groups, in the hope of getting good tips. The sedan-chair carriers line up on the bank. The moment they get into a boat they tell the boatman to hurry and row across to the Tuanchiao area, and get lost in the crowd. Therefore, in that area before the second watch (ten o'clock), the place is filled with noise and music bands in a weird, boiling confusion, like a roaring sea or a landslide, or a nightmare, or like bedlam let loose, with all the people in it rendered deaf for the moment. Large and small boats are tied up along the bank, and one can see nothing except boats creaking against boats, punting poles knocking punting poles, shoulders rubbing shoulders, and faces looking at faces. Soon the feasting is over, the officials leave, the yamen runners shout to clear the way, the sedan-chair carriers scream for fare, the boatmen give warning that the city gates will soon be closed. A grand procession of torches and lanterns, with swarms of retainers, passes on. Those on land also hurry to get into the city before the closing of the gate, and very soon almost the entire crowd is gone.

Only then do we move the boat to Tuanchiao. The rocks have become cool by this time, and we spread a mat on the ground and invite ourselves to a great drink. At this time the moon looks like a newly polished mirror, the hills appear draped in a new dress, and the face of the lake is like a lady after a fresh make-up. Those who have been hiding themselves under a tree and enjoying a quiet sip come out now also. We exchange names and invite them to join us. There we have charming friends and famous courtesans; cups and chopsticks are in place, and the songs and music begin, in the chilly dream world of moonlight. The party breaks up at dawn, and we get into the boat again and move it into the miles of lotus-covered surface, where we catch a nap in an air filled with its fragrance, and have a perfect sleep.[15]

ON ZEST IN LIFE by Yuan Chung-lang

I find that zest is a rare gift in life. Zest is like hues on the mountains, taste in water, brilliance in flowers, and charm in women. It is appreciated only by those who have understanding, and is difficult to explain in words. True enough, it is common nowadays to find people who affect a taste in certain diversions. Some cultivate a love for painting, calligraphy and antiques, and others are fascinated by the mystics and the recluses and the life of a hermit. Still others are like the people of Soochow who make a hobby of tea and incense, turning it almost into a cult. These are superficial, and have nothing to do with real zest and understanding of the flavour in living.

This zest for living is more born in us than cultivated. Children have most of it. They have probably never heard of the word 'zest', but they show it everywhere. They find it hard to look solemn; they wink, they grimace, they mumble to themselves, they jump and skip and hop and romp. That is why childhood is the happiest period of a man's life, and why Mencius spoke of 'recovering the heart of a child', and Laotse referred to it as a model of man's original nature. The peasants who live near the mountains and forests do not make a cult of these things; in their life of freedom and absence of social conventions, they enjoy the beauties of nature all as a part of their living. The more degenerate men become, the harder they find it to enjoy life. Some are fascinated by merely sensual enjoyments and call it 'fun', and find their pleasure in meats and wines and sex and riotous living and defiance of social customs, saying they are thus liberating themselves. Often as one progresses in life his official rank becomes higher and his social status grows bigger; his body and mind are fettered with a thousand cares and sober duties. Then knowledge, learning and life experience stop up even his pores and seep down to his hardened joints. The more he knows, the more befuddled he becomes, and the more removed he is from understanding this zest in living.[16]

THE WEDDING NIGHT by Shen Fu

This was on the 16 July in the year 1775. In the winter of this year one of my girl cousins was going to get married and I again accompanied my mother to her maiden home. Yun was of the same age as myself, but ten months older, and as we had been accustomed to calling each other 'elder sister' and 'younger brother' from childhood, I continued to call her 'Sister Su'.

At this time the guests in the house all wore bright dresses, but Yun alone was clad in a dress of quiet colour, and had on a new pair of shoes. I noticed that the embroidery on her shoes was very fine, and learned that it was her own work, so that I began to realize that she was gifted at other things, too, besides reading and writing.

Of a slender figure, she had drooping shoulders, and a rather long neck, slim but not to the point of being skinny. Her eyebrows were arched and in her eyes there was a look of quick intelligence and soft refinement. The only defect was that her two front teeth were slightly inclined forward, which was not a mark of good omen. There was an air of tenderness about her which completely fascinated me.

That night, when I came home from my relatives' place in the country, whither I had accompanied my female cousin the bride, it was already midnight, and I felt very hungry and asked for something to eat. A maidservant gave me some dried dates, which were too sweet for me. Yun secretly pulled me by the sleeve into her room, and I saw that she had hidden away a bowl of warm congee

and some dishes to go with it. I was beginning to take up the chopsticks and eat it with great gusto when Yun's cousin Yuheng called
out, 'Sister Su, come quickly!' Yun quickly shut the door and said:
'I am very tired and going to bed.' Yuheng forced the door open
and seeing the situation, said with a malicious smile at Yun, 'So,
that's it! A while ago I asked for congee and you said there was no
more, but you really meant to keep it for your future husband.'
Yun was greatly embarrassed and everybody laughed at her, including the servants. On my part, I rushed away home with an old
servant in a state of excitement.

Since the affair of the congee happened she always avoided me
when I went to her home afterwards, and I knew that she was only
trying to avoid being made a subject of ridicule.

On the 22 January 1780 I saw her on our wedding night, and
found that she had the same slender figure as before. When her
bridal veil was lifted we looked at each other and smiled. After the
drinking of the customary twin cups between groom and bride, we
sat down together at dinner and I secretly held her hand (which was
warm and small) under the table, and my heart was palpitating.
I asked her to eat and learned that she had been keeping a fast for
several years already. I found that the time when she began her fast
coincided with my smallpox illness, and said to her laughingly:
'Now that my face is clean and smooth without pockmarks, my dear
sister, will you break your fast?' Yun looked at me with a smile and
nodded her head.

This was on the 22nd, my wedding night. On the 24th my own
sister was going to get married, and as there was to be a national
mourning and no music was allowed on the 23rd we gave my sister
a send-off dinner on the night of the 22nd, and Yun was present at
table. I was playing the finger-guessing game with the bridesmaids
in the bridal chamber and being a loser all the time, fell asleep drunk
like a fish. When I woke up the next morning Yun had not quite
finished her morning toilet.

That day we were kept busy entertaining guests, and towards the
evening music was played. After midnight, on the morning of the
24th, I, as the bride's brother, sent my sister away and came back
towards three o'clock. The room was then pervaded with quietness,
bathed in the silent glow of the candle-lights. I went in and saw
Yun's woman servant taking a nap behind the bed, while Yun had

taken off her bridal costume, but had not yet gone to bed. Her beautiful white neck was bent before the bright candles, and she was absorbed in reading a book. I patted her on the shoulder and said: 'Sister, why are you still working so hard? You must be quite tired with the full day we've had.'

Quickly Yun turned her head and stood up saying: 'I was going to bed when I opened the bookcase and saw this book and have not been able to leave it since. Now my sleepiness is all gone. I have heard of the name of *The Western Chamber* for a long time, but today I see it for the first time. It is really the work of a genius, only I feel that its style is a little bit too biting.'

'Only geniuses can write a biting style,' I smiled and said.

The woman servant asked us to go to bed and left us and shut the door. I began to sit down by her side and we joked together like old friends after a long separation. I touched her breast in fun and felt that her heart was palpitating too. 'Why is Sister's heart palpitating like that?' I bent down and whispered in her ear. Yun looked back at me with a smile and our souls were carried away in a mist of passion. Then we went to bed, when all too soon the dawn had come.

As a bride, Yun was very quiet at first. She was never sullen or displeased, and when people spoke to her, she merely smiled. She was respectful towards her superiors and kindly towards those under her. Whatever she did was done well, and it was difficult to find fault with her. When she saw the grey dawn shining through the window, she would get up and dress herself as if she had been commanded to do so. 'Why?' I asked. 'You don't have to be afraid of gossip, like the days when you gave me that warm congee.' 'I was made a laughing-stock on account of that bowl of congee,' she replied, 'but now I am not afraid of people's talk; I only fear that our parents might think their daughter-in-law is lazy.'

Although I wanted her to lie in bed longer I could not help admiring her virtue, and so got up myself, too, at the same time with her. And so every day we rubbed shoulders together and clung to each other like an object and its shadow, and the love between us was something that surpassed the language of words.[17]

CHAPTER XV

The Novels of the Ching Dynasty

THE Manchus were more subtle in ruling over the Chinese than the Mongols had been. They massacred those who resisted them, but did not create a caste-system, like the Mongolians, in which the Chinese were relegated to the bottom of the social order. The Manchus respected Chinese traditions and culture; in fact, many Manchus were brought up under Confucian teachings, and learned to read and write Chinese better than many a Chinese.

Towards the *literati* the Manchu emperors in the early years of their rule adopted a policy of winning their loyalty by giving them official positions. If an old man was well-educated, or a good poet or writer, he could still be given an official position without having to sit the official examinations, so long as he was properly recommended. For the young generation there was the Civil Service examination, which was based on the skill of writing *pa ku wen* and poetry. The other aspect of the policy was shown whenever the emperors felt that they had failed to win such loyalty from the scholars; they then killed ruthlessly. Many Chinese scholars died simply because their writings were suspected of having hidden meaning and 'disrespectful insinuation' or 'hostile sentiments' toward the foreign rulers. Nevertheless the Manchu rulers encouraged research, which was already quite popular at the time under the leadership of Huang Tsung-hsi (1601–1695), Ku Yen-wu (1613–1682) and Wang Chuan-shan (1619–1692). During the Kang Hsi Period (1662–1722), the *Kang Hsi Dictionary* and the *Ku Chin Tu Shu Chi Cheng* (*Grand Encyclopaedia*) were compiled, and during the Chien Lung Period (1736–1795) *Sze Ku Tsung Shu* (*The Library of Classics, History Books, Philosophy and Literary Works*) was compiled. However, during the ten years (1773–1782) when this was being done, the Manchus also burned 538 titles or more than 13,000 volumes.

As a result, literature with the exception of *hsiao pin wen* and fiction was at rather a low ebb during the Ching Dynasty. But that great writers did exist in the Ching Dynasty was proved by the author of *Red Chamber Dream*. Apart from this, there were *Ju Lin Wai Shih* and *Ching Hua Yuan*, both of which were unique in content.

1. *THE NOVEL OF SOCIAL SATIRE:*
THE SCHOLARS

Ju Lin Wai Shih (*The Scholars*) was written by Wu Ching-tse (1701–1754), and although it was the first of its kind remains the best Chinese satirical novel. It is, strictly speaking, not a novel but a loosely linked collection of short stories. Its popularity can be attributed to the author's warm and humorous style. Wu was not bitter, and his language was not abusive. Many Chinese scholars liked to think that the popularity of this book was due to the fact that there were no sexual scenes in it, but this view does not seem to hold good today, judging by the popularity of many present-day novels. But, perhaps more important, *The Scholars* poked fun at the scholars, a privileged and respected class which had held sway over society (in the common view) for too long. Wu is also said to have published a collection of essays and another book, entitled *Commentaries on Poetry*.

Wu himself was born into a family of scholars, in the Province of Anhwei. His ancestors were all scholar-officials. With such a background he was well equipped to poke fun at scholars. According to his biographer, Cheng Chiu-fang, Wu Ching-tse was very intelligent and gifted, but he did not like to study *pa ku wen*, and he did not know the value of money, so that when his father died and he was left in charge of the family fortune, he squandered it all within a few years in drinking and feasting, and by giving it to the poor who asked for his help.

Nor did he want to become an official. When the Governor of Anhwei, Chao Kuo-ling, hearing of his literary fame, summoned him and tested his abilities, and recommended him as a candidate to participate in the National Civil Service Examination, Wu declined. Having no means of making a living he became poorer and poorer. At last, he moved to Nanking where, it is believed, he wrote his novel and supported his family by selling his books, and presumably writing eulogies for people on special occasions. Cheng Chiu-fang said that in the winter when it was bitterly cold and Wu had no wine to drink he would often go out beyond the city walls with a few friends and walk around, shouting, singing and reciting poems until day broke. They called these nocturnal outings 'foot-warming exercises'.

Cheng also mentioned that one of his great-uncles was related to Wu, and often helped him out with daily necessities. One autumn it rained for three or four days, and Cheng's great-uncle said to his sons, 'The price of rice has gone up quite a bit since the rain. I wonder how Ming Hsien (Wu Ching-tse's courtesy name) is faring. Take three *tou*[1] of rice and two thousand cash over to him.' His sons went and found that Wu had not had a grain of rice to eat for two days. 'But once Wu had money he would spend it on drinking and sing-song girls, and never worried about the future.'

He was not unhappy in his Bohemian life, and had many friends. It must have been during this period that he and his friends raised money to build a temple on Rain Flower Hill in memory of 230 worthies of ancient times, starting with Tai Po of the Kingdom of Wu.[2] When their funds were exhausted Wu sold his house to raise money. He became even poorer, but he couldn't help himself. It is impossible now to know who the 230 worthies were, but if Tai Po was one of them it is safe to say that they were people who despised fame and fortune, and liked to be just themselves.

He expressed himself probably in the words of the remarkable tailor he described at the end of *The Scholars*:

Chung Yuan is a tailor of some fifty years old, and he runs a shop in Three Mountains Street. Every day he plays on a lyre and writes poems after work. His friends ask him, 'If you want to be a man of culture why don't you give up tailoring and befriend people from the Academy?'

'I play on the lyre and write poems not because I want to be a man of culture, but because I like to,' he would answer. 'I am a tailor simply because my father and my father's father were in this trade. It isn't as though when one knows how to read and write it is beneath one to be a tailor. Furthermore, the people at the Academy have their own ideas. They would never condescend to befriend us! Now I earn six or seven *fen*[3] of silver a day, and have enough to eat.

I play on my lyre and write my poems and am free to do whatever I like. I ask not for wealth or fame, and don't have to wait upon others. Neither heaven nor earth interfere with me. How can I be any happier?'

People often say that Wu based the characters of his novel on people he knew, and that Tu Shao-ching, the scholar who thinks nothing of money and is always willing to help people, was meant by the author to represent himself.

But if he saw the humorous side of scholars, he saw the dilemma they were in, too, and pitied them. His biographer Cheng said that when Wu discovered that Cheng had become very poor because he had failed in the examinations, Wu wept and said, 'To think that you should have become as destitute as I am!'

The Scholars is said to have contained fifty-five chapters originally, but two different versions, having respectively fifty-six and sixty chapters, were widely circulated. It was the first novel to be written in the Mandarin dialect, a form of which later became the national language of China. This perhaps also added to its popularity.

Here are two short excerpts from the novel. One lampoons the hypocrisy of a scholar in mourning. The other shows the fantastic ideas which had been instilled in the minds of Chinese scholars and women by the Neo-Confucians of the Sung Dynasty, who thought that it was better to die of starvation than to fail in observing womanly propriety.

They came in. First Mr Chang paid his respects and then Fan Chin went up and saluted Mr Tang, the Magistrate, treating him as if he were his teacher. The Magistrate repeatedly declined the honour and asked them to be seated, and had tea served. He first talked to Mr Chang, saying that it had been a long time since they last met and how was Mr Chang keeping, and what not. He then praised the high quality of Fan Chin's essays and asked, 'Why don't you sit for the higher examination?'

Only then did Fan Chin say, 'My mother has died. I am in mourning, according to the prescribed custom [which requires that a man hold his social and political activities in abeyance while he is observing the mourning of the death of a parent, which can last up to three years].'

Magistrate Tang was taken aback. He hastily called for a suit of

329

plain clothes and changed into it, and bowed them into the hall at the rear of the Magistrate's residence. A table was laid out and wine was served. Among the dishes served there were bird's-nest soup, chicken and duck, and two special dishes from Kwangtung Province. . . . The cups and chopsticks were inlaid with silver, and Fan Chin looked embarrassed and hesitated to use them. The Magistrate was puzzled until Mr Chang said with a laugh, 'I think Mr Fan is reluctant to use these cups and chopsticks while he is in mourning.' The Magistrate hurriedly ordered that an earthenware cup and a pair of ivory chopsticks be brought for Fan Chin, but the latter still would not start eating.

'He would not use these chopsticks either,' said Mr Chang.

Finally a pair of white bamboo chopsticks was brought and everything was satisfactory. The Magistrate was worried that since Fan Chin seemed to follow every letter of the prescribed behaviour for a man in mourning, he would not drink wine and eat meat, for he had no vegetarian dishes ready. Therefore he was very much relieved when Fan Chin picked a large shrimp-ball from the bowl of bird's-nest soup and put it in his mouth. . . .

The following excerpt explains why during and after the Literary Revolution in the first decade of this century there was the outcry of 'Man-eating Religion of Propriety'.

When Wang Yu-huei arrived in the home of his son-in-law, some twenty *li* away, he saw that the son-in-law was indeed critically ill, and the medicine prescribed by the doctor did not seem to have any effect. After a few days his son-in-law passed away. . . . When her husband had been embalmed and encoffined Wang Yu-huei's third daughter came out to bow to her parents-in-law and her father.

'Father,' she said, 'my eldest sister has been widowed and come home to depend on you for a living. Now my husband also has died. I do not want to come home and become your burden also. You are a poor scholar, you cannot support so many daughters!'

'What are you going to do?' asked Wang Yu-huei.

'I would like to take leave of my parents-in-law and you and seek the way of death, so as to follow my husband to where he is!'

Upon this her parents-in-law were frightened and said to her, weeping, 'My daughter, are you crazy? Even an ant strives to live.

How could you say such a thing! You have married our son. Alive, you are a member of this family; dead, you are this family's ghost. We will of course support you so you don't have to depend on your father. Now stop talking such nonsense!'

'You are both old,' she said. 'If I could not serve you well, but have to cause you worry, how am I supposed to feel? It will be better for me to die!

'It will be a few days before I die,' she added. 'My only request is that Father should go home and send Mother to me, so that I can say farewell to her.'

'My child, so long as you have decided,' said Wang Yu-huei, 'I would not think of stopping you. Your name will be recorded in the history book! You go ahead and do what you think is right. I shall go home today and send your mother over to say good-bye to you.'

In spite of the objection of his daughter's parents-in-law Wang would not change his mind, and went straight home to tell his wife.

'How is it that the older you are the more stupid you become?' said his wife. 'If our daughter should think of seeking the way of death you should try to stop her instead of encouraging her. What nonsense is this!'

'People like you would not understand things like this,' Wang Yu-huei answered.

Upon this his wife burst out crying and immediately sent for a sedan-chair to go and try to dissuade her daughter. Wang Yu-huei remained at home and continued to read his books and practise calligraphy, all the time waiting to hear the news of his daughter's death. In the meantime his wife tried her best to dissuade her daughter, but all her efforts were in vain. Her daughter would sit with her after doing the morning toilet and refuse to eat and drink. On the sixth day she became too weak to get up from bed, and Mrs Wang, her heart pierced and her every nerve shaken by the sight, fell sick and was brought home. Another three days passed, when at about the second watch in the evening several men, carrying torches, came and reported, 'Third Young Mistress, having starved for eight days, died today at noon.' Upon hearing this Mrs Wang fainted. When she came to she cried continuously. Wang Yu-huei went to her bedside and said to her, 'Old wife, you really are a fool! Our daughter has now become an immortal and it is nothing to cry about! I only wish that I had such a good cause to die for!' He then lifted his head and laughed. 'It's a good way to die! It's a good way to die!' Roaring with laughter he walked out of her room. . . .

Two months later, after a day of memorial services held in honour of Wang Yu-huei's deceased daughter, a great feast was arranged in Ming-lun Hall by all the Confucian scholars of the district. They invited Wang Yu-huei to be the honoured guest, in homage to his bringing up such a good daughter, whose death added glory to the Confucian teachings. But by this time Wang was seized with remorse and declined to join them. The next day he went to pay a visit to Mr Yu, the teacher at the local government academy, and said, 'At home I see my wife's grief-stricken face every day. I have not the strength to stand it and wish to go away for some time. . . .'

When he arrived in Soochow he went to visit Hu Chiu. On the way he went into a teahouse and ordered a cup of tea. Outside there were many large pleasure houseboats on which people were burning incense and had laid out banquets under the carved beams. After a while Wang Yu-huei saw some boats carrying courtesans sailing by. The curtains on the boats were not lowered and girls in bright-coloured clothes sat drinking with their clients. Wang Yu-huei was thinking that 'the custom here in Soochow is bad. A woman should not come out of her room. How can any woman think of sailing on a boat on this river?' when presently he saw a young woman dressed in white on a boat, who reminded him of his daughter. His heart was seized by grief, and hot tears rolled from his eyes.

2. THE LOVE ROMANCE: RED CHAMBER DREAM

Hung Lou Meng (*Red Chamber Dream*) is to the Chinese novel what the *Book of Poetry*, *Li Sao*, *Historical Record*, the poems written by Li Po and Tu Fu, and Northern Drama written by Kuan Han-ching and Wang Shih-fu are to their various genres. The Chinese so admire this novel that a 'Redology' has existed for some fifty years, with scholars arguing and advancing theories about the author's identity, the meaning of the novel, etc. But it is now generally agreed that *Red Chamber Dream* was written by Tsao Hsueh-chin, who lived from *c.* 1719 to 1763.

Tsao was a Chinese whose ancestors migrated to Manchuria some time during the latter part of the Ming Dynasty. It was probable that through a mixed marriage his ancestors became Manchus. When the Manchus overthrew the Ming Dynasty, Tsao's ancestors followed them back to China proper and were treated as belonging to the conquering class. From 1663 to 1728, beginning with Tsao's great-grandfather, the family was in charge of the Nanking Silk Bureau. The chief of this bureau was the buyer for the imperial household of jewellery, clothes and other goods. But more important still, only the confidants of the emperor were appointed to such posts, for they were charged with the responsibility of reporting directly to the emperor the important events which took place in their areas. The post was therefore a most lucrative and important one, although it did not rank very high. In the sixty-five years that three generations of Tsao's had held the post, Emperor Kang Hsi stayed five times in the official residence of the Bureau Chief during his inspection tours in the Yangtse Valley. Six years after Emperor Yung Cheng acceded to the throne, however, Tsao Fu, Hsueh-chin's father, was relieved of his post, and Tsao Hsueh-chin, then aged ten, went back with his family to live in Peking. The fortunes of the family suffered great reverses. A theory has been advanced that since Yung Cheng used all kinds of intrigue and plots to remove other aspirants to the throne, he felt obliged to adopt harsh measures to establish his own authority after he became Emperor, and this was the reason Hsueh-chin's father, whom Emperor Kang Hsi had trusted, was among the first to go. But there might have been a host of other reasons for the family's subsequent persecution and downfall. Perhaps the jealousy and grudges of other people helped.

Tsao Hsueh-chin used his own experience of the decline of a family and his memory of the 'good old days' as the background of *Red Chamber Dream*, which is the first great tragedy in Chinese literature of an unfulfilled, triangular love story, that of Pao-yu, Black Jade and Precious Clasp. When Tsao began to write his novel, perhaps in his thirties, he was already living in greatly reduced circumstances. In 1762 his son died and, deeply grieving, he fell sick and died on New Year's Eve, 1763. He was in his early forties, and only eighty chapters of his novel had been finished.

The existing version of *Red Chamber Dream* has 120 chapters. The majority of scholars and sinologists seem to agree that the last forty chapters were written by Kao Ngo. But all Kao Ngo says in his preface to the novel is: 'My friend Cheng Wei-yuan showed me the manuscript of the novel he had brought. "I have taken a lot of trouble to collect this manuscript . . ." he said. "Since you have time now, would you help me edit it?" I consented.' Perhaps Kao was being modest.

Red Chamber Dream is a novel of huge canvas, with a total of more than 400 characters.

The novel begins with the arrival of Black Jade in Nanking after her mother's death, to live in the Chia family, which was at the height of its power and wealth. The girl is beautiful, talented, sensitive and jealous, and falls in love with Pao-yu almost from the moment they meet. Pao-yu is a clever, spoiled brat who likes the company of his sisters and maids. He is given to moods, and perhaps life in a ducal family bores him. Certainly the fact that he was born with a piece of jade in his mouth, and had a grandmother who doted on him because of it, allowed him to have things almost always his own way. His first remark to Black Jade when he meets her is 'I have seen you somewhere before'. He was serious when he said this, for he was supposed to have helped Black Jade gain human form in her previous incarnation when she was a plant, and he gave her water. Black Jade is moved to tears. Pao-yu turns to his grandmother and says, 'What makes her eyes so red? Indeed, we shall have to call her Cry-baby if she cries so much!'

Soon Precious Clasp, daughter of Pao-yu's aunt, also comes with her mother to live in the Chia family, and the three cousins become good companions. Precious Clasp is almost the exact opposite of Black Jade. She is in good health while Black Jade suffers from tuberculosis. She is reserved and diplomatic, while Black Jade is impetuous and doesn't care whom she hurts with her caustic tongue. But Black Jade is full of fun, and Pao-yu falls in love with her. Although they have sworn their love for each other they quarrel also, and in general live the carefree, idyllic life of the spoiled young people of a very wealthy family, against the background of a fantastically beautiful ducal garden. The family's eldest daughter is made an imperial concubine, and the family enjoys great wealth and power. The many cousins who live in the garden play games, versify, indulge in petty quarrels and jealousy, even while the seeds of tragedy are being sown. For voracious members of the elder generation get into trouble with the authorities, bringing tragedy into the family in the deaths of several of the girls, and Pao-yu's playfulness itself also ends in the death of his favourite maid. In the interplay of fate and character, Pao-yu loses his piece of jade, and his senses at the same time. The entire household is in a turmoil over this, and the grandmother decides to arrange a marriage for the spoiled boy in the hope of cheering him up. Unknown to Black Jade and Pao-yu, the family decides that Precious Clasp is the girl for him. A great conspiracy is on to keep the news from Pao-yu and Black Jade until the ceremony is actually under way. But Black Jade hears of it, and becomes very ill, while Pao-yu, under the impression that he is going to marry Black Jade, eagerly awaits the date of his marriage. On the day of his marriage the elders borrow Black Jade's maid to escort the bride to the ceremonial hall, in an effort to deceive the bridegroom, while Black Jade lies dying in her rooms. When Pao-yu discovers that he has married the wrong girl Black Jade is already dead. Torn with grief Pao-yu loses his senses completely. Very much later he recovers and looks back on his adolescence, realizing how very remarkable it has been. The family's decline comes very swiftly after this, when the imperial concubine dies, and Pao-yu's uncle is deprived of his rank for oppressing the people in the province and his property confiscated. Chia Cheng, Pao-yu's father, in trying to stop corruption, succeeds only in getting himself impeached for maladministration. Gone is the glory and splendour of old, like a dream. When Pao-yu comes to his senses he for the first time knows the real values of life, and tries to restore honour and good fortune to the family by studying and preparing for the Civil Service examination. But when the examination is over he disappears. When the results are published, and Pao-yu's name is seventh on the list of successful candidates, it would seem that honour and good fortune could have returned to the Chia family, but Pao-yu is nowhere to be found, even when the Emperor orders him to appear at Court for an audience.

One night, on a journey by river, Pao-yu's father suddenly sees a person who looks like his son in the moonlight, with the shaved head, bare feet and garb of a monk, prostrate in front of him and kowtowing. Chia Cheng stands up in surprise and confusion. He sees the sad and compassionate expression on the person's face. Before he can speak Pao-yu is gone, escorted by a Buddhist monk and a Taoist priest. Chia Cheng runs after them, but they have vanished as suddenly as they came.

It is impossible to do justice to a novel of this type by a synopsis of a few hundred words. The merit of *Red Chamber Dream* as a novel lies in its memorable characterization, which is so vivid that today these characters are still alluded to when we criticize someone, saying that this girl is like Phoenix, or that girl is like Precious Clasp.

Here is a short passage from the novel:

Black Jade was taking an afternoon nap when Pao-yu went to see her, and he did not want to awaken her. Purple Cuckoo (Black Jade's maid) was sitting on the veranda sewing, and Pao-yu walked up to her. 'Did she cough a little less last night?' he said.

'It was better last night,' Purple Cuckoo said.

'*Omitofu*!' Pao-yu said. 'It had better be!'

'Since when have you been a devout Buddhist? That's an innovation!' said Purple Cuckoo.

'Well, necessity is the mother of invention,' Pao-yu said with a smile, watching as Purple Cuckoo took off her thin quilted garment. She was wearing only a green satin vest underneath. Pao-yu stretched out his hand and felt her and said, 'Do you want to get sick too, sitting in the draught with so few clothes on? We will all be in a fix then!'

'You must keep your hands to yourself from now on if you want to have a chat with me,' said Purple Cuckoo. 'Aren't you afraid of gossip? It isn't as though we were still children, you know. The Young Mistress often tells us not to be too friendly with you. Look at her! She's only afraid she can't get far enough away from you!'

Taking her sewing she vanished inside the house.

Stunned, Pao-yu stood there for a long time looking vacantly at Tsuma planting the bamboos in front of the house, and then went and sat down on a rock, shedding tears. He did not know what to do.

After some time Snowgoose came from Mrs Wang's [Pao-yu's mother] house with a bowl of ginseng, and saw someone sitting on a rock under the peach trees, with his hands on his cheeks, and staring into space. Upon a closer look she discovered that it was none other than Pao-yu. 'What is he doing there?' she thought. 'Spring is a time for illness. I expect he's off in one of his trances again.'

She walked over to him and said, smiling, 'What are you doing here?'

Pao-yu was startled. 'What are you talking to me for?' he said. 'Haven't you all been forbidden to speak to me? Aren't you afraid of gossip? Go on home!'

Snowgoose thought that he must have quarrelled again with

Black Jade, and went on into the house and left the ginseng with Purple Cuckoo. 'Who upset Pao-yu?' she asked Purple Cuckoo. 'He's sitting there crying.'

'Where?' said Purple Cuckoo.

'Under the peach trees behind the pavilion.'

Purple Cuckoo put her sewing down at once and said, 'Please mind the house a minute for me. If the Young Mistress calls say I won't be long.' She left the house and went to look for Pao-yu. She was standing right in front of him when she said with a smile, 'I was only saying those things a minute ago for everybody's good. There's no need to sit here and sulk and cry! If you get sick what will happen?'

'I'm not sulking,' said Pao-yu. 'I was thinking over what you said, and finding it most reasonable. Soon nobody will speak to me any more, and that's why I started to cry.'

Purple Cuckoo sat down beside him.

'You'd better not sit beside me then,' Pao-yu said with a smile.

'I want to ask you about the bird's nest,' she said.

'Oh, that,' said Pao-yu. 'Well, I brought it up to the Old Mistress and Sister Phoenix the other day. I hear that you people are being given an ounce of it a day.'

'So it was you,' said Purple Cuckoo. 'We must thank you, then.'

'Black Jade must have it every day,' Pao-yu said. 'If she takes it regularly for two or three years she will recover.'

'Yes, but once she starts having it she will miss it when we go back south next year, for we shan't be able to afford it then.'

Pao-yu cried, 'Who is going back south?'

'Black Jade is going back to Soochow.'

'You're teasing me again,' Pao-yu said. 'She may have come from Soochow, but why should she go back now that her mother is dead, and there is no one to look after her? Isn't that the very reason why you were sent for to come here? That proves you are lying.'

'Well, don't be so sure of it,' said Purple Cuckoo. 'Do you think that she has no one to go to? Her family may be small, but it is not so small that they cannot look after their own people. When the Old Mistress sent for her it was because Black Jade was small, and the Old Mistress wanted to look after her herself. But now Black Jade is grown up, and the Lin family is not the kind to let her impose on other people for ever. Therefore, come the spring, or the autumn at latest, we will be going. If we don't go the Lin family will send someone to fetch her. Last night the Young Mistress told me to tell you to sort out all the playthings she ever gave you and return them to her. She will return your things too.'

Pao-yu was thunderstruck. He could not speak. Purple Cuckoo was going to say something else when Blue Cloud came and said, 'The Old Mistress wants you. Is this where you have been?'

'He's been asking about my Young Mistress's illness. Take him away,' Purple Cuckoo said, smiling, and returned to her own house.

Pao-yu was sweating, and veins were swelling in his face. Blue Cloud took him back to his own house.

Hsi-jen [Pao-yu's personal maid] was alarmed when she saw him. He was perspiring all over, and saliva was running out of his mouth. His eyes stared ahead without seeming to see. He lay down when told to lie down, and sat up again when she told him to sit up, and drank the tea when she told him to drink the tea. Everyone was alarmed, but no one dared to report to the Old Mistress. They decided to send for Lee Momo.

Lee Momo [Pao-yu's old wet nurse] came and felt him on the cheeks, and pinched him on the upper lip. She pinched so hard that she left a deep mark on it, but there was no reaction from Pao-yu.

'Oh, this is bad!' she said, and letting out a 'Yah!' she took his head in her arms and began to wail loudly.

'We asked you to come and tell us what to do, not to cry,' cried Hsi-jen.

Lee Momo said, 'I have taken care of him in vain! I have lavished a lifetime's care on him for nothing! He's good for nothing any more!'

Hsi-jen thought that old Lee Momo must know what she was talking about, and began to weep too. Blue Cloud told Hsi-jen that Pao-yu had been talking to Purple Cuckoo before becoming this way, and Hsi-jen left immediately for Black Jade's house to find her.

Purple Cuckoo was giving Black Jade her medicine when Hsi-jen walked up to them without ceremony and said, 'What did you tell our Pao-yu just now? Go and look at him, and then tell the Old Mistress! I'm through!'

Black Jade saw that Hsi-jen was angry and in tears, too, and said, 'What's happened?'

Hsi-jen said after a while, 'I don't know what Purple Cuckoo told him, but that idiot's lost his senses! His hands and feet are cold, he is staring straight ahead of him without seeing, and has lost his power of speech as well. Lee Momo pinched him and he didn't even feel it. It doesn't look as if he is going to live . . . he may already be dead. Lee Momo is already wailing.'

When Black Jade heard this she vomited the medicine she had just taken, and had a paroxysm of coughing and wheezing. Afterwards she lay down panting and said, pushing Purple Cuckoo away, 'Don't bother about me any more. Better get a rope and hang me.'

'I didn't say anything, honestly,' Purple Cuckoo said. 'I only teased him a little and he thought I meant it seriously.'

'You should know that fool by now,' said Hsi-jen. 'He can't tell when you are joking and when you are serious.'

'What did you say to him?' said Black Jade. 'You'd better go and explain that it was a joke, maybe he'll come out of his trance.'

Purple Cuckoo immediately returned with Hsi-jen to Pao-yu's residence. But the Old Mistress was already there.

When the Old Mistress saw Purple Cuckoo she cried, 'You useless thing! What did you say to him?'

'Nothing, nothing, I was only joking with him,' Purple Cuckoo cried.

At the sight of Purple Cuckoo, however, Pao-yu cried 'Aiyah!' and seemed to come out of his trance. He started to weep, and everyone was relieved to see it. The Old Mistress grabbed Purple Cuckoo and wanted her to apologize to Pao-yu, for she thought that she had said something to offend him. But Pao-yu also seized Purple Cuckoo and said, 'Take me with you!'

At last Purple Cuckoo had to explain that what she had said about Black Jade going back was only in fun.

'Oh, is that all?' said the Old Mistress. 'I thought it was something more serious. But you are a clever girl, you shouldn't tease him, knowing what he is like.'

Aunt Hsueh said, 'Pao-yu is a good, honest boy, and has been so close to Black Jade. I don't blame him for being upset at the thought of her leaving. Come to think of it we would all be very upset if that were to happen. But now there is nothing to worry about. He will be all right after he has taken one or two medicinal brews.'

She was still talking when someone said, 'Lin Chih-hsiao and Lai-ta's wives have come to see how the Young Master is.'

339

'Let them come in, it is nice of them,' said the Old Mistress.

But upon hearing the word 'Lin' Pao-yu cried, 'No, no! The Lin family have sent them to come and take Black Jade away! Tell them to go away!'

When the Old Mistress saw the way he was she too said, 'Tell them to go away!' and turned to Pao-yu, saying, 'It wasn't anyone from the family of Black Jade. Her people are all dead. No one is coming to take her away!'

'I don't care who it was!' said Pao-yu. 'Only Black Jade is allowed to have the surname Lin!'

'There is no one here by the name of Lin,' said the Old Mistress. 'Anyone who has the surname of Lin has been told to go!' She told the others, 'Tell Lin Chih-hsiao not to come onto the estate again, and none of you must use the word "lin" again. Mind you obey me, children!'

Nobody dared to laugh, and everyone promised.

3. *THE NOVEL OF IDEAS:*
FLOWERS IN THE MIRROR

The persecution of Chinese scholars by Manchu emperors was at its severest during the reigns of Yung Cheng (1723-1735) and Chien Lung (1736-1795), when an innocent remark about Chinese history could lead to a writer and his entire clan being put to death, if the remark could be construed to be a slur upon the sovereign. Chinese scholars were so cowed by these persecutions that they buried themselves in heaps of papers and devoted themselves to doing philological and exegetical work on the Confucian classics—a safer occupation. After some time this became the vogue of the *literati*, and Chinese scholars became obsessed with erudition and, with a few exceptions, would not dream of creating a work of art purely out of the imagination.

Li Ju-chen (1763?-1830), who wrote *Ching Hua Yuan* (*Flowers in the Mirror*), was a conspicuous exception. At a time when men with great knowledge of Chinese classics were alone considered scholars, he was distinguished for his scholarship and knowledge of philology. Yet his novel, on which he spent over ten years, revealed none of the stodgy spirit with which other scholars were apt to air their erudition.

Like Wu Ching-tse, Li Ju-chen did not want to learn how to write *pa ku wen*, and thus failed to pass the Civil Service examination. His keen mind, however, led him into the fields of astrology, calligraphy and chess, at all of which he distinguished himself. But he was best known during his time for his work on phonetics, published as *Li's Phonetics*. He learned phonetics from Lin Ting-kan (1755–1809), an authority on ancient music and phonetics, when he first went to live in Haichow. Li was then a youth of twenty, and since he was not interested in taking part in the Civil Service examination he spent much time studying with Lin, and became proficient enough to compare ancient pronunciations of the Chinese language with those of his time, and to form theories of his own. In *Flowers in the Mirror* he devoted almost three chapters to this subject, and made a great mystery out of his theory of phonetics by saying that it was the 'national secret' of the Country of People of Split Tongues. Today, his theories on the combination of consonants and vowels seem elementary to many people, but it was at his time something new.

Li was lucky to have an understanding elder brother, Ju-huang, with whom he lived for almost twenty years. Ju-huang never seemed to grudge him the freedom to pursue his interests but supported him almost all his life, except for a short period in 1801 when Li Ju-chen went to a district in Honan Province to be an assistant to the Magistrate. While there the Yellow River, the 'sorrow of China', flooded, and the dike was broken. The rebuilding of the dike and the dredging of the river later on became material for his novel.

It is obvious that he had a very active mind. For many people would have been satisfied to pass their time drinking and writing poetry and consorting with courtesans when they were free from the worries of making a living. Li, while he may have done these things as well, also became an authority on chess, mathematics, painting, medicine, gardening, classical texts, poetry and a few other things. He wrote *Flowers in the Mirror* 'to amuse himself' when he was in his fifties, and spent more than ten years on it. It was published in 1828, and two years later he died.

Flowers in the Mirror has 100 chapters. The story begins as the Goddess of One Hundred Flowers and the Moon Goddess quarrel in Heaven. The Moon Goddess conspires with the Heart-Moon Fox when the latter is being sent to earth to become Empress Wu of the Tang Dynasty, to make all flowers on earth bloom at the same time. As a result, the Goddess of One Hundred Flowers and the spirits of a hundred flowers are punished for negligence by the Western Divine Mother, and sent down to earth to become a hundred mortal women.

The Goddess of One Hundred Flowers becomes the daughter of Tang Ao, a brilliant scholar who has won third place in the National Civil Service Examination, but is deprived of his newly won rank because the Empress suspects him of conspiring with rebels to overthrow her and bring back the Emperor, whose throne she has usurped. Tang is greatly disappointed, and seeking refuge from worldly worries sets out on a long journey overseas with his brother-in-law, Lin Chih-yang, a merchant. It is this journey which forms the major part of the novel, in which they meet the spirits of the different flowers as they visit many strange countries with strange people, such as the Country of Women, the Country of Intestineless People, the Country of Giants and the Country of Two-faced People, which gives the author a chance to discourse on the many fields in which he was an authority. At last, many of the flower spirits and the Goddess of One Hundred Flowers herself return to the capital of Chang-an, where the girls distinguish themselves by passing a 'Civil Service examination for women'. Together with the young men whom they marry, who are the rebels working for the Emperor's cause, they overthrow Empress Wu and bring the Emperor back to the throne. However, only the Goddess of One Hundred Flowers cultivates enough 'Tao' to separate her spirit from the temptations of the mortal flesh, and she returns to Heaven.

The loosely woven structure of the story served only as a platform for the author to express his ideas on many subjects, social, artistic and otherwise. But many of these were uniquely expressed, as we see in the chapter on the Country of Gentlemen, when customer and shopkeeper reversed their roles, and the customer insisted on overpaying the shopkeeper for his goods, while the shopkeeper insisted that his goods were not worth the money. In the Country of Women, Li Ju-chen, plumping for equal rights for women, had a man mistaken for a woman and go through all the discomforts society imposes upon women. The late Dr Hu Shih, in his erudite preface to an edition of the novel, said that inequality of the sexes was one of the main themes the author wanted to expound in the novel. 'The author believes that in education and politics, men and women should have equal opportunity.' Dr Hu also pointed out that the strange things Li's characters saw overseas were used to call attention to inequality of social practice in China, and compared the work to *Gulliver's Travels*. The description of the thirty-odd countries his characters visited added up, in one way or another, to the author's idea of a perfect society, and as such, *Flowers in the Mirror* may be said to belong to Utopian literature.

Here is an excerpt[1] from the novel. Tang Ao and his brother-in-law, arriving in the Country of Two-faced People, decided to go ashore and look around. But brother-in-law Lin Chih-yang forgot to change his clothes, and went ashore looking like a poor man, next to Tang Ao in his scholar's scarf and silk costume. When the pair returned to the junk Old Tuo, the helmsman, asked them about their experiences.

'Why, you are wearing each other's clothes,' Old Tuo remarked.

'We walked over ten *li* after you left us before we met any two-faced people,' said Tang Ao. 'But everyone was wearing a turban at the back of his head, so we couldn't see both of their faces at once. I went up to some of them and had a nice chat. I asked them about the customs of the country, and they were all smiles, and spoke to me most respectfully and in the most cordial manner. I thought they were charming, lovely people, quite different from the people we've met anywhere else.'

'But as soon as I put in a few words they all looked at me, stopped smiling, and became cold and reserved and were most reluctant to have anything to do with me,' said Lin. 'Afterwards we wondered if it hadn't something to do with our clothes, so we changed round, and sure enough, they began to treat me with the utmost respect, and to give Brother Tang the cold shoulder.'

'So that is what is meant by being two-faced,' said Old Tuo.

'Not only that, but when brother-in-law was talking I sneaked around the back of one of these people and stealthily lifted his turban,' said Tang Ao. 'When I saw what was underneath I received the fright of my life and screamed. There was an ugly face with rat's eyes, hooked nose and a furious expression on it, and when this face saw me the bush-like eyebrows gathered in a deep frown, it opened its basin of a mouth and stuck out its long tongue at me. I was over-powered by an extremely vile odour which made me almost faint. When I turned around again brother-in-law was on his knees.'

'Why did you do that?' Old Tuo asked.

'You see, this man was talking to me in a most pleasant way when

Brother Tang lifted his turban and revealed not only his other face but his true nature. Then his good face turned green, too, and stuck out its tongue at me. I was so surprised I didn't know if he was going to kill me next. Somehow my knees buckled, I sank to the ground and kowtowed to him repeatedly, and then ran for my life. Have you ever heard of such a thing, Old Tuo?'

'It's nothing surprising,' said Old Tuo. 'I've met many people of this kind in my long life. The difficulty lies in recognizing them for what they are. But if you are more careful about whom you speak to, you can save yourself many unpleasant surprises.'

Here is a passage telling of the travellers' adventures in the Country of Sexless People.

Tang Ao said, 'I have heard that the people of this country do not give birth to children. Can that be true?'

'I have heard that it is so,' said Old Tuo, 'because there is no distinction between men and women among them. I have been here before, and indeed the people look neither like men nor women.'

'But if they don't reproduce shouldn't they all have died long ago?' asked Tang Ao.

'No, because their bodies do not corrupt after death, but they come back to life again after 120 years. Thus, their numbers neither increase nor decrease. They think of death as sleep, and life as a dream, for well they know that all mortal strife ends in a long sleep. Therefore, they don't crave fame and power and personal gain. They know that these things don't last, and that if they succeed in winning them in one life, they will only wake up 120 years later to find that they have to struggle for them all over again. Needless to say these people also eschew violence.'

'How foolish we must seem to them then,' said Lin, 'when we don't even come back to life again, and yet struggle so hard for wealth and fame!'

'If you can look at matters that way,' said Tang Ao, 'all you need to do is to place a different value on these very things.'

'That's easy to say, and theoretically I can see that wealth and fame are of dubious value when we think that life is like a fleeting dream. Yet, when I find myself embroiled in a real situation, it is as though I were crazed, and I cannot help becoming excited and engaged in

344

the struggle and the strife. However, in the future, when I find myself in that state, I should be happy if someone would pinch me. Then I would wake up at once to the futility of it all.'

'Ah, but when you are in that state I'm afraid that you would not listen if I tried to remind you of the futility of it all, but, on the other hand, turn around and bawl me out for interfering with you,' said Old Tuo.

'That's true,' said Tang Ao. 'Lust for fame and fortune are like an intoxication. While a man is intoxicated he doesn't realize it. It is only when all is over that he realizes that everything is an illusion. If men could realize this all the time there would be much less trouble in the world, and there would be happier people on earth.'

'But I hear that the people here eat the soil, is that true?'

'Yes,' said Old Tuo. 'They don't farm, and they don't like the fruit which grows on trees, but prefer to eat the soil. Perhaps because by nature they are really an earthy lot!'[4]

CHAPTER XVI

The Literature of Modern China (I)

1. THE LITERARY REVOLUTION

TRADE between China and foreign countries has existed for many thousands of years. In the early period it was conducted by overland routes via Chinese Turkestan, notably by the famous silk road, but the volume of trade was relatively small. In the nineteenth century, with industrialization and the subsequent search for raw materials and markets, western countries discovered the legendary old Cathay, and forced an expanded trade upon her through the seaports, and thus broke her 'closed-door self-sufficient' policy. It is not the purpose of this book to say whether the 'gun-boat' policy adopted by the western countries was wise or necessary, but the consequent Opium War of 1840–1842, which was the first of a series of wars waged by western countries to protect their interests and promote a trade which China did not want, seems to have proved to the Chinese people that the foreigners were indeed barbarians, as they had long suspected. For profit they would traffic in anything! The reaction of the Chinese to the 'gun-boat' policy was natural enough: 'We must also get gun-boats and have guns.' It was thought that nothing else could be or need be learned from the West.

Before China could formulate a coherent programme an Anglo-French Expedition struck again. They attacked Tientsin, advanced to Peking, the capital, burned the summer palace, forced the court to flee to the north-west and compelled China to sign an even more humiliating treaty with them in 1860. Together with the Taiping Rebellion which erupted in south China and almost brought down the Ching Dynasty, the too apparent signs of ineptitude on the part of the Manchu rulers made many Chinese launch independent schemes of reform. They established arsenals, shipyards, railroads, telegraph and telephone networks. It gradually dawned on them that it was not only the manufacture of gun-boats and guns, but that western methods of management, too, seemed to be better than those of the Chinese. Grudgingly they accepted science and technology as necessary imports.

When in 1895 tiny Japan, which China had looked down upon as some kind of a vassal, defeated China, in spite of China's bigger naval fleet, the shock drove her to an agonizing reappraisal of her efforts at meeting the foreign challenge. For China and Japan had started to adopt western science and technology at about the same time, but Japan, in carrying out the Meiji Restoration Programme, went all the way and rejected nothing western. Perhaps there was something more to learn from the 'barbarians'? Again, grudgingly, the Chinese intelligentsia admitted that western laws and political institutions apart from science and technology should be studied. They maintained, however, that Chinese philosophy, ethics and the basic principles upon which society was founded should not be influenced. In fact, these were superior to the western system. This idea was epitomized in the famous saying of Chang Chih-tung (1837–1907), 'Chinese learning as the basic structure, western learning for practical application.' This proposal in its divergent forms was hotly debated in China in the 1920s and controversy is raging even now in Taiwan. The confrontation of two different cultures with national survival seemingly involved is necessarily an explosive situation, and gives rise to problems in almost every aspect of life and, of course, academically.

While China was thus changing, translations from western languages were beginning to be introduced. First came the Holy Bible, then scientific works, then western history books and social science manuals. These rapidly increased in range and volume. It is significant to note that in 1896, one year after the defeat of China by Japan, Huxley's *Evolution and Ethics* became the first western work of philosophy to be translated into Chinese, by Yen Fu (1853–1912), one of the two outstanding translators of the nineteenth century. Yen Fu went on to translate Spencer's *Sociology* and John Stuart Mill's *System of Logic* and, because he used the classical literary style, won the respect of the scholars of his time, and exerted much influence over them.

While Yen Fu devoted his time to translating non-fiction, the other outstanding translator of the time, Lin Shu (1882–1924), translated fiction. The latter did not read any foreign language, but 'translated' 171 works, of which 99 were by English writers, 33 by French writers and 20 by American writers. He depended on interpreters, who read the stories in the original and told them to him, and he then wrote the stories down with great skill. His translations were very popular, and perhaps exerted some influence over Chinese novelists of the time. A number of exposé novels appeared in the last years of the Ching Dynasty. Among the best-known are *Strange Things of the Last Twenty Years* by Wu Yu-yao (1867–1910), *Kuan Chang Hsien Hsing Chi* (*The Official World*) by Li Po-yuan (1867–1906) and *Nieh Hai Hua* (*A Flower in the Sea of Sin*) by Tseng Pu. While these reflected the deteriorating social and political climate of the time, they also showed some western influence in novel writing.

A Flower in the Sea of Sin was perhaps the best. It was published in 1907 and reissued in 1927, and tells of the romance of Hung Chun, a famous scholar who later became the Chinese Ambassador to England, and Fu Tsai-yun, a well-known courtesan, whom he made his concubine. Later, when Fu Tsai-yun went back to Shanghai to resume her profession after her husband died, she was able to influence Count Waldersee, with whom she had previously been friendly, when he came as Commander of the Armies of Eight Countries to occupy Peking in 1900 during the Boxer Rebellion. Through this story the author was able to lambast the officials and scholars of the time, and show his sympathies with the revolutionaries, including Dr Sun Yat-sen, the founder of the Chinese Republic.

These exposé novels were written in vernacular prose, like the storyteller's texts of the Sung Dynasty, and that used by short-story writers of the Sung, Yuan and Ming Dynasties, and the novelists of the Yuan, Ming and Ching Dynasties. For novelists had found that the vernacular language was better suited to fiction than the classical language which Yen Fu and Lin Shu used in their translations. Some novels were even written in local dialects, the best of which was *Hai Shang Hua Lieh Chuan* (*The Lives of Courtesans*), written in the Shanghai dialect. The best of the vernacular fiction writers was Liu O (1857–1909), who wrote *The Travels of Lao Tsan*. This book became widely known to English readers through an edition published in Nanking in 1947 under the title *Mr Decadent*, and one published in London in 1948 with the title *Mr Derelict*.

Fiction came to the fore at this time also because scholars were beginning to realize the importance of the novel as a tool to awaken and inform the people. It was a good instrument through which to criticize the government and air the idea of revolution. Many scholars published articles emphasizing this, among whom Liang Chi-chao (1873–1929) was the most prominent. The language was changing under the pressure of the times, and Liang wrote in a bold style, freely mixing the new with the old, using Buddhist terms, imported scientific terms and poetic allusion as the need arose. His prose style was, as it were, a bridge between the classical style and the vernacular style which was soon to become dominant.

Because Liang wrote in a persuasive style his commentaries on the current scene found response in many readers. The deep frustration and near despair of the people was soon to erupt in a Literary Revolution which could not disengage itself from politics.

Change was reflected in poetry of this time also. Poets began to use imported terms, and experiment with new forms. Huang Tsun-hsien (1848–1905) adopted the expressions and style of the folk songs of his home town, Meihsien, to write poems, and boldly announced, 'I write as I talk. The rules of writing poetry in ancient times cannot bind me. The expressions of the common people are incorporated in my poems.'[1]

Huang was a career diplomat and was assigned successively to Tokyo, San Francisco, London, Malaya and finally appointed to be Minister to Japan, but he resigned before he took up this last post. His travels abroad brought him into close contact with western ways of living, and added a new dimension to his poetry. Liang Chi-chao praised his efforts and said that he was the finest poet of his time. He is best remembered for his sad satirical poems about the Sino-Japanese War of 1895, the Boxer Rebellion, and the subsequent invasion of China by the armies of eight countries.

While the trend in fiction, poetry and prose was towards greater use of the vernacular language, and experimenting with new methods of presentation, the national situation which it reflected closely was rapidly growing worse. Resentment against the corrupt administration of the Manchu and the fate suffered by the Chinese at the hands of foreign invaders, and a strong urge to regain the glory of the past and become a strong and prosperous nation again finally culminated in the Revolution of 1911 led by Dr Sun Yat-sen, which overthrew the Ching Dynasty, and established the Republic of China, the first republic in the Far East.

The Revolution, however, did not relieve the situation, and what followed was chaos. There appeared on the scene war lords who occupied and ruled over different parts of the country, and some even attempted to restore the monarchy. This persisted until 1927 when, after the completion of the Northern Expedition launched by the Kuomintang, national unity was achieved, at least in name. Actual unity was realized only in 1937 when, faced with Japanese invasion, all the factional forces rallied behind the leadership of the Nationalist Government. This, too, turned out to be short-lived as conflict between the Nationalists and Communists, which flared up sporadically, increased in intensity towards the end of the Sino-Japanese War, and led to a split which persists today, with the Communists established in mainland China and the Nationalists in Taiwan. The end of this conflict is not yet in sight.

The Literary Revolution, which erupted in 1919, had two important contributing factors apart from the ones I have mentioned. One was the attempt by scholars to develop new systems of romanizing written Chinese in an endeavour to increase the literacy of the population. Another was the establishment by the Ministry of Education of a Committee for the Standardization of Chinese Pronunciation in 1912 soon after the Republic was founded. For Chinese characters, scholars were realizing, were extremely difficult to learn when compared with the twenty-six letter alphabet of the West. The Committee proposed a set of thirty-nine 'phonetic symbols' (*Chu yin fu hao*) to denote pronunciation. In 1919 a new set of symbols was proclaimed, and in September of the same year a *Dictionary of National Phonetic Symbols* was published. These symbols were promoted for a time as a phonetic substitute for Chinese characters, so that one could 'spell' out each word by its pronunciation instead of having to memorize a different character for each word. But presumably because of the great difficulties encountered in overcoming tradition, and also because in each province each character may be pronounced in many different ways, these attempts were not successful. In the 1930s there were again movements to romanize characters; these met with little success. The Chinese Communists took the question up again after they came to power in 1949, but with little result. They have, however, established a system of simplification of Chinese characters, which the Chinese elsewhere, however, have not generally adopted.

During the years before the Literary Revolution the need for a national dialect became obvious. Eventually, it was decided by the government that *Kuan Hua*, or Mandarin, should be the national dialect, as it was spoken in six provinces in Northern China and eight in the Yangtse Delta. People from the remaining four of the eighteen provinces then constituting China also knew a little *Kuan Hua*.

The success of magazines written in the vernacular brought to it political weight as well as literary influence. Of the many which were published at this time, *Hsiu Hsiang Hsiao Shuo* (*Illustrated Novels*) and *Hsin Hsiao Shuo* (*New Novels*) did a lot to emphasize the importance of novels. Liang Chi-chao, editor of *New Novels*, was most influential. He said, 'To establish a new morality we must first create new novels. To found a new religion we need first new novels. To have better government we must first have new novels. To have new science and technology we must first create new novels. . . . Why? Because novels possess enormous power to influence people.' Liang was also editor of *Hsin Min Tsung Pao* (*The New Citizen*), in which he commented on national affairs, and he became the mentor of the youth of his time.

When Chen Tu-hsiu (1879–1942) founded *La Jeunesse* in September 1915, the influence of magazines on national affairs and literature was already great. In the November issue of the magazine Chen wrote an article, 'A Discussion of the History of Modern European Literature', in which he said, 'Owing to the rise of science since the end of the nineteenth century . . . Europe entered a new era. All the old moral principles, thoughts and institutions were destroyed. Literature and art, too, changed and passed from romanticism to realism and then to naturalism.' In so far as Chinese literature was concerned, he said later, in answering a reader's letter, 'It remains in the stages of classicism and romanticism. Hereafter, it will develop into that of realism.' By this he meant presumably that Chinese literature was comparable to that of the West in the eighteenth and nineteenth centuries. It was probably the first attempt of a Chinese intellectual to apply what he understood to be the European process of development in literature to that of China, and predict its future development.

Chen's opinion drew support from Hu Shih (1891–1962), who was then a student in America. Hu thought that Chinese literature should be realistic. He expressed this in a letter to Chen, mentioning what he later called 'Eight Don'ts for a Chinese Literary Revolution'. These he expanded later in an article 'Suggestions for the Reform of Chinese

Literature' published in the January 1917 issue of *La Jeunesse*. The 'Eight Don'ts' were:

1. Don't use classical allusions.
2. Don't use clichés.
3. Don't use the parallel construction of sentences.
4. Don't purposely avoid slang.
5. Don't ignore grammar.
6. Don't be over-sentimental.
7. Don't imitate ancient literature.
8. Don't write meaningless articles of no substance.

It will be noted that Hu now called his suggestions those for a 'Literary Reform', not 'Revolution' as he first did. But Chen was less patient and tactful. He wrote a leading article in the very next issue of *La Jeunesse* calling for:

1. Doing away with the ornate and obsequious literature of the aristocratic few and creating a simple and lyrical literature of the people.
2. Doing away with the cliché-ridden and grandiose literature of classicism and creating a fresh and honest literature of realism.
3. Doing away with the pedantic and obscure literature of escapism and creating a plain-speaking and popular literature of society in general.

Chen's proposals won the support of Chien Hsuen-tung (1887–1939), a famous professor of Chinese phonetics, etymology and semantics at Peking University. This greatly strengthened the position of those in favour of a literary revolution, for if a famous scholar of Chinese classics was in favour of a 'literature of the people', there must be something wrong with the old literature. In literary circles, too, Chien's word carried weight. But Hu Shih still counselled caution. He wrote to Chen Tu-hsiu saying, 'The validity of these principles (for a literary revolution) cannot be determined overnight, or by one or two persons. . . . We should not advocate that our views are absolutely right and leave no room for correction.'[2] Chen replied, however, that 'It is indeed a basic principle for intellectual progress to tolerate opposition . . . but when it concerns using the vernacular as the only or principal medium for literature, what we advocate is so obviously right that we need not leave room for discussion . . .'. Chen's attitude was perhaps no different from that of any revolutionary who believes in his cause, and it was due more to him than Hu Shih that the cry for a literary revolution attracted so much attention, both favourable and otherwise.

From January 1918 *La Jeunesse* was co-edited by six professors of Peking University and was published entirely in the vernacular, which was later to be called *Kuoyu* or the 'national language'. This was an important development. For, before that time, even Chen Tu-hsiu and Hu Shih wrote in *wen yen* or the classical style. It was thus appropriate for Hu, who had returned to China and joined the faculty of Peking University and who was one of the editors of the magazine, to publish in April of that year his article 'On a Constructive Literary Revolution', proclaiming the death of the classical literature and advocating the creation of a 'literature written in the national language and a national language suitable for literature'. He started experimenting with writing poems in the vernacular in that year, the result of which was published in 1920, a work entitled *Experiments*, representing the first sample of the new poetry-writing. A new type of essay, short and caustic, also appeared in the magazine. This was called *Sui Kan Lu* (*Random Jottings*), which developed into the often temperamental and sometimes penetrating epigrams for which Lu Hsun (1881–1936) became famous. Lu Hsun also wrote his *Diary of a Madman* for *La Jeunesse*, which incidentally remains one of the best Chinese short stories. When the magazine published a special issue on Ibsen in 1918 it signalled the start of the new drama movement and introduced to China the 'play' as it is understood in the West.

Thus, plunging headlong into action, the literary revolutionaries or reformers (depending on one's view of them) of *La Jeunesse* and their supporters in *New Tide* (a magazine published by students in Peking University) aroused opposition on the part of some professors of classics at the same university, notably Liu Shih-pei (1884–1914), Huang Kan (1886–1935) and Ma Hsu-lun. But the most colourful and influential of them was Lin Shu, the translator. He wrote short stories which were published in the *New Shanghai Times* ridiculing the literary revolutionaries. Opposition flared up sporadically, but became widespread when in 1922 Professors Wu Mi, Hu Hsien-su and Mei Kuang-ti of Nanking Higher Teachers' College published *Hsueh Heng* (*Critical Review*), in which they criticized the creation of a literature based on the spoken language. In 1925, Chang Shih-chao, then Minister of Education, published the *Chia Yin Chou Kan* (*Tiger Weekly*) in Peking and came out against the literary revolution. But none of these efforts could turn the tide, and vernacular literary works appeared in increasing volume, and were accepted by the reading public.

The success of the Literary Revolution was expedited by the May Fourth Student Movement of 1919 which was touched off by the failure of Chinese diplomatists at the Versailles Peace Conference to recover from Japan the areas in Shantung Province which she occupied. Students in Peking organized huge demonstrations demanding the dismissal of the three Chinese representatives at the Conference. This unrest spread to other cities, and there were many strikes. The editors of *La Jeunesse*, in spite of the fact that they had agreed not to get involved in politics, found themselves supporting the students against the then warlord government. They helped to distribute handbills in the streets. Chen Tu-hsiu was arrested and jailed for eighty-three days. This brought about a merger of the literary movement with the student movement, which had influence over almost every aspect of the life of the literate Chinese.

After a new dictionary of Chinese using phonetic symbols to indicate pronunciation of words was published in 1919, the Ministry of Education proclaimed that in the following year students of the first two years in primary schools should be taught exclusively in the vernacular. Two years later textbooks for primary schools were prepared and issued, and secondary schools and colleges decided voluntarily that their textbooks should also be written in the vernacular. Thus, vernacular Chinese, or *pai hua*, gained recognition as the standard language. As some scholars seem to have thought that it was the lack of official recognition which delayed the development of a 'literature of the national language', it appeared to many that the Literary Revolution had at last succeeded, and it was now up to the writers to create the kind of literature the people wanted.

The development of Chinese literature since that time can best be seen by the change in ideas of the literary groups formed by leading men of letters.

Briefly, in the period of the May Fourth Movement, writers were against the traditional idea that 'literature is the instrument for the teaching of moral principles', or 'Literature as the vehicle of Tao', as it is put in Chinese. The Society for the Study of Literature, which was founded in 1921 with a membership of 172 leading writers, advocated what Chou Tso-jen called a 'literature of humanity'. In the summer of the same year a group of young Chinese returned students from Japan, including Kuo Mo-jo, Yu Ta-fu, Chang Tse-ping and Tien Han, organized the Creation Society in Shanghai. They stood for 'creative writing', and produced individualistic and romantic writing, heavily tinged with melancholy. After the May Thirtieth Incident of 1925, which was caused by the shooting of a Chinese worker by a Japanese foreman in a cotton mill in Shanghai and which subsequently caused nationwide anti-British and anti-Japanese strikes, the Creation Society gave up its individualistic idea of 'art for art's sake' and called for a 'revolutionary literature' to fight against imperialism and warlordism. The Society for the Study of Literature also felt the impact of the Incident and its members split into two groups. The first was the Yu Sze Sheh or 'Random Talks Society' with Lu Hsun, Chou Tso-jen, Sun Fu-yuan, Lin Yutang and Chien Hsuen-tung among others as members, which stood for realism and humanitarianism in literature, and the continuation of the idea of a 'literature of humanity'. The other group was called the Crescent Society, with Hu Shih, Hsu Chih-mo, Wen I-to and others as members and stood for symbolism.

The end of the Chinese Nationalist and Communist co-operation in 1927 after the Northern Expedition brought political conflict to the literary scene. The Creation Society began to come out for 'proletarian literature'. And in 1930 the Communists, having won Lu Hsun over, launched the League of Leftist Writers. Opposing them was a new group led by Huang Chen-hsia, Wang Ping-ling and others which called for a 'Nationalist literature'. In a way, what they both advocated was the same 'literature as an instrument for the teaching of moral principles' concept which the literary revolutionaries had fought against a few years earlier. Only Lin Yutang, Chou Tso-jen and others outside these two groups maintained that literature should be the expression by individuals of their personal experience. This found expression in three magazines Lin Yutang started, *The Analects*, *This Human World* and *Cosmic Wind*. In October 1936, in view of imminent Japanese aggression, Lu Hsun, Lin Yutang, Kuo Mo-jo, Mao Tun, Pa Chin, Chen Wan-tao, Hung Shen and others issued a Manifesto of the Literary Circle calling for unity to resist oppression and respect the freedom of speech. However, no unity in the literary field was ever achieved. During the Sino-Japanese War from 1937 to 1945, literature continued to go the way of 'an instrument of moral instruction', and with a few singular exceptions, could not disengage itself from it. When the Chinese Communists came to power on the mainland of

China, Chinese literature became completely an instrument of propaganda, or 'vehicle of Tao', if that term is preferable. In Taiwan, too, the literary work produced has been more concerned with an anti-Communist stand than with literature itself.

This, then, is the brief background of modern Chinese literature. In the following sections I shall try to present the development of its different aspects.

2. *MODERN CHINESE POETRY*

Hu Shih was the first of the leaders of the Literary Revolution to try his hand at writing poems in the vernacular. His *Experiments*, published in 1920, consists of two parts. The first part was actually not very different from those poems written in the classical style. He himself said that he was more satisfied with those contained in the second part. But they seem to us now to be almost juvenile either in content or in method of presentation. However, they were the bold and conscientious efforts of a great scholar to create a new prosody. He worked on the natural rhythm of verse and the natural harmony of words. Other poets of that period, including Liu Tai-po and Yu Ping-po, do not seem to have been capable of freeing themselves from the influence of the traditional classical poetry. Later Kuo Mo-jo was noted for the pantheistic content of his poems. Generally speaking, the poets of the day tried, and failed, to write 'free verse'. These efforts, without form or rhyming, found little favour with the Chinese who had been used to the sonority and rhyming of traditional poetry. What is this? they said with contempt. It is nothing but a piece of poorly written prose broken up into so many lines and passing as poetry. To a great extent their verdict was right!

Soon the Poetry Supplement of the *Peiping Morning Post*, with the support of poets educated in England and America, came out for some kind of stanzaic structure. Hsu Chih-mo and Wen I-to were the leaders of this group. Wen stressed the 'balance of metre' and uniformity in the length of the lines of a poem. Hsu, however, was a great romantic, overflowing with enthusiasm and talent, and got better results. These two poets had many followers, notably Chen Meng-chia, Pien Chih-lin, Ho Chi-fang and Feng Chih. The last-named later wrote his famous sonnets which successfully employed the poetic form of the West to express his feelings.

At about the same time other poets, especially Lee Chin-fa, started to write poems in the style of the French symbolists. They ignored structure of form in pursuit of the beauty of imagery, and tried to make mosaic-like works with words. What they managed to convey was often colourful, yet it did not in itself mean very much. Among the poets of this group Tai Wang-shu was one of the more successful ones.

The Sino-Japanese War, which broke out in 1937, brought Chinese poetry abruptly back to free verse and steered it away from being the expression of personal feeling towards appeals for patriotism. Ai Ching, Chuang Keh-chia and Tien Chien became known to the public during the years of the war. They went on to suggest a new form of poetry, *lang sung* poems, or 'poems for reading aloud'. This had its effect, but the standards were never high.

It must be mentioned here that traditional Chinese poetry still has its practitioners and enjoys a revival in Taiwan. Of the poets of the old school, Yu Yu-jen, the old revolutionary, is perhaps the best. The reason for the continued existence of traditional poetry-writing is attributable at least partly to the scanty results achieved in modern poetry so far. There are, however, modern poets who strive to combine the ambience of traditional poetry with the vernacular language, and who experiment in evoking associations by using classical poetic phrases and rhymes and definite stanzaic construction.

Here is a selection of the best modern poetry by Chinese writers.

THE FATHOMLESS SEA by Hsu Chih-mo[3]

The fathomless sea and heaven I do not want,
Nor do I wish to fly a giant kite
To catch the upper wind from every side;
I only want a gleam of light,
I only want a crevice—
Like a child in a dark room
Curled in the window seat,
Gazing upon the ever-open gap
Below the western sky—
Merely for one minute,
A gleam of light.

IN THE MOUNTAINS by Hsu Chih-mo[4]

The courtyard is an oasis of quiet
Surrounded by the clamour of the town;
Shadows of pines are woven on the ground,
Bright and beauteous is the full moon.

Nobody knows in the mountains of tonight
What scenery there will be:
Pine-trees perhaps, and moonlight,
And deeper quiet.

O, to swim in the waves of the moon,
To become a gust of ethereal wind
And frolic in deep mountains
And rouse the spring-intoxicated pines!

I would puff a fresh green needle
Towards your window, so it would alight
Gently, like a tender sigh—
Your tranquil slumber not to stir.

EARTHQUAKE by Kuo Mo-jo[5]

The earth revives,
All beings tremble,
But this is only for a second,
Then all is hushed.

There is silence after the heave,
A silence like annihilation,
Sunshine smiles to the children,
To the dazed and terrified children.

I remember this once happened in my youth,
Mother told me 'twas an enormous turtle opening
    and shutting its eyes.
Under the earth is there truly a giant turtle?
I saw it with the eye of a youthful mind.

Now the enormous turtle is dead
And yet I see it soaring through the air,
I know that the quake was caused by a volcano
But how does this knowledge benefit my soul?

A CHAT IN THE WOOD by Tai Wang-shu[6]

Walking into the gloomy wood
One feels a sudden chill at heart.
Dear, do you feel chill at heart
Enfolded in my arms
When our lips meet?

Dear, do not smile,
To weep a little is proof of tenderness.
Weep, dear, weep upon my knees,
On my shoulder, on my breast:
To weep is so unlike brief happiness.

'Follow you to the world's end.'
Do you persist in saying so?
Perhaps you're joking! Go chase the heavenly wind across
    the plain.
I am lighter and lighter than the heavenly wind:
You will never overtake me.

Ah, crave no more this useless heart of mine!
Go search for trees of coral in the mountain
And flowers in the sea.
'Where is the keepsake of our happy days?'
Here, sweet, here:
The poignant sorrow, sorrow brown of hue.

ANXIETY by Tai Wang-shu[7]

Say it's the sadness of the lonely autumn,
Say it's a longing for the far-off sea.
If people ask the cause of my anxiety,
I dare not speak your name.

I dare not speak your name
If people ask the cause of my anxiety,
Say it's a longing for the far-off sea,
Say it's the sadness of the lonely autumn.

SONNETS by Feng Chih

I

We are prepared to savour fully
Unexpected miracles.
After long, tedious years,
A comet suddenly appears, a storm rises.

In that instant, as in our first embrace,
Our lives
And the sadness and happiness of the past,
Turn before our eyes into immovable form.

We praise the tiny insects:
They end their beautiful lives
After mating once

Or once encountering danger.
The purpose of our whole life is to meet
A sudden storm, a falling star.

2

We wave to each other, and once parted,
Find ourselves in two different worlds.
We feel cold and suddenly see the great expanse
In front of us—just like two new-born babies.

O, each leave-taking is like being born once more,
We've borne hardship of work,
To warm up what is cold, to ripen what is raw,
We each tend our own world.

In order to meet again, like the first time we met,
With a thankful feeling, thinking of things past.
As when we first met and instantly felt the existence

Of previous lives. There are springs and autumns
In a lifetime. We feel the change of seasons
But not the years of this human world.

ON THE WAY HOME by Pien Chih-lin[8]

Like an astronomer turning from his telescope,
Amid the noise I hear my own slow steps.
Is it beyond the sphere outside my own sphere?
The road through dusk is like some grey despair.

THE AUTUMNAL WINDOW by Pien Chih-lin[9]

Like a man in the middle age
I look back on the traces of the past,
Blank desert after desert at each step,
Waking out of a disconcerting dream
To hear the crows of evening over half the sky.

The sunset on grey walls
Reminds me of a consumptive
Who images the rosy cheeks of youth
In the faint twilight of an ancient mirror.

AUTUMN by Ho Chi-fang[10]

Scattering all the pearly dews of morning,
The noise of timber-felling riddles the deep ravine,
Sickles sated with rice are put aside,
Plump melons and hedgerow-fruits are loaded in baskets.
Autumn lingers about the farmhouses.

Round nets are cast in the chilly mist on the river's brim,
Flat fish-like shadows of maple-leaves are gathered,
The awnings are covered under films of frost,
As they row homeward gently sway the oars.
Autumn dallies about the fishermen's boats.

3. *MODERN CHINESE SHORT STORIES*

The first Chinese story written in the western style to appear in *La Jeunesse* was Lu Hsun's *The Diary of a Madman*. As with efforts at westernization in other fields, it was inspired by a master in the West to an extent that bordered on imitation. In this case the inspiration came from Gogol. However, where inspiration ends and imitation begins is a fine point to define, and perhaps at this stage of development of the Chinese short story even imitation could be forgiven. In any case, Lu Hsun brought his own talent to the story, and later proved himself to be an author in his own right. The novelty of *Diary* probably had something to do with its immediate success. It drew a great many readers, and remains to this day one of the best short stories of modern China.

Lu Hsun laced his writings with messages and social protests. His best-known work, *The Story of Ah Q*, was an obvious satire on the social history of his time. In 1923 he published these two stories and twelve others in a collection entitled *Na Han* (*Outcries*), which title neatly sums up the nature of his stories. In 1926 another collection of his short stories, *Pang Huang* (*Hesitation*), was published, and Lu Hsun's name as a writer was firmly established. He seemed to think quite highly of himself also, for in his preface to *Hesitation* he wrote this short poem:

> Lonely is the new literary scene,
> Peace reigns over the old battlefield;
> Of the two opposing sides, only one soldier
> Remains, shouldering his gun, and hesitates.

It was really a pity that he, the one soldier who remained, was later to devote almost all his time to writing epigrams which were angry and satirical comments thrusting at his real and imaginary enemies of passing significance. Otherwise, he might have produced more stories of quality.

Yu Ta-fu won fame for his *Chen Lun* (*Lost*), a collection of three short stories. He depicted in them the melancholia and disappointment of youth in a chaotic country at a time of transition of moral standards, especially the conflict between a search for platonic love and the need to satisfy sexual desire. These stories cast an immense spell over a great number of young people. Kuo Mo-jo's translation of Goethe's *Sorrows of Werthe* gained tremendous popularity, perhaps for the same reasons.

Yeh Shao-chun's stories had a simple, concise and realistic style. The fact that he could not read any foreign language was probably a blessing in disguise, for he was able to avoid the prevalent practice of writers of using long, involved sentences which passed as 'Europeanization'. In his story collections, entitled *The Barrier*, *Under Fire*, *In the City*, etc., he tried to convey the sentiment that the combination of natural beauty and love through understanding was the highest ideal of life, but this idea did not receive the recognition it deserved.

Other short-story writers of note were Chang Chih-ping, Ping Hsin, Ling Shu-hua, Lo Hua-sheng, Chiang Kuangtse and Ting Ling.

From 1929 short stories became more and more popular, and improved with their authors' mastery of technique. There were many notable writers, including Pa Chin, Lao Sheh, Ouyang Shan, Ai Wu, Wu Tsu-hsiang, Wei Chin-chih and Peng Chia-huan. But the most accomplished and representative writers were perhaps Shen Tsung-wen (b. 1902), Chang Tien-yi (b. 1907) and Hsu Yu (b. 1910).

Shen Tsung-wen is best known for his descriptions of clerks in the army, peasants, small shopkeepers, boatmen, people of the Miao tribe and innocent youth in the western region of Hunan Province. He said in his preface to *Border Town*, perhaps the best of his works:

> I have an indescribable affection for peasants and soldiers. This shows in all my writing, and I have never tried to hide it. I was born and brought up in the kind of country town which I write about. My brothers, like my grandfather and father, were all in the army, and they either died fighting or remained in their posts until the last day of their lives. . . . For they were upright and honest and their lives had been both great and common, their temperament both moving and critical. In writing about them I have just put them down truthfully and simply. . . . This may make them seem remote to the educated people and those who were brought up in cities.

His stories proved to be to the taste of educated and city people as well. His style is polished, concise and vivid, and he was able to infuse his writing with an admiration for innocence in human beings, even innocent crookedness. He apparently feels that people don't need knowledge to possess happiness, and that innocence is the prerequisite of virtue. There is not the crude preaching in his stories which is so obtrusive in Lu Hsun's work. His skill at presenting the pastoral beauty of small towns and the charming and innocent country people has as yet found no peer in Chinese literature.

While Shen Tsung-wen's stories are noted for their beauty of style and affirmation of life, Chang Tien-yi's stories are known for their fast pace, dramatic action and brazen ideological bias. Chang is observant and analytical, and his stories ring true. He has written a great many of them, and published eight collections of them in the ten years before the Sino-Japanese War, of which *From Vacuity to Fullness* was perhaps the best.

Hsu Yu wrote more about the bourgeoisie and life in the coastal cities under western influence. His characters captured the mood of the time, when the young, educated Chinese were timorously trying to ape the West in fashion and in assessing values in life. He probably has a greater command of vernacular prose than many of his contemporaries, and writes stories of great lucidity.

Here is an excerpt from Shen Tsung-wen's *The Husband* which I have chosen because it is one of the best known of his short stories. It opens with a short description of a river scene in which there are many small boats tied to the stilt-houses on the river bank. These are used by women from the nearby countryside to practise the oldest profession in this small river town. This was fairly common, for life was hard on the farms, and many young farmers had their young wives 'trading' on the river boats to help out. After a period of long separation the couple would reunite on a festival day, when the young farmer changed into clean clothes and went to visit his wife.

The farmer in this story is surprised at the manners and the make-up his wife has learned to use from the town people, and only when she asks if he has received the money she sent him and if the old sow has given birth to another litter does he regain his composure. When night comes the husband withdraws himself to the rear of the boat as swaggering customers arrive, and looks into the river, thinking of his chickens and piglets, feeling that only the small animals are his friends. He falls asleep, but at midnight his wife comes and puts a piece of brown sugar in his mouth, for she remembers that he likes it. Whatever he says she puts a piece in his mouth and goes back to entertain her customers.

In the morning, while his wife goes to burn incense at the temple, the rough waterfront 'protector' of the river boats appears, and the farmer tells him that he is the girl's husband. The protector orders him, 'Tell her not to receive any guests tonight. I am coming back.' The young man waits until noon and his wife does not come back. Despondent, he decides to go back to the farm. On his way he meets his wife.

In the street he meets his wife coming back with Wu Tou [a young girl on the boat] who has a new *hu chin* [a musical instrument] in her hand.

'Where are you going?' his wife said.

'I want to go home.'

'I asked you to watch things while we were gone, and you want to go home! Who offended you to make you so mean?'

'I want to go home. You just let me go.'

'Come back to the boat!'

He saw that his wife was even angrier than her voice revealed, and knowing that the *hu chin* had been bought for him he followed her back to the boat. She made him feel wanted again, and asked him to try out the *hu chin*, which further soothed his feelings.

When night fell the matted cover was drawn over the front of the boat. The young man played on his *hu chin* and Wu Tou started to sing. Later, Old Seven [his wife] joins her. Over the glass chimney of the old lamp a makeshift lampshade of red paper casts its warm glow over the boat and filled it with the festive air of the New Year. The young man's heart filled with happiness. But soon there were drunken soldiers walking on the river bank who heard the two girls.

Two drunkards staggered to the boat, their hands dirty with mud. Holding on to the mooring they croaked, as though they had walnuts in their mouths, 'Who's singing there? Make known your name! We will reward you. . . . Five hundred. . . . Have you heard? Five hun—dred!'

In the boat the music stopped suddenly, and there was silence.

The drunkards kicked at the sides of the boat, making dull thumping noises. They tried to push back the mat cover, but could not find the fastenings, and gave up. 'Don't you want reward, you bitch born prostitute? . . . Playing deaf and dumb? Who dares to make merry here? I am afraid of no one! Not even the Emperor! No, sir, I'm a louse if I'm afraid of him! Our Commander and Division Commander are bastards. I'm not afraid of them!'

The other one shouted, 'Sexy broad! Come and help me up!'

They began to throw stones at the mat cover, cursing furiously. Everyone on board was frightened. The old woman [the procuress] hurriedly turned down the light and walked over to push back the covering. The young man, frightened by the scene, picked up his *hu chin* and went to the rear of the boat. In a minute the drunkards came on board and came into the open cabin. While still mouthing obscenities they fought to kiss Old Seven, the old woman and Wu Tou. One of them asked in a hoarse voice, 'Who was singing here and making music? Get the *hu chin* player to play for me!'

The old woman dared not answer, and Old Seven did not know what to say. The drunkards cursed loudly, 'You stinking slut! Get the pimp to play for me! I'll give him one thousand! Not even Premier Tsao Meng-teh was that generous! I'll give him one thousand, one thousand pieces of sweet potato. Hurry up, don't make us angry! . . .'

'*Ta-yeh*! It was only the few of us in the family, making music for fun. . . .'

'No, no, no! Old whore, you are no good. Too old, like a shrivelled-up orange! Go and get the *hu chin* player! Bastard! I want to play it! I want to sing!' So saying, he stood up and made for the rear of the boat. The old woman was frightened, and her mouth fell open. Old Seven finally regained control of herself. She took the drunkard's hand and put it on her breast. He sat down. 'All right, good. I can pay. I'll sleep here tonight!' He started to hum a few bars of a well-known air.

After this the drunkard lay down beside Old Seven, and the other soldier who did not say anything lay down on the other side of her.

The young man, after a while, called softly to the old woman from the rear of the boat. The old woman crawled quietly over to him. 'What happened?' he said.

'Soldiers from the barracks, drunken and acting like wolves. They'll go away after a while.'

'They'd better. I forgot to tell you a square-faced man who acted like a big shot came this morning. He said to tell you not to entertain any customers, he is coming tonight.'

'The one who wears a pair of big boots and speaks very loud, as though a gong were being struck?'

'Yes, yes. He wears a huge gold ring.'

'He is Old Seven's godfather. Did he come this morning?'

'Yes. He talked to me for a long time and ate some chestnuts before he left.'

'What did he say?'

'He said he will definitely come, and that you must not have any customers here. Also, he said he would buy me drinks.'

What is he coming for, the old woman wondered. Is he coming to stay the night? Could it be that he has noticed me? Although as a procuress she was used to all kinds of situations she was still feeling hurt because she was told that she was no longer any good. She crawled back to the front cabin and finding the obnoxious goings on there, she cursed, 'Swine!' and went back to the rear

'Well?'

'Nothing.'

'Well, have they gone?'

'No, sleeping.'

'Sle—eping?'

The old woman understood the tone of his voice although she could not see his face. 'Elder brother, you hardly ever come to town. Why don't we go up and have some fun? I'll treat you to a gallery seat at a show.'

The young man just shook his head.

After the soldiers left Wu Tou, the old woman and Old Seven joked about the drunken manners of the soldiers in the front cabin. The young man remained in the rear, and did not come out to join them. The old woman went to call him twice, but he would not answer. The old woman turned around and began to examine the four banknotes the soldiers had left behind, for she knew how to differentiate between forgeries and genuine notes. These were good banknotes. She showed Old Seven how to tell the difference, and under the light pointed out the watermarks in the notes. Then she put the banknotes under her nose and sniffed at them, and said that the soldiers must have received them at the Moslem beef shop, for they smelled of butter.

Wu Tuo went to the door again. 'Elder brother, they have gone. Come on, let's finish the song. . . .'

Old Seven stopped her.

Everyone was silent. The young man at first plucked at the strings of his *hu chin* and made small noises. Then he stopped. The noises of cymbals, drums and pipes from the riverside street floated to them. A merchant was celebrating something, and entertaining his guests by inviting a theatre troupe to give a show in his place, which would last the whole night.

After a while Old Seven crawled to the rear cabin, but returned almost immediately.

Old Seven shook her head and heaved a sigh. 'Stubborn as a mule, let him be.'

They felt that the Protector would not show up now, and the old woman, Old Seven and Wu Tou all lay down and slept in the front, and left the young man alone in the rear cabin.

At midnight the Protector led a team of police to search the boats.

Four armed policemen stood in the bow, and the Protector and an Inspector entered the front cabin, shining their torches. By then, the old woman was lighting the lamp, and from experience she knew that there was nothing very serious involved. Old Seven sat up in bed, put her clothes around herself, and addressed them respectively as 'Daddy' and 'Inspector Master' and called for Wu Tou to serve tea. Wu Tou was sleepy, thinking about picking berries in March that she had dreamt about.

The young man, roused up from his sleep, was dragged to the front cabin by the old woman. Speechless at the sight of the Protector and the big man in black uniform, he wondered what had happened. The Inspector immediately became officious. 'Who is this?'

'Old Seven's husband,' said the Protector. 'He has just come for a visit.'

Old Seven said, 'Inspector, he came only yesterday.'

The Inspector looked at the young man, then at the young woman, and pursued the matter no further. He went about the cabin, poking into things here and there. When he looked at the jar of dried chestnuts (which the young man had brought for his wife) the Protector took a big handful of them and put them into the Inspector's big pocket. The Inspector smiled and said nothing.

After a while they left to search other boats. The old woman was on the verge of putting the cover back on the boat when a policeman returned and said, 'Tell Old Seven that the Inspector is coming back to inspect her carefully, understand?'

'Right away?'

'After he has searched all the boats.'

'Serious?'

'When did I lie to you, old whore?'

The young man was surprised to see her happy expression, for he could not understand why the Inspector should want to come back to inspect Old Seven. Now, looking at his sleepy wife, he was no longer angry with her, but wanted to make peace with her and lie down in bed with her and talk about affairs at home and discuss one thing with her. He sat down on the edge of her bed, hardly moving.

The old woman seemed to know what the young man was thinking about. She sensed his desire and knew that he did not understand the situation. So she reminded Old Seven, 'The Inspector is coming soon!'

Old Seven bit her lips, not making a sound, as if she were lost.

Early next morning the young man got ready to leave. He did not say a word, but put on his sandals, found his pipe, and packed his things. Then he sat down on the edge of the low bed. He had a hard time saying what he wanted to say.

Old Seven asked him, 'Didn't you promise Daddy to have lunch with him at his place?'

He just shook his head.

'He ordered a banquet especially for you! Four dishes, four bowls and wine! It's an honour. Would it be right not to accept his hospitality?'

He did not answer.

'Don't you want to see a show?'

He did not answer.

'The pork dumplings at Man Tien Hung Restaurant will not be ready until lunch time. They are what you like best!'

He did not answer.

He insisted upon leaving. Old Seven didn't know what to do. She went to stand dumbly in the bow for a time, and came back and took from her purse the banknotes the soldiers gave her. She counted them and crumpled them up and stuck them into his left hand. The young man did not say anything and Old Seven felt she knew what he wanted. 'Would you give me the other three banknotes,' she said. The old woman gave her the money and Old Seven pressed it into the young man's hand as well.

The young man shook his head, threw the notes on the ground, and covering his face with his big, coarse hands, started to cry like a child. At this, Wu Tou and the old woman fled to the rear cabin. How strange, Wu Tou thought. To think that such a big fellow would cry, how funny! But she did not laugh. She stood at the stern, looked at the *hu chin* hanging from one of the beams, and wanted desperately to sing a song. But somehow she could not even make a noise.

When the Protector came to take his guest for the banquet he found only the old woman and Wu Tou on board the boat. Upon inquiring, he learned that the young couple had left early that morning to return to the country.

CHAPTER XVII

The Literature of Modern China (II)

1. *MODERN CHINESE PROSE*

IN the first years after the Literary Revolution it was in the field of essay-writing that the new men of letters accomplished the most. This was because essay-writing had long been practised in China, while the art of drama, poetry, novel and short-story writing as these were practised in the West was still being learned by the leaders of the Revolution. The *hsiao pin wen*, written by Yuan Chung-lang and others in the late Ming Dynasty and by Chin Sheng-tan, Yuan Mei and others in the Ching Dynasty, are indeed very much akin to modern essays in spirit. It was thus easier for writers of this period to express themselves in this particular literary form, combining the traditional and other techniques they had picked up from reading the works of writers like Montaigne and Lamb. The best-known essayists were Chou Tso-jen, Chu Tse-ching, Yu Ping-po, Hsu Chih-mo, Hsia Ping-hsin, Lu Hsun, Chen Yuan and Lin Yutang.

Hsu Chih-mo's essays were often romantic, poetic prose. His *The Cambridge I know* was perhaps the most widely read and admired of his essays. Yu Ping-po and Chu Tse-ching excelled in quietly expressing deep feelings in a refined manner, while Hsia Ping-hsin was best in expressing 'naïve happiness' and 'innocent tears' to her 'small readers'. Lu Hsun, Chen Yuan and Lin Yutang all wrote satirical and critical essays on various questions of the day. Chou Tso-jen, on the other hand, was a master at expressing various feelings in a simple, subtle style. He was seldom obvious, and for this reason his essays were compared to strong Chinese green tea, which leaves a lingering taste in one's mouth.

It has often been said that there are a rebel and a hermit in the soul of every Chinese man of letters. In other words, that Chinese essays were either 'vehicles of Tao' or of 'self-expression'. Most essayists in the period immediately after the Revolution took the latter standpoint. Lu Hsun translated Kuriyahawa Hakuson's *Out of the Ivory Tower*, a pamphlet which advocates the self-expressionist approach to writing essays, and Chou Tso-jen quoted the literary theory of Yuan Chung-lang, of the Ming Dynasty, to support his 'self-expressionist' stand.

It was in 1924, when the magazines *Hsien Tai Ping Lun* (*Contemporary Review*) and *Yu Sze* (*Random Talks*) were published, that 'rebellious' essays began to flourish. It is interesting to note that Lin Yutang said in an article which appeared in *Random Talks* that 'All independent thinking persons who honestly hold their personal opinions will, at some time or other, become abusive. But this abusiveness is exactly what upholds the dignity of scholars. The scholar who never criticizes anything, only loses his self.' For in 1932 he and Chou Tso-jen and other contributors to the magazine published *The Analects* and came out again in favour of the self-expressionist approach to essay-writing. In 1934 he published *This Human World*, and in 1935 started another magazine, the *Cosmic Wind*, bringing the writing of literary essays to a height that was not reached even in its heyday in the late Ming Dynasty.

Lu Hsun, almost alone among the contributors to *Random Talks*, maintained his 'vehicle of Tao' approach. Although he admitted that 'the achievements in essays were greater than those in the novel, drama and poetry in the May Fourth Movement', he went on to say that 'naturally essays reflected the struggles and battles waged in that period, but because many essayists tried to learn the technique of writing essays from English essayists, their work was sometimes humorous and graceful, their styles decorous and polished. But the purpose was to show that what the classical Chinese literature could do, the new vernacular literature could also do. The future of Chinese essays lies obviously in continuously waging struggles and battles (against what is wrong with China).' He therefore devoted the last twenty-odd years of his life to writing *tsa wen*, which were short and incisive commentaries on matters of current interest. In the 1930s, admirers of his *tsa wen* style published two magazines, *Tai Pai* and *Wan Chung*, to compete with *This Human World* and *Cosmic Wind* for readership, but their circulation was rather small.

Apart from these two 'groups', Ho Chi-fang, Lee Kuang-tien and Liang Shih-chiu were the best-known essayists. After the Sino-Japanese War erupted in 1937 essays received less attention from writers, and for a time journalistic reporting was in great vogue, but it soon died out. The high tide of the development of Chinese essays seems to have passed.

Here are some samples of Lu Hsun's epigrams, and an essay by Lin Yutang.

SOME EPIGRAMS OF LU HSUN[1]

There is a favourite way with those who know old literature. When a new idea is introduced they call it 'heresy', and must bend all their efforts to destroy it. When that new idea, after a hard struggle, has won a place for itself, they then discover that 'it's the same thing as was taught by Confucius'. They object to all imported things saying that this is 'to convert Chinese into barbarians', but when the barbarians become rulers of China, they discover these 'barbarians' are also descendants of the Yellow Emperor.

The Chinese have only two names for foreign races: one is 'foreign races', the other is 'Your Majesty'.

When the Chinese are in power, and see that others cannot do anything to them . . . they are autocrats and have no use for moderation; and when they are out of luck, then they begin to speak of 'fate'. They would be content even with being slaves and find themselves in perfect harmony with the universe.

Who says that the Chinese do not change? When new things are introduced they want to reject them, but when they begin to see that there is something in them they begin to change. But they do not change by adapting themselves to new things, but by adapting the new things to themselves.

A friend of mine has said, 'The question is not whether we can preserve our national heritage, but whether the national heritage can preserve us.' To preserve ourselves is the first thing. The question is whether it has or has not the power to preserve us, and not whether it is a 'national heritage'.

SPRING FEVER by Lin Yutang[2]

I had come back from the trip to Anhwei to find spring in my garden. Her steps had lightly tripped over the lawn, her fingers had caressed the hedgerows, and her breath had touched the willow branches and the young peach trees. Therefore, although I had not seen her coming, I knew she was here. The rose bugs, of the same green as the stem on which they thrived, were again in evidence, earthworms again put in their appearance by throwing up little clusters of mud in the garden beds, and even those poplar branches that I had chopped up into small sections, of one or two feet long lying in a heap in the yard, performed a miracle by putting forth green and merry leaves. Now after three weeks I could already see the shadows of leaves dancing on the ground on a sunny day, a sight that I had not seen for a long time.

What is happening to men and animals is a different story. There is sadness all around. Perhaps it isn't sadness, but I have no other word for it. Spring makes you sad and spring makes you sleepy. It shouldn't, I know, and if I were a peasant boy, or if everyone in my household from master to cook had only to look after buffaloes, I am sure we would not feel sad about it. But living in the city in spring is different. Consciously nothing is happening. But the unconscious self, with the heritage of millions of years, tells us that we are deprived of something, missing something.

I think I have found the word now: it is called 'spring fever'. Everyone is having a spring fever, including Chubby, my dog. I had cured my spring fever by taking a trip to Anhwei and seeing those emerald pools near Yulingkuan. But I had boasted of my trip before my cook and he happened to be from Anhwei and it made him extremely sad. For he is washing dishes and cutting carrots and cleaning kitchen utensils in spring, and that makes him sad. My boy, a tall husky farmer from Kiangpei, is polishing windows and mopping the floor and sticking letters in the letter box and pouring out tea the whole day for me, and that makes *him* sad. Then we have the cook's wife in our household as washerwoman—by the way, I like her extremely, because she is fairly good-looking and has all the virtues of a good Chinese girl; she keeps her mouth shut and works the whole day, moving about on her little half-emancipated feet, ironing and ironing and ironing and not saying a word, and she does not giggle but laughs in a natural, quiet way when she laughs, and talks in a low voice when she talks. Perhaps she alone is not feeling sad, for she is grateful that we have spring in the garden already, and there is so much green and so many leaves and so many trees and such good breeze. . . . But her husband, the cook, a handsome dandy, is growing impatient of his work and giving us worse food than usual. He is listless most of the time, and makes his wife wash all the dishes in order that he may go out early. Then Ah Ching, the 'boy'— he is really a tall man—came one day to me and said that he wanted leave for an afternoon. A leave from Ah Ching! I was completely surprised. I had told him to take a day off every month, but he had never done so. And now he wants a half-day's leave to 'arrange an important matter with a friend from his native district'. So *he*, too, has caught the spring fever. . . .

While Ah Ching was taking leave from my home somebody else was taking leave from office to visit my garden. It was the messenger boy from the K—— Book Company. He had not appeared for a long time, for a grown-up man had been delivering the manuscripts and proofs in the last month or so. Now the boy must take his place and deliver the proofs, or perhaps a single letter, or a copy of a magazine, or even to convey me a good wish. That boy—I know he is living down in the eastern district, where you can see only walls and back doors and refuse cans and cement floors, with not a green leaf around. Yes, green leaves could grow from the crevices of rocks, but *not* grow from the cracks of cement floors. . . .

There is sadness, too, among the animals. Chubby has been a monk, and so long as spring isn't here, he is a contented dog. I always thought my garden big enough for him to play about, so I never let him out. . . . But now the garden isn't big enough for him, not by a long shot, in spite of all the bones and the delicious left-overs. Of course, it isn't that. I understand him. He wants *her*, no matter blonde or brunette, pretty or ugly, so long as she is a she. But what could I do? Chubby is very sad.

Then a tragedy happened in our little household of pigeons. There is really only a couple. There were six or seven of them when I took over the house, but all left and only this sweet couple remained. They had tried to raise a family in the loft of my garage, but always had no luck. Two or three times the young was hatched and then it would learn to fly before it could walk and would fall dead. I didn't like that look in the parents' eye, twinkling and twinkling, and they standing silently on the opposite roof to contemplate the funeral. This last time it looked as if they were going to be successful, for the young one was growing bigger every day, and had even come out to the loft window and gazed at the outside world and could already flap its wings.

But one day our whole household was thrown into a flurry by the announcement by the rickshaw boy that the young pigeon was dead. How had he died? The rickshaw boy had seen him just roll on the ground and die. It called for a Sherlock Holmes brain like mine.

Mysteriously I felt over the body of the dead young pigeon. The pouch under the neck which used to be full of food, was evidently empty. Two eggs were lying in the nest. The mother pigeon had been hatching again.

'Have you seen the father pigeon lately?' I opened the query.

'Not for a few days already,' said the rickshaw boy.

'When did you see him last?'

'Last Wednesday.'

'Hm—hm!' I said.

'Have you seen the mother about?' I asked again.

'She didn't leave the nest much.'

'Hm—hm!' I said.

It was evident there had been desertion. The spring fever had done it. It was death from starvation beyond the shadow of a doubt. The mother pigeon could not leave the nest, and she could not find food for the young one.

'Like all husbands,' I muttered.

Now with her husband deserting her, and her young one dead, the mother pigeon would not even sit on the eggs. The family has been broken up. Sitting for a while at the opposite roof corner, and taking a last look at her former happy home (where her two eggs still lay), she flew away—I don't know where. Perhaps she will never trust a male pigeon again.

2. MODERN CHINESE NOVELS

The modern Chinese novel was the slowest of all literary forms to develop after the Literary Revolution. Although there were Chang

Tse-ping's *Tai Li* and other novels about the conflicts between love and desire, and Wang Tung-chao's *Dusk*, which reflected the mood of the youth of the time, the 'new' novel did not come of age until Mao Tun's *Disillusion* was published in 1928. Perhaps it was because novels needed a longer incubating period than poems, short stories, etc., and Chinese writers were waiting until almost all the famous novelists of the West, including Wilde, Flaubert, Maeterlinck, Louis Aragon, Anatole France, Goethe, Schiller, Sinclair and Signoret were introduced to China and their works had been read and appreciated before they attempted to write novels as they were understood in the West. *Disillusion* and Mao Tun's two other autobiographical novels, *Vacillation* and *Pursuit*, were later given a collective title: *Eclipse*. Mao Tun had always been a strong supporter of the Communist movement, and was a propagandist of the Political Department during the Chinese Nationalist Northern Expedition in 1925–1927, which started with Communist support but ended with the elimination of the Communists from the ruling circle by the Nationalists. *Eclipse*, as the title indicates, showed the author's disappointment with the turn of things. Although the trilogy made Mao Tun famous, it was, however, *Midnight*, which was published in 1932, which made him the foremost novelist of his day.

In the same year that Mao Tun published his first novel *Disillusion*, Yeh Shao-chun also published his *Ni Huan-tse*. Its canvas was smaller than Mao's trilogy, but they both used the Northern Expedition as the background, and both had tragic endings. Also, they were both honest efforts by the authors to portray what they considered to be the effect on the people, especially the young, of the failure of the expedition to bring about a new phase in the history of the Republic. On the whole, *Ni Huan-tse* is a better novel. It has a tighter plot and is less contrived.

Pa Chin, who published his short novel *Destruction* in 1929, was one of the most prolific novelists. He wrote the *Love Trilogy*, consisting of three short novels: *Fog*, *Rain* and *Lightning*, and the *Swift Current Trilogy*, consisting of three novels: *Family*, *Spring* and *Autumn*, as well as many other novels, short novels and short stories. He is not really a good novelist, but, being an anarchist, his anger with the *status quo* and his romantic ideas about revolution seemed to inform his writing with a yearning for a better future which struck the hearts of a multitude of young students. In the 1930s, Pa Chin was no doubt the idol of the greatest number of young students, many of whom identified themselves with the characters of his novels and novelettes.

Lao Sheh is the only humorous novelist China has so far produced. He started writing fiction in 1925 and has since written many novels, including *Biography of Niu Tientse*, *Divorce*, *Four Generations under One Roof* and *Rickshaw Boy*, the last one being his best. He is of Manchu descent, which is singular in Chinese literary circles, and wrote his best work in a pure Peking vernacular, which is also singular. He excelled in telling a story with many humorous episodes. Now, however, living in Communist China, his work has the stamp of Communist propaganda all over it, and no longer has any literary value.

Apart from these as it were giants there were other novelists in the 1930s, including Chang Tien-yi, who wrote *The Strange Knight of Shanghai*; Ting Ling, who was noted for *Tien Village*; Lee Chieh-jen, who wrote *The Big Wave*; Hsiao Chun, who wrote *Village in August*; and Tuanmu Hung-liang, who wrote *The Khorchin Grasslands*.

Since the Sino-Japanese War the efforts of the veteran novelists have produced less notable results. Mao Tun's *Maple Leaves Red Like Flowers in February* and Lao Sheh's *Four Generations Under One Roof*, although major efforts produced during the war bear no comparison to their earlier works. Pa Chin was perhaps the exception. His *Fire*, again a trilogy, was on a par with his earlier novels, and his *Leisure Garden* and *Cold Nights* showed his determination to write psychological novels. His style, too, improved, becoming less flat. Among the new novelists, the most talked about within academic circles was Chien Chung-shu. His only novel, *The Besieged City*, published in 1947, did not gain great popularity. It is a rather old-fashioned novel, using a return journey the hero takes during the war between Shanghai and the interior of China as the thread of the episodes. But the author writes with great gusto and wit, and there is some good characterization in the book, although the attention paid to the novel was due perhaps more to his erudition than to the merits of the novel itself.

In the last thirteen years on mainland China, the most talked-about novels have been Ting Ling's *Sun Over Sangkan River* and Chao Shu-li's *San Li Wan*. Both are novels about peasants, the first about the Land Reform carried out in Nuanshui Village near Cholu City, along the Sangkan River, the second, about the founding of a co-operative in San Li Wan Village. *Sun Over Sangkan River* is decidedly the better of the two novels. It at least paints a gallery of vivid characters, in spite of the political aim every literary work in Communist countries has to serve.

In Taiwan many new novelists have emerged. Their works, however, follow a set formula of anti-Communist themes. Glaring weaknesses in characterization and plot render many of these novels of doubtful literary value. Chiang Kwei's *The Whirlwind* and Wang Lan's *Blue and Black*, both ambitious works, covering respectively a period from 1919 to the earlier years of the Sino-Japanese War, and from the 1930s to the time the Chinese Communists came to power in mainland China, are among the better novels written there.

In my opinion, Mao Tun's *Midnight* remains the best modern novel written in Chinese, and better achievements by Chinese novelists in recent years are those written in English, free from political partisanship, such as Han Suyin's *A Many-splendoured Thing* and Lin Tai-yi's *The Eavesdropper* and *The Lilacs Overgrow*.

Midnight describes the rise and fall of the fortunes of Wu Sun-fu, a powerful 'national capitalist' during the 1930s, when a Kuomintang politician Wang Ching-wei, in alliance with the warlord Feng Yu-hsiang, rose in military revolt against the Central Government and labour was restive in Shanghai and other big cities. Briefly, the novel tells how Wu, after having modernized his silk mills, goes on to merge his company with smaller ones in spite of strikes and the economic recession brought about by the civil war. He has the vision of establishing an empire, selling his products in every corner of the country. He also founds a finance company to facilitate his business transactions, and is confident that by better management and cutting down costs he will ultimately realize his aims. But his financial commitments turn out to be greater and the strikes staged by the workers in his factories backed by the Communists more difficult to break than he expected. He also did not take into consideration the threat of foreign competition. In frustration he speculates on the Stock Exchange. He is successful to a certain extent, but the dominant figure in the Stock Exchange, Chao Po-tao, a comprador backed by foreign interests, gets to know of the difficulties Wu is in, and offers to buy out Wu's interests. Wu has always been contemptuous of compradores, and now, his pride hurt, challenges Chao's position in the Stock Exchange. In the ensuing duel Wu throws everything he has into the battle, but his brother-in-law doublecrosses him and Wu goes bankrupt.

To write a brief summary of a novel is to be unfair to the novelist

This is particularly so with *Midnight*. It has a wealth of sub-plots and characters. And in trying to describe faithfully the odds against which a national capitalist had to work in the 1930s, the author also furnished the reader with the results of his research, albeit tinted by Marxism. Wu Sun-fu was the typical Chinese industrialist of the 1930s, fighting for his ideals single-handed, caught in the chaos created by tumultuous forces at work in an awakening country. Chao Po-tao was, of course, the sensuous, smug, sneering comprador backed by foreign interests with whom every Chinese in the big cities was familiar. Mao Tun was successful not only in vividly presenting these two characters, but the many scenes he described were authentic. Here is a short scene from the novel:

From the depth of the area of the squatters' huts a shadow quietly crawled out, like a dog on the prowl, hunting with his nose for a weak spot in the police cordon. High above in the deep blue sky, stars seemed to be winking, and together with the frightened cries of a baby in one of the huts, there went the shrill police whistle! By slow and steady movement the shadow finally moved out of the cordon, and thereupon it moved faster. Winking stars followed the shadow through twists and turns into a dirty alley. At the back door of a house at the end of the alley the shadow tapped three times, and slipped into the house as soon as the door was opened a crack.

In the front room upstairs there were three dilapidated beds (without mosquito nets) and a square table. Under a 15-watt electric lamp a young girl was seen lying on a bed by the window, talking in a low voice to another young girl sitting near her. The latter suddenly turned around and exclaimed:

'Why, Sister Yueh, you—you have come alone?'

'Sister Hsiu and Ah Hsin were arrested, didn't you know?'

'I did! I am asking about Chu, Chu Kwei-yin, isn't it? The new member, why hasn't she come?'

'I couldn't go to look for her! I was almost unable to come myself. They do keep a tight watch!'

Chen Yueh-o shook her head and spat. She sat down at the square table, poured herself a cup of tea and started to drink slowly. The girl on the bed slapped at the shoulders of her companion.

'It is the same as in Hung-kou. Ma Chin, the general strike has failed again!'

Ma Chin grunted, her sparkling eyes trained on Chen Yueh-o's face. Chen Yueh-o was listless, or at least, confused. Conscious that Ma Chin was watching her, she put down her cup and turned around and asked anxiously, 'What are we going to do? Tell me quickly?'

'When Old Ke is here we shall start the meeting. Tsai Cheng, what time is it? Why hasn't Old Ke shown up? Even Su Lun is not here yet.'

'Seven-twenty already! I can't wait too long. I have to attend a meeting at half-past eight in Hung-kou. Oh, what a bother!'

Tsai Cheng heaved heavily and sat up. She embraced Ma Chin, lightly gnawing at her neck. Impatiently, Ma Chin wrung herself free and laughingly remonstrated, 'What's this, you nymphomaniac! But Sister Yueh, how's the "fighting spirit" of the little sisters in your factory? All right? Here in Chapei the girls are firm enough. This morning, when they heard that part of the girls in your factory had returned to work, they automatically tried to break into your factory. If only the little sisters in your factory had been firmer, the general strike would be able to go on. But you have now unconditionally gone back to work. This is bad! If this time we should fail we shall never be able to strike successfully again!'

'But this strike is not over yet, Ma Chin! I suggest that we try our damn best tonight to organize the girls. Tomorrow, we shall again try to break into the factories,' said Tsai Cheng. 'We shall throw everything we have into it. If we fail it will be a glorious defeat! Ma Chin, after due consideration, I believe we shall go back to what I suggested in the first place: don't be afraid of sacrifice, be prepared for glorious defeat!'

She ran to Chen Yueh-o and embraced her and put her cheek against hers. Chen Yueh-o blushed, twisting her body in embarrassment. Tsai Cheng laughed hysterically, and throwing herself on to the bed shook the bed so furiously that it creaked.

'Quiet, Tsai! . . . Glorious defeat, indeed!'

Cursing softly, Ma Chin went to sit opposite Chen Yueh-o by the table and asked about the details of the situation in her factory. But they had exchanged only a few words when two men came in together. The one walking in front sat himself down abruptly by the table, took out a watch, glanced at it, and began to rap out orders:

'It's already half-past seven! Hurry, hurry! Ma Chin, stop talking!

Tsai Cheng, get up! You are not showing the right spirit at all!'

'Old Ke, you are late, too! Hurry, Ma Chin! Sister Yueh! I have to go to Hung-kou at half-past eight!'

So saying, Tsai Cheng jumped up from the bed and sat down beside Ke Tso-fu. Ke was not yet thirty years old, a bit taller than Tsai Cheng. His pale, thin face was not particularly distinguished, except that his two firmly clamped lips showed that he was wilful. The other youth was somewhat fatter than Ke. He had a pair of lively eyes, around which were lines of fatigue. He smiled at Ma Chin and sat down beside her.

The atmosphere in the room suddenly became tense. With the weak yellow lamp shining over them, Ko Tso-fu first said to the young man:

'Su Lun, your work is awful! This afternoon at the meeting of the activists in the factory your leadership was wrong! You could not take the revolutionary emotions of the masses and bring the struggle from one stage to the next, expanding its scope all the time! Your leadership was tainted with right-wing sentiments, holding your work to the *status quo*. You have become the tail of the masses. Now that the strike at the silk factories has reached a critical stage you must overcome this "tailism"! Ma Chin, your report on the work at Chapei!'

'Hurry up, make it snappy. I have to leave at half-past eight!' Tsai Cheng urged, drumming the table with a pencil.

Ma Chin spoke calmly for five minutes. She raised an important point: 'More than half the progressive elements among the women workers in the factory had been lost owing to the harsher measures adopted by the employers. Their support from the masses is therefore weaker.' Ke Tso-fu listened impatiently. He glanced at Ma Chin several times and then at his watch. His two thin lips became more tightly closed.

'I am against Ma Chin's conclusion! New progressive elements will be forged and brought forth in struggles, the support of the masses should also be strengthened in struggles. This psychosis of fear is also an expression of tailism!' Tsai Cheng said hurriedly, shooting a glance at Su Lun, sitting opposite her. Now, she was insisting on what she considered her first suggestion. For the placid Ke Tso-fu had started out by criticizing rightists and tailism, and she had always felt whatever Ke said was right.

Ke Tso-fu did not speak. His lips were even more tightly shut. As a rule, he was the one to pronounce conclusions and make decisions.

Su Lun, who had received a glance from Tsai Cheng, was in sympathy with what Ma Chin said. Naturally, he could not admit his tailism and he said suavely, 'What Tsai Cheng talked about is theory, while Ma Chin was talking about facts. We should not ignore reality. Old Ke said that I made mistakes in the meeting of activists this afternoon. Perhaps I did. But the meeting was not properly organized. Only half the activists showed up. Their reports were not realistic, or to the point. And they expressed themselves in a most chaotic fashion. This fully exposed the poor ability of our cadres of lower echelons and it was a hopeless task trying to lead them! If I committed the error of tailism, then every lower echelon cadre is guilty of the same thing! Tsai Cheng and Ma Chin, who are directly responsible for the strike, have also become the tail of the lower cadres!'

'Why am I also a tail. . . .'

'Let's stop this nonsense and quickly decide on the steps to be taken in our work. Sister Yueh has something to say!'

Ma Chin stopped Tsai Cheng and Su Lun from arguing and drew Ke Tso-fu's attention to Chen Yueh-o. Ke Tso-fu turned his head slightly toward Chen Yueh-o, his eyes large and expectant.

'What shall we do? Please tell me quickly. The two other comrades in our factory have been arrested and there's only me left. The girls went back to work today because they were forced to. If we could propose a sound arrangement we can get them to go on strike again tomorrow! But please tell me quickly what we should do!'

Chen Yueh-o was anxious and excited. She had difficulty in understanding the jargon Ke Tso-fu and Su Lun used and could not find appropriate words to express her ideas. She felt what Ma Chin said was right, since Ho Hsin-mei and Chang Ah-hsin were arrested, wasn't it true that with only herself left their strength was weakened? But she didn't dare express her disagreement with what Tsai Cheng said, which she vaguely understood to be the gospel of the Revolution. After she had expressed herself with difficulty she turned to look anxiously and expectantly at Ke Tso-fu.

Ke Tso-fu's plain, thin face suddenly looked grim. He glanced once again at his watch and said, 'You must mobilize every resource, work harder tonight to heighten the fighting spirit of the masses.

Tomorrow the workers must not go back to work. Especially in Yu Hua Factory where you must get the workers to go on strike again! You must overcome every difficulty to bring about the strike again! Your slogan to the masses should be: Oppose the use of hooligans by the Capitalists! Oppose the arrest of workers by the Capitalists!'

In the momentary silence which followed there came into the room the sound of a dumpling pedlar striking his hollow bamboo section in the alley, and the cries of a baby in the neighbourhood. The yellow light of the 15-watt electric light shone weakly overhead and finally Ma Chin said calmly, 'Almost all our supporters in Yu Hua Factory have been arrested and the masses are now under strict surveillance. Before we reorganize our organization we cannot risk having another strike!'

'What? Reorganize? It is now the critical moment of the general strike. There is simply no time for you to reorganize. Tonight you must reorganize, recruit new activists and start your offensive!'

'It is impossible to do all this in one night! Our organization has been completely destroyed. Our enemies are keeping a tight watch— this is a gamble! Even if we manage to start a strike it will immediately be crushed, and what is left of our work will be entirely wiped out!'

Ma Chin was adamant, her black eyes glared at the others. Ke Tso-fu was silent, his lips were tightly pressed together. He appeared to be just as firm in his opinion as Ma Chin. It seemed that they had reached deadlock. Tsai Cheng let out a sudden cry, but didn't say anything. Her 'second suggestion', which had been pushed to the back of her mind, was now struggling with her 'first suggestion', which she preferred. She bit her lips undecidedly while Chen Yueh-o waited anxiously. Then Su Lun tried to bring them round.

'Ma Chin, tell us your ideas.'

'I believe that we should make slight changes in our stand about the general strike. Those factories which can go on with the strike should naturally fight on. Others which have suffered great losses must not risk it again, but must have a breathing space. We should rapidly re-group ourselves, develop our organization and preserve our strength, so that when the time comes we can again . . .'

Without waiting for her to finish Ke Tso-fu severely reprimanded her: 'You are in fact saying we should stop the general strike! To retreat at the critical stage of the high tide of Revolution is cowardly! Yours is a rightist idea!'

'Exactly! You want to break up the front of the general strike, while at the same time you want other factories to go on with the strike. This is self-contradictory!' Tsai Cheng said hurriedly. Now in her mind it was again her 'first suggestion' which had won over. Ma Chin suddenly looked flustered. She was nevertheless unmoved.

'Why should it be contradictory? It can be done. To gamble is to commit suicide!'

'If there is a good way of doing things our factory can go on strike again tomorrow. But there are now so few of us and the masses are afraid of persecution. Were we to depend on the same method of two days ago we could hope to start another strike! The most important thing is to devise a new approach!' said Chen Yueh-o, looking at Ma Chin. She was able to express her ideas in such a manner only with great effort, but Ke Tso-fu and Tsai Cheng did not pay any attention to her. Su Lun agreed with Ma Chin and realized what Chen Yueh-o wanted to say, so he tried again to reconcile the different opinions expressed:

'Sister Yueh's opinion is based on facts! She wants a new approach which means a change of tactics. Am I right? I suggest that since our cell in Yu Hua Factory has been undermined we must try to re-organize. If one night is not enough let's give it another day. We will strike two days from now. Thus, we shall keep the battle-line of the general strike intact!'

'No! If we cannot expand the scope of the struggle tomorrow the general strike will fail! If Yu Hua Factory were to start working tomorrow the working masses would vacillate!' Tsai Cheng said vehemently.

Unable to contain herself any longer Ma Chin reacted acrimoniously. 'If this is the case then the time for the general strike was not ripe! It was an impetuous action, a gamble!'

At this Ke Tso-fu boiled with rage. He pounded on the table and ordered sternly, 'Ma Chin! You are criticizing the General Line of the Party! Your rightist mistake is most serious! The Party wants to eliminate such rightist opinion resolutely! If the workers of Yu Hua Factory are not made to strike tomorrow it will mean that the general strike will have been sabotaged and the General Line been disobeyed. The Party will have to award severe punishment.'

'But what if this will send our comrades into the hands of the enemy?'

Ma Chin remained adamant. Her face was all red, but her lips pale. Ke Tso-fu shouted angrily, pounding on the table, 'I warn you, Ma Chin! The Party exercises iron discipline! No one is allowed to disobey orders! Go immediately with Sister Yueh to prepare for tomorrow's struggle! No matter what the sacrifice will be, go and do it! This is an order!'

Ma Chin lowered her head and was silent. Ke Tso-fu glared angrily at her and turned abruptly to talk to Tsai Cheng and Su Lun. 'Intensify your work in Hong-kew, Tsai Cheng! Resolutely carry out the orders and eliminate all rightist opinions! Su Lun, tell the girls the important resolutions on the general strike just passed by the General Union of Silk Workers.'

Having said this, Ke Tso-fu again looked at his watch, stood up and left.

3. *MODERN CHINESE DRAMA*

Modern Chinese drama as such means plays written in the western style. This is because the leaders of the Literary Revolution found it difficult to write traditional Chinese operatic verses in the vernacular which they were anxious to propagate. Also, as these leaders were fired with the desire for reform, they found it easier to follow the examples set by western playwrights. So it was natural that Ibsen and Bernard Shaw, the reformers, were the first playwrights to be introduced to China.

But it was not until 1921, when Hung Shen returned from America and joined the Drama Association, that China could claim to have started her own dramatic movement. For it was then that the theories and practical production methods of the stage received attention. The next year Tien Han, another prominent figure in the development of modern Chinese drama, founded the Nan-kuo Society.

These two groups produced many plays, and Tien Han and Hung Shen both wrote plays about the problems of war, women, marriage and poverty. Other playwrights, including Ouyang Yu-ching and Kuo Mo-jo, wrote historical plays. Apart from Ting Hsi-lin, who wrote mostly one-act humorous plays, all the playwrights tended to use the stage as a pulpit. This can perhaps be traced back to the Chinese tradition of using operas to convey a lesson or a moral, but it is difficult to say whether this was in fact the reason.

In 1927 Tien Han founded the Shanghai University of Arts, in which there was a Department of Drama. Although the University proved to be short-lived, there has been since then an institute for the study of the dramatic arts. The consciousness of the importance of the dramatic arts led to the founding of the first professional drama troupe, the China Travelling Drama Company, in 1934. This culminated in the establishment of the National School of Dramatic Arts in Nanking in 1935.

The year 1934 saw also the publication of Tsao Yu's *Thunderstorm* and its production the following year on the stage by the Fu Tan Drama Society upon the recommendation of Hung Shen. Directed by Ouyang Yu-ching, the production was a great success, and very probably *Thunderstorm* has become the most frequently produced modern Chinese play. Tsao Yu went on to write *Sunrise*, *The Wilderness*, *Metamorphosis*, *Peking Man* and *The Family*, among other plays, and his position as one of the leading Chinese playwrights was firmly established.

But the playwrights who contributed most to the development of modern Chinese drama were perhaps Tien Han, Hung Shen and Ouyang Yu-ching. Apart from their being the first to participate in the production of new plays, to organize dramatic troupes and schools, Tien Han and Hung Shen were probably the most prolific playwrights. Tien's plays reflect the changes in the thinking of the Chinese intellectuals, from his earliest sentimental and romantic *One Night at a Café* and other plays written in the 1920s to the patriotic *Huei Chun Chih Chu* (*The Song of Recovery*) and other plays in the 1930s to his play of disillusion, *Song of Autumn Noises*, and new operas, including *Songs of the Kiang-han Fishermen*, in the 1940s. Hung Shen wrote plays on many different subjects. His *Wu-Kuei Bridge*, *Flavourful Rice* and *Green Dragon Pool* represent his most ambitious attempts at depicting village life: how the powerful gentry dominated the lives of the peasants, how the peasants suffered even when the harvest was good and how education alone could not help solve the problems of the peasants. His *Pao Te-hsin* deals with the problem of conscription during the war, and was the first play to be written in the Szechuan dialect. Ouyang Yu-ching's contribution lay primarily in promoting new operas, although his long association with modern drama and his historical plays are worthy of note.

It was during the Sino-Japanese War that modern Chinese drama matured. Not only were lighting and design improved, but playwrights produced plays on many themes. Apart from those already mentioned there were Chen Pai-chen, who wrote *Spring Returns to the Earth*; Yuan Chun, who wrote *The Model Teacher of All Times*; Shen Fu, who wrote *Twenty-four Hours in Chungking*; Yu Ling, who wrote *A Walk in the Long Night*; Hsia Yen, who wrote *The Fascist Bacillus*; Wu Tsu-kuang, who wrote *Wen Tien-hsiang*; Lao Sheh, who wrote *The Problem of Face*; and Sung Tse-ti, who wrote *The Motherland is Calling*.

On the whole, however, plays remained the entertainment of the educated people of the cities, while efforts at modernizing traditional opera have not yet produced good results.

I would like to introduce the reader to a short scene from Tsao Yu's *Thunderstorm*. This play has four acts with a prologue and an epilogue. It depicts a day in the life of the Chao family, which consists of Chao Po-yuan, director of a coal mine, his wife Huan-yi, his elder son Ping, borne out of wedlock by Sze-ping, who had an affair with Po-yuan while working as a maid in the Chao household and who was thought to have committed suicide twenty-seven years ago, and his second son Tsung. Other characters are Lu Kwei, a family servant, Phoenix his daughter, also a maid in the household, his wife Lu Sze-ping, and Lu Ta-hai. Lu Ta-hai is Sze-ping's and Po-yuan's second son, whom Sze-ping took with her when she was banished from the family.

The play opens with Ping's impending departure for his father's coal mine to get away from his stepmother, with whom he had had an affair two years before. He has been tormented by this, because he is now in love with Phoenix and feels guilty towards his father. Huan-yi, jealous of Phoenix, has arranged for Mrs Lu to visit her and take Phoenix away. Her father Lu Kwei, on the other hand, approves of Phoenix and Ping's romance because of the money he hopes to get out of it, and having found out about her affair with Ping, is confident he can dissuade Huan-yi from getting rid of Phoenix. Tsung is also in love with Phoenix, but his love is not of a possessive kind. Po-yuan knows nothing of his two sons' love-affairs, neither, of course, does Mrs Lu, who is unaware that the head of the Chao family is the father of her two sons. Lu Ta-hai, who has come as the workers' representative to see his employer, is also ignorant of the fact that the owner of the coal mine is actually his father.

On a humid day, with a thunderstorm brewing, these characters meet in the Chao home. Ping, evading Huan-yi's efforts to stop him leaving, seeks comfort from Phoenix, who is torn between her love for Ping and for her mother. Mrs Lu decides to take Phoenix away and Po-yuan, satisfied that his former mistress will not make trouble for him, tries to give her money to quieten his still active conscience, but Mrs Lu refuses, asking only to see Ping once again for the last time. Unhappily when he comes in she is forced to witness her two sons fighting one another and decides to leave at once with Phoenix. Phoenix's father is relieved of his job but, unaware of the relationship between his wife and Po-yuan, he still thinks he can benefit from Ping's love for Phoenix and goes back to blackmail Huan-yi into re-employing them both. Lu Ta-hai, who has found out that Ping has slept with Phoenix, threatens to kill him—not knowing that Ping is his brother—if he does not marry the girl, believing that this is his mother's wish also. Ping promises to marry Phoenix and later agrees to go away with her immediately. Here is the *dénouement* of the play.

(*Phoenix drags Ping to the centre door. The door opens. Mrs Lu comes in with Lu Ta-hai.*

Within two hours Mrs Lu has become a different person. Her voice has become hoarse through shouting and crying, her eyelids droop, wrinkles mark her forehead and her movements are slow and deliberate after having suffered tense emotions. She has become the epitome of suffering. Her clothes are partially dried after being soaked in the rain. Her temples are covered with matted and dishevelled hair. She is trembling and walks slowly into the room.)

PHOENIX (*frightened*): Mama!

MRS LU (*stretching her hands out painfully to her daughter*): Come, Phoenix!

(*Phoenix runs to her mother and kneels down*)

PHOENIX: Mama! (*She hugs her mother's knees.*)

MRS LU (*caresses her daughter's head and says with pain*): My child, my poor child!

PHOENIX (*sobs*): Mama, forgive me! Forgive me! I've disobeyed you.

Mrs Lu (*helps her up*): Why didn't you tell me?

Phoenix (*lowering her head*): I love you, Mama. I was afraid. . . . I didn't want to make you unhappy in any way or make you look down upon me—I dared not tell you.

Mrs Lu (*in anguish*): It was all because of my blindness to the facts. I should have known. But God! Who would have thought that such a thing could have happened, and happened to my children! It is because of you that your mother has suffered this fate!

Ta-hai (*with restraint*): Mama, let's go. Phoenix will come back with us first—I have arranged with him (*pointing to Ping*). He will leave for the mine first and then come back for her.

Mrs Lu (*confused*): Who says so? Who says so?

Ta-hai (*looking coldly at Mrs Lu*): Mama, I know what you want and will do accordingly. So I shall not talk about the Chao family and have nothing more to do with them.

Mrs Lu (*confused, she sits down*): What, leave them be?

Ping (*hesitating*): Mrs Lu, please believe me. I will treat her well. We have decided to leave right away.

Mrs Lu (*taking Phoenix's hands, trembling*): Phoenix, you—you are leaving with him!

Phoenix (*bowing and pressing hard her mother's hands*): Ma, I will have to leave you for the time being.

Mrs Lu (*cannot stop herself*): You two cannot be together!

Ta-hai (*surprised*): Ma, what are you talking about?

Mrs Lu (*standing up*): No! No!

Phoenix (*anxiously*): Ma!

Mrs Lu (*ignoring Phoenix while grabbing her hand*): Let's leave. (*Turns to Ta-hai*) Go and call a rickshaw. Phoenix may not be able to walk. Let's go. Hurry!

Phoenix (*desperately tries to break away*): Ma, you can't do this.

Mrs Lu (*woodenly and mechanically*): Come, come.

Phoenix (*imploringly*): Ma, do you want to see your daughter die of agony before your eyes?

Ping (*walking towards Mrs Lu*): Mrs Lu, I know I've done you wrong, but I can try to mend my ways. Now that the situation is like this, you—

TA-HAI: Ma, this time, I—I can't understand you!

MRS LU: Phoenix, you listen to me. I would rather that you no longer exist than let you go away with him—let's go.
(*When Ta-hai walks to the door Phoenix lets out a wail*)

PHOENIX (*wailing*): Oh, Mama, Mama! (*she faints and falls towards her mother*).

MRS LU (*holding her*): My child, you—

PING (*anxiously*): She has fainted.
(*Mrs Lu feels Phoenix's forehead, calls softly to her and sobs. Ping runs towards the dining-room*)

TA-HAI: You don't have to go. It's not serious. Just give her some water. She has been like that ever since she was a child.
(*Ping sprinkles water on Phoenix's face. She slowly comes to, her face deadly pale*)

MRS LU (*forces some water into Phoenix's mouth*): My good child. You come back, you just come back—my ill-fated child.

PHOENIX (*her mouth and eyes slowly open, and she draws a breath*): Oh, Mama!

MRS LU (*confused*): My child, don't blame your mother for her hard-heartedness. She can't even begin to talk about her misery.

PHOENIX (*heaving a sigh*): Ma!

MRS LU: What, my child?

PHOENIX: I, I can't tell you, Ping!

PING: Phoenix, are you feeling better?

PHOENIX: Ping, I've kept it from you. I didn't want to tell you.
(*Turning toward her mother and looking at her imploringly*) Mama, you—

MRS LU: What, my child, tell me quickly.

PHOENIX (*sobbing*): I, I . . . (*boldly*) am already carrying . . . (*she cries*)

MRS LU (*anxiously*): What, you said you are . . . (*she is stunned*).

PING (*taking Phoenix's hand*): Phoenix! What, really, you. . . .

PHOENIX (*cries*): Yes.

PING: Since when? Since when?

PHOENIX (*lowering her head*): About three months.

PING (*happily*): Oh, Phoenix. Why didn't you tell me, my . . .

MRS LU (*murmurs*): My God!

PING (*goes over to her*): Mrs Lu, you must not be stubborn any longer. It was all my fault. I beg of you! (*He kneels down*) Please let her go. I can assure you that I will try to be worthy of her, and you.

PHOENIX (*stands up and walking to her mother kneels down*): Mama, have pity on us, give us your approval and let us go.

MRS LU (*sitting down, dazed*): I'm in a dream. My daughter, my own children, in thirty years—Oh, heavens above! (*she covers her face with her hands, crying, and then gestures for them to leave*) Go away. I don't know who you are. (*She turns away from them.*)

PING: Thank you. (*He stands up*) Let's go, Phoenix.
(*Phoenix stands*)

MRS LU (*she turns around and says involuntarily*): No! You cannot go!
(*Phoenix kneels again*)

PHOENIX (*pleading*): Mama, why are you like this? My mind is made up. I don't care whether he is rich or poor, or if he is anybody—I am his. He is the first man to whom I promised myself, and I don't care about any other man. Ma, now that I am in such a condition I'll have to go where he goes and become what he is. Mama, don't you understand, I . . .

MRS LU (*gestures for her to stop and says in agony*): My child.

TA-HAI: Mama, since younger sister is already this way you might as well let her go.

PING (*darkly*): Mrs Lu, if you won't let her go we'll have to disobey you and go anyway. Phoenix!

PHOENIX (*shaking her head*): Ping! (*She is still looking at her mother*) Mama!

MRS LU (*deeply grieved, speaking softly*): Oh, God knows who is the offender, who is the cause of this. They are my pitiful children, not knowing what they have done. Heavens above! If anyone is to be punished it is me. I am the offender—it was I who went astray. (*Heart-broken*) Now, I understand. I understand what is done is done, and it is no use blaming the unjust gods. When one has committed a sin this will unavoidably be followed by another. (*Caressing Phoenix's head*) They are my innocent children. They should live well and be happy. Only I know of the sin, and I alone should bear the cross. Who knows, their happiness might not be sinful? They are young, they did not mean to commit a sin. (*She stands, raising her head to the sky*) Tonight, it is I who let them go away together. I know this is wrong, but I, it is I, who am responsible. I have caused all this. My children are good and innocent. Oh, God! If there is to be punishment, mete it out to me! (*Turns her head*) Phoenix. . . .

PHOENIX: Ma . . . what is the matter? I don't know what you are talking about.

MRS LU (*turns around, speaks kindly*): Never mind. (*She smiles*) Get up, Phoenix. You may leave together.

PHOENIX (*gets up, and deeply moved, embraces her mother*): Mama!

PING (*quietly*): Hurry, there are only twenty-five minutes left. Call for the car. Come on, let's go.

MRS LU (*quietly*): No, this time you are slipping away. You must not bother the others. (*She turns to Ta-hai*) Go out and get a car. I want to go home. You go to the railway station with them.

TA-HAI: Yes.

(*Ta-hai exits through the middle door*)

MRS LU (*speaking sadly and softly to Phoenix*): Come, my child, let me hold you for a while. (*Phoenix comes and embraces her mother. Mrs Lu turns to Ping*) You come, too, let me have a look at you. (*Ping comes over, his head bowed. Mrs Lu stares at him and wipes away her tears*) All right! You may go now—I want you two to promise me one thing before you leave.

PING: Please tell us.

MRS LU: If you don't promise me I will not let Phoenix go.

PHOENIX: Tell us, Ma. I promise.

MRS LU (*looking at them*): You two must go far away from here, the farther the better, and never return. After today, whatever may happen to us, you must not come to see me.

PHOENIX (*greatly distressed*): But Ma . . .

PING (*catches Phoenix's eyes and whispers to her*): She says this because she is upset. Later on she will change her mind.

PHOENIX: Well, all right. . . . Ma, let's go.
(*She kneels down and kowtows, while weeping, to her mother. Mrs Lu fights to restrain herself*)

MRS LU (*waves her hand*): Let's go.

PING: Let's go out through the dining-room. I have a few things there.
(*When they are near the dining-room the dining-room door opens and Huan-yi walks out. They are surprised*)

PHOENIX (*can't help herself*): Tai-tai!

HUAN-YI (*gravely*): Where are you going? It's still thundering outside!

PING (*to Huan-yi*): Why, you hid yourself in there and eavesdropped on us!

HUAN-YI: Yes, not only me, there's someone else. (*Turns and calls toward the dining-room*) Come out, you!
(*Tsung comes out timidly*)

PHOENIX (*surprised*): Second Young Master!

TSUNG (*uneasily*): Phoenix!

PING (*displeased with his younger brother*): Tsung, how could you be so inconsiderate!

TSUNG (*amazed*): Ma asked me to come! I didn't know what you were supposed to be doing.

HUAN-YI: Now you know.

PING (*harassed*): What are you trying to do?

HUAN-YI (*sarcastically*): I only asked your younger brother to say good-bye to you.

PING (*angrily*): You are really a . . .

TSUNG: Elder brother!

PING: I am sorry, Tsung! (*Suddenly he turns to Huan-yi*) But there is no mother like you in the whole world!

TSUNG (*perplexed*): Ma, what is this?

HUAN-YI: See for yourself! (*She turns to Phoenix*) Phoenix, where are you going?

PHOENIX (*hesitating*): I . . . I . . .

PING: Don't lie. Tell them, openly and proudly, that we are going away together.

TSUNG (*understands*): What, Phoenix, are you going away with him?

PHOENIX: Yes, Second Young Master, I, I'm . . .

TSUNG (*demanding*): Why didn't you tell me?

PHOENIX: It wasn't that I didn't want to tell you; I have told you not to see me again, because I . . . I'm not a nice girl.

PING: No, why say you are not a nice girl? Tell them (*pointing at Huan-yi*), tell them that you are going to marry me!

TSUNG (*somewhat surprised*): Phoenix, you . . .

HUAN-YI: Now, you know. (*Tsung lowers his head*)

PING (*flares up and accuses*): You are heartless! Do you think your son would take revenge—would want to come between Phoenix and me? Tsung, whatever you have to say, say it! I'll forgive you. (*Tsung looks at Huan-yi, at Phoenix, and then lowers his head*)

HUAN-YI: Tsung, say it! (*She stops for a while, and adds hurriedly*) Tsung, why aren't you saying anything? Why don't you ask Phoenix? Why don't you ask your elder brother? (*She pauses again. Everyone is looking at Tsung, but Tsung remains speechless*) Say something, Tsung! Why, are you deaf? Dumb? Stupid? When you see your sweetheart being taken away from you, don't you feel anything?

TSUNG (*looks up and like a lamb says*): No, no, Ma! (*He looks at Phoenix and lowers his head*) If Phoenix is willing I have nothing to say.

PING (*walks over to Tsung and holds his hand*): Oh, my good brother, my understanding brother!

TSUNG (*wondering, trying to think*): No, no, I suddenly discover . . . I feel . . . as if I don't really love Phoenix. (*Emptily*) I . . . I was only fooling myself!

PING (*grateful*): But, Tsung . . .

TSUNG (*Ping's demonstrativeness makes him quiet*): No, take her away, only be good to her.

HUAN-YI (*her hope entirely vanished*): Oh, you! (*Suddenly furious*) You are not my son! You are not like me—you are a dead swine!

TSUNG (*humiliated*): Ma!

PING (*shocked*): What are you trying to do?

HUAN-YI (*dazed*): You don't act like a man. If I were you I would strike her! You are a clot, a lifeless clot. You are your father's little lamb. Now I know—you are not mine, you are not my son.

PING (*indignant*): Aren't you his mother? To talk about him like this!

HUAN-YI (*painfully*): Ping, you may tell, you may tell all; I am not afraid, you tell them that I am no longer his mother!

TSUNG (*woefully*): Ma, why are you like this?

HUAN-YI (*drops all restraint*): When I asked him to come I had forgotten all about myself. (*She turns to Tsung hysterically*) Don't think that I am your mother. (*Raising her voice*) Your mother has died long ago, died of your father's oppression and of loneliness. I am not your mother, but a woman who has come back to life after meeting Chao Ping. (*Throws every consideration overboard*) She, too, wants to have a man to love her, wants to live fully!

TSUNG (*grieved*): Oh, Mama!

PING (*catches Tsung's eye*): She's sick. (*He turns to Huan-yi*) Come, let's go upstairs. You need a rest.

HUAN-YI: Nonsense! I am not sick, I'm not sick, I'm not mentally sick! Don't ever think that I'm talking nonsense. (*She wipes away her tears and speaks distressfully*) I have suffered for many years. For eighteen years I have been living in Hell, in this prison, cesspool of a family. But my heart is not dead. Your father could only make me give birth to Tsung; my heart, and my whole being, remained my own. (*She points to Ping*) Only he wanted everything that I was. But he doesn't want me now, he no longer wants me.

TSUNG (*heart-broken*): Ma, my dearest Mama! What is all this?

PING: Don't pay any attention to her, she is mad!

HUAN-YI (*fiercely*): Don't imitate your father! Not mad—I am not mad! I want you to tell, I want you to tell them—this is my last revenge.

PING (*heartlessly*): What do you want to say? I think you'd better go upstairs to sleep.

HUAN-YI (*laughs coldly*): Don't pretend. Tell them that I am not your stepmother.

(*Everyone is taken aback. There is momentary silence*)

TSUNG (*helplessly*): Ma!

HUAN-YI (*heedless*): Tell them, tell Phoenix. Tell her.

PHOENIX (*cannot stand it*): Mama! (*she throws herself at her mother*).

PING (*looks at Tsung and then turns to Huan-yi*): What is this for? Why talk about things past? You are making Tsung miserable.

HUAN-YI (*shouts*): I have no child, I have no husband, I have no family, I have nothing. I only want you to say that I—I am yours.

PING (*harassed*): Oh, younger brother! Look how pitiful he is, if you have any trace of pity left in you . . .

HUAN-YI (*revengeful*): Now, you have learned to act like your father, you hypocrite! Remember, it is you who have cheated your brother, me and your father!

PING (*angrily*): Rubbish! I have not cheated him! Father is a good man, he has led a morally upright life! (*Huan-yi laughs coldly at this, and Ping turns to Phoenix*) Don't pay any attention to her, she is mad. Let's go!

HUAN-YI: Don't go. You can't go out anyway, I've locked the front door. Your father is coming right away, I have sent someone to ask him to come.

MRS LU: No, *Tai-tai*!

PING: What are you trying to do?

HUAN-YI (*coldly*): I just want your father to see his future daughter-in-law before you leave. (*She calls*) Po-yuan, Po-yuan!

TSUNG: Ma, please don't!

PING (*walks over to Huan-yi*): Mad woman, if you dare to call for him again!
(*Huan-yi runs to the door of the study and calls again*)

MRS LU (*frightened*): Phoenix, let's go.

HUAN-YI: No, he's coming!
(*Po-yuan enters through the door of the study. Everyone is immobile. A silence, like death, descends*)

PO-YUAN (*at the door*): What is all the shouting? Why aren't you upstairs sleeping?

HUAN-YI (*haughtily*): I want you to meet your good relatives.

PO-YUAN (*sees Mrs Lu and Phoenix, is surprised*): Oh, you, you, what are you doing here?

HUAN-YI (*drags Phoenix over to Po-yuan*): Meet your daughter-in-law. (*Pointing at Po-yuan, she speaks to Phoenix*) Call him father! (*She then points to Mrs Lu and says to Po-yuan*) You, too, should meet this old lady.

MRS LU: *Tai-tai!*

HUAN-YI: Ping, come over here. Come and kowtow to this your mother, in front of your father.

PING (*embarrassed*): Father, I, I . . .

PO-YUAN (*as if he understood*): What . . . (*To Mrs Lu*) Sze-ping, you have come back after all.

HUAN-YI (*taken aback*): What?

MRS LU (*frightened*): No, no, you are wrong.

PO-YUAN (*repentant*): Sze-ping, I thought you would come back.

MRS LU: No, no! Oh, my God!

HUAN-YI (*greatly surprised*): Sze-ping? What, is she Sze-ping?

PO-YUAN: Yes. (*Annoyed*) Huan, don't ask me this again. She is Ping's mother whom I thought dead thirty years ago.

HUAN-YI: Heavens, no!

(*After a moment Phoenix groans and looks at her mother, who, heart-broken, stares at the floor. Ping, his mind in a turmoil, looks confusedly at his father and Mrs Lu.*) *In the meantime Huan-yi suddenly becomes aware of a more tragic life than her own and turns more sympathetically towards Ping. She is sorry she acted so badly before, and quickly regains the normal feelings of a mother, looking remorsefully at her son.*

PO-YUAN (*grimly*): Ping, come here. Your mother has not died. She is still alive.

PING (*half out of his mind*): Not her! Father, please tell me it's not her!

PO-YUAN (*severely*): Blast it! Ping, don't talk nonsense! She may not have come from a wealthy family, but she is nevertheless your mother.

PING: Oh, Father!

PO-YUAN: Having the same mother as Phoenix may be embarrassing, but you must not lack respect for your mother because of it.

PHOENIX: Oh, Mama!

PO-YUAN: Ping, forgive me. All my life I've committed only this one grave error. I never thought that she would be still alive, and that she would come here today. I think this must be fate. (*He turns to Mrs Lu and sighs*) I am now an old man. I was full of remorse after I told you to leave, and prepared to send you twenty thousand dollars. Now that you are here I think that Ping, being a dutiful son, will look after you well. What I have done wrong he will make up to you.

PING (*turns to Mrs Lu*): You—you are my . . .

MRS LU (*involuntarily*): Ping . . . (*she sobs*).

PO-YUAN: Kneel down, Ping. Don't think that you are dreaming. She is your mother.

PHOENIX (*her mind deranged*): Ma, this cannot be true.
(*Mrs Lu sobs*)

HUAN-YI: Ping, I never thought that it was—like this, Ping. . . .

PING (*laughs insanely*): Father! (*He turns to Mrs Lu, still laughing*) Mother! (*He looks at Phoenix, pointing at her*) You . . .

PHOENIX (*she and Ping stare at each other and laugh. Suddenly, it becomes more than she can bear*): Oh, Heavens above! (*She runs out through the door in the centre. Ping throws himself on a sofa and Mrs Lu stands still, lifeless.*)

HUAN-YI (*calls out hurriedly*): Phoenix, Phoenix! (*She turns to Tsung*) I don't like the look of her. Quickly, go after her.
(*Tsung runs out through the centre door, calling Phoenix's name*)

PO-YUAN (*comes over to Ping*): Ping, what is this?

PING (*bursts out*): Father, you shouldn't have brought me into this world!
(*He exits through the dining-room door. From afar come Phoenix's cries, and Tsung's desperate shouts for Phoenix and then his cries*)

MRS LU *and* HUAN-YI: Phoenix, Phoenix! What happened? Tsung, my son. Oh, my son!
(*Together they run out through the central door*)

PO-YUAN (*walks hurriedly over to the window, draws back the curtain and asks in a trembling voice*): What happened? What happened?
(*A servant enters through the central door*)

SERVANT (*panting*): Master!

PO-YUAN: Quickly, what has happened?

SERVANT (*catching his breath*): Phoenix is dead.

PO-YUAN: What about Second Young Master?

SERVANT: Also ... also dead.

PO-YUAN (*trembling*): No, no ... how?

SERVANT: Phoenix stumbled on to the faulty electric cable, and Second Young Master didn't know it. He tried to help her up and they were both electrocuted.

PO-YUAN (*almost fainting*): No, this couldn't—this cannot have happened.

(*Po-yuan runs out with the servant. Ping comes out from the dining-room. He is deadly pale, but composed. He walks to the desk in which Lu Ta-hai has left his pistol. He opens the drawer, takes it out, and with his hand slightly shaking, walks slowly into the study on the right-hand side. Outside, there is a tumultuous sea of voices, cries and screaming. Mrs Lu comes back through the centre door, her expression stony. An old woman servant follows her, holding a flash-light.*)

OLD WOMAN (*comfortingly*): Old Lady, don't just stand there. This won't do. You cry, you need a good cry!

MRS LU (*spiritlessly*): I can't cry!

OLD WOMAN: This is God's will, nothing can be done about it ... but you must cry.

MRS LU: No, I just want to be left alone. (*She stands there dumbly*)
(*The centre door is pushed wide open. Many servants crowd around Huan-yi. It is difficult to tell if she is crying or laughing*)

SERVANT (*speaking outside the house*): Go in, *Tai-tai*, don't look now.

HUAN-YI (*she is half pushed and half carried in through the centre door, where she leans on the door and laughs strangely*): Tsung, why do you open your mouth as if you were laughing at me? Oh, my boy, you silly boy.

PO-YUAN (*comes to the middle of the centre door, his face tear-stained*): Huan-yi, come in! My hands are numb, please don't look at him any longer.

OLD SERVANT: *Tai-tai*, come in. He is scorched, and there is nothing we can do for him.

HUAN-YI (*comes in, moans*): Tsung, my good boy. A moment ago you were all right. Why should you have died, and so pitifully? (*She stands there transfixed*)

PO-YUAN (*having come in*): You should rest. (*He wipes away his tears*)

HUAN-YI (*laughs hysterically*): Tsung, you should die, die! Having such a mother, you should die!
(*There come the sounds of a scuffle*)

PO-YUAN: What is that? Fighting at this time?
(*The old woman servant goes out to see. In a moment another servant comes in*)

PO-YUAN: What's going on outside?

SERVANT: Lu Ta-hai, that fellow who came this morning has come back. We tried to stop him from coming in.

PO-YUAN: Tell him to come in!

SERVANT: Master, he has run away through the side-door after he kicked and struck several of us down.

PO-YUAN: Run away?

SERVANT: Yes, sir.
(*The servants exit. There are only Po-yuan, Mrs Lu and Huan-yi left*)

PO-YUAN (*sadly*): I've lost a son. I can't afford to lose another.
(*They all sit down*)

MRS LU: You might as well let him go. I know that he hates you, he won't come back to see you.

PO-YUAN (*quietly, feeling surprised*): That the young ones should die before us, and leave us, the old. . . . (*Suddenly*) Where is Ping? Where is the elder Young Master? Ping? Ping? (*No one answers*) Hey, boys, come here! (*No one answers*) You go and find him for me. Where is my eldest son?
(*There is the report of a pistol shot from the study*)

HUAN-YI (*suddenly*): Oh! (*She runs into the study. Po-yuan stands rooted. In a moment Huan-yi runs out shouting*) He . . . he . . .

PO-YUAN: He . . . he . . .
(*Po-yuan and Huan-yi together run into the study. Mrs Lu stands, stumbles for a few steps and near the centre of the room she falters and kneels down. The light gradually fades. Strains of Bach's Mass in B minor seem to come from afar and become louder as the stage darkens. The curtain falls. . . .*)

NOTES

INTRODUCTION

1. A famous Buddhist monk of the Liang Dynasty (A.D. 502–556).

2. The Chinese way of phonetic spelling, by joining the initial or consonant sound of a word to the end or vowel sound of another word.

3. Chen Yin-keh, *Three Questions Concerning the Theory of Four Tones*, Journal of Ching Hua University, quoted in *The History of the Development of Chinese Literature* by Liu Ta-chieh (Chunghua Bookstore, Shanghai, 1941).

4. A famous critic (A.D. 1876–1927), especially known for his studies of the oracle bones of the Yin Dynasty and the development of Chinese drama.

5. A *chueh chu* or 'stop-short' poem consists of four lines of five or seven words to a line. Rhyming occurs at the end of the second and fourth lines, having been set in the first. In some 'stop-short' poems, each two lines form a couplet, but this is not as a rule required.

6. A *lu shih* or 'regular' poem consists of eight lines of five or seven words each. Rhyming also occurs at the end of each even-numbered line, and in 'soft' tones. The tones, either 'soft' or 'hard', of each word used in the poem must conform to one of several sets of patterns established to bring out the contrast of tones and rhymes. Each two lines of this type of poem form a couplet and the middle two couplets must be real couplets, i.e. all the words must be balanced against corresponding words in the other line, both in meaning and tone.

7. One of the *nien hao* or royal designation of the years of an Emperor's reign, that of Emperor Hsuan Tsung of the Tang Dynasty (A.D. 713).

8. Another *nien hao* of Emperor Hsuan Tsung of the Tang Dynasty.

9. The leaders of this revolution were, among others, Hu Shih and Chen Tu-hsiu. They stood for a *pai hua*, or vernacular literature, and against *wen yen*, or classical, stylistic literature. They were against almost everything traditional, and for almost everything new, or western—democracy, for instance. So the scope of this revolution was not limited to literature, although it first started with the need for literary reform. One of their proposals for establishing a new literature was that a man must write only when he had something to say.

10. A.D. 772–842.

11. Notes on the hundred poems which he sent in lieu of a letter to Po Chu-yi.

12. A.D. 775?–826. A younger brother of Po Chu-yi.

13. By Chou Mi towards the end of the thirteenth century, in ten volumes. Wu Ling was another name for Hangchow.

14. The most famous is *Chin Pen Tung Shu Hsiao Shuo* (*Popular Stories of the Capital*).

15. One of the *nien hao* of Emperor Huei Tsung of the Sung Dynasty.

16. By Wang Shuo of the Sung Dynasty. It is a book about the development of Chinese music.

17. 'Life of Confucius', translated by Lin Yutang, *The Wisdom of Confucius*, Random House, New York, 1943. Michael Joseph, 1958, p. 85.

18. A book said to have been written by Tso Chiu-ming to furnish details of the events baldly set down in *Chun Chiu*, which was written by Confucius.

19. A seven-stringed musical instrument.

20. Huns.

21. By Hsieh Yung-yo of the Tang Dynasty.

22. The official singing and dancing institute set up by Emperor Hsuan Tsung.

CHAPTER I

1. This is the traditional Chinese view. Opinions advanced by some scholars opposing this view seem to me unconvincing. They say that Confucius referred twice to 'three hundred poems' as an established corpus and that he quoted one poem which was not included in the *Book of Poetry*. This, they claimed, Confucius would not have done if he had edited the book. The thing is, nobody knows when Confucius referred twice to the 'three hundred poems' as an established corpus. He might have done so after he himself edited the book, and to quote one poem which was not included in the *Book of Poetry* is, I think, not a right which is to be denied an editor. After all, in *Tso Chuan* more than ten poems were quoted which were not included in the *Book of Poetry*, which shows that there were quite a number of well-known poems besides the three hundred poems. Some other scholars said Confucius talked derisively about the music of Cheng and contended that had he edited the *Book of Poetry* he would not have done so. This opinion is based on the premise that the 'music of Cheng', which Confucius referred to, is *cheng feng* or folk songs of Cheng included in the *Book of Poetry*. There is no proof of this. On the other hand, we see in *The Analects* that Confucius discussed with his disciples some of the folk songs of Cheng which were collected in the *Book of Poetry*, which shows that *cheng feng* is not the 'music of Cheng'. It seems reasonable to abide by the

traditional interpretation until convincing evidence to the contrary is provided.

2. *Lun Yu* (*The Analects*) is a record kept by Confucius' disciples about what the Master said and what he did. It is impossible to say who the editor was. Many scholars consider it, however, to be the most reliable source of information about Confucius.

3. *Sung* and *ya* poems are two of the three kinds of poems making up the *Book of Poetry*.

4. *The Wisdom of Confucius*, p. 170. In this quotation Dr Lin translated *Shih Ching* as the *Book of Songs*, which is of course also right. For the sake of uniformity I have taken the liberty of calling it the *Book of Poetry*.

5. *Book of Songs*, translated by Arthur Waley, Allen & Unwin Ltd, 1937, p. 49.

6. *Lyrics from the Chinese*, translated by Helen Waddell, Constable & Co Ltd, 1951, p. 16.

7. *Book of Songs*, p. 45.

8. *Chinese Poetry in English Verse*, translated by H. A. Giles, Bernard Quaritch, 1898; also in *Select Chinese Verses*, Shanghai, 1937.

9. Ibid.

10. *Book of Songs*, p. 113.

11. Ibid., pp. 247–9.

12. Ibid., p. 232.

13. Ibid., p. 161.

CHAPTER II

1. *The Wisdom of Laotse*, translated and edited by Lin Yutang, Random House, New York, 1948. Michael Joseph, 1958, p. 51.

2. Ma Hsu-lun, among others, is of this opinion. See his *Laotse Chiao Ku*, Ku Chi Press, Peking, 1956.

3. *The Works of Motse*, translated by Y. P. Mei, Probsthain & Co, pp. 81–2.

4. 'Main Currents of Thought by Chuangtse', translated by Lin Yutang, *The Wisdom of Laotse*, p. 45.

5. 'The Book of Mencius', translated by Lin Yutang, *The Wisdom of Confucius*.

6. 'A husband is one whom one looks to for support for life.'

7. *Mencius*, IV, Part 2, II.33, translated by James Legge, 1874.

8. *The Wisdom of Laotse*, p. 293–5.

9. Ibid., p. 178.

10. Ibid., p. 179.

11. *The Wisdom of China and India*, translated and edited by Lin Yutang, Random House, 1942, p. 690.

12. Ibid., p. 234.

13. *Chuangtse*, Chap. 26, 'Wai Wu'.
14. *The Wisdom of Laotse*, p.25.
15. Ibid., p. 222.
16. Ibid., pp. 223–4.
17. Ibid., pp. 172–3.
18. Ibid., p. 173.
19. *The Wisdom of China and India*, p. 691.
20. *Chuangtse*, Chap. 24, 'Hsu Wu Kwei'.
21. *The Wisdom of Laotse*, p. 44.
22. Wei-lu, a mythical hole in the bottom of the ocean.
23. Mythical rulers before the Three Kings.
24. *The Wisdom of China and India*, pp. 682–7.

CHAPTER III

1. Szema Chien, 'The Life of Chu Yuan', as translated by David Hawkes in his *Ch'u Tz'u: The Songs of the South*, Oxford University Press, 1959, p. 12.
2. Sung Yu, another poet mentioned by Szema Chien as one who excelled in writing '*sao*'-style poems.
3. Cheng Chiao, *Tung Chih*, 'Kun Chun Tsao Mu Liao Hsu'.
4. The term Tsu Tse has been used to designate poems written by Chu Yuan and those of others who imitated his style. Here, the term refers only to those written by Chu Yuan.
5. Szema Chien, 'The Life of Chu Yuan', *Historical Record*.
6. Words which are rather similar to prepositions and conjunctions in English.
7. By Tai Sheng of the Han Dynasty.
8. *Wu* is not unlike a priest who conducts sacrificial and religious rites, except that because of the animistic attitude of the Tsu people he also serves as the embodiment of the spirits or gods for whose favours the rites are held.
9. 'Record of Geography', *History of the Han Dynasty*.
10. See Lin Yutang, *Wisdom of Confucius*, pp. 216–18. Cf. also Couvreur, *Li Ki*, Tome II, cap. XVII, III, pp. 86–90.
11. *Hsin Hsu*, 'Chieh Shih Pien'.
12. *Shuo Yuan*, 'Shan Shuo Pien'.
13. Szema Chien, 'The Life of Chu Yuan', *Historical Record*.
14. *Ch'u Tz'u: The Songs of the South*, p. 23.
15. Ibid., p. 27.
16. 'The Life of Chu Yuan', in *Historical Record*.
17. *Ch'u Tz'u: The Songs of the South*, p. 24.
18. Ibid., p. 25.
19. Ibid., pp. 76–7.

20. Ibid., pp. 104–5.
21. Ibid., p. 26.
22. Ibid., pp. 43–4.
23. Ibid., pp. 37–8.
24. Ibid., p. 38.
25. Ibid., pp. 65–6.
26. Ibid., pp. 31–4.
27. Not the Nine Songs of Tsu Tse, but those of the State of Chi.

CHAPTER IV

1. *Historical Record*, or *Shih Chi* in Chinese, is an abbreviated version of the original title of the book *Ta Shih Kung Shu*, written by Szema Chien.

2. The rulers of the vassal States of Chou promoted themselves to the ranks of duke and king when the power of Chou declined and they themselves became more powerful.

3. The original is *San Chin*, which means Han, Chao and Wei, the three splinter states of the State of Chin. But here it seems right to suppose that Lu Lien meant only the State of Wei.

4. When the Han Dynasty was established and an effort was made to find Confucian classics, Fu Sheng, an old scholar, dictated the classics from memory and they were recorded. Later, these were accepted as the standard version. However, Confucian classics were later found in the walls of the palace of King Kung of Lu, many passages of which were different from the accepted version. This created many hotly debated controversies, which are called the dispute between *Chin Wen* (accepted version) and *Ku Wen* (the version which was found in the walls).

5. *Ping Tsuen Shu*, or the chapter on currency in the *Historical Record*.

6. Szema Tan was himself a famous scholar. His work, *The Essence of Six Schools of Thought*, is considered to be the best dissertation on Chinese philosophy of his time.

7. Whose job was to help guard the palace.

8. It is difficult to say which part of the *Historical Record* was written by Szema Tan. Pan Ku, the author of *History of the Han Dynasty*, seemed to think that Szema Tan wrote at least those parts which concern philosophy, for Szema Chien was a Confucian while his father believed in Taoism, and it was Pan Ku's opinion that the author of the chapters on philosophy respected Taoism more than Confucianism.

9. *Shih* means poetry. Here it refers to the *Book of Poetry*. *Shu*, which means books, refers to the *Book of History*.

10. Szema Chien: a letter in reply to Jen An.

11. The *Book of Changes*.

12. *Li*, the *Book of Rites; Yueh*, the *Book of Music*.

13. Preface to the *Historical Record*.

14. Szema Chien: a reply to Jen An's letter.

15. *Ch'u Tz'u: The Songs of the South*, p. 12.

16. Reply to Jen An's letter.

17. Ibid.

18. It is impossible to say when Szema Chien died. But it is generally agreed that he died in the last years of Emperor Chao's reign, that is, from 89 to 86 B.C., when he was fifty-seven to sixty years old.

19. Reply to Jen An's letter.

20. The *Annals of Emperor Wu* we now have was written by Chia Shao-sun of the Han Dynasty.

21. One of the *nien hao* of Emperor Wu.

22. Ten of the original chapters were lost and replaced by those written by Chia Shao-sun and others.

23. Situated in the south-west of the present Ling Pao district of Honan Province.

24. It flows from Li Mountain into the Wei River in Shensi Province.

25. About seventeen *li* to the east of the present Ling Tung District in Shensi Province.

26. East of the present Chang An District of Shensi Province.

27. Nominally, both the Duke of Pei and Hsiang Yu were still serving under King Huai of Tsu. Therefore, the Duke would not address Hsiang Yu as 'Your Majesty'.

28. To his subordinates King Hsiang was, of course, 'His Majesty'.

29. At this period the Chinese did not use tables and chairs but squatted on mats on the ground.

30. A piece of round jade with a hole in the middle.

31. Li Mountain is situated to the west of Hung Meng.

32. To the east of Chang-an in Shensi Province.

CHAPTER V

1. Despite the fact that he raised Confucianism to a status higher than other schools of thought, and established an examination system which selected scholars on the basis of their knowledge of Confucianism for official careers, Emperor Wu effectively restricted the extent to which various schools of thought other than Confucianism could hope to win the minds of the scholars.

2. A collection of folk songs by Kuo Mou-ching of the Sung Dynasty.

3. *Ch'u Tz'u: The Songs of the South*, pp. 105–6.

4. ?–141 B.C.

5. 162–? B.C.

6. ?–122 B.C.

7. Great astronomer, A.D. 78–139.

8. The present Shou Chang and Tung Ping Districts of Shantung Province.

9. The present Chun Chia District of Szechuan Province.

10. Both these states have long been assimilated and become part of China. Yeh Lang is situated somewhere to the east of the present Tung Chih District of Kweichow Province and Peh Chung somewhere to the west of the present Yi Pin District of Szechuan Province.

11. Today the Chinese still refer to Szechuan as Pa-shu, or simply as Shu.

12. Chun was a state which was situated to the south-east of the present Hsi-chang District, Cho to the south-east of the present Han Yuan District, in Szechuan Province.

13. All small tribal states in the present Szechuan Province.

14. *Sao Ti*, the style of *Li Sao*. In other words, poems written in the style of *Tsu Tse*.

15. Preface to his *Liang Tu Fu* (*Two Capitals*).

CHAPTER VI

1. *Yueh Fu* originally meant the Office of Music, set up by Emperor Wu of the Han Dynasty, but has come to mean folk songs. The folk songs of the Han Dynasty that have come down to us are songs 'of the streets and fields' ('Record of Music', *History of Chin*). The most comprehensive anthology of such folk songs is Kuo Mou-chiang's *Yueh Fu Shih Chi* (*Anthology of Folk Songs*).

2. See the first section of Chapter VII for details of this theory.

3. A.D. 479–501. His *Shih Pin* (*Criteria of Poetry*) is a famous book devoted to the criticism of five-word poems.

4. Arthur Waley, *Chinese Poems*, George Allen & Unwin, 1961, p. 45.

5. Ibid., p. 47.

6. A.D. 507–583. His *Yu Tai Hsin Yung* in ten volumes is an anthology of poems written before the Liang Dynasty (502–557).

7. Prince Chao Ming (501–531) of the Liang Dynasty. His *Selected Master-pieces of Chinese Literature* is a well-known anthology.

8. The general for whom Szema Chien spoke up as a result of which he was punished by castration.

9. Of the Liang Dynasty. His *Wen Hsin Tiao Lung* (*The Carved Dragon of the Literary Mind*) is a well-known book of literary criticism.

10. 'On Poetry', in *Wen Hsin Tiao Lung*.

11. *Nien hao* of Emperor Hsien of the Han Dynasty, A.D. 196.

12. A.D. 1673–1769.

13. Emperor Kuang Wu of the Han Dynasty moved his capital to Lo-yang in A.D. 25. The period before that, from 246 B.C. to A.D. 8, is called the Western

Han Dynasty. During this period the capital of the Han Dynasty was Chang-an.

14. *Shuo Shih Chiu Yu (Comments on Poetry)*.

15. *Chinese Poems*, p. 55.

16. Ibid., p. 40.

17. Shan Tao, Yuan Chi, Hsi Kang, Hsiang Hsiu, Liu Ling, Yuan Hsien and Wang Jung.

18. Jerome Ch'en and Michael Bullock, *Poems of Solitude*, Abelard-Schuman, 1960, p. 13.

19. *Tung-po Shih Hua (Tung-po's Comments on Poetry)*.

20. *Chinese Poems*, p. 91.

21. Ibid., p. 93.

22. Translated by Lin Yutang, *The Importance of Understanding*, World Publishing Company, Cleveland, Ohio, 1960, pp. 124–5; William Heinemann Ltd, 1961.

CHAPTER VII

1. Memo to Emperor Wu of the Liang Dynasty from Kuo Tsu-shen, quoted in Volume 70, *History of Southern Dynasties*, edited by Lee Yen-shou of the Tang Dynasty.

2. *Kuang Hung Ming Chi*, in thirty volumes, was written by Tao Hsuen, a Buddhist monk, to propagate Buddhism.

3. As quoted in Cheng Chen-to's *History of Chinese Literature*, Commercial Press, Shanghai, 1932, p. 193.

4. 'Three Questions Concerning Four Tones', as quoted in *The History of the Development of Chinese Literature*, p. 285.

5. Sin-lo and Po-chi were two states in what is now Korea.

6. Tibet.

7. The present Turfan district in Sinkiang Province.

8. *Mao*, a staff or switch with woven-wool top, which served as a symbol of the authority given to a general by the Emperor.

9. Han Hai, north of the Mongolian Desert.

10. *Hu Chin*, a four-stringed musical instrument. Some people call it the Chinese violin.

11. *Pi Pa* is not unlike a mandolin. Its four strings are made of gut and the head of the handle is bent back.

12. Some scholars contend that Sui Yeh is Suyub, the modern Tokmak in what is now the Soviet Republic of Turkestan, while others think that it was the transliteration of the name Syria. According to the 'Record of Geography' in the *New History of the Tang Dynasty*, Sui Yeh was a town under the jurisdiction of Yen Chi Protectorate Government, which belonged to the Government for the Pacification of Western Regions. Yen Chi is now a district in Sinkiang Province.

13. One of the sixteen states established in the north-west of China during the period between 314 and 439, with her capital first in Tun-huang and later in Chiu Chuan in Kansu Province.

14. *Han Lin Hsueh Shih Li Kung Mu Pei* or 'Memorial of Academician Li, to be inscribed on the tablet of his tomb'.

15. Li Po's courtesy name.

16. 'Records of Arts and Letters', in the *History of the Han Dynasty*, mentions that there are twenty-four volumes of Feng Ku and Liu Chia. They are books about the mystical technique of Tun or 'escape'.

17. This happened in 487 B.C. when Confucius visited Tsu. The song goes like this:

> O phoenix! O phoenix!
> What has happened to thy character?
> Let bygones be bygones
> But make amends for what still lies ahead.
> Alack-a-day! A thousand pities for the Rulers of the day!

18. 'Three Bailiffs' refer to his three poems which have the word bailiff in their titles: *The Bailiff of Hsin-an, The Bailiff of Shih-hao* and *The Bailiff of Tung-kuan Pass*. 'Three Departures' refer in the same way to *The Departure of the Newlyweds, The Departure of the Homeless* and *The Departure of the Aged*.

19. All five poems are translated by Witter Bynner from the texts of Kiang Kang-hu in *The Jade Mountain*, Allen & Unwin Ltd, 1929, pp. 53, 205, 216, 54, 59 and 67; Alfred A. Knopf, New York, 1929.

20. Lin Yutang, *My Country, My People*, John Day, New York, 1937, p. 257; William Heinemann Ltd, 1936.

21. Robert Payne, *The White Pony*, John Day, New York, 1947, pp. 194-5; Allen & Unwin Ltd, 1949.

22. Ibid., p. 219.

23. Ibid., p. 230.

24. Ibid., p. 253.

CHAPTER VIII

1. *Kung, shang, chiao, cheng* and *yu* are the five notes of the Chinese musical scale. Here it refers to the tonal harmony of the words.

2. Biography of Lee O, *History of the Sui Dynasty*.

3. *Tsung Shuo*, or 'General Comments' on the *Carved Dragon of the Literary Mind*.

4. *Li Yuan Pien*, or 'On Writing', of *Ching Lou Tse*, in the collection of his works.

5. Biography of Lee O, op. cit.

6. *Chuan Tang Wen* (*Literary Works of the Tang Dynasty*).

7. See Lin Yutang, *The Importance of Understanding*, p. 98.

8. Postscript to the *Memorial of Ouyang, a Student*.

9. The area which covered the upper reaches of the Huai River.

10. A letter in reply to Chiao Shih.

11. Postscript to *Commentaries of Mr Liu I*.

CHAPTER IX

1. This book was thought to have been written by Pan Ku in the Han Dynasty, but is now considered by scholars to have been written by an unknown author in the Wei or the Chin Dynasty.

2. A.D. 531–591 of the Liu Sung Dynasty.

3. Of the North Chi Dynasty.

4. Edited by Tao Shin, a Buddhist monk of the Tang Dynasty.

5. By Wu Chun (460–520) of the Liang Dynasty.

6. In *Sequel to Yuyang Miscellany*, Vol. 4.

7. Or *Ho Tung Chi*, collected in *Tai Ping Kuang Chi* (*Tai Ping Encyclopaedia*).

8. Famous Buddhist monk and translator of the Tang Dynasty who went to India to study Buddhism. He translated seventy-five works issued in more than thirteen hundred volumes.

9. Lee Fu-yen and Fei Hsin were both of the late Tang Dynasty, but the years of their birth and death are unknown.

10. 780–848.

11. Of the late Tang Dynasty.

12. The letter is translated by Lin Yutang, *Importance of Understanding*, pp. 138–9.

CHAPTER X

1. *Yuan Shih Nieh Pien* (*On Poetry*).

2. *O Pei Shih Hua* (*Talks on Poetry*) in *O Pei*, Vol. 3.

3. Written by Tu Yu of the Tang Dynasty. It is a history book covering the changes and developments in economics, examinations, music, military affairs, law and punishments, local government and national defence in China from ancient times down to the Tien Po period of the Tang Dynasty.

4. The modern Wu Wei of Kansu Province.

5. In Kuche and Shaya Districts in Sinkiang Province.

6. There are two books called *History of the Tang Dynasty*. The first one, edited by Liu Shun of the Later Chin Dynasty (936–946), is called *Old History of the Tang Dynasty*. The second one, edited by Ouyang Hsiu and others of the Sung Dynasty, is called *New History of the Tang Dynasty*.

7. One of the folk songs of the State of Wei, or *Wei Feng*, included in the *Book of Poetry*.

8. Now forms a part of Chu Tsu-mou's *Chien Chun Yi Shu* (*Chien Chun's Book Finds*).

9. Edited by Chao Tsung-cho in the third year of Kuang Chen (940).

10. This refers to his homesickness, for the State of South Tang was to the east of the capital, Pien Liang, of Sung.

11. *Hua Meng Lu* by Chang Shun-min of the Sung Dynasty.

12. Of the Sung Dynasty in two volumes.

13. By Liu I-ching of the Yuan Dynasty in ten volumes.

14. According to Chao Teh-lin's *Hou Chin Lu* which was written in the Sung Dynasty.

15. Lee Ching-chao, *Chao Hsi Yu Ying Tsung Hua* (*Miscellany of a Fisherman Hermit in Chao Hsi*).

16. Recorded in *Sequel to Tsui Chien Lu* by Yu Wen-pao of the Sung Dynasty.

17. The fifteenth day of the first month of the year, also known as the Festival of Lanterns.

18. Utopia.

19. Tao Chien.

20. South of the Yangtse River, or what was left of Chinese territory.

CHAPTER XI

1. *Chu* is both the new poetic form and the libretto of Chinese opera. Here, it is used to mean the former, because it is an earlier development.

2. Designation of the reign of Emperor Hui Tsung of the Sung Dynasty.

3. Tseng Min-hsing, *Tu Hsing Tsa Chih*, Vol. 5.

4. Among the better-known *san chu* writers were Kuan Han-ching, Pai Po, Wang Shih-fu, Ma Chih-yuan and Chang Keh-chiu.

5. This was developed on the basis of a *tsan chun* play which has only two actors, one hero and one clown. In the Sung Dynasty and in the State of Chin these shows were called respectively *tsa chu* and *yuan pen*. There were one actor, one clown, one extra, one director and one stage manager.

6. See Chapter XII, first section, for details of *pien wen*.

7. They are Tung Chia-yuan's *Western Chamber*, Liu Chih-yuan (author unknown), and Wang Po-chen's *Tien Po Yi Shih* (*Stories of the Tien Po Period of the Tang Dynasty*).

8. This is one of the seventeen 'keys' of music (six *kung* and eleven *tiao*) used in the Chin and Yuan Dynasties. For details see *Tse Yuan* by Chang Yen and *Yen Yueh Kao Yuan*.

9. There were four castes of people under Mongolian rule: first, Mongolians;

second, people of the Western Regions of China and of Europe who were subjects of the Mongols; third, Tartars and the Chinese in Northern China who were ruled by the Tartars; fourth, the Chinese in South China.

10. *Tan* means leading actress.

11. From *Yu-chuen Chu Hua* (*Comments on Chu*) by Li Tiao-yuan.

12. A great sophist of the State of Chi in the Warring States Period. It was said that he served King Huei of the State of Yuan loyally, but was victimized and sentenced to jail. In bitterness he cried out, and although it was June snow fell.

13. Elder sister.

14. Preface to *Chou Hsin Fu*, part of the *Collected Works of Yu Ming Tang*.

15. This is a little forced. The author simply wanted to insert here the name of the hero, which is Liu (Willow) Meng-mei (Dream of Plum).

CHAPTER XII

1. This is apparently based on Buddhist sutras, for Saddharma-pundarika, Jakata-mala and other sutras were written partly in prose and partly in verse.

2. Of the 'Five Dynasties'.

3. Written in 1147.

4. Written by Chou Mi towards the end of the thirteenth century when the Sung Dynasty had fallen.

5. Published in the Ching Dynasty.

6. *Three Monsters of Tingchow* was found in *Ching Shih Tung Yen* (*Stories to Warn Men*); *The Debauchery of King Liang of Chin* was found in *Hsing Shih Heng Yen* (*Stories to Awaken Men*). Both collections were compiled by Feng Meng-lung.

7. *The Debauchery of King Hai Ling of Chin* is an alternative title for the story *The Debauchery of King Liang of Chin*.

8. This is a conservative estimate. Other scholars are of the opinion that there are twenty-seven *hua pen* stories of the Sung Dynasty extant. But without positive proof it is perhaps better to be prudent.

9. Cyril Birch, *Stories from a Ming Collection*, The Bodley Head, 1958, pp. 55–8; Indiana Press, Bloomington, Indiana, 1959.

CHAPTER XIII

1. The five dynasties established consecutively in the fifty-three years (907–960) after the Tang Dynasty was overthrown and before the Sung Dynasty was established.

2. Both are books on Chinese drama. *Lu Kwei Pu* means literally *Records*

of Ghosts and was written in the Yuan Dynasty, while *Tai Ho Cheng Yin Pu* (*Spectrum of Classical Music*) was written in the Ming Dynasty.

3. Lee Cho-wu, *Tung Hsin Shuo* (*On Innocence*).

4. Sequel to *Lu Kwei Pu*.

5. As quoted in Chou Mi's *Kwei Hsin Tsa Shih* or *Miscellany*.

6. Preface to *All Men Are Brothers*, 120-chapter edition.

7. Translated by Pearl S. Buck, *All Men Are Brothers*, Methuen & Co Ltd, 1933, pp. 458–62; John Day Company, New York, 1933.

8. *Monkey*, translated by Arthur Waley, Allen & Unwin Ltd, London, 1942; Penguin Books, 1961, pp. 81–7; John Day Company, New York, 1943.

9. *The Golden Lotus*, translated by Clement Egerton, Vol. IV, Routledge & Kegan Paul Ltd, 1939, pp. 112–15.

CHAPTER XIV

1. The first two were the leaders of a group known as 'Seven Scholars of an Earlier Period', the last two were leaders of 'Seven Scholars of a Later Period'.

2. Second letter to a Mr Ho.

3. Biography of Lee Pan-lung, *History of the Ming Dynasty*.

4. Ibid.

5. Also known as Lee Chih.

6. Letter to Keng Ting-hsiang.

7. *On Innocence*.

8. The *Book of Poetry*, the *Book of History*, the *Book of Rites*, the *Book of Music*, the *Book of Changes*, and *Chun Chiu*.

9. Preface to *Collected Poems of Hsiao Hsiu* (his younger brother Yuan Chung-tao).

10. Tang and Yu are the dynasties founded by the legendary Yellow Emperor and Emperor Shun, while the Three Dynasties are Hsia, Shang and Chou Dynasties.

11. Yuan Tsung-tao, *On Writing*.

12. Yuan Chung-tao, preface to *The Complete Works of Chung-lang*.

13. Yuan Chung-lang, *Shang Chen* (*Rules of Drinking*).

14. Preface to *Collected Poems of Hsiao Hsiu*.

15. Translated by Lin Yutang, *Importance of Understanding*, pp. 159–61.

16. Ibid., pp. 112–13.

17. Ibid., pp. 126–9.

CHAPTER XV

1. One *tou* is roughly 2·2 gallons.

2. One of the many states of the Warring States Period.

3. One *fen* is one-hundredth of a tael, which is roughly 1.1 oz.

4. From *Flowers in the Mirror*, translated by Lin Tai-yi for UNESCO.

CHAPTER XVI

1. *Jen Ching Lu Shih Tsao* (*Poems of Jen Ching Lu*).
2. Letter dated 9 April 1916.
3. Harold Acton and Chen Shih-hsiang, *Modern Chinese Poetry*, Duckworth, 1936, p. 76.
4. Ibid., p. 85.
5. Ibid., p. 86.
6. Ibid., p. 146.
7. Ibid., p. 148.
8. Ibid., p. 122.
9. Ibid., p. 126.
10. Ibid., p. 69.

CHAPTER XVII

1. Translated by Lin Yutang, *The Wisdom of China and India*, p. 1089.
2. Lin Yutang, *The Importance of Understanding*, pp. 151–4.

BIBLIOGRAPHY

1. CHINESE LITERATURE: GENERAL BACKGROUND AND HISTORIES

Chao Chia-pi, *Chung-kuo Hsin Wen-hsueh Ta-hsi* (*A Comprehensive Anthology of Modern Chinese Literature*). Liang Yu Press, Shanghai, 1935.

Chen Shou-yi, *Chinese Literature*, Ronald Press, New York, 1961.

Chen Tse-chan, *Chung-kuo Wen-hsueh Shih Chiang-hua* (*Lectures on the History of Chinese Literature*). Pei-hsin Press, Shanghai, 1933.

Cheng Chen-to, *Chung-kuo Wen-hsueh Shih* (*A History of Chinese Literature*). Commercial Press, Shanghai, 1932.

Chien Mu, *Kuo Shih Ta Kang* (*Introduction to the History of China*). Reissued by the Commercial Press, Taipei, 1956.

Chow Tse-tsung, *The May Fourth Movement: Intellectual Revolution in Modern China*. Harvard University Press, Cambridge, Mass., 1960.

Giles, H. A., *A History of Chinese Literature*. D. Appleton & Co, 1923, reissued by Grove Press, New York, 1958.

Hightower, J. R., *Topics in Chinese Literature*. Harvard University Press, 1953.

Hu Shih, *Hu Shih Wen Tsun* (*Collected Essays of Hu Shih*, 1921–1930). Shanghai.

Lin Yutang, *Wisdom of China and India*. Random House, New York, 1942.

Liu Ta-chieh, *Chung-kuo Wen-hsueh Fa-chan Shih* (*The History of the Development of Chinese Literature*). Chung-hwa Book Store, Shanghai, 1941.

2. POETRY

Acton, Harold, and Chen Shih-hsiang, *Modern Chinese Poetry*. Gerald Duckworth & Co Ltd, London, 1936.

Bynner, Witter, *The Jade Mountain*. Alfred A. Knopf, New York, 1929; Allen & Unwin Ltd, London, 1929.

Chang Hui-yen, *Tse Hsuen* (*A Selection of Tse*).

Hawkes, David, *Ch'u Tz'u: Songs of the South*. Oxford University Press, 1959.

Ke Hsien-ning, *Chung-kuo Shih Shih* (*A History of Chinese Poetry*). Chinese Cultural Press, Taipei, 1960.

Lu Kan-ju and Feng Yuen-chun, *Chung-kuo Shih Shih* (*A History of Chinese Poetry*). Ta Kiang Book Store, Shanghai, 1931.

Payne, Robert, *The White Pony*. John Day Company, New York, 1947; Allen & Unwin Ltd, London, 1949.

—— *Contemporary Chinese Poetry*, Routledge, London, 1947.

Waley, Arthur, *Book of Songs*, Allen & Unwin Ltd, London, 1937.

—— *Chinese Poems*, Allen & Unwin Ltd, London, 1961.

Wang I, *Tsu Tse Chang Chu* (*Annotations of Tsu Tse*).

Wang Kuo-wei, *Jen Chien Tse Hua* (*Comments on Tse*).

Wang Shih-chen, *Chuen Tang Shih Shuo.* (*Poetry of the Tang Dynasty*).

Yao Chi-heng, *Shih Ching Tung Lun* (*Introduction to the Book of Poetry*). Reissued by the Chung-hwa Book Store, Shanghai, 1958.

3. FICTION

Birch, Cyril, *Stories from a Ming Collection*. The Bodley Head, London, 1958; Indiana University Press, Bloomington, Indiana, 1959.

Buck, Pearl, trs., *All Men Are Brothers*. John Day Company, New York, 1933; Methuen & Co Ltd, London, 1933.

Egerton, Clement, *The Golden Lotus*. Routledge & Kegan Paul, London, 1939.

Hsia, C. T., *A History of Modern Chinese Fiction*. Yale University Press, New Haven, Conn., 1961.

Hu Lun-ching, *Chuan-chi Hsiao-shuo Hsuen* (*A Selection of Short Stories of the Tang and Sung Dynasties*). Cheng-chung Press, Taipei, 1960.

Ke Hsien-ning, *Chung-kuo Hsiao-shuo Shih* (*The History of Chinese Fiction*). Chinese Cultural Press, Taipei, 1959.

Kung Ling-ching, *Chung-kuo Hsiao-shuo Shih-liao* (*Source Material for the History of Chinese Fiction*). Commercial Press, Taipei, 1959.

Lu Hsun, *A Brief History of Chinese Fiction*. Foreign Language Press, Peking, 1959.

Waley, Arthur, *Monkey*. Allen & Unwin Ltd, London, 1942; John Day Company, New York, 1943; Penguin Books, 1961.

4. PROSE

Prince Chao Ming, *Wen Hsuen* (*Selected Literary Masterpieces*).

Chen Chung-fang, *Chung-kuo Yun-wen Tung Lun* (*Introduction to Chinese Rhymed Prose*). Chung-hwa Book Store, Taipei, 1958.

Lin Yutang, *The Importance of Understanding*. World Publishing Company, Cleveland, Ohio, 1960; William Heinemann Ltd, London, 1961.

Mao Kun, *Tang Sung Pa Ta Chia Wen Chao* (*A Selection of the Masterpieces of Eight Prose Masters of the Tang and Sung Dynasties*).

Wu Tiao-hou and Wu Tsu-tsai, *Ku Wen Kuan Chih* (*The Best of Chinese Classical Prose*). Reissued by the Commercial Press, Hong Kong, 1961.

Yuan Chung-lang, *Yuan Chung-lang Chuen Chi* (*The Complete Works of Yuan Chung-lang*). Reissued by the World Press, Taipei, 1957.

5. DRAMA

Chi Ju-shan, *Kuo Chu Yao Liao* (*The Fundamentals of Chinese Drama*). Chinese Cultural Press, Taipei, 1958.

Jen Na, *San Chu Kai Lun* (*Introduction to San Chu*).

Wang Kuo-wei, *Sung Yuan Hsi Chu Shih* (*A History of the Drama of the Sung and Yuan Dynasties*).

Wu Mei, *Yuan Chu Yen-chiu* (*A Study of the Drama of the Yuan Dynasty*).

6. BIBLIOGRAPHY

Yuan Tung-li, compiler, *China in Western Literature: A Continuation of Cordier's Bibliotheca Sinica*. Yale University Press, 1958.

TABLE OF CHINESE DYNASTIES

Dynasty	Dates	Remarks
(Mythical)	2697–2200 B.C.	Legendary
Hsia	2205–1784 B.C.	Together with Chou, these are called
Shang (Yin)	1783–1123 B.C.	'Three Dynasties' Classic period
Chou	1122–222 B.C.	Spring-Autumn Period, 722–481 B.C. Warring States Period, 403–221 B.C.
Ch'in	221–207 B.C.	Reunified China
Han	206 B.C.–A.D. 219	Eastern Han from A.D. 25
Wei	220–264	Wei, Wu and Shu formed the Three Kingdoms from about A.D. 200
Chin	265–419	Eastern Chin from 327. Barbarians' kingdoms in North China, 304–439
Northern-Southern Dynasties		
Sung	420–478	These are called North and South
Chi	479–501	Dynasties for distinction. Together
Liang	502–556	with preceding Wu and Eastern
Chen	557–588	Chin, called 'Six Dynasties', a term referring to southern culture
Sui	589–617	Reunified China
Tang	618–906	
Five Dynasties		
Liang	907–922	
Tang	923–935	These are called Five Dynasties to
Chin	936–946	distinguish them from other dynasties
Han	947–950	of the same name
Chou	951–959	
Sung	960–1276	Southern Sung from 1127 onwards with Northern China under Tartars and Mongols
Yuan (Mongol)	1277–1367	Foreign rule
Ming	1368–1643	Restored to Chinese rule
Ching (Manchu)	1644–1911	Foreign rule
Republic	1911	

INDEX

of, 6; in Sung Dynasty, 214; conquers N. China, 222, 226; one literary work of, 229–30; conquered by Mongols, 237

Ch'in, state of, in Warring States Period, 62–5, 67–8, 77, 82

Chin Chia, five-word poems of, 118

Chin Dynasty, 124–5, 291; Buddhism in, 137; supernatural stories of, 185

Ch'in Dynasty, 17, 82; poetry of, 7, 62, 121

Chin Kuan, 215–16, 220, 222; tse of, 224; mentioned, 301

Chin Sheng-tan, 3, 245, 320; and All Men Are Brothers, 292–3; essays of, 370

China Travelling Drama Company, 386

Chinese language, classical and vernacular, vii, 348–9; translating Buddhist sutras into, 3–6, 125, 138–9; four tonal differences of, 4, 139; early pictographs of, 15–16; Western books translated into, 347–8; changing nineteenth-century, 349; attempts at romanizing written, 350; need for national dialect, 351; 'national' (Kuoyu), 353; vernacular (pai hua) recognized as standard, 354

Chinese Revolution (1911), 349–50

Ching Dynasty (Manchu), novels of, 3, 326–45, 348; prose of, 3, 319–20; chuan chi of, 236; Western impact during, 346; overthrow of, 349–50

Ching, Emperor, 100

Ching hsi opera, 237

Ching Hsiang, King of Tsu, 64–7

Ching Pen Tung Shu Hsiao (Popular Stories of the Capital), 257–69

Ching Ping Shang Tang Hua Pen (compiled by Hung Pien), 258, 270

Ching Shih Tung Yen (Stories to Warn Men), 258

Ching-ling School, 319–20

Chitse in Northern Drama, 232–3

Chiu Hu Pien Wen (The Story of Chiu Hu), 6, 256

Chou Dynasty, vii, 19, 27, 37–8; poetry of, 17–18, 27, 169; prose of, 36; music of North, 207

Chou Mi, 291; Reminiscences of Things that Happened in Wu Ling of, 9, 257

Chou Pang-yen, 216, 221–2

Chou people, 58

Chou Tso-jen, 3, 354–5, 370–1

Chou Yang, 100

Chou Yu, 4; Rhymes of Four Tones (Sze Sheng Chieh Yun) of, 114

Chu Chih songs, 207

Chu Chuen, Tai Ho Cheng Yin Pu of, 282

Chu Kuang-hsi, 143, 156

Chu kung tiao, 6–7, 10, 229–32

Chu poems, 2, 4, 9, 12, 226–37

Chu Tse-ching, 370

Chu Yuan, 62–8; Tsu Tse of, 68–75; sao ti poems of, 7; Nine Songs (Chiu Ko) of, 11, 60, 68–71; influenced by Book of Poetry, 57–8; On Encountering Sorrow (Li Sao) of, 57, 63–5, 67–9, 72–5, 88, 110, 245; use of 'empty words' by, 58, 62; influenced by tse songs and music, 59–60, 69; Szema Chien's Life of, 62, 64, 68, 88; Confucianism of, 63, 67–8; banishment of, 64–7; new poetic form of, 66–7, 69; death of, 67; festival commemorating, 68; poems of, 68–75; Questions asked of Heaven (Tien Wen) of, 68; The Summons of the Soul (Chao Hun) of, 66, 68, 71, 98; Nine Declarations (Chiu Chang) of, 68; The Spirit of the Fallen (Kuo Shang) of, 69–70; mentioned, 42, 147. See also Tsu Tse

Chu Yu-tsun, 319–20

Chuan chi (Southern Drama), 3, 234–6; sung in kun chiang, 236; merged with hua pu, 236–7; of Tang Hsien-tsu, 246, 249; Yu Ting Chih of, 301

Chuan Chi (Fei Hsin), 191

Chuan chi hsiao shuo (short story), 2, 170, 188–92; example of, 192–204

Chuan Hsiang Ping Hua Wu Chung (Story-tellers' Five Stories), 281–3

Chuang Keh-chia, 357

Chuangtse, 2, 41–9, 63; on Sophisms, 39; caustic comments of, 42–6, 50; on life and death, 46–8; prose style of, 50; given title of Chen-jen, 151; on fiction, 184

Chuangtse, vii, 2, 49–56, 188, 245; extracts from, 42–9, 51–6; popularity of, 124; Su Tung-po on, 219

Chueh chu, see 'Stop-short' poems

Chung Hsing, 319